Imperial Co-Histories

Imperial Co-Histories

National Identities
and the British and Colonial Press

Edited by
Julie F. Codell

Madison • Teaneck
Fairleigh Dickinson University Press
London: Associated University Presses

Associated University Presses
2010 Eastpark Boulevard
Cranbury, NJ 08512

Associated University Presses
Unit 304, The Chandlery
50 Westminster Bridge Road
London SE1 7QY, England

Associated University Presses
P.O. Box 338, Port Credit
Mississauga, Ontario
Canada L5G 4L8

The paper used in this publication meets the requirements of the American National Standard for Permanence of Paper for Printed Library Materials Z39.48-1984.

Library of Congress Cataloging-in-Publication Data

Imperial co-histories : national identities and the British and colonial press / edited by / Julie F. Codell.
     p.   cm.
   ISBN 0-8386-3973-9 (alk. paper)
   1. Great Britain—Colonies—Press coverage.   2. British—Foreign countries—press coverage.   3. Great Britain—Colonies—History—19th century.   4. National characteristics, British—Press coverage.   5. Imperialism—Press coverage.   I. Codell, Julie F.
   DA16.147   2003
   070.4′4932532′094109034—dc21   2002015673

This book is dedicated
to colonized people everywhere—
those who struggled in the past
and those who continue to struggle in the present.

Contents

Illustrations

Acknowledgments

THE EDITOR AND AUTHORS WISH TO THANK THE FOLLOWING PUBLICA-
tions for permission to publish versions of essays from their completed or forthcoming publications:

David Finkelstein's essay, "Imperial Self-Representation: Constructions of Empire in *Blackwood's Magazine*, 1880–1900," is published with permission from Pennsylvania State University Press
based on material in a forthcoming book in the press's Empire and
Media collection. Thanks to Marti Hendershot for this permission.

Tony Hughes-d'Aeth's essay, "History by Installment: Australian
Centenary and *Picturesque Atlas of Australasia*, 1886–88," is based on
Chapter 3 of *Paper Nation: The Story of the Picturesque Atlas of Australasia 1886–1888* (2001) and is published here by permission of Melbourne University Press. Thanks to Melissa Mackey for this
permission.

Aled Jones's essay, "Welsh Missionary Journalism in India, 1880–
1947," is published by permission of the University of Wales Press
and is based on his chapter in *Life, Love and Labour—Exploring Ethnic
Diversity in Wales*, forthcoming. Thanks to Paul O'Leary for this permission.

I wish also to thank the authors who have worked hard to prepare
these essays over a two-year period; Christine Retz, our editor, who
was so patient and helpful; our careful copyeditor Pat Lichen; and
the other staff of Fairleigh Dickinson University Press and the Associated University Presses who have worked with us to prepare this
book.

Imperial Co-Histories

Introduction: Imperial Co-Histories and the British and Colonial Press

Julie F. Codell

What is theoretically innovative, and politically crucial, is the need to think beyond narratives of originary and initial subjectivities and to focus on those moments or processes that are produced in the articulation of cultural differences. These "in-between" spaces provide the terrain for elaborating strategies of selfhood—singular or communal—that initiate new signs of identity, and innovative sites of collaboration, and contestation, in the act of defining the idea of society itself.
—Homi K. Bhabha, *The Location of Culture*

In recent years, readings of the colonial and postcolonial "conditions" have identified a central deliriousness in the working of imperial history. . . . the hesitancies and uncertainties that colonialism seemed so adept at producing. . . . the discursive ambivalences of imperialism. . . . spaces of bewilderment and loss . . .
    Englishness has been consistently been defined through appeals to the identity-endowing properties of place. . . . *as* a Gothic cathedral, the Victoria Terminus, the Residency at Lucknow, a cricket field, a ruined country house, and a zone of riot. . . . Englishness has been *generally* understood to reside within some type of imaginary, abstract, or actual locale. . . . to control, possess, order, and dis-order the nation's and the empire's spaces.
—Ian Baucom, *Out of Place: Englishness, Empire, and the Locations of Identity*

THE ROLE OF THE PRESS IN WRITING EMPIRE

THE PRESS, A LOCALE AT ONCE "IMAGINARY, ABSTRACT, OR ACTUAL," IN IAN Baucom's words, is one such place where identity can be discursively ambivalent, hesitant, and bewildering. The press often presumes to speak for a nation or a people or a "public," but it speaks conditions and identities always in process and always multi-voiced. This book's essays collectively examine the press's production of "co-histories" in its unique virtual spaces where joint histories, simultaneous, ideal, and "real," intervene in one another's texts in a dialogue between

15

Britain and its empire and intercolonially between colonized readers. As Joanne Shattock and Michael Wolff explained twenty years ago in their ground-breaking study of the Victorian press, the press was "the context within which people lived and worked and thought, and from which they derived their . . . sense of the outside world."[1] I would add that as the nineteenth century progressed, readers also derived their sense of their own and others' places and spaces from the press, which offered a major site for the production and re-production of national identities. Dialogues among readers, editors, and writers were attenuated over time, as well as over space, through published responses and comments to articles and through serialization. New, unstable and destabilized ("dis-order") identities emerged, shaped by the press's dialogic, or rather multi-logic, nature.

As scholars increasingly recognize, metropole and colony, however convenient an abstract dichotomy, were never fixed or discrete but always overlapping and intersecting. Antoinette Burton argues against binary formations of identities (British or "native"), while recognizing that "one discourse may, under certain historical conditions, manage and even discipline another,"[2] an interdiscursive set of relations this book attempts to explore in the context of imperial identities represented in the press. Burton recognizes a sea change in current studies of the relations between "home" and "colony": "Traditional imperial history, which wrestled with the core-periphery model down to the 1980s, has begun to question some of the polarities and the exclusions that have structured its practice from the nineteenth century onward." This questioning has "redirected the focus of empire to the domestic cultural scene" to the point of now examining "the impact of empire on British national identities in the Victorian period."[3]

British culture was profoundly changed by the influx of ideas, fashions, culture, and food from the colonies, an influx still barely touched upon by scholars.[4] As Raymond Williams has shown in *The Country and the City*, relations between perceived "centers" and their peripheries generate constant conflict, appropriation, and re-modeling, to produce what Simon Gikandi calls "a culture of mutual imbrication and contamination."[5] In addition to the movement of people, goods, and ideas, the most popular and powerful determinant for bridging "home" or "mother" country and its colonial peripheries was the press. English newspapers and periodicals circulated to the colonies, and news from the colonies bounced back to London, as well as to the rest of the British Isles and from colony to colony. The colonial press, both Anglo and native, quoted

English papers regularly for readers in India, South Africa, Australia, New Zealand, and the Middle East. Everyone read the news from metropole and from colony simultaneously as news circulated in print and later in telegraphic news services. The press vanquished distances between "centers" and "peripheries" and juxtaposed differences through images as well as texts. News was both geographically located and dislocated from place into print virtuality to produce new identities not definable as "British" or "native," two categories themselves not monolithic, homogeneous, or stable. Anglo-Indians,[6] for example, had their own press that was neither "Indian" (and Indians had both English-medium and vernacular newspapers and periodicals) nor "British," and they expressed their own sometimes new, sometimes hybrid ideas and desires not otherwise represented in native or metropole newspapers. Their newspapers articulated views unique to the British living in India with their own set of cultural identities so well examined thirty years ago by Benita Parry in *Delusions and Discoveries* (1972).[7] Likewise, through their own English-medium and vernacular presses, colonized populations generated and composed their own identities that were not simple hybrids of "British" and "Other."

This book explores the intersecting national and imperial discourses in the Victorian press at home and abroad—in newspapers, the wire service, periodicals, and special publications, such as the Centennial Atlas of Australia and the *Journal of Indian Art and Industry* published by the art schools established in India under the British Raj. These essays map identities created in and by the press, as Michael Wolff so clearly understood: "an attitude, an opinion, an idea, did not exist until it had registered itself in the press, . . . an interest group, a sect, a profession, [would] come of age when it inaugurated its journal."[8] One can say the same about national, gendered, racial, and imperial or supranational identities that emerged in colonial and British periodicals.

In this book scholars from the United States, Britain, Australia, India, and Canada explore these intersections from a variety of national perspectives and from countries whose historical and textual relationships to Empire were diverse. These essays participate in the disciplines of history, literature, anthropology, and art history, and in new interdisciplinary fields such as gender and media studies, to explore ways in which gender, religion, art, and literature cut across national and imperial boundaries. The resulting interdisciplinary study of periodicals offers, as Lyn Pykett observes, opportunities to explore texts in new ways, not simply to analyze or deconstruct them, but also to examine relationships in the press among mean-

ings and modes of production. Venues of production include readers' receptions and each periodical's political position or ideology
and socioeconomic niche, and not all of these were internally consistent or even intended. Not simply a venue for direct or frontal dog-
matic statements, the press constituted a shifting and often fumbling
imperial discourse, to revise Pykett's description of the press as "social discourse, rather than as direct 'social statement.' "[9]

Authors in this collection suggest that on imperial topics, the
press wrote co-histories, a term I use from a concept Edward Said
borrowed from Franz Fanon: "Despite its bitterness and violence,
the whole point of Fanon's work is to force the European metropolis
to think its history *together with* the history of colonies awakening
from the cruel stupor and abused immobility of imperial domination. . . ." (italics are Said's).[10] The press generated these co-
histories in which Britain and the colonies textually constituted
themselves and each other with and against each other and in each
other's constant presence, real or imagined. All sides addressed orientalizing prejudices, the distribution of power, imperial policies,
local and national histories, religious doctrines, and the appropriation of cultures, whether British or colonial or native. The press sustained a shared locale for the coexistence of Britain and the colonies
in a virtual printed space in which authors, writing themselves and
the imperial co-histories of two places at once, evaporated the dichotomy of center and periphery, and reshaped the imagined, the
virtual, the geopolitical, and perhaps even the physical geographies
between Britain and the colonies.

Periodicals appealed to an imperial scopophilia with images of indigenous art, bodies, architecture, and monuments to satisfy readers' curiosity and reaffirm their concepts of their own and others'
identities. Press content ranged from jingoism to critiques of imperial administration, both supportive and critical of colonial wars and
imperial policy. Empire was by no means unanimously applauded by
British citizens; publications describing various wars, policies,
events, celebrations, and ethnographic discoveries contained some-
times-virulent debates over events and policies. The British public
often had to be won over about such events as General Eyre's Jamai-
can massacres, the Sepoy "Rebellion," the tactics of Cecil Rhodes or
Rajah James Brooke of Sarawak in Borneo, the legitimacy of the
Zulu Wars or the Boer Wars—the press was as capable of eliciting
sympathy for colonized and resistant natives as it was for inciting
public support for repression-as-retaliation. Multi-voiced expressions in the press offered nuanced political and psychological
debates imposed by often discontinuous historical and spatial expe-

riences of empire in each colony and intercolonially, as well. Most dramatically, the press offered a platform for subject peoples to speak; periodicals regularly published articles by colonial subjects from the Middle East and throughout Asia, and these contained dynamic, resistant views of empire, modern images of colonies, and precolonial native histories and mythologies.

As Aled Jones cogently argues, the press was a crucial "agent of change" that could profoundly affect public opinion because of "its role in disseminating information and ideas along a wide front to large populations of readers" who "read and responded to the knowledge provided by the news and to the ideas that informed it" and in their turn "conditioned the ways in which journalism was organised and professionalised."[11] The dialogic, or multi-logic, nature of the press was the outcome of its mass readership and powerful influence, as well as the function of the various and diverse ways in which the press was read and in which the press reported colonial events to effect many unpremeditated colonial decisions and policies.

Yet the press was not neutrally pluralistic. Foucault's notion of discourse as a defined set of priorities and boundaries operated in the press: "the delimitation of a field of objects, the definition of a legitimate perspective for the agent of knowledge, and the fixing of norms for the elaboration of concepts and theories . . . a play of prescriptions that designate its exclusions and choices."[12] The press was not only an agent of change, but was also a component of larger colonial enterprises of surveillance and observation to gather information for imperial control and domination. Using Antonio Gramsci's notion of hegemony in its historical, as well as theoretic, application, Gauri Viswanathan points out that colonial force was accompanied by, and often preceded by, cultural domination through the institutionalization of educational and cultural policies (Louis Althusser's kinder, gentler ideological state apparatus) that formed part of Empire's means of coaxing or coercing native cooperation with British domination.[13] The press had a major role in these "educational" processes. Communication in various newspapers for various publics and in various sites and languages meant that versions and revisions of accounts of imperial events were obsessively reiterated and disseminated around the globe.[14] The press served a vast culture of propaganda that embraced everything from postcards to the cinema, propaganda societies, and school textbooks, as John MacKenzie as documented.[15] Through institutions of education and culture, the British perpetrated the belief, according to a brief in 1838, that they were " 'more wise, more just, more humane, and more anxious to improve their condition than any other ruler they [Indians] could possibly have'" (cited in Viswanathan, 113). Viswanathan argues convincingly that the British "proved" themselves fit to rule more by representation than by actual behavior (Viswanathan, 114). Thus, representations of British ideals served to justify Empire at home and imperial control abroad, and the press was a major venue for such representations and their political uses (Viswanathan, 115–18).

Print technology in the Empire not only permitted the proliferation of British ideas and domination; it also opened opportunities for colonized writers to express themselves to global audiences, both English and native. Between 1800 and 1835, Indian writers in Bengali, Hindi, Marathi, Tamil, Telugu, and Urdu were shaping a modern prose in their respective languages, a modernization possible partly through the print medium and its wide dissemination, as Vinay Dharwadker points out.[16] According to J. Don Vann and Rosemary T. VanArsdel, from the early colonization of the nineteenth century,

> the press was influential in providing the "contact point" between the settlers, or colonists, and the native people and/or the people of previous European arrivals. In almost every colony, periodical literature also faced, head-on, the problems of multilingualism. . . . in some instances identical editions of the same copy were produced in the different tongues; occasionally two or three translations were bound together.[17]

Colonial and colonized readers and authors were not simply mimicking British ways, but critiquing, ridiculing, resisting, modifying, and upending them. Dharwadker argues for four subject positions among Indian colonial subjects, for example: "resistance, collaboration, cosmopolitanism, and revivalism" (Dharwadker, 114). Recently scholars have recognized that colonial subjectivities developed along their own lines and their own traditions and articulations: "the ineluctable and uncontainable hybridity of this print culture, without precedent in the West or elsewhere, ensured that it did not and could not replicate in India the conditions, processes, and outcomes of the Enlightenment, print capitalism, or romantic nationalism of Europe." This hybridity (from many sources) distinguished it from the "sovereign" subjectivity assumed to exist under British rule (Dharwadker, 114).

The notion of "place" is also at play in this book. The press manufactured an imaginary empire, at the same time that its nature was assumed by readers to be the "real," a transmitter of "true" events.

It also manufactured a new public sphere as powerful as any physical place and one in which imperial coercion and resistance to that coercion could take place.[18] The press public sphere, however, was still as bourgeois as the concept of public sphere introduced by Jürgen Habermas; the press offered a voice to those, including colonial nationalists, who had education and sufficient leisure to read it and write for it.[19] But this was less true of readers of the vernacular press in the colonies for whom the press's history as lived experience, offered immediacy and discursive flexibility so important to collective, native resistance to colonial domination, as Frantz Fanon noted.[20]

Place and identity have a dialectical relationship, as many of these essays argue. Agent of change, of hegemony, of resistance, and of many other inflected ideologies and opinions in between, the press voiced many colonial experiences to and from readers who inhabited a real and a virtual Empire "at home" and "abroad." The representation of the Empire in the press called on readers to support or reject policies for places they would never see and for people they would never meet except in texts and images. Each colony had its own relationship to Britain, to imperial life and authority, to its own history and to its own unstable, struggling national identity. Complex and shifting social and political alliances of memsahibs, for example, exposed "the complex part played by Western women in both sustaining imperialism and resisting or undermining it."[21] Colonies had their own pre- and post-conquest multiple histories and trajectories shaped by civil servants, families, imperial agents, and adventurers who "adopted" identities of the exotic other, "going native" while retaining their "Britishness." Being in another country offered a freedom from often-restricted identities of home, to which one could return when desired and from which one never entirely left.

SITES OF AUTHORITY: IMPERIAL DOMINATION AND PRESS INTERVENTION

The press made co-histories possible, and these essays historicize empire in its most timely form—the press that recorded momentary changes and fluctuations of the meanings of nation and empire in dynamic discourses and in powerful images. Recently, several scholars have explored the intersection of empire and the press by focusing on a particular periodical or event. Peter Sinnema's *Dynamics of the Pictured Page: Representing the Nation in the Illustrated London News* focuses longitudinally on one periodical's representation of the intersection of empire and nation in both image and text. Paula Krebs's *Gender, Race, and the Writing of Empire: Public Discourse and the Boer War* focuses on the treatment of an imperial war across public representations in a variety of periodicals. Essays in *Imperial Co-Histories* employ both kinds of examination, of particular periodicals and of issues or sets of issues across periodicals.[22]

The first section of the book examines the press's intervention to align native identity with British imperial authority and domination. Deepali Dewan examines the *Journal of Indian Art and Industry* through which Indian and British scholars and colonial administrators produced knowledge about South Asia's visual past that created notions about Indian art "traditions." The journal was associated with the art schools the British established throughout South Asia and was illustrated by new reproduction techniques. These new print technologies enabled the dissemination of information about Indian art which was based upon narratives of historical development and decay, and produced colonial knowledge that served imperial political and social agendas at a time when many believed that art symbolized the level of a culture's civilization and progress. But, of course, Indian art created its own spheres of authority and attraction quite apart from imperial ideologies and domination.

Michael Hancher's study of Walter Graham Blackie's *Imperial Gazetteer* identifies that mid-Victorian reference work as a newspaper reader's companion, a *vade mecum* that enabled the reader at home to construct the world and its Other identities out of what the press reported. An advocate for geography as an intellectual and imperial discipline, Blackie pledged objectivity, but the richly imagined account of India in his *Gazetteer* belies that ambition. Like other dictionaries, the *Gazetteer* was made out of other books, a circumstance that limited its authority if not its import, but which guaranteed its wide dissemination and influence.

Alex Nalbach explores the role of the telegraphic news agencies in their own imperial partition of the world into colonized "news" territories divided among Reuters (United Kingdom), Havas (France), and Wolff (Germany). These three agencies collaborated to dominate world information markets, transforming events in a variety of ways that magnified even minor events to make Empire newsworthy. These agencies, Nalbach argues, were the software of empire-building and empire-maintenance. Their own cartel, however, was undermined by their advocacy of New Imperialism and the accompanying European rivalries, the very forces they condoned and reflected in their news and in their own monopolistic infrastructures.

David Finkelstein examines the press's representation of Empire in *Blackwood's Magazine* from 1880 to 1900. Using archival records, as well as material published in *Blackwood's,* Finkelstein points out the close family ties between the magazine and the Indian Civil Service. The magazine assumed it held a dominant presence in India and the British colonies through its readership of civil servants and colonial administrators to which it catered. Finkelstein explores whether the magazine's Tory politics in its domestic and literary content was equally applied to its colonial coverage.

J. Lee Thompson examines the Imperial Press Conference of 1909, the first in a series of twentieth-century conferences. Close ties between attending journalists and British politicians bound the press to British nationalism and imperialism. Thompson analyzes the effect these bonds had on the colonies' contributions to the defcnsc of England in 1914 and their identification with Britishness, and journalists' cooperation in the creation of the Empire Press Union.

Dorothy O. Helly and Helen Callaway explore the press's construction of South Africa in the journalistic writings of Edmund Garrett, Randolph Churchill, and Flora Shaw during the early 1890s. Despite differences among these authors, they shared similar views about the representation of South Africa's various ethnic groups and their roles in the future development of the region's mineral wealth and political economy. They also instilled in British readers of all social classes patterns of political awareness and patriotic response that would serve to interpret the shattering events of the Jameson Raid at middecade and the Boer War that followed, events that raised critical issues not only about South Africa's place in the Empire, but Britain's own imperial identity.

Sites of Fracture: Resistance and Autonomy in Colonial Representations

In the second section, authors explore conflicts and contradictions in the periodical press through its representations of empire, including colonial and native self-representations. Often the experience of Empire split identities, sometimes through a reconstruction of gendered identity provoked by travel, and sometimes through a dialectic between a colony's historical origins—or imagined origins—and its contemporary place—or imagined place—in the Empire.

Catherine Pagani argues that the images of Chinese art and artifacts in the British press embraced a range of information, from politics to art and social customs. Focusing on the representation of Chinese culture in the popular *Illustrated London News* coverage of two major exhibitions in 1842 and in 1865, Pagani explores ways in which art objects became signifiers of a nation or "race" and their ownership a sign of European cultural and moral superiority. Art of the colonies helped define Englishness, as well as Chinese "alterity," constituted by the images and texts about these exhibitions. Pagani demonstrates that despite demonizing the Chinese in political articles, the press dealt more subtly with Chinese art while still maintaining British claims of cultural superiority and legitimate colonial power.

Denise Quirk's essay examines the role of the women's press in a colonial circuitry of people, practices, and discourses that shaped Victorian patterns of imperial identity formation. She explores the contradictions and tensions produced in the women's press as it featured images and reports of new feminist claims about women's subjectivity, the incorporation of India under the Raj, contested theories of "race," and shifts in consumer culture in the 1860s and 1870s. Focusing on representations of "Anglo-Indians," "woman's-rights women," and "true Englishwomen," Quirk argues that the press was performative, constructing and circulating interdependent notions of gender and race that contributed to the gendering of imperialism and the creation of new forms of British and colonial national identities.

Julie Codell looks at writings by Indian colonial subjects in the mainstream British press in the last quarter of the nineteenth century on three topics: imperial policies and administration, women, and Islam. Over one hundred articles appeared from 1840 on, and these were written by well-educated, Anglicized, and often politically prominent and highly nationalistic colonial subjects. They wrote to affect British imperial policy through an imaginary pact with British readers, strategically employing their "authenticity" as natives. Their identities were complex and conflicted, often shifting in a single article and claiming and rejecting both British and subaltern allegiances. These shifts and alliances were revealed in their rhetoric of reverse Orientalism and their own Enlightenment personae, as well as in their merging a defense of Empire with implications of dangers and threats to it.

Tony Hughes-d'Aeth explores the content of the *Picturesque Atlas of Australasia* produced for the Australian Centenary to demonstrate how the pictures and texts of this atlas combined history, memory, and visuality to produce a national identity that captured the desire of Australian readers to justify their discrete nationalism, while simultaneously masking the ambiguities of their historical and colonial condition. Here place and identity were joined as twinned and bound constructions of imagination, visualization, history, and ambition.

Aled Jones studies the multiple identities of Welsh missionaries who represented the British Empire. They produced their own journals and many of them were women who spoke Bengali and Welsh, making their relations with English-speaking colonial administrators complex and ambivalent. Once considered "heroic," these women were denigrated in modern postwar Wales as an imperial embarrassment. This change reflected the ambivalences of Britishness in twentieth-century Wales, as the missionaries' writing expressed their own conflicts about their "real" and "imagined" identities as Welsh and British, and their identification with colonized Indians.

Douglas Peers presents a study of J. W. Kaye in connection with the Anglo-Indian and British press. Kaye presented imperial heroes as evangelical, masculine, and chaste, underscoring differences between imperial military and administrative heroes (Elphinstone, the Lawrence brothers), and those he felt were outside this model—Indians and even some Anglo-Indians. Kaye himself was a member of different communities throughout his life—British, Anglo-Indian, and Indian. Kaye's narrative of Empire drew upon Victorian constructions of race and gender and upon his own dual experiences of writing in both India and England.

NOTES

I wish to thank Antoinette Burton for her very helpful suggestions and comments on this introduction.

1. Joanne Shattuck and Michael Wolff, eds., *The Victorian Periodical Press* (Leicester: Leicester University Press, 1982), xiv–xv.

2. Antoinette Burton, *At the Heart of the Empire: Indians and the Colonial Encounter in Late-Victorian Britain* (Berkeley and Los Angeles: University of California Press, 1998), 22.

3. Antoinette Burton, *Burdens of History: British Feminists, Indian Women, and Imperial Culture, 1865–1915* (Chapel Hill: University of North Carolina Press, 1994), 19.

4. See Julie F. Codell and Dianne Sachko Macleod, eds., *Orientalism Transposed: The Impact of the Colonies on British Culture* (Aldershot: Ashgate, 1998); see Nupur Chaudhuri, "Shawls, Jewelry, Curry, and Rice in Victorian Britain," *Western Women and Imperialism*, eds. N. Chaudhuri and M. Strobel (Bloomington: Indiana University Press, 1992), 231–46, for a compelling study of how memsahibs channeled the flow of Indian goods to Britain. See also John MacKenzie, *Orientalism* (Manchester:

Manchester University Press, 1995), for discussions of the influence of colonial visual cultures on British art and architecture.

5. Raymond Williams, *The Country and the City* (New York: Oxford University Press, 1973), 1–3; Simon Gikandi, *Maps of Englishness: Writing Identity in the Culture of Colonialism* (New York: Columbia University Press, 1996), *xviii*.

6. In the nineteenth century, "Anglo-Indian" referred to those British living in India, while "Eurasian" referred to those of mixed "race."

7. Benita Parry, *Delusions and Discoveries: Studies on India in the British Imagination, 1880–1930* (Berkeley and Los Angeles: University of California Press, 1972).

8. Michael Wolff, "Charting the Golden Stream," *Victorian Periodicals Newsletter,* 13 (1971): 26–27.

9. Lyn Pykett, "Reading the Periodical Press: Text and Context," *Investigating Victorian Journalism,* eds. L. Brake, A. Jones, L. Madden (London: Macmillan, 1990), 15. See also Pykett, "Reading the Periodical Press: Text and Context," *Victorian Periodicals Review,* 22 (1989): 107.

10. Edward Said, "Representing the Colonized: Anthropology's Interlocutors," *Critical Inquiry,* 15 (1989): 223.

11. Aled Jones, *Powers of the Press* (London: Scolar, 1996), 2–3.

12. Michel Foucault, "History of Systems of Thought," *Language, Counter-memory, Practice,* ed. D. F. Bouchard (Ithaca: Cornell University Press, 1977), 199.

13. Gauri Viswanathan, "Currying Favor: The Politics of British Educational and Cultural Policy in India, 1813–54," *Dangerous Liaisons: Gender, Nation, and Postcolonial Perspectives,* eds. A. McClintock, A. Mufti, and E. Shohat (Minneapolis: University of Minnesota Press, 1997), 113–14.

14. For a study of this circulation of imperial news, see C. A. Bayly, *Empire and Information* (Cambridge: Cambridge University Press, 1996).

15. John M. MacKenzie, *Propaganda and Empire* (Manchester: Manchester University Press, 1984).

16. Vinay Dharwadker, "Print Culture and Literary Markets in Colonial India," *Language Machines,* eds. J. Masten, P. Stallybrass, and N. Vickers (London: Routledge, 1997), 112–13.

17. J. D. Vann and R. VanArsdel, *Periodicals of Queen Victoria's Empire* (Toronto: University of Toronto, 1996), 5.

18. Ato Sekyi-Otu, *Fanon's Dialectic of Experience* (Cambridge: Harvard University Press, 1996), 82, on the relation between place/space and coercion.

19. Jürgen Habermas, *The Structural Transformation of the Public Sphere,* trans., Burger and Lawrence (Cambridge: Harvard University Press), 1989.

20. Frantz Fanon, *The Wretched of the Earth.* trans., Constance Farrington. Preface by Jean-Paul Sartre (New York: Grove Press, 1963).

21. N. Chaudhuri and M. Strobel, eds., *Western Women and Imperialism* (Bloomington: Indiana University Press, 1992), 12.

22. Peter Sinnema, *Dynamics of the Pictured Page: Representing the Nation in the Illustrated London News* (Aldershot: Ashgate, 1998); Paula Krebs, *Gender, Race, and the Writing of Empire* (Cambridge: Cambridge University Press, 1999).

Part 1

Sites of Authority:
Imperial Domination
and Press Intervention

Scripting South Asia's Visual Past: *The Journal of Indian Art and Industry* and the Production of Knowledge in the Late Nineteenth Century

Deepali Dewan

In THE PAST DECADE, DISCIPLINES IN THE SOCIAL SCIENCES AND, MORE RE-cently, in the humanities, have traced their origins to postenlighten-ment thinking and, more particularly, to the forms of knowledge fa-cilitated by and produced in the colonial context. This is also true for the discipline of South Asian Art History. Illustrated publications played a central role in producing forms of art historical knowledge. In this essay, I examine *The Journal of Indian Art and Industry,* a major illustrated journal of South Asian art published in the latter half of the nineteenth and early part of the twentieth centuries. I show how particular forms of knowledge about South Asia's artistic past were produced within its pages through the choice of subject matter, manner and sequence of illustration, and the relationship between image and text. As a periodical, *The Journal of Indian Art and Industry* had a regularity that other illustrated text books did not, and was able to standardize certain ideas about Indian art through its circula-tion and reach. Benedict Anderson has pointed out the central role that the print literature, especially press media, has had in produc-ing imagined communities (1991). The illustrated press in the latter half of the nineteenth century, for the case of South Asia, played a similar role in producing an intellectual community that shared particular forms of knowledge about South Asian art. This knowl-edge, I would argue, has become a part of disciplinary knowledge in the discipline of South Asian Art History today.

The production of knowledge in the discipline of South Asian art history has been explored in the important volume *Perceptions of South Asia's Visual Past* (1994) edited by Catherine Asher and Thomas Metcalf. The introduction lays out a ground work for Euro-pean perceptions of South Asian art that builds upon Partha Mitter's *Much Maligned Monsters* (1977). It argues that points of debate about

Indian art reflected theories of the rise and decline of civilizations, producing an "orientalist canon" in the process (3–4). As a result, the past became a site around which narratives of South Asian visual culture were constructed. While the essays examine the work of particular scholars or scholarship on particular monuments now a part of the canon (see especially the 1994 Tartakov essay), the role of the illustrated press in disseminating ideas about Indian art is conspicuously absent. The insightful volume edited by Tim Barringer and Tom Flynn, *Colonialism and the Object* (1998), explores the intersection of art objects and colonialism through institutions such as annual exhibitions and museums (see also Guha-Thakurta 1998). While these institutions are key components in the production and circulation of objects in the nineteenth century, the role of art schools is absent. My examination of *The Journal of Indian Art and Industry* attempts to fill these gaps by foregrounding the central role played by art schools and the illustrated press in producing knowledge about South Asian art. It attempts to bridge scholarship in the Humanities with that in the Social Sciences by historians and anthropologists who have been examining how culture, particularly notions of "tradition," were produced in the interstices of colonial policy (Mani 1989; Dirks 1992, 1997; Cohn 1996; Raheja 1999).

THE JOURNAL OF INDIAN ART AND INDUSTRY
AND CHROMO-LITHOGRAPHY

The Journal of Indian Art and Industry (hereafter *JIAI*) was published quarterly from 1884 to 1917 (fig. 1). There were a total of seventeen volumes (136 issues). The journal was initiated by Edward Charles Buck, the Secretary to the Government of India in the Revenue and Agricultural Department, in collaboration with Thomas Holbein Hendley and John Lockwood Kipling, principals of the main art schools on the subcontinent at Jaipur and Lahore, respectively. As stated in the first issue of the journal, its purpose was to: increase demand of Indian art industries; facilitate their supply through trade agencies; call on authorities abroad to help direct progress; shape tastes of consumers, suppliers, and producers toward older artistic forms; and give art school students an education based on indigenous models by having them produce the illustrations (*JIAI* 1: *iii–iv*). Kipling wrote the first two issues and contributions to subsequent issues were made by a range of authors, both British and Indian. In 1894, the name of the journal was changed from *Journal of Indian Arts* to *The Journal of Indian Art and*

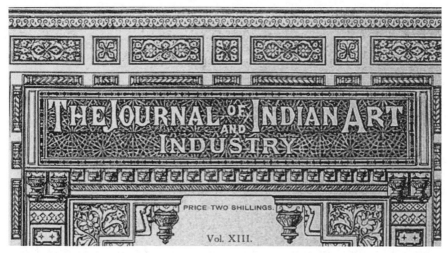

Figure 1. Cover detail. *Journal of Indian Art and Industry,* Volume XIII, Number 108 (October 1909).

Industry. Topics included reports on art industries such as textiles, architecture, and metalwork, or on particular regions of the subcontinent such as Punjab, Rajasthan, and Madras. Further, reports on the many annual exhibitions that took place during the course of the nineteenth century, such as in London, Paris, Jaipur, and Calcutta, were also included.

JIAI was the first journal devoted to the study of Indian art.[1] Each issue of *JIAI* contained either a series of articles or a monograph on a specific topic. It published articles by some of the main figures involved in art education in South Asia and England in the latter half of the nineteenth century such as art school principals, museum directors, exhibition organizers, industrialists, art enthusiasts, and government officials. Other than the individuals already mentioned, authors included E. B. Havell, H. H. Cole, James Burgess, Vincent Smith, Henry Cousens, Sir George Birdwood, Alfred Chatterton, Cecil Burns, Lady Herringham, O. C. Gangoly, and Ananda Coomaraswamy. In this way, the journal reflected the evolution of thought about South Asian art, from colonial ideologies expressed by Hendley and Kipling to the nationalist concerns of Coomaraswamy in the last issues.[2]

The journal was also important as an illustrated publication in an age when illustrations, especially in color, were few and expensive. In a 1894 conference on art education, Hendley urges those present that the importance of producing art publications was not for the text but for the illustrations themselves: "The truth is that any one who has the opportunity of merely illustrating rare works of art is doing inestimable service . . ." *(Papers* 21). Each issue of the *JIAI* contained two to ten illustrations to accompany the text. These illustrations were usually bound in the issue after the text and were black and white and in color. The illustrations in the *JIAI* documented works of art from South Asia's artistic past deemed worthy of emulation by art schools officials. Towards the end of its run, Hendley explained the chief purpose of the *JIAI* was to "put on permanent record, by illustration and description, good works of the past, and so to set up standards to which . . . to conform . . . " *(JIAI* 15: 51). Through the journal, these illustrations were dispersed to art schools for students to copy. As examples of good design, they were also meant to shape consumer taste.

The *JIAI* was one of the first journals to mass-produce color illustrations. *The Illustrated London News,* for example, had increased the desire for popular illustrated literature, but could only afford the reproduction of black and white etchings. Up until the end of the nineteenth century, color illustrations had to be colored by hand at great expense, or through aquatint engraving, which was limited to two or three inks (Hardie *vii,* 87). The *JIAI* was among the first publications to mass-produce color illustrations in a relatively affordable manner. This was achieved by William Griggs, a London publisher who had been the official publisher to the East India Company and the Indian Museum.[3] He was the major publisher of large-scale art books of South Asian art and contributed to the development of a new technology called photo-chromo-lithography that allowed the production of color illustrations at a cheap rate. While he was not the sole inventor, he was responsible for its continued use in the late nineteenth and early twentieth century (Hardie 225). In a pamphlet made in 1882 to advertise his publishing business, Griggs promoted the new method by calling photography a handmaid to the manufacturing arts (Griggs 3). Photography allowed for an accuracy of detail that the early illustrative technologies could not match.[4] Further, the combination of photographic and printing technologies produced a method of mass production that was both accurate and affordable. The *JIAI* remained at a low cost of Rs 2 throughout its run (with a short span at its beginning when it sold for Rs 1 per issue).

The case of Grigg's career alludes to the fact that the development of color-illustrated literature was forged primarily by publications about geographical areas considered the West's Other. European interest for the exotic and images of curiosity was facilitated by imperialist expansion and colonial policies in surveying and documenting of conquered lands and cultures. The *JIAI* is one example in which the development of new technologies of color illustration was facilitated by colonial policies. The colonial context provided the means for the surveying of South Asia's artistic past and colonial art education required the documentation and dispersal of images of South Asia's artistic past for the promotion of traditional arts. Thus colonialism produced the conditions that allowed for and then necessitated the use of photographic technologies in the mass production of color illustrations. In this way, the *JIAI* is an important example of the way in which colonialism facilitated the project of modernity.

Although it did not achieve a large subscription base—often being published at a loss—the *JIAI* played a role in dispersing ideas about Indian art to a wide audience (*Papers* 20). Like many nineteenth-century publications, one issue was passed around and read by many individuals, thus becoming accessible to people beyond an individual subscriber. Further, individual issues or articles from the journal were republished later as monographs that became important texts in art history scholarship.[5] The journal ceased in 1917 with no indication by postscript or note of its cessation, suggesting that it was possibly an unforeseen event. Ray Desmond suggests that the journal stopped due to a wartime shortage of paper (Desmond 204). Yet the reasons remain unclear. The journal seemed to have been largely the efforts of Buck, Hendley and the publisher Griggs, who often served as editor. Grigg's death in 1911 followed by the deaths of Buck and Hendley in 1917, whose obituaries are included in the last few issues, were the likely cause for the journal's abrupt closure. This underscores the central role of a few key players not only in the production of the journal, but in shaping and disseminating ideas about Indian art via the print medium that would reach a wide audience through the emerging nineteenth-century illustrated press. The *JIAI* produced knowledge about South Asia's artistic past that would have a lasting impact in a number of ways. These ways form the focus of my examination for the remainder of this essay.

Producing "Tradition"

The Journal of Indian Art and Industry was part of the promotion of traditional arts in the arena of art education in the latter half of the nineteenth century, which consisted of art schools, annual exhibitions, and museums as part of an institutional triangle. The agenda of art education had shifted from an earlier focus on the promotion of western ideals of naturalistic drawing to the promotion of traditional Indian arts (Mitter 1994). One avenue for this promotion was the publication of articles and images on traditional industries and monuments. The journal was conceived when Buck had written to Hendley to ask how to obtain photographs of objects from the Jeypore Exhibition of 1883, one of the major nineteenth-century exhibitions on the South Asian subcontinent heralded as displaying excellent examples of traditional arts (*JIAI* 17:84). The objects on display were from the Maharaja of Jaipur's private collection and were considered by art administrators as examples that could be used in art schools to promote traditional art production. Photographs of such works could be distributed to arts schools as a way for students and craftsmen to study and emulate good examples beyond the close of an exhibition. The journal was conceived as a venue for the distribution of such images. In this way, the *JIAI* was the print component of a network of institutions and individuals, and had a profound influence for the circulation of ideas about Indian arts not possible for static structures like museums and exhibitions or individual people.

One way *JIAI* produced knowledge of South Asia's artistic past was simply the choice of subject matter in the articles. The subject matter of the articles together came to constitute what was considered "traditional" Indian arts. Of the 136 issues of the journal, the majority of articles were on textiles. This is not surprising, as South Asia's textile industry had constituted a major portion of the export market from the subcontinent to Britain since the eighteenth century. Publications on the technical and visual aspects of textile production were desirable by both British textile mills and art schools as a way to emulate examples of commercially and aesthetically successful products. The second most common subject matter in the *JIAI* was architecture, of which almost half the articles focused on Mughal monuments such as Fatehpur Sikri, the Taj Mahal, and Akbar's Tomb at Sikandra. The third most common subject was metalwork, followed by reports on annual exhibitions, pottery, wood carving, and enameling in descending order. The reports on annual exhibitions are interesting for they focus on a variety of decorative art practices and presented them, even contemporary productions, as "traditional" Indian art. The subject matter of the articles together defined what came to constitute the "traditional" in Indian art and industry. Those art-making practices that were not written about in some form or another became largely absent in what was being constructed as a canon of Indian art. The journal, for example, is one way certain monuments came to constitute "Mughal architecture" and how Mughal architecture, in turn, came to hold a major position in the canon of South Asian architecture.

Further, articles that combined mediums were often defined along regional lines. For example, articles such as "Decorative Art in Rajputana" (*JIAI* 2) and "The Industries of Madras" (*JIAI* 3) were organized by political boundaries of native royal states or British presidencies. The categorization of art industries along these lines implied and then naturalized stylistic coherency within these regions. It conflated political boundaries with stylistic regions, producing a manner of talking and thinking about South Asia's visual culture along regional lines, suggesting a distinct aesthetic division between political regions which may not necessarily have been there.

Mughal architecture and other select components of South Asia's artistic past were valorized in the pages of the *JIAI* because they fit in with ideas about good design generated in the nineteenth century as a result of the intersection of colonial and metropolitan art education. In the early part of the nineteenth century, England was distressed over the waning commercial interest (in both export and domestic markets) in her art manufactures. In attempts to revive its art industry, England instituted a scheme of art education in 1837 to teach the principles of design and manufacture (Sparkes 33–41; Macdonald 73 ff; see also Efland 1990). At the 1851 Great Exhibition, the first of its kind, the decorative arts of South Asia were heralded as displaying the aesthetic ideals of design and could be used to teach students in British schools. The type of design that was particularly attractive to British art schools was abstract or geometric designs that ornamented a surface without masking the function of the object. This aesthetic ideal was seen as far superior to the current Victorian style of decoration that overwhelmed the surface of an object with naturalistic ornamentation. In this way, the textile arts and the arts of Islamic South Asia were foregrounded as being particularly suitable models for decorative design.[6]

The study of select monuments from South Asia's visual past as models of good design also determined how they were represented in image and text as well. The textual content of articles on textiles focused on the technical processes in their production and explained the process in detail from the beginning. For example, issue 108 from October 1909 focuses on silk industries of India and details silk production from the initial stage of gathering the silkworm to the production of the fabric. The illustrations parallel the textual narrative by depicting the different species of worm, their cocoons, and the resulting moths. Further, there are images of the traditional methods of production and illustrations of fabric samples and their designs (fig. 2). These do not parallel the textual narrative but are a result instead of the use of images in art school curriculum, as a way to study examples deemed of good design to use for the basis of new production. The illustrations of the sample fabrics are close-up views of particular designs. They do not show the whole fabric, or uses of the fabric, but rather the designs on the surface. As images on a flat page, they are decontextualized from their original object and made available for copying onto any surface. In this way, the illustrations in the *JIAI* both worked with the text and constituted an independent component as patterns for use in art schools.

Similarly, articles on architecture served the journal's function as a pattern book. The textual content of articles on architecture focused on the architectural ornament. In the illustrations, usually a

Figure 2. "Indian Poppy" design on silk (detail). Photo-chromolithograph by William Griggs. In "The Silk Industries of India," by Thomas Holbein Hendley, *Journal of Indian Art and Industry*, Vol. XIII, no. 108 (October 1909), plate 4.

view of the whole monument was presented first, situated in a landscape indicated by a few trees or figures. Subsequent illustrations detailed the ornamentation rendered as flat designs (figs. 3, 4). These were meant to serve as patterns that not only documented South Asia's visual past but provided a design that could be reproduced on surfaces of contemporary manufacture. The progression of illustrations from an overview of the monument to a series of details was like a lens that studied an object with increasing scrutiny. This linear visual progression replicated Enlightenment methodology of scientific study that moved from the general to the specific, from whole to detail. This same format is still the way the scholarly analysis of a monument or art object, narrated through image and text, is presented in the discipline of South Asian art history today. The study of select monuments through image and text in the print space of the *JIAI* led to their continued central place as "traditional" arts in the canon of South Asian art history.

Reproducing the Narrative of Decline

In addition to a valorization of certain forms of South Asia's artistic past, the 1851 Great Exhibition also produced a concern in official British art circles about the seemingly recent decline of South Asian art industries. It was believed that South Asian art had significantly declined from a higher aesthetic achievement in the past to one degraded by commercialization, industrialization, and bad taste. The condemnation of art practices marked by industrialization was informed by the growing arts and crafts movement led by William Morris. This movement condemned synthetic materials and mass production in favor of hand-crafted, natural materials, and traditional designs. The 1883 gathering of art schools officials at the Calcutta exhibition, out of which the *JIAI* was born, was primarily intended to establish a scheme to stop degradation in Indian arts through a joint effort that would involve art schools, exhibitions, and museums (Mitter 1994).[7] The primary means was to record information on traditional art practices and disseminate it through a variety of formats, such as a system of awards in schools and at exhibitions, a scheme of display in museums, and through the print medium.

In order to "save" South Asian art, information about the artistic past had to be recorded and distributed as a way to educate people in what were good artistic forms. The articles in *JIAI* not only provided examples of good artwork to British art schools, but provided

Figure 3. Wazir Khan Mosque, Lahore. Drawing by Sher Mohammad, Drawing Master, Mayo School of Art, Lahore. Chromolithograph by William Griggs. In "The Mosque of Wazir Khan, Lahore," by John Lockwood Kipling, *Journal of Indian Art and Industry*, Vol. II, no. 19 (October 1888).

Figure 4. Wazir Khan Mosque (detail). Drawn by Mohamed Din, Allah-ud-din and Amir Baksh, students of Lahore School of Art. Chromolithograph by William Griggs. In "The Mosque of Wazir Khan, Lahore," by John Lockwood Kipling, *Journal of Indian Art and Industry*, Vol. II, no. 19 (October 1888).

examples of good objects from South Asia's past in order to stop the decline in Indian art industries. A discourse of decline came to be the ideological fulcrum around which ideas about Indian art were formed. This narrative of decline for Indian arts associated examples from the past with good design and examples from the present with bad design. Most books, reports, and articles published on Indian art in the latter half of the nineteenth century in some way reflected or were marked by this belief in decline.

In attempts to curb decline in contemporary production, the journal assumed an authority and discretion as to which objects from South Asia's visual past were worthy of study and emulation. In the space of the journal, a few people had control over the circulation and evaluation of images. In looking backward in order to define artistic models worthy of emulation, the discourse of decline asserted and then naturalized an equation between good and traditional. What was "bad" was the new. In equating good with traditional, what was deemed good came to define, in turn, what was traditional. In this way, images chosen as good models formed a canon of works that would be the foundation of later scholarship.

Articles on present-day industries illustrated examples that proceeded from good examples to bad ones. The good examples were
often cited as "old" examples fortunate enough to be preserved in
private collections. For example, in an article on "Phulkari Work in
the Punjab" by Mrs. F. A. Steel, the illustrations at the end of the
text start with examples of older phulkari embroidery (*JIAI* II). The
first two illustrations are labeled "Very Old Work" and "Very Old
Border, Showing Highly Decorative Darning Work." The reader is
to take these examples as good specimens in comparison to the illustrations that follow. The last two images in the series of twenty-nine
plates are labeled "Manchester Bagh, Specimen of the Cause of
Phulkari Deterioration. Result of Native Bad Taste" and "Jubilee
Bagh, Result of English Bad Taste." These examples are modern
work, as indicated by their labels. While Steel blames both English
and Indian "bad taste" for the creation of the bad designs, the older
samples are held up as the models to follow. In this way, the very
order of illustrations produced a narrative of decline—from good to
bad—that overlapped a chronological degradation—from old to
new. In this way, the narrative of decline was reinforced not only in
text but through the illustrations as well.

Producing the "Native Craftsman"

The notion of "tradition" and the narrative of decline come together in the figure of the "native craftsman." In almost every article examining an industry from South Asia's visual past or present,
there is an illustration of a "native craftsman" at work. This image
features quite prominently in the nineteenth-century arena of art
education. At exhibitions in India and London, photographs or
drawings of the "native craftsman" were presented beside the objects on display. In some instances, craftsmen themselves were
brought in to demonstrate their process of production to the viewing public. In many ways, the native craftsman offered a sense of authenticity to an art object, that is, he solidified the "traditional" in
what came to be defined as traditional Indian art. At the same time,
he became identified with the source of Indian arts decline as the
agent whose bad taste produced the art industries in need of revival.
The image of the "native craftsman" conveyed both associations.[8]

In both text and image, the *JIAI* constructed a romanticized notion of the "native craftsman" (fig. 5). In him, art administrators
sought a refuge from the industrialization of the late nineteenth
century. The "native craftsman" became a specific site for the nos-

Figure 5. "Wood Carver." Drawn by John Lockwood Kipling, Simla, 1870. In "Industries of the Punjab," by John Lockwood Kipling, *Journal of Indian Art and Industry,* **Vol. II, no. 20 (October 1888).**

talgia for a pre-industrial past. Qualities heralded by the Arts and Crafts Movement were the very qualities used by the colonial administration to describe the colonized native. Nonindustrial meant "not progressive," "not modern," and bound by the past. These characteristics were also deployed by the British to justify their presence, claiming that Indian natives needed British authority as a way to civilize, modernize, and advance. The "native craftsman," then, as a symbol of tradition and nonindustrialization, became a site of contention and justification for Empire. He embodied qualities that were, on the one hand, to be praised and, on the other hand, to be condemned, controlled, and improved. In the context of debates around Indian art industries, the "native craftsman" became a repository of tradition and of degradation. As a repository of tradition, he was the last link to a preindustrial age and knowledge of the old techniques. On the other hand, as a colonized subject and thus perceived as being inferior in the skills of rational thinking, judgment, and discernment—qualities of the British "experts"—the "native craftsman" was also viewed with suspicion. He was perceived to be susceptible to industrialization and commercialization, and thus the cause of Indian art's decline.

Illustrations of the "native craftsman" in publications like *JIAI* visualized the contradiction. Always presented in the mode of doing work, his body in labor came to stand for the transmission of traditional knowledge as well as for the potential transmission of degraded aesthetic form. The presence of the image of the "native craftsman" at work validated such publications as the *JIAI* that were meant to both promote "tradition" and stop the decline of Indian art. This presence of the figure of the "native craftsman" authenticated the textual information written therein. The proximity of the image to the text suggested that the knowledge presented was similar to the traditional knowledge possessed by the "native craftsman." Yet the proximity of the image of the "native craftsman" to the text also suggested his close surveillance by colonial authority, whose presence was represented by the journal itself. In this way, the figure of the "native craftsman" was produced by the colonial illustrated press and in turn played a role in shaping its discursive content.

Conclusion

In this essay, I examine *The Journal of Indian Art and Industry* as a preliminary examination of the role of the illustrated press in producing forms of art historical knowledge in the latter half of the nineteenth century. In particular, I examine the relationship between image and text in three broad areas—producing the notion of "tradition," the narrative of decline, and the figure of the "native craftsman." Scholars in colonial studies have pointed out that the process of gathering information that was so much a part of the colonial context, was hardly as passive and objective an act as the terms "survey," "compile," and "collect" imply. Rather, the process of gathering was an act that not only recorded information but produced knowledge about the colonized. The production of art historical knowledge is an emerging arena of analysis. While certain

avenues have been explored, art education in one area remains un-
examined. *The Journal of Indian Art and Industry* was a result of many
of the debates in colonial art education in the latter half of the nineteenth century. It is one example of how colonialism and the press
intersected to produce and distribute knowledge about South Asia's
visual past. At the same time, it cannot be understood solely within
a framework of colonialism as many of the art debates were shaped
by movements taking place outside the colonial context. In this way,
the nineteenth-century illustrated press serves as an important example of how colonialism and modernity were not separate but profoundly interconnected processes.

NOTES

1. An earlier journal was published by Dr. Alexander Hunter, the founder and
first Principal of the Madras School of Arts. Called the *Indian Journal of Art, Science,
Manufacture*, eight issues were published between 1850–51 and another four in
1856. Two supplementary issues, the *Illustrated Indian Journal of Arts*, were published
in 1851, which featured images meant to be used in art education. This journal
differed from *The Journal of Indian Art and Industry* in that it contained lessons in
drawing alongside reports on geology and scientific experiments in paper-making.
It was meant as an art school textbook and to encourage local industries. It was
short-lived, was largely written by Hunter, and had a limited circulation within the
Madras Presidency save a few copies sent by Hunter abroad. *The Journal of Indian Art
and Industry*, in contrast, contained studies of particular art industries and patterns
students could use in art production, had a lengthy run, published contributions
from many authors, and had a wide circulation. Hunter's journal is interesting as a
document of the very early phases of colonial art education in South Asia as it includes reprints of early lectures by Hunter at the Madras art school. Further, it reflects the state of colonial art education before the shift in art school policy toward
the preservation of traditional Indian arts which was the ideological foundation for
the later *Journal of Indian Art and Industry*.
2. In this analysis, I focus on the content of the journal prior to appearance of
nationalist-inspired articles, which merit separate consideration.
3. Born in 1832, Griggs began work at the age of twelve (Desmond 122). His first
involvement with Indian arts was at the Indian Court of the 1851 Great Exhibition
where he worked as a carpenter. He would later serve in various capacities in service
of the Indian Court at exhibition in Paris in 1855 and 1857, in London in 1871,
and in Vienna in 1873 (*JIAI* 15:31). He worked as Technical Assistant under Forbes
Royle at the East India House in setting up displays of the East India Company's
collections of Indian objects and later under Forbes Watson, Reporter on the Products of India, after the collection was transferred to the India Museum (Desmond
123 and *JIAI* 15:31). His main role was as photographer, and he was employed on
many of the early photographic documentation projects of the people and culture
of the Indian subcontinent. In 1863 he was made main photographer on the *People
of India* (1868–75), a collection of photographs of Indian royalty and people, for
which he selected photographs in the museum's collection and made all the prints

for two hundred sets of the volumes (Desmond 98). He also photographed every fragment of the Buddhist Stupa of Amaravati that had been sent to the Indian Museum by surveyor Colin MacKenzie as part of the process to collect and preserve monuments from India's ancient past. These photographs were then used by James Fergusson, one of the earliest historians of Indian art, as illustrations in his study of Buddhism, *Tree and Serpent Worship in India* (1874) which Griggs printed (Desmond 160). Throughout the time Griggs worked at institutions involved in collecting and displaying Indian objects of interest, he worked at adapting photography with the printing process in efforts to produce a method of mass production at an affordable cost. In 1868, he gave a paper on the marriage of photography and chromolithography to the London Photographic Society, using the case study of his work at the India Museum on a volume of Indian textile design (Griggs 3). Griggs career is interesting as a point of convergence for a number of elements in the late nineteenth century that set the conditions of the proliferation of illustrated publications on South Asian art: surveying, exhibition displays, museum collections, colonializm, illustration technologies, and mass production.

4. For a introduction to the nineteenth-century uses of photography in imaging empire, see John Falconer's entry in Chris Bayly, *The Raj* (London: National Portrait Gallery, 1990), 274–308. For a more recent examination, see Vidya Dehejia, ed., *India Through the Lens: Photography 1840–1911* (Washington, D.C., Ahmedabad, and Munich: Freer Gallery or Art and Arthur M. Sackler Gallery with Mapin and Prestel, 2000).

5. For example, a series of monographs on *Art and Industry through the Ages* was published in the late 1970s and early 1980s by Navrang.

6. The use of particular Mughal monuments, especially Fatehpur Sikri, as the basis for the style of Indo-Sarcenic architecture produced by British architects in South Asia, underscores the connection between knowledge about South Asia's artistic past produced in the arena of art education (of which the *JIAI* is one manifestation) and the production of a new kind of visual culture in the late nineteenth and early twentieth century. In turn, the production of a new kind of visual culture that was deliberately based on past models further secured those models a place in what was considered the "traditional" arts of the subcontinent.

7. For a larger discussion on the intersections of metropole and colony in the arena of art education, see Deepali Dewan, "Crafting Knowledge and Knowledge of Crafts: Art Education, Colonialism and the Madras School of Arts in Nineteenth-Century South Asia" (Ph.D. diss., University of Minnesota, 2001).

8. For a fuller discussion of the figure of the "native craftsman" at work, see Deepali Dewan, "The Body at Work: Colonial Art Education and the Figure of the 'Native Craftsman,'" in Satadru Sen and James Mills, eds., *Confronting the Body: The Politics of Physicality in Colonial and Post-Colonial India* (London: Anthem Press, forthcoming).

An Imagined World: *The Imperial Gazetteer*

Michael Hancher

What, they lived once thus at Venice where the merchants were
   the kings,
Where Saint Mark's is, where the Doges used to wed the sea with
   rings?

Ay, because the sea's the street there; and 'tis arched by . . . what
   you call
. . . Shylock's bridge with houses on it, where they kept the
   carnival:
I was never out of England—it's as if I saw it all.
                                    —Robert Browning, "A Toccata of Galuppi's"

As THE SPEAKER OF "A TOCATTA OF GALUPPI'S" GROPES HIS WAY TO A
recognition of eighteenth-century Venetian culture, prompted by
music of that time and place, it becomes apparent that his understanding has already been informed by what he has read and seen
in print or (as with Shylock's bridge) has encountered in theatrical
representations of print. "I was never out of England—it's as if I saw
it all." Galuppi's marvelous music is not evocative by itself: the prior
marvel is that printed words and images enable its learned auditor
to imagine a distant place, time, and cultural identity. The mer-
chant-kings, the ritual wedding, the distinctive canals "there" and
the bridge "where" the carnival took place—thanks to the experience of print, all those exotic, local particulars can easily be imagined from the Victorian perspective.

Contemporary with Browning's poem, the hefty book under examination in this chapter, *The Imperial Gazetteer: A General Dictionary
of Geography, Physical, Political, Statistical and Descriptive, Compiled from
the Latest and Best Authorities,* worked as a verbal and visual gloss on
the foreign world that members of the British middle class constantly read about and thought they knew in their magazines and
daily newspapers. Itself a pastiche of received accounts and images
(as the last phrase of the subtitle acknowledges), this *Gazetteer* sup-

plied the reading public at home with essential ingredients for the imaginative construction of a world and its peoples elsewhere—a world that was increasingly important to the British empire, in those remnants not actually subsumed by it.

The Scottish firm of Blackie and Son began to publish *The Imperial Gazetteer* in parts in 1850. When the thirty-sixth and last part was published in 1855, the entire work was put on sale, bound in two volumes (fig. 6). The parts sold for 2s. 6d. each; the two volumes sold for £4. 15s.[1] In many ways this work was a characteristic Blackie production. Useful and informative, practical and improving, it took its place in a long line of intellectual tools for the rising lower-middle-class, which included such works as William Grier's *The Mechanic's Calculator, or Workman's Memorial Book* (1832), Thomas Andrew's *Cyclopedia of Domestic Medicine and Surgery* (1842), and *The Popular Encyclopedia* (7 volumes, 1841). Matched in the Blackie catalogue by numerous works of piety and popular theology, such works overshadowed occasional works of belles lettres, often of Scottish inflection—Alexander Whitelaw's *Casquet of Literary Gems*; Thomas Hogg's stories and poems; the poems of Robert Burns. Published in relatively inexpensive parts, *The Imperial Gazetteer* continued the firm's tradition of packaging knowledge for the impecunious.[2]

However, the economy of the publishing arrangement was disguised by the grandeur of the title. The *Imperial* epithet, which up to midcentury connoted not imperialism so much as nationalism and seriousness of purpose (and which more particularly denoted a large format of paper[3]), was virtually a Blackie brand name: before *The Imperial Gazetteer* there was *The Imperial Dictionary* (1847–50), and before that *The Imperial Family Bible* (1841); later there would be *The Imperial Atlas of Modern Geography* (1859) and *The Imperial Bible-Dictionary* (1864–66).[4] The matrix of concepts named in these titles identifies much of the power of the printed word. If mass literacy was the product of domestic Bible reading, especially in Scotland, it required not only capital such as the Blackies supplied, but also a developed lexicography; and it led to the inventorying of the world.[5]

Originally, as Noah Webster knew, a gazetteer was "[a] writer of news, or an officer appointed to publish news by authority."[6] Secondarily, the term was apt to figure as "[t]he title of a newspaper." Only later did the term come to designate "[a] book containing a brief description of empires, kingdoms, cities, towns, and rivers, in a country or in the whole world, alphabetically arranged; a book of topographical descriptions." The Blackies' *Imperial Dictionary* repeated all three of Webster's definitions verbatim—the standard, derivative practice in that work.

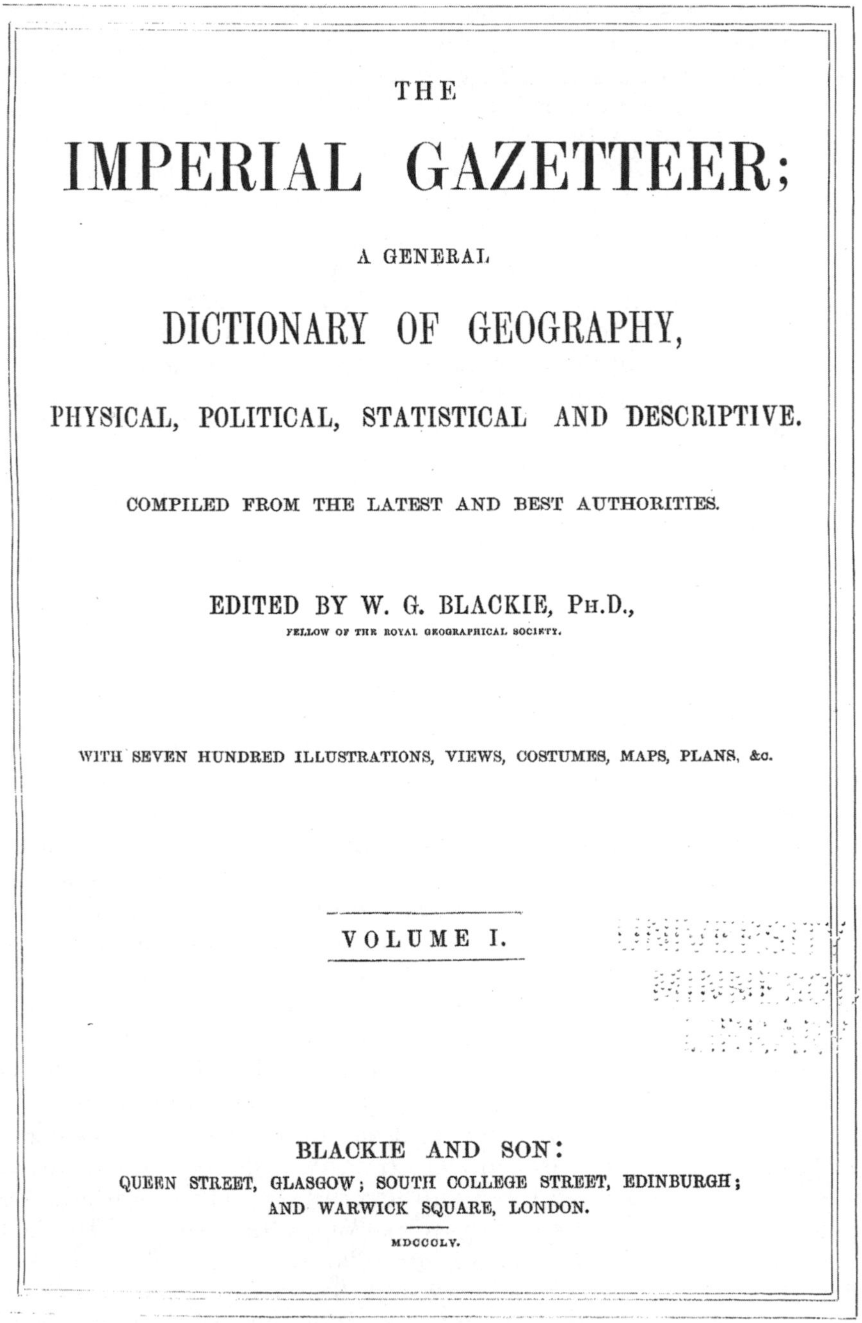

THE
IMPERIAL GAZETTEER;

A GENERAL

DICTIONARY OF GEOGRAPHY,

PHYSICAL, POLITICAL, STATISTICAL AND DESCRIPTIVE.

COMPILED FROM THE LATEST AND BEST AUTHORITIES.

EDITED BY W. G. BLACKIE, Ph.D.,
FELLOW OF THE ROYAL GEOGRAPHICAL SOCIETY.

WITH SEVEN HUNDRED ILLUSTRATIONS, VIEWS, COSTUMES, MAPS, PLANS, &c.

VOLUME I.

BLACKIE AND SON:
QUEEN STREET, GLASGOW; SOUTH COLLEGE STREET, EDINBURGH;
AND WARWICK SQUARE, LONDON.

MDCCCLV.

Figure 6. Title page of *Imperial Gazetteer* (1855), Volume I.

Neither Webster nor the Blackies' lexicographer, John Ogilvie, considered how "gazetteer" came to acquire a geographical denotation. At the turn of the century, however, the *New English Dictionary* would uncover the explanation of the shift. In 1692 the historian Laurence Echard had published a book called *The Gazetteer's, or Newsman's Interpreter: Being a Geographical Index of all the Considerable Cities, Patriarchships, Bishopricks, Universities, Dukedoms, Earldoms, and Such Like; Imperial and Hance Towns, Ports, Forts, Castles, &c. in Europe.* Evidently a gazette's printed news, especially news of the world, required interpretation and explanation, for the reader if not indeed for the writer. This need, Echard suggested in his title, could be met quickly by taking up his alphabetized "geographical index." When the success of his volume led Echard to produce Part II, in 1704, he justified it in a phrase that changed the meaning of the word: "The kind Reception the Gazetteer has met with in the World . . . [has] induced us to go on with a second Part."[7] And so the writer became the written, and *gazetteers*, so called, came into being, explicitly as an aid to reading the printed word, implicitly as a way of rewriting the world.

The Blackies characterized their *Imperial Gazetteer* as a *Dictionary of Geography*. If doing so had market implications, extending the commercial success of *The Imperial Dictionary*, it also acknowledged the essentially discursive and lexicographical nature of their geography, and identified the world as a construction of words. But not of words only: for a subtitle boasted of "seven hundred illustrations, views, costumes, maps, plans, &c." The world could be seen, as well as said, in this *Imperial* work (fig. 7). A visually flat, double-column recital of purported facts, relieved by finely detailed wood engravings that open to an often three-dimensional and implicitly colorful (though black-and-white) world, repeats a formula that had been handsomely deployed in their *Imperial Dictionary*—the first extensively illustrated dictionary in English, to which this work was meant to be a "companion."[8] The Blackies, who were printers as well as publishers, were commercial rather than fine printers; but their work always had a clarity and dignity that enhanced its utilitarian ambitions.[9]

The modesty of the *Gazetteer*'s subtitle, "*Compiled from the Latest and Best Authorities,*" was consistent with the firm's slightly down-market identity. The Blackies and their authors did not make knowledge so much as retail it in less expensive packages: they did not think it necessary to innovate facts. Also, compilation cost less than origination. The text of *The Imperial Dictionary*, for example, owed more to the estate of Noah Webster than the Blackies felt called upon to pay.

The preface recalled a promise made in the prospectus to this hundred sail of ships. It is protected by a battery of five guns, with a martello tower of one gun in its centre, walled in at the back, with loop holes facing the harbour.

CAVARZERE-DESTRO-E-SINISTRO, a vil. Austrian Italy, gov. of, and 25 m. S.S.W. Venice, traversed by the Adige, which divides it into two parts. It contains a parish and three auxiliary churches, and has a considerable trade in cattle, corn, hay, wood, and silk. Pop. 7000.

CAVASO, a market tn. Austrian Italy, gov. Venice, prov. of, and 20 m. N.W. Treviso. It contains a parish church, and several chapels and oratories; and has manufactures of woollen and linen cloth, and hats, dye-works, and fulling-mills. Pop. 2500.

CAVE, two tns. and two pars. England, E. Riding, York:—1, Cave (North), the town, situate on a plain, consists of two principal, regular, and well-kept streets; houses in the modern style, and built of brick. Amply supplied with excellent water. It has a parish church, and a Methodist and a Friends' meeting-house, and two schools. Area of par. 6360 ac. Pop. 1217.—2, Cave (South), the town, 2 m. from N. Cave, stands at the foot of a hill called 'Mount Airy;' and has a parish church, and an Independent and a Methodist meeting-house, and two schools. Good supply of excellent water. In the neighbourhood is Cave Castle, an old Gothic edifice. People chiefly agriculturists. Area of par. 7480 ac. Pop. 1852.—(Local Correspondent.)

CAVENDISH, par. Eng. Suffolk; 3450 ac.   Pop. 1353.
CAVENHAM, par. Eng. Suffolk; 2080 ac.   Pop. 277.
CAVERS, par. Scot. Roxburgh, 24 m. by 8.   Pop. 1709.
CAVERSFIELD, par. Eng. Bucks; 1200 ac.   Pop. 178.
CAVERSHAM, par. Eng. Oxford; 5100 ac.   Pop. 1642.
CAVERSWALL, par. Eng. Stafford; 5380 ac.   Pop. 1505.

CAVERY, a river, Hindoostan, to the waters of which Mysore and the Carnatic owe much of their agricultural wealth. It rises from several head streams in Coorg and Mysore, near the coast of Malabar, and between lat. 11° 37' and 13° 20' N., flows E. through Mysore, Coimbatoor, and the Lower Carnatic, and after a winding E. course of about 450 m., falls into the Bay of Bengal, by numerous mouths, in the province of Tanjore, the plains of which are fertilized by its S. branches. In N. Coimbatoor the Cavery forms an island, called Sivana Samudra, near to which are two magnificent cataracts. The cataract of Gargana Chuki occurs in the N. Channel, where the water falls over a perpendicular rock 200 ft. high; the S. cataract, called Birra Chuki, has a fall of 100 ft. in 10 or 12 streams. The Cavery is filled by the monsoon rains in May and July, but is not navigable excepting by small boats.

CAVERYPAUK, a tn. Hindoostan, Carnatic, 57 m. W.S.W. Madras; lat. 12° 53' N.; lon. 79° 31' E. It is meanly built, and the adjoining fort, at one time a place of some strength, is now in ruins. A victory was gained here by the British over the French and their allies, in 1754. Near the town is an immense water-tank, 8 m. long by 3 broad, which fertilizes a large tract of country, and is, perhaps, the finest work constructed in S. India for the purpose of irrigation. The tank is faced on the inside with large stones, and supported by a mound of earth 30 ft. high.

CAVI, a tn. Papal States, 28 m. E.S.E. Rome. It stands in a beautiful district, and is finely built on a tufa rock on the slopes of Mount Mentorella. Near it is a fine modern bridge of seven arches, built over a deep torrent, one of the tributaries of the Iacco. Cavi was built by the Colonna as early as the 11th century, and is memorable for the peace signed here, in 1557, between the Duke of Alba and the Caraffeschi. Pop. 2000.

CAVIANA, an isl. Brazil, prov. Para, in the mouth of the Amazon, N. the isl. of Marajo, on the equator. It is of irregular form, measures 50 m. N.W. to S.E., and about 20 m. broad. It is well wooded.

CAVITÉ, a tn. and prov. isl. Luzon, one of the Philippines. The TOWN is situated at the extremity of a point of land which projects, in a N.E. direction, into the Bay of Manila, E. coast; lat. 14° 29' 30" N.; lon. 120° 56' E. (R.); about 11 m. S.W. Manila. It is capital of the province, is well fortified, and is the place of residence of the governor.

It contains a church, barrack, convent, and hospital; houses nearly all of stone. A manufactory of cigars, lately established, has added considerably to the commercial importance of the town. Cavité has a reputation for salubrity, and is much resorted to on this account by invalids from Manilla. Its docks and arsenals were at one time famous, but have been long going to decay.——The PROVINCE is situated partly on the Bay of Manilla, which, with the province of Tondo, bounds it on the N., the Lac de Bay on the E., the province of Batangas on the S., and the sea on the W. It is advantageously situate, but is not very fertile, although much more could be made of it by a more industrious people than that by which it is inhabited, who are extremely indolent, and so viciously disposed, that it is said more criminals come from this province than from any other in the island. The chief productions are rice, sugar, indigo, and coffee, some of the latter is said equalling, if not surpassing, that of Mocha. A great variety of fruits likewise are grown, including mangoes, dates, bananas, water-melons, oranges, and lemons. There is also some traffic in cattle, sheep, and swine. Fish is another principal source of subsistence. Cavité is celebrated for its pastry and confections. Pop. of prov. 84,495.

CAVOR, or Cavour, a tn. Sardinian States, Piedmont, div. Turin, prov. of, and 7 m. S.S.E. Pinerolo. It stands in a fertile plain at the foot of the Alps, contains a communal college; and has manufactures of linen; tanneries, silk-mills, some trade in corn, and two annual fairs. It suffered much by an earthquake in 1808. Marble and slates are quarried in the neighbourhood, Pop. 6000.

CAWDOR, a par. Scotland, 4 m. square, chiefly in co. Nairn, but partly in co. Inverness, remarkable only for containing the remains of the castle in which, as tradition asserts, though on more than doubtful ground, King Duncan was murdered, an event immortalized by Shakespeare. The present castle, a fine specimen of ancient fortalice, was built in the 15th century, rendering it impossible it could be the same in which the Scottish monarch was assassinated, that tragedy having taken place in the 11th century, or about 400 years before. Macbeth's second title was Thane of Cawdor. P. 1212.

CAWKWELL, par. Eng. Lincoln; 540 ac.   Pop. 47.

CAWNPOOR, or Caunpore, a tn. and dist. Hindoostan, presid. Bengal, N.W. provs. The TOWN, r. bank, Ganges, which is here about a mile in breadth, is 115 m. N.W. Allahabad; lat. 26° 30' N.; lon. 80° 12' E. It is of considerable extent, but is, on the whole, mean-looking and dirty, with exception of the chowk or principal street, which is composed of well-built brick houses, two or three stories high, with balconies in front. Hardly any of its temples or mosques are worth noticing, with exception of one small musjid, an

MOSQUE AT CAWNPORE.——From an Original Drawing by Capt. R. Smith, 44th Regt.

elegant little structure, ornamented with three egg-shaped domes, a large one in the centre, and a smaller on each side, and having a tall and graceful minaret at either end. Saddlery, harness, gloves, and jewellery are manufactured here to some extent. Cawnpoor is one of the most important military stations in India. The cantonments extend along the r. bank of the Ganges for nearly 7 m., comprising many hundred bungalows, the barracks for the troops, and the bazaars, the

VOL. I.   80

Figure 7. Page 633 of *Imperial Gazetteer* (1855), Volume I.

work "to consult, in the compilation, the most recent and authentic works, both home and foreign" (vii);[10] and the editor boasted that the firm had amassed a large geographical library—some twenty-five hundred volumes—in many (Western) languages.[11] The illustrations, too, came mostly from books: "They are derived partly from original drawings, but principally from engravings and expensive illustrated works . . . the authorities from which they are taken. . . . serve to authenticate the drawings" (vii). The Blackies are not troubled by the paradox that the authenticity of their representing the world should depend upon derivativeness and mediation.

It is fitting that a chief ally for the Blackies' project of compiling the world should have been a librarian—and not just any librarian, but Thomas Watts, the amazing polyglot who was responsible for buying most of the foreign-language books in the British Museum.[12] Watt's powers as a linguist, which included mastery of dozens of languages of the East as well as the West, were matched by his mnemonic control of the British Museum book collection.[13] This is the same Watts, who as *The Imperial Gazetteer* was first appearing in print, read a visionary paper to the Philological Society in London, titled "On the Probable Future Position of the English Language," observing that "at present the prospects of the English language are the most splendid that the world has ever seen. It is spreading in each of the quarters of the globe by fashion, by emigration, and by conquest."[14] He welcomed the "prospect . . . so glorious" (212): "It will be a splendid and a novel experiment in modern society, if a single language becomes so predominant over all others as to reduce them in comparison to the proportion of provincial dialects" (214). The *Imperial Gazetteer* project contributed to and benefited from the success that Watts envisioned.

The man in charge of this project was Walter Graham Blackie, the second and most scholarly son of the founder of the firm, John Blackie (fig. 8 shows him in a contemporary photographic portrait).[15] Though well educated (after distinguishing himself in classics at the University of Glasgow, he took a Ph.D. in classics at the University of Jena), Blackie had no particular geographical interest or knowledge when he began his work on the *Gazetteer.* But he took his work seriously, and became a dedicated armchair geographer, responsible for the accumulation of the geographical library already mentioned; and ultimately an advocate and proselytizer for establishing geography as an academic discipline in Great Britain. Though Kant and other German philosophers had begun to formulate the discipline early in the century, and a professorship was established at Berlin as early as 1820, geography had hardly gained a

Figure 8. "W.G. Blackie, Ph.D., LL.D., *circa* 1855." Photograph by Maull and Polyblank, London. In *Walter Graham Blackie* by Walter W. Blackie (1936), facing page 90.

foothold in British universities before the nineteenth century came to an end.[16] Blackie, noting that the midcentury reform of the Indian Civil Service called for close scrutiny of the literary, philosophical, and mathematical competence of applicants, argued in a paper presented to the Scottish Literary Society on 4 March 1858, not long after he completed the *Gazetteer,* that a competent knowledge of geography (or, as we would aptly say today, "geographical literacy") was much more relevant to such a calling, and also that it was high time to establish departments of geography in the leading universities.[17]

When Blackie read this paper, British rule in India had reached a crisis that he did not mention. The Sepoy Rebellion of 1857, widely publicized and condemned as the Indian Mutiny, had foreclosed any ameliorative "reform" of the East India Company; instead, Her Majesty's Government would take direct control of the subcontinent by an act of parliament on 2 August 1858. Sensational press coverage of the rebellion seared a half dozen geographical names into the consciousness of thousands who read and millions who did not read *The Imperial Gazetteer.*

India, a country that would eventually become the personal property of Queen Victoria, loomed large in Blackie's imagined world. It is likely that one man, Henry Beveridge, wrote all of the entries in *The Imperial Gazetteer* that concerned India.[18] A family memoir reports that Beveridge "wrote a large part . . . as much as half" of the original edition of *The Imperial Gazetteer,* and "was paid for this at the rate of 1s. for 104 words or 15s. for a page of 1,560 words." The author of this memoir, his grandson, calculated on this basis that Beveridge "must have written some two million words of highly valued information in the *Gazetteer* and must have earned nearly £1,000."[19] The success of *The Imperial Gazetteer* soon led Blackie and Beveridge to launch a timely and ambitious three-volume project, again first issued in parts, *A Comprehensive History of India, Civil, Military, and Social, From the First Landing of the English to the Suppression of the Sepoy Revolt; Including an Outline of the early History of Hindoostan . . . Illustrated by Above Five Hundred Engravings* (1862; the first parts appeared in 1858). Apparently this more shapely work was more to Beveridge's taste than his work on the *Gazetteer.* It was generally well received in the *Athenaeum*; the reviewer commended Beveridge's "two-sided" effort to be impartial, though he faulted Beveridge's "careless fluency" (perhaps the result of his having been paid by the word).[20] Beveridge constructed this substantial account of a whole continent from his researches in the British Museum library: apparently he never visited India.

Beveridge's *Imperial Gazetteer* article on the city of Delhi (assuming it to be his), which credits "Government returns" and the *Journal of the Statistical Society* for its information, includes an engraved vignette of the Palace of the King, adapted from "the Hon. C. S. Hardinge's Recollections of India" (figs. 9 and 10).[21] Charles Stewart, later Viscount Hardinge, was the son of Henry Hardinge, the first Viscount, who at the time that this image was first published as a lithograph (1847), had succeeded his brother-in-law, Lord Ellenborough, as governor-general of India. Instrumental in spreading Western reforms among the population, he later would succeed the Duke of Wellington as commander-in-chief of the British army. In that post he contributed to the maladministration of the Crimean War, and also authorized the introduction of the Enfield Rifle, which would become notorious as the proximate cause of the Indian Mutiny.[22] This drawing by the first Viscount's son, as lithographed by J. D. Harding (no relation[23]), shows a scene of past opulence and present indolence. The anonymous wood engraver for the Blackies took few liberties with the composition, editing away some of its detail to fit the much-reduced space of the vignette—which, however, asserts its presence by expanding beyond the width of a single column of type.

Beveridge's letterpress celebrates the faded glories of this palace, as seen from the perspective of a belated tourist:

The interior of the palace corresponds with the noble entrance, and sufficient yet remains to show that in the days of the meridian glory of the

Figure 9. "PALACE OF THE KING, DELHI.—From the Hon. C. S. Hardinge's Recollections of India." Wood engraving. *Imperial Gazetteer* (1855), Vol. I, p. 819.

Figure 10. "DELHI. PALACE OF THE KING." Lithograph by J.D. Harding, after drawing by Charles Stewart Hardinge. *Recollections of India* **(1847). Courtesy of the Ames Library of South Asia, University of Minnesota Libraries.**

empire, it was a place worthy to be seen on account of the richness of its decorations, and the splendour of the court. In many places the walls only remain, and these, from want of repair, are tumbling down and threatening ruin to the inmates.[24]

The crumbling walls are taken to symbolize depredations wreaked upon the city at the turn of the nineteenth century by "the Maharattas," who degraded the Mogul Emperor:

[They] took possession of his capital, of his gardens and houses, and used his name to oppress and impoverish the people by fraud and extortion. From this miserable state of desolation and ruin, the city was rescued by the British in 1803; when it was entered and taken possession of by Lord Lake, after he had defeated the army of Dowlub Row Scinda in the neighbourhood. Peace and order were now restored to the city and territory, and a handsome annual allowance made to the Emperor and family (1:819).

In the second edition (1874) it was necessary to add a paragraph that incriminated a "nominal representative of the Great Mogul, who held the sovereignty of the place under British protection," for his complicity in the rebellion, and to report the Mogul's punishment (exile under arrest). The report concludes, "[a] great part of the place was reduced to ruins in the mutiny and siege, but it has since recovered much of its former appearance, and has also been much improved in its sanitary condition."[25]

Cawnpoor (also spelled "Cawnpore"), identified in the first edition as "one of the most important military stations in India," is described as "of considerable extent, but . . . on the whole, mean-looking and dirty," aside from a presentable main street.

> Hardly any of its temples or mosques are worth noticing, with the exception of one small *musjid*, an elegant little structure, ornamented with three egg-shaped domes, a large one in the centre, and a smaller on each side, and having a tall and graceful minaret at either end (1:633) (fig. 11).

Quite a different social space was marked off by the troops at Cawnpoor—a simulacrum of British civilization, which would not last undisturbed:

> Within the cantonments are a handsome suit of assembly-rooms, supported by voluntary subscription; and a commodious and elegant theatre, a public drive, called the Course, a fashionable resort after sunset; a race-course, and several club-rooms. There are here, also, a Protestant church, a R. Catholic chapel, and schools for the children of the soldiers (1:634).

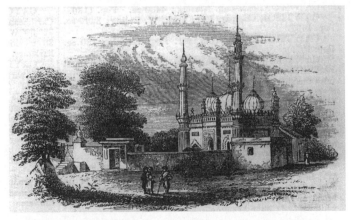

Figure 11. "MOSQUE AT CAWNPORE."—From an Original Drawing by Capt. R. Smith, 44th Regt." Wood engraving. *Imperial Gazetteer* (1855), Vol. I, p. 633. Courtesy of the Ames Library of South Asia, University of Minnesota Libraries.

In the aftermath of the rebellion, the revised edition of the *Gazetteer* had to represent another building in Cawnpore, the notorious building where the British "women and children . . . helpless prisoners," were "slaughtered, and their bodies . . . thrown into a well (July 15*th*)."[26] A dark wood engraving, raked by sunlight, represents the courtyard of "The 'Slaughter House,' Cawnpore, in which the Massacre took place" (fig. 12). In the foreground three pointed arches, Indian in origin but Gothic in their solemnity, frame a view of a meaner building, which is pierced by three plain doorways in graded stages of closure and derangement. Two vultures perch on the roofline, conspicuous within one arch, as others approach in the distance. A melancholy officer leans against one of the arches, and gazes at the slaughterhouse for the reader. This compact black-and-white scene, which arrests the reader's attention by extending into the adjacent column of letterpress, is the skillful reduction of an imposing colored lithograph (brown, blue, and black), that measures 16 by 11 inches on a sheet 26 by 19 inches (fig. 13)—one of twenty in the lavish folio *Views in India, from Drawings Taken during the Seapoy Mutiny* by D. Sarsfield Greene (1859). Featuring by way of frontispiece a large lithographed portrait of Adelaide, "The Queen Dowager of Great Britain, Ireland, and Hanover," after a painting (1849) by the Queen's favorite portrait painter, Franz Winterhalter, and dedicated "by gracious permission" to "His Royal Highness The Duke of Cambridge," then commander-in-chief of the British army,

Figure 12. "THE 'SLAUGHTER HOUSE,' CAWNPORE, in which the Massacre took place.—From Green[e']s Sketches in India during the Mutiny." Wood engraving. *Imperial Gazetteer, Supplement* (1868, 1876), Vol. I, p. 86.

Figure 13. "THE SLAUGHTER HOUSE, CAWNPORE. Interior." Lithograph after drawing by D. Sarsfield Greene. *Views in India, from Drawings Taken during the Seapoy Mutiny* (1859), plate IX.

this work was subscribed to by, among others, The Royal Library, The Royal Artillery Institution, the Earl of Cardigan (who led the famous and ill-fated charge of the Light Brigade in the Crimean War), and Lord Stanley (a member of the Board of Control of the East India Company).

In his preface Blackie remarked that the illustrations in *The Imperial Gazetteer* derive "principally from engravings and expensive illustrated works" (1:vii).[27] The deluxe format of *Views in India* sorts oddly with the morbid, even prurient fascination that it elicits. Though the large images it presents are desynchronized from violence—as with the "Slaughter House" lithograph, which gives a belated view, after the fact—the handsomely printed letterpress can court disgust.[28] The writer for the *Gazetteer Supplement* is more circumspect in his account, and puts the British revenge quickly behind him, preferring to dwell on the commemorative present:

> On the following day the victorious progress of [General] Havelock forced the rajah to retreat, and the British soldiery inflicted a terrible retribution on the sanguinary sepoys. For some time after these events Cawnpore was little better than a heap of ruins, but having been partly

rebuilt it is beginning to resume its previous appearance. A church per-
petuates the record of the Cawnpore massacre, and memorial gardens
inclose the cemetery, the well, and other sites of the melancholy catastro-
phe. The approach to the gardens is exceedingly barren and uncultivated, but on entering the gates everything looks fertile and green. The
gardens are beautifully laid out, and are irrigated by miniature canals
conveying water to them a distance of 15m., so that their verdure is kept
up even during the dry season. Close by the site of the bungalow or
house in which the women and children were murdered is the well, over
which an octagon building of beautiful architecture has been erected,
entered by steps and a bronze gateway. In the interior is a kind of tomb,
also octagonal, of carved stone, with an inscription round the base, and
surmounted by a figure of Mercy in white marble. There is no roof to
the building, the idea of a well being preserved as much as possible.[29]

In a suggestive article, "Representing Authority in Victorian
India," Bernard S. Cohn has pointed out that, "[f]or the Englishman in the later half of the nineteenth century, travelling in India
as visitors or in the course of their duties, there was a regular Mutiny
pilgrimage to revisit the sites of the great events—the Delhi Ridge,
the Memorial Well and the Gardens in Kampur," among others.[30] In
passages such as the one just quoted, *The Imperial Gazetteer* enables
the homebound reader to participate in that pilgrimage.
    In addition to many articles about particular locales, *The Imperial
Gazetteer* devotes two general articles to India, one under the old
name "Hindoostan," and the other under the more bureaucratic
title "India (British)"—the latter being more of a statistical and political accounting. "India (British)" has charts (tables) but no pictures; "Hindoostan" has several pictures (of natives) but no chart.
Two of the pictures recycle images from John Luard's *Views of
India*.[31] The first, captioned "Coolies," dramatically focuses upon a
detail in Luard's panoramic illustration of a mountain view near
Simla, north of Delhi (figs. 14, 15). In this skillful engraving, figures
that appear incidental or at best ornamental in the lithograph take
on an monumental quality even though squatting. The text identifies Coolies as one of several "native tribes" (like the "Bheels . . .
Catties, Coles, Gonds, &c.") that were "by no means exterminated"
by the invading Hindoos, and that remain "uncivilized, or owning
only a few importations of Hindoo superstition or civilization"—a
nice equivocation (1:1218). This is the original meaning of the word
"coolie": the Victorian reader would be more familiar with the secondary meaning of laborer (often involuntary), but Blackie's *Imperial Gazetteer* dutifully foregrounds the original meaning.[32]
    Whether coded as laborers or idlers and natives, the coolies de-

Figure 14. "FAGOO." Lithograph by John Luard. *Views on India* **(1838). Courtesy of the Ames Library of South Asia, University of Minnesota Libraries.**

Figure 15. "COOLIES.—From Luard's Views in India." Wood engraving. *Imperial Gazetteer* **(1855), Vol. I, p. 1218.**

picted are male. A corresponding illustration of "Nautch girls," adapted from Luard's *View of India*, shows women as dancers (figs. 16, 17). They illustrate an aspect of the caste system, to which the *Gazetteer* devotes three long paragraphs. The writer repeatedly draws analogies between that system and European society:

> The institution of *caste*, so characteristic of society throughout nearly the whole of India, cannot be considered entirely peculiar to that region, since prejudices of rank and position prevail even in Europe, in many curious respects, similar to those which divide the classes of the population in Hindoostan; but nowhere are such prejudices and distinctions pursued to such ramifications, and in so arbitrary and often merciless a manner, as in that portion of the globe under consideration (1:1220).

"[A]s indeed in Europe," some of the professions identified with and by the caste system "are held to be much more honourable and worthy than others," although no European analogue is offered for "outcasts . . . of no rank whatever" (1:1220). One's caste is predestined—not a word that Beveridge uses—and he does not comment on the comparative implications that follow from that fact:

> With all these fine-drawn diversities of rank and respectability, the division into superior and inferior castes is not attended in Hindoostan with

Figure 16. "A NAUTCH." Lithograph by John Luard. *Views in India* (1838).
Courtesy of the Ames Library of South Asia, University of Minnesota Libraries.

Figure 17. "NAUTCH GIRLS—From Luard's Views in India."
Wood engraving. *Imperial Gazetteer* (1855), Vol. I, p. 1221.

any feeling of humiliation on the part of the latter. Every caste, and sub-division of a caste, forms a little distinct society in the general commu-nity. Its members enjoy the sense of equality among themselves, whilst their position, in all respects, towards the other members of the general community, is determined before their birth. The divine origin of castes being universally admitted, there is no ground for personal animosity. The members of the higher castes feel no malice or pity for, but rather indifference towards, those of the lower, nor the latter any envy or ha-tred of the former (1:1221).

Caste can be degraded through bad dietary practices, "or intermar-rying with persons of a lower caste (which, it may be said, is, in a minor degree, the case even in Europe)." One device to reduce the threat of such intermarriage is female infanticide. "Such," the writer comments, "are a few of the peculiarities of the social system of the Hindoos."

It cannot be wondered at that, with a debasing superstition, and institu-tions that have oppressed and split its people into a multitude of unsym-pathizing sections, India, with a vast population and abundant resources, should have been, during all its history, the prey of one invader after another (1:1221).

The status of the Great Britain as the last such invader is only im-plied.

Having thus concluded his description of the caste system, Beveridge continues to discuss it, to draw attention to a particularly interesting caste that he has not mentioned:

> The institution of caste, thus arbitrarily stereotyped upon the Hindoos, has produced a multitude of monstrous anomalies which pervade the whole framework of society in India. In one caste, and one alone, the females are permitted to cohabit, or form matrimonial alliances with Europeans; from another caste, a certain proportion of the females, regarded as incapable of marriage, are contributed to be brought up as *bayaderes*, *nautch*, or dancing-girls in the Brahminical temples, where they minister to the appetites of the priesthood (1:1221).

The accompanying illustration (fig. 12), looks decorous enough, though slotted in directly above the phrase "where they minister to the appetites of the priesthood." A book for family consumption, *The Imperial Gazetteer* could be as suggestive in its text as its companion volume, *The Imperial Family Bible.*

More generally, Beveridge shows a voyeur's interest in the women of Hindoostan:

> The females of the inferior ranks are diminutive, and by no means attractive; but those of the higher are frequently quite the reverse, possessing graceful forms, finely tapered and rounded limbs, soft dark eyes, long fine hair, and a glowing complexion. As to dress, the labouring population of both sexes go almost naked; a turban, and a cotton covering around the loins, constituting the whole of their apparel. . . . (1:1218).

But the implied reader of at least some passages may be female—a woman interested in the dress of "the upper classes":

> Amongst the upper classes, the dress of the females, particularly, is elegant; consisting of a jacket, with half-sleeves, fitting closely to the shape, and often made of rich silk; a flowing garment, of silk or cotton, called a *shalice*, and so disposed as to fall in graceful folds; embroidered slippers; and the hands, arms, ankles, and ears, profusely ornamented with rings and jewelry (1:1218).

Yet our interest is returned to the other side of the cloth—not dress, but nakedness: "The prevalence of ornament extends throughout nearly all ranks of the population; and it is common to see females adorned with gold armlets, anklets, &c., but with scarcely a shred of clothing" (1:1218–19).

Eliding within the same paragraph from questions of dress to questions of moral substance, Beveridge renders a confused judgment that anticipates the débâcle of the rebellion:

> Subtlety and shrewdness are the most conspicuous mental characteristics of the Hindoos; and they have been properly described as 'the acutest buyers and sellers in the world.' In their manners they are mild and retiring; timidity and indecision are all but universal qualities; and yet, when officered by Europeans, they have proved themselves faithful and obedient soldiers, and courageous in the field. Artifice and deceit, a want of probity and candour, are amongst their conspicuous failings (1:1219).

In 1868, writing a preface to the second edition of *The Imperial Gazetteer*, which attached an alphabetically ordered supplement to the original range of articles, W. G. Blackie remarked that "[t]he plan adopted in the SUPPLEMENT is identical with that of the GAZETTEER. The descriptions and accounts have been taken almost solely from original authorities, and confined as far as possible to statements of fact; opinions and suppositions, as such, being studiously and uniformly excluded."[33] In his later history of the firm, Blackie reiterated the factual nature of the illustrations: "[e]very illustration being necessarily a separate and distinct fact" (*Sketch*, 53). As a printer and publisher, Blackie may be forgiven for identifying the representations of "original authorities" with facts. He would have been surprised by the fact that his facts were as often as not opinions and suppositions, not scientific reports but acts of social imagination.

When the first volume of *The Imperial Gazetteer* appeared in print, the reviewer for the *Athenaeum* found "two reasons why a new gazetteer on a comprehensive scale is likely to be acceptable at the present":

> In the first place, the knowledge to be gained from such a work was never so valuable as now, because freedom of intercommunication between different countries and different parts of the same countries was never so great, nor the inducements to it so strong—particularly in reference to British subjects. Again, the rapid progress that has been going on of late in various parts of the world—more especially in America and in our own dependencies—gives an additional value to a new work founded on the most recent information. A knowledge of geography in its widest sense is now essential, not merely to the merchant, the emigrant, and the politician,—but to *the ordinary newspaper reader who wishes to understand and appreciate what he reads.* Such a knowledge may be derived from this excellent book of reference, which is correctly described in the above title [given in full—including the phrase "*Compiled from the*

latest and best Authorities"], and contains all that is really worth knowing of each place mentioned in it.[34]

Containing "all that is really worth knowing" is truly an imperial, not to say totalitarian, ambition. Furthermore, in the passage emphasized above the reviewer happily, if unwittingly, recovers the early sense of *gazetteer* as a gloss on a newspaper—a newspaper now become the telegraph-charged medium of "intercommunication" between countries and "parts of countries." National identity arguably derived in the nineteenth century from the shared reading of such documents.

Beveridge and the Blackies wrote *The Imperial Dictionary* out of other documents: they imagined their world in the domed reading room of the British Museum library. They were never out of the library—it's as if they saw it all. Could they have done otherwise? Even had they left that room and taken passage to India, would it have made any difference? The question is easier to ask than to answer.[35]

NOTES

Robert Browning, *The Poems*, ed. John Pettigrew and Thomas J. Collins, 2 vols. (New Haven: Yale University Press, 1981), 1:550. First published in 1855 and probably written not before 1850, these verses are closely contemporary with *The Imperial Gazetteer*.

1. Agnes A. C. Blackie, *Blackie and Son, 1809–1959* (London: Blackie and Son 1959), 22. *Publishers' Circular*, 1 May 1855, 166, 176. Volume 1 had appeared separately, priced at two guineas (*Publishers' Circular*, 16 Dec. 1852, 467).

2. Michael Hancher, "The Number Trade at Blackie and Son," Seventh Annual Conference, Society for the History of Authorship, Reading, and Publishing; University of Wisconsin–Madison, 15–18 July 1999.

3. This usage dated back to the seventeenth century (*OED*). Alan M. Clark, in his *Catalogue: Exhibition, 150 Years of Publishing—Blackie and Son, 1809–1959* (Glasgow, 1959), registers several titles, including *The Imperial Gazetteer,* under the rubric "The Imperial Era," commenting that "between the 1840s and 1870 a series of large and impressive works of reference were issued under the suitable label of *Imperial*. These books are impressive from all points of view" (23). He duly reports the format of these books as "Imperial 4to" or "Imperial 8vo."

4. However, Blackie didn't invent the label. From 1801, parliament was known as Imperial Parliament, in recognition of the union of Ireland with Great Britain, itself an integration of England, Wales, and Scotland. The epithet strictly applied in such titles as *British Imperial Calendar* (1810), and it was deployed in other contexts for its evident prestige; for example, *The Imperial Magazine* (1819–34); Henry Moore's *New and Grand Imperial Family Bible* (London, 1813); *The Imperial Journal of Art, Science, Mechanics, and Engineering* (1840). An older prestige had attached to such titles as *The Imperial Magazine; or, The Complete Monthly Intelligencer* (1760–62), and *Biographical and Imperial Magazine* (1789–92). See also Michael Hancher, "Gaz-

ing at *The Imperial Dictionary*," *Book History* 1 (1998), 159–60, regarding emergent "imperialist" connotations circa 1850.

5. For the leading analysis of this matrix see Benedict Anderson, *Imagined Communities: Reflections on the Origin and Spread of Nationalism* (London: Verso, 1983).

6. Noah Webster, *An American Dictionary of the English Language*, 2 vols., 1828 (reprint, New York: Johnson Reprint Corporation, 1970). Webster referred the first definition to Johnson and to Pope—whom Johnson cited to illustrate a secondary sense, akin to the modern "spin doctor." The primary sense was simply "[a] writer of news." (Samuel Johnson, *A Dictionary of the English Language*, 2 vols., 1755 [reprint, New York: AMS Press, 1967].)

Illustrating the word *gazette*, Johnson paraphrased a remark of Locke's that closely identified geography, gentility, and print: "An English gentleman, without geography, cannot well understand a *gazette*." Locke made the remark in his brief essay, "Some Thoughts Concerning Reading and Study for a Gentleman," first published in 1750: "an English gentleman . . . without it [viz. 'geography in general'] . . . cannot well understand a Gazette"; *Works of John Locke*, 10th ed., 10 vols. (London, 1801), 3: 273. Compare P. C. Chamberlayne, *Compendium Geographicum; or, a More Exact, Plain, and Easie Introduction into All Geography, Than Yet Extant, After the Latest Discoveries, or Alterations; Very Useful, Especially for Young Noblemen and Gentlemen*, 2nd ed. (London, 1685), [A3r]: "Methinks he that is ignorant of it [i.e., Geography], (especially if a Man of parts) must needs blush every time he reads the Gazette, and cannot give an account in what *Country* is seated such a *Place*, or *Town* of note." See also Jonathan M. Smith, "State Formation, Geography, and a Gentleman's Education," *Geographical Review* 86 (1996): 91–100, especially 95–96.

7. Quoted from *The Oxford English Dictionary*, 13 vols. (Oxford: Clarendon Press, 1933), which reproduced and supplemented *A New English Dictionary on Historical Principles*, 10 vols. (Oxford: Clarendon Press, 1928). Words beginning with the letter *G* appeared in volume 5 of the *NED* (1901), which had previously been issued in parts.

8. So it was advertised in *Blackie's Literary and Commercial Almanack, 1854* (Glasgow: Blackie and Son, 1853), 65.

9. "Fine printing" may be an unfair standard, since what is usually called "modern fine printing" is a late-nineteenth- and twentieth-century phenomenon. However, the publisher William Pickering (1796–1854) and his printer Charles Whittingham (1795–1876) did inaugurate a revival of high-quality standards in a business that had suffered from commercial success. Though the Blackies did not compete in that league, they did work to a relatively high standard for their day.

10. Quote is from p. vii. Apparently quoting from the "full Prospectus" (which was included in the first part, but which I have not seen), the advertisement for *The Imperial Gazetteer* in *Blackie's Literary and Commercial Almanack, 1854*, emphasizes that "[i]n its compilation, *the most recent and authentic sources* will be consulted" (65).

11. "Besides the use that has been made of several public libraries, a private library, extending to nearly 2500 volumes, has been collected, exclusively for the compilation of the *Imperial Gazetteer*, including works in French, Italian, Spanish and Portuguese, German, Dutch, Danish, and Swedish" (*vi*).

12. Robert Cowtan, *Memories of the British Museum* (London: Richard Bentley and Son, 1872), 116–19, 267.

13. Once, confronted with a list of "some twenty-three books" that Robert Blackie, the art editor for the *Gazetteer*, could not find in the Museum catalogue, Watts rattled off all the necessary details from memory—which book was in the print room, and too old anyway to be useful; which was lost, or at the binder's; what

the "press-marks" (call numbers) for the others were. W. G. Blackie, *Sketch of the Origin and Progress of the Firm of Blackie and Son, Publishers* (Glasgow: printed for private circulation, 1897), 54.

14. Thomas Watts, "On the Probable Future Position of the English Language," *Transactions of the Philological Society* 4 (1848–50): 212.

15. Walter W. Blackie, *Walter Graham Blackie, Ph.D., LL.D. (1816–1906)* (London and Glasgow: printed for private circulation by Blackie and Son, 1936), facing p. 90.

16. The first such chair appears to have been established at Oxford, in 1887, followed by one at Cambridge, in 1888. Glasgow University established a Department of Geography in 1897.

17. W. G. Blackie, *Remarks on the East India Company's Civil Service Examination Papers, As Illustrative of Some Defects in the Course of Academical Education in Scotland* (Glasgow: printed for private circulation, 1858).

18. The preface to the *Supplement* and First Revised Edition (1868) credits Beveridge explicitly as regards that edition at least, as having written "a large number of important articles" (*viii*); identifying him as "Author of the 'Comprehensive History of India,'" this credit implies that his contributions mainly concerned India. W. G. Blackie's *Sketch* later identified Beveridge as one of several writers who contributed to the first edition (52).

19. These numbers may well be exaggerated; but certainly Beveridge needed the money. Success as a student at the University of Edinburgh had led to a career as a preacher in the Church of Scotland, which he let lapse after marrying an heiress no longer young, who had £8,000. Becoming an Advocate to the Scottish bar did nothing to increase Beveridge's income; business investments led to bankruptcy; but working as "a bookseller's hack" saved him in the end. William Henry Beveridge, *India Called Them* (London: Allen and Unwin, 1947), 16.

The author's name appears on the title page of *India Called Them* simply as Lord Beveridge. A Fabian economist who directed the London School of Economics from 1919 until 1937, he chaired the Inter-Departmental Committee on Social Insurance and Allied Services (1941) and produced *Social Insurance and Allied Services*, widely known as "the Beveridge report"; it was a key document in the shaping of the welfare state in Great Britain. See José Harris, *William Beveridge: A Biography*, 2nd ed. (Oxford: Clarendon Press, 1997).

20. *Athenaeum*, 12 April 1862, 495–96.

21. Charles Stewart Hardinge, *Recollections of India, Drawn on Stone by J. D. Harding from the Original Drawings by the Honourable Charles Stewart Hardinge* (London: Thomas M'Lean, 1847).

22. The second Viscount Hardinge sympathetically reviewed his father's career in *Viscount Hardinge, Rulers of India* 19 (Oxford: Clarendon Press, 1892).

23. Briton Cooper Busch, *Hardinge of Penshurst: A Study in the Old Diplomacy* (Hamden, Conn.: Shoe String–Archon, 1980), 319 n. 4. Busch sketches C. S. Hardinge's career in a paragraph on p. 15.

24. W. G. Blackie, ed., *The Imperial Gazetteer: A General Dictionary of Geography, Physical, Political, Statistical and Descriptive*, 2 vols. (Glasgow: Blackie and Son, 1855), 1:819.

25. W. G. Blackie, ed., *The Imperial Gazetteer: A General Dictionary of Geography, Physical, Political, Statistical, and Descriptive; With a Supplement, Bringing the Geographical Information Down to the Latest Dates*, 2 vols. (London: Blackie and Son, 1876), *Supplement* 1:117.

26. Ibid., 1:86.

27. Years later Blackie continued to emphasize the deluxe nature of these source

volumes: "the most rare and costly publications both home and foreign" (*Sketch*, 53).

28. The commentary on the preceding plate, an exterior view of "The Slaughter House" (Plate 8) concludes:

> When Cawnpore again came into our possession, a gallows was erected close to this House, and all rebels and mutineers who here paid the penalty of their crimes, were first made to lick the now dried, but still too plainly perceptible blood of our women and children. This was the greatest punishment that could be inflicted, as by the laws of their religion it entailed the loss of caste; they were flogged until they complied, and then met a death only too easy for the bloody deeds committed by them.

29. *Supplement*, 1:86–87.

30. *The Invention of Tradition*, ed. Eric Hobsbawm and Terence Ranger (Cambridge: Cambridge University Press, 1983), 179; quoted by Ian Baucom, *Out of Place: Englishness, Empire, and the Locations of Identity* (Princeton: Princeton University Press, 1999), 107. In chapter 3 Baucom traces a dominant English narrative of India that binds intimacy and betrayal, war, memory, mapping, and tourism.

31. John Luard, *Views in India, Saint Helena and Car Nicobar: Drawn from Nature and on Stone* (London: J. Graf, printer to Her Majesty, 1838). Luard's military career in India and Afghanistan is reviewed by James Lunt, *Scarlet Lancer* (London: Rupert Hart-Davis, 1964). He often recorded his surroundings in a sketchbook.

32. The word is not reported in the original edition of Blackie's *Imperial Dictionary*. It does appear in the *Supplement* that was incorporated into the second edition (1868), but with the secondary meaning only given: "In the *East Indies*, a porter or carrier."

33. The second edition was itself revised in 1872, and often reissued. Reference here is to the issue of 1876 (1:*vii*).

34. Unsigned notice of *The Imperial Gazetteer*, vol. 1, *Athenaeum*, 7 May 1853, 561; emphasis added.

35. Thanks are due to Gordon Hirsch, who helpfully commented on a draft of this chapter; and to Donald C. Johnson, curator of the Ames Library of South Asia, and Charles F. Thomas, digital-projects coordinator at the Elmer L. Andersen Library (like the Ames Library, a unit of the University of Minnesota Libraries) for providing figures 5, 7, 9, and 11. I presented a version of this chapter at the conference "Material Cultures: The Book, the Text, and the Archive," sponsored by The Centre for the History of the Book, The University of Edinburgh, 28–30 July 2000.

"The Software of Empire": Telegraphic News Agencies and Imperial Publicity, 1865–1914

Alex Nalbach

IN JANUARY 1870, SIX MONTHS BEFORE THE OUTBREAK OF THE FRANCO-Prussian War, representatives of the three most powerful media organs in the world—a sixty-year-old entrepreneur from London, a distinguished Prussian privy councilor, and a French Bonapartist company director—gathered quietly in an upstairs office in the Rue Jean-Jacques Rousseau in Paris to conclude a secret imperialist pact of breathtaking scope: a partition of the globe for the collection and distribution of the world's political and commercial telegraphic intelligence.

The negotiators unrolled a map of the world, bent over it, and began to draw lines. To the British went England, Holland, and their dependencies; to the French, Western and Southern Europe; to the Prussians, Germany, Scandinavia, and the Russian metropoli. Other territories—Austria, the Low Countries, the Balkans, North America—would be shared. In these exclusive spheres of influence, each firm secured a monopoly over the sale of information and, by implication, its collection as well. To save costs and out-perform outsiders, they agreed to exchange their intelligence with one another, which each could then compile into a world report unmatched by any potential competitor. The negotiators inked this division of spoils into a tripartite "treaty," to be renewed every twenty, and later every ten, years. Never published and only reluctantly revealed to official circles, the alliance remained shrouded in secrecy. Under this arrangement, the domination of world information markets by three firms—the telegraphic news agencies *Reuters* of London, *Havas* of Paris, and *Wolff* of Berlin—remained virtually uncontested for decades.[1]

Studies of the relationship between the press and *fin-de-siècle* imperialism have overlooked the central position of the British, French,

German, and American telegraphic news agencies. Because of their monopolistic control over both foreign and imperial-colonial intelligence, the agencies served as "gatekeepers" for nearly all cable intelligence, whether headline political news, market data, palace gossip, or cricket scores. They filtered information flowing both inbound from the colonies to the capitals, and outbound from the metropole to the periphery. They therefore served as important magnifiers of distant crises, multiplicators of imperialist sentiment, and weapons in imperialist rivalries.

By the outbreak of the First World War, however, their cartel was cracking apart. Statesmen and diplomats, editors and publishers, pamphleteers and patriots all railed against the cosmopolitan information alliance. Europe had entered the age of the sensational New Journalism of the penny press, the boisterous New Politics of mass parties, and the adventurous New Imperialism of jingoists and strategists. These developments, each reinforcing the other, both swelled the demand for telegraphic information from overseas, and at the same time strained the gentlemanly commercial contract of 1870. To accommodate their patrons and their critics that their respective news empires expand at the expense of their allies, the agencies punched holes and scribbled exceptions into the once elegantly simple "treaty," or simply violated the contract outright. But imperialist publicity, both within and outside of an agency's "sphere," often went ignored or provoked angry reactions from editors if it exceeded the commercial needs of the press itself: the telegraphic news agencies found it difficult to compel newspaper editors to run more stories on empire than subscribers cared to read. Nevertheless, despite this important caveat, the agencies could, and did, play a significant role in generating an imperialist mindset by limiting the range of material from which editors compiled their cable news columns to stories promoting imperialism.

The major telegraphic news agencies were founded in the middle third of the nineteenth century by a handful of polyglot entrepreneur-adventurers. In 1835, a French speculator, Charles-Louis Havas—a mercantile favorite of Napoleon in his youth, but clinging to the ragged edge of ruin in middle age—opened a translation office at Paris, abstracting the foreign press for French newspapers and banking houses. Experimenting with couriers, carriages, and carrier pigeons, Havas employed the latest and most expensive technology to gather intelligence by the 1840s: the electric telegraph. At the end of the decade, two expatriate translators in the *Agence Havas* left Paris to return to their native Prussia and start their own telegraphic news agencies. In 1849, Dr. Bernhard Wolff opened the

Wolff Bureau at Berlin, while Paul Julius Reuter established a relay-station between the ends of the French and German telegraph networks at Aachen, before moving to London in 1851 to furnish intelligence off the new Channel cable for speculators on the Exchange. Meanwhile, across the Atlantic, six press barons formed the *Associated Press* at New York in 1848 to expedite the gathering of foreign and telegraphic news.[2]

The methods of the early telegraphic information services were simple. "Stringers" (part-time agents) in distant cities would gut the local press for market quotations and headlines, and telegraph the main items of interest to a central office, conveniently located near the stock exchange or the main branch of the telegraph service. At agency headquarters, the information would be translated for domestic clients, and delivered in lithographic copies or flashed by special electric lines to the offices of brokers and editors.

Despite their limited operating capital and scant plant, Havas, Wolff, Reuter, and the *Associated Press* rapidly achieved quasi-monopolies over foreign intelligence in their respective national territories. The press of their day was fractured by regional, confessional, and political divisions. The meager budgets of special-interest rather than information journals, unable to attract a mass audience and ignored by potential mass advertisers, could scarcely sustain high telegraph tolls or the salaries of special correspondents. For their news columns and market quotations, they turned to the telegraphic news agencies. By dividing costs among the greatest number of clients, the agencies turned the complex and expensive task of gathering information from all points by the swiftest technology into a profitable and powerful enterprise. No individual paper could match them for speed or completeness of foreign coverage, and many gave up trying. "The public may believe that there are many [French] newspapers," grumbled Honoré de Balzac in 1840, "but in fact, there is only one: the *Agence Havas*."[3]

These national monopolies blocked one another from selling news abroad. A decade of bitter turf wars between the European agencies in the 1860s gradually convinced each of the founders that the elimination of his counterparts was impossible. Dreams of a global intelligence monopoly were abandoned in favor of a global oligopoly. In January 1870, they partitioned Europe into "spheres of influence" for the collection and distribution of news abroad.[4] In 1876, *Reuters* and *Havas* further divided up overseas territories: South America and the Ottoman Empire passed to *Havas*; India, China, Japan, the Straits, Australia, and New Zealand went to *Reuters*; Egypt and any other nonreserved territories would remain "neutral," open to the exploitation of any party.[5] The pattern had been set. National monopolies were established at home, and exclusive empires demarcated abroad. This alliance, broken briefly by war but unfailingly renewed in 1890, 1900, 1910, and throughout the 1920s, would dominate the world's political, financial, and general information for three quarters of a century.

This monopoly was especially powerful with respect to colonial news. In an age in which only the very wealthiest papers could afford permanent correspondents even in the great capitals of Europe, high cable rates, enormous distances, hazardous conditions, and the infrequency of headline-worthy news from overseas rendered independent coverage of imperial news unprofitable for individual journals. Even when the great dailies made efforts to acquire their own coverage of colonial crises, the reports of their special correspondents were usually filed by post because of high cable costs, and the telegraphic news agencies dominated the flow of electronic news from overseas. When the French invaded Madagascar in 1895, French correspondents largely left telegraphy to *Havas*. "Why should we send telegrams?" one Frenchman asked his counterpart of the *Pall Mall Gazette*. "The *Havas Agency* sends all the news by wire, and with the exception of events such as a big battle, it matters little whether it is published three weeks sooner or later."[6]

Agency reports were not only the fastest but often the *only* coverage of imperialist developments. During the Fashoda crisis of 1898, *Reuters* monopolized telegraphic intelligence. Detesting reporters, Kitchener quarantined them all at Cairo with one exception: the *Reuters* correspondent.[7] Where French journalists acquiesced in the *Havas* monopoly, however, the British press was outraged by such favoritism. The *Daily News* protested:

> If the decree had been that no correspondent at all would be allowed, it might conceivably have been capable on grounds of military expediency. But this is not the case. Sir Herbert Kitchener, it seems, does not object to correspondents altogether. What he objects to is the presence of independent correspondents.[8]

As the *Daily News* implied, by the turn of the century, the agencies maintained close relations with their respective national governments. Censorship, suppression, indictments for *lèse majesté*, and the blacklisting or expulsion of correspondents were common hazards of journalism: agency managers learned quickly to accommodate the regime of the day.

The agency-state relationship went beyond a mere avoidance of trouble, however. As an American critic noted in 1912:

A large portion of the news must be obtained from official sources. The
first information of wars and rumors of wars, treaties, naval and military
affairs, projected legislation, court gossip, and governmental activities of
all kinds comes from those who are interested in maintaining things as
they are. And boys, just remember when we were "cubs," how carefully
we protected the source of news; and now when we have grown big, and
the source of news has grown from the policeman on the beat to a great
nation, let us admit that we do not interfere with the source.[9]

Favorable relations with official sources were as vital in the colonies as at home. In 1858, after the Anglo-Indian War thrust the Raj
into European headlines, Reuter approached the British Foreign
Office to ask that he be included among newspaper editors receiving copies of Foreign Office telegrams.[10] Later, when Reuter established his own network to collect and distribute news in India itself,
he still relied heavily upon official sources. In 1865, Reuter appointed his son's young tutor, Henry M. Collins, to India. Establishing a *Reuters* service from the East entailed a threefold mission:
establishing an office at Bombay, appointing stringers throughout
India, and striking a deal with the Government of India at Calcutta.
In exchange for a service of *Reuters* telegrams, Governor-General
Lord Lawrence offered the *Reuters* agent the first crack at the Government's official news.[11]

In times of imperial war, when physical danger, confusion, communication bottlenecks, and censorship confounded correspondents, official sources became even more important. Because of
their wide-ranging influence and their political reliability, agency
correspondents enjoyed privileged relations with military command-
ers on the periphery. Kitchener's favoritism of the *Reuters* correspondent in the Sudan has been mentioned. Likewise, *Associated Press*
General Manager Melville Stone recalled that during the Spanish-
American War, "A capable reporter was installed upon the flag-ship
of each of the squadrons, and both Sampson and Schley [command-
ers of American naval forces] gave them every possible facility to enable them to do their work."[12]

Governments enjoyed more than a stranglehold on the most important sources of news—they also monopolized most of the fastest
means of *transmitting* news. All the European overland telegraph
networks were state monopolies after 1870: the agencies cozied up
to the state for rate reductions or communication priorities. For
overseas news, *Reuters* was able to make favorable arrangements with
the state for the use of submarine cables laid to link the British Empire;[13] the press rate on such lines was eventually reduced to a penny
a word between points in the British Commonwealth.[14]

Governments could also be induced to underwrite an agency's profitability more directly. The business of news involved high initial costs: far-flung correspondents, the latest, most expensive technologies, and 'round-the-clock schedules. And the expense of news gathering rose constantly. Imperialism, multilateral diplomacy, and the growing demand for detailed "human interest" stories increased the scope and complexity of news. These combined pressures deprived *Reuters* shareholders of dividends for the first time in 1884.[15] By the last decade of the nineteenth century, the information branches of *all* the European agencies found it impossible to show profits. "I am sorry to have again to make the admission that news gathering and distribution is an unremunerative business," the Chairman announced to *Reuters* stockholders in 1908. "Did we not fortunately possess other sources of revenue, we could not possibly afford for news telegrams what we at present spend."[16]

Each European agency became reliant upon sources of income besides the sale of news to the press: commercial and financial data services, advertising and banking branches, private dispatch services, and state assistance. Each received special "subscriptions" from official quarters, in truth thinly disguised subsidies. Such subsidies were essential in the colonies—remote areas with underdeveloped presses, unlikely to become profitable without massive official support. In May 1867, for example, the Government of India commissioned the *Reuters* agent at Karachi to deliver telegrams to imperial officials. Renewed in 1873, this "Government subscription" was now described as a "subsidy." The agency itself seemed unashamed of the expression: three years later, the firm asked the Viceroy for an increase of this "subsidy." The minutes of the Board later recorded satisfaction with the doubling of "the subsidy granted to the Company."[17]

In Egypt, too, the weakness of the local press forced the agency to rely on special government "subscriptions": for twenty-five years, the Khedive paid *Reuters* and *Havas* £1,000 a year for cabling messages to and from the Egyptian government.[18] The *Reuters* general manager for Egypt recalled:

> We took up the role of a news agency in this country on condition that the Government would support us in various ways, principally as a subscriber to our telegrams, and the existence of our organization in this country depends upon the continuance of that support.[19]

The pattern became familiar throughout the British Empire. In May 1911, the British government agreed to pick up the additional cable costs involved in carrying whole, rather than summarized, texts of important speeches by ministers to *Reuters* subscribers throughout the Empire.[20]

The case was similar in French North Africa. Like French mining and railway firms, *Havas* counted confidently upon the encouragement and even support of the French government to sustain its presence in Morocco. The agency reminded its local agent in late 1906:

> Given that the French government certainly has interest in seeing us achieve a serious place in Morocco, it seems to us that it should afford us a more effective support. You know that at Algiers the Governor still pays us 500 francs per month, and that at Tunis we receive from the residency a subscription of 1,000 francs. Because we are installed in Morocco in extremely difficult business conditions, it appears that we have the right, without possible discussion, to support at least as serious as that which is given to us at Tunis.[21]

Within a month, the head of the French Legation at Tangier had offered three thousand francs.[22] In 1912, the French Residency took an annual subscription for ten thousand francs. "I am quite disposed to pay a higher price for this subscription when the resources of the protectorate, currently quite limited, permit it," he added.[23] The Residency was true to its word: the subscription reached fourteen thousand francs annually.

Given the importance of official sources, state telegraph facilities, and subsidies, it was not long before the agencies wholly identified themselves with their respective national interests. This identification relieved the state of having to wield more overt forms of influence over the national news agencies. To be sure, the official sponsors of the agencies could, and did, review managerial appointments, survey political reports, and insert favorable stories and correctives into the daily news service. In general, however, the relationship was more subtle. The holders of power received from the agencies a grateful recognition of the importance of the state to their affairs. As the nations prospered, the national news agencies prospered; as the governments' influence expanded, so their influence expanded; as the empires grew, their telegraphic empires grew. The agencies demonstrated an eagerness to serve, willingly and without compulsion or supervision, the interests of the regime of the day.

But the agencies were keen that their official relations not be too obvious. *Havas* expressed anxieties that its Tangiers agent considered himself too closely connected to the French Legation. "By giving too complacent an ear to inspirations from an official source," it pointed out, "we too often risk playing the role of dupes."[24] In addition, *Havas* insisted upon the distinction between a "subscription" and a "subsidy"—a fine point frequently lost on its Moroccan representatives.[25]

Reuters was even more bold in its denials of official support. Despite a subsidy it virtually extorted from the Foreign Office in order to maintain its presence in China in 1909, the annual report to *Reuters* shareholders in 1913 audaciously quoted the Peking correspondent of the *Daily Telegraph* as follows:

> *Reuter's Telegram Company* has procured a special news service with English correspondents in all China who report immediately on any event. A special characteristic of this excellent service consists in that native newspapers in all parts take more and more subscriptions and place great stock in them. The Chinese press already comprises hundreds of daily papers and will soon reach a thousand. Public opinion hereby is promoted and its growth supported in healthy manner, and Englishmen can be pleased that they contribute to the fostering of this opinion in broad measure, not through the support of the government, but rather thanks to the skill inherent in their race.[26]

It was often the appearance of "independence" itself, so carefully maintained by the agencies for professional reasons, which multiplied the value of the agencies for official publicity. The most important agencies were either cooperatives owned by the newspapers themselves, or joint-stock firms in the hands of private individuals or banking houses. This "autonomy" improved their political value by obscuring the origins of official propaganda. It also permitted disassociation from embarrassing mistakes.[27]

Like other imperialist ventures, then, telegraphic news-gathering began as a purely private undertaking, but soon embroiled reluctant officials in murky questions of privilege, protection, and pelf. Indeed, some telegraphic news moguls had considerable experience with similar, more explicitly "imperialist" undertakings. In 1872, the recently ennobled Baron de Reuter obtained from the Shah of Persia a staggering seventy-year exclusive concession for the economic development of the entire country: railroad construction, irrigation, forest and mineral resource development, a bank under state guarantee, the management of a six million pound loan on the London market, and a twenty-five year customs monopoly.[28] Persian corruption and Russian intrigue stymied the concession for sixteen exhausting years. Reuter appealed again and again to the British Foreign Office for aid against the machinations of the Shah and the

Russians: papers at the British Foreign Office on the concession between 1872 and 1876 alone comprise three volumes of some thirteen hundred pages.[29] Reuter assured the Foreign Secretary of his wish "to render the scheme of the highest value to Great Britain,"[30] but the Foreign Office remained cool to Reuter's plans, until at last the baron's second son traveled to Persia to effect a withdrawal.[31] But other imperialist ventures of Reuter met with greater success. In 1865, with the aid of bankers and traders in India and China, he reorganized his small news-gathering firm as a limited liability company in order to raise capital for a submarine telegraph cable between England and the Norderney on the north German coast, a line which could become the western-most link of a future overland telegraphic system to India.[32] Reuter's cable became enormously profitable, and the success of the Norderney cable helped finance the expansion of Reuter's news-gathering operations overseas in the following years.[33]

Reuter was not the only baron of telegraphic news-gathering to dabble in imperialist projects like submarine telegraphy. In 1879, the *Agence Havas* was purchased by émigré financier Baron Frédéric-Émile d'Erlanger. As a young man, d'Erlanger had journeyed to the Orient, and met the young French Consul at Cairo, Ferdinand de Lesseps. Like Lesseps, d'Erlanger became a leading member of the French Saint-Simonians, champions of industrialization and imperialism who envisioned a united world bound together peacefully and profitably by letters of credit, steel, steam, and copper wire. It was to Erlanger that France owed its electronic links to Algeria, Egypt, India, Australia, China and Indochina, and even the New World.[34]

The telegraphic news ventures of Reuter and d'Erlanger were no less imperialist than the Persian concession or cable investments. Like submarine telegraph cables, the telegraphic news agencies served a vital function in holding the colonial empires together. If cables were the hardware of the new imperialism, the agencies became the software of empire.

First, news agencies made their intelligence-gathering networks available to their governments. Reuter furnished his telegrams for free to high officials and the palace: by 1878, Queen Victoria referred to him as one "who generally knows."[35] When *Reuters* later lobbied for a Foreign Office subsidy in 1894, the agency agreed to "to place at the disposal at [*sic.*] the F.O. all the intelligence they receive from their agents all over the world, much of it of a confidential nature and which is never published."[36]

Such reports became of particular value during times of imperial crisis. During the Boer War, though both the British and the Boers allowed *Reuters* correspondents to be stationed in their camps, the *Reuters* general manager for South Africa made his intelligence available to Kruger's enemies, the British authorities. Henry Collins, who oversaw the Capetown bureau, recalled:

> throughout the war the whole of Reuter's extensive cable services from home, and the telegrams received from the numerous correspondents at the front, were regularly supplied to the authorities at Cape Town, and to every [British] military command in the field—an act of courtesy which was greatly appreciated, and for which the Agency received, at the close of hostilities, the special thanks of the Government in a graceful letter from the High Commissioner.[37]

The agencies flashed not only vital hard political-military news and market data, but also "soft" gossip and human interest material, between colonial outposts and the metropole, bearing both imperial power and imperial sentiment. Because its principal clients were British, most *Reuters* reports concentrated upon news of the British government or the British Empire: the agency, whether by serendipity or by design, became an agent of imperial publicity. As *Reuters* historian Graham Storey noted:

> For British merchants in India, China, and throughout the Far East, *Reuters'* market prices and quotations became one of the necessities of existence. For the British in India, civil servants, Army officers, their families and appendages, *Reuters'* telegrams in newspapers and clubs soon became a direct link with home.[38]

The agencies later guided public opinion in the budding periphery press, becoming, in the words of one *Havas* administrator, instruments of "intelligent and pacific penetration." *Reuters* dispatches dominated the cable columns of the emerging Indian and Australian press, just as *Havas* monopolized the overseas intelligence of the press of North Africa.

At the same time, the agencies generated publicity of colonial activity in metropolitan newspapers. "As foreign news is now managed," noted *Vanity Fair* in 1872, "it is not too much to say that he who has control of telegrams has control of public opinion in foreign affairs."[39] By keeping "empire" in print day after day, they exaggerated the significance of what were in many cases minor skirmishes on the periphery, and made their satisfactory resolution into political imperatives. The omnipresence of empire in their services accustomed the reading public to imperialism. Constant references to the empire gradually made it impossible for the public to

conceive of a world without "our" colonies. Once acquired, imperial possessions would be difficult to part with, not only for strategic
but now also for domestic political reasons. The impact of telegraphic dispatches from the empire upon the public was amply
demonstrated during the Boer War, when a *Reuters* correspondent
in South Africa managed to smuggle news of the relief of the outpost of Mafeking through enemy lines, scribbled on a dispatch hidden inside of a sandwich. When the news broke in London,
euphoria was so immediate, raucous and widespread that the expression "mafficking"—a riotous public celebration—became part
of English vocabulary. By keeping the empires steadily in the preoccupations of a wide public at home, telegraphic news agencies encouraged both imperial expansion and the maintenance of empire.

The agencies went beyond simply propagating imperial information and sentiment, however: their editorial policies actively supported or promoted the regime or policy of the day. Telegraphic
propaganda was less a question of *coloring* the news through willful
distortion than the *selection* of information. "Spin" was expensive: to
explain takes more words than simply to report.[40] Indeed, the agencies upbraided correspondents who engaged in imperialist editorializing. One *Havas* director wrote his Moroccan representative:

> Remain calm, relate events without heat and without acrimony; add
> nothing to the facts, which should suffice in themselves, do not com
> ment, do not forecast, and do not allow your correspondents to com
> ment or forecast. Prune their service as much as necessary; you have
> every latitude to proceed to excisions which seem prudent to you. This
> should be the entirety of your *politique marocaine.*[41]

Jingoism by allied agencies was even less tolerable. During the
Spanish-American War, *Havas* complained of the exaggerations and
drum-beating of the American cooperative, surpassed only by the
jingoist Hearst. "The seriousness of our agencies," *Havas* grumbled
to *Reuters,* "does not lend itself, as is perhaps the case in America, to
these exaggerations."[42]

Rather than editorializing, official publicity through the telegraphic news agencies was more often a matter of the suppression
of damaging information, and the propagation of flattering intelligence. *Havas* exercised extreme caution in its reports from Morocco, reminding its agent, "A *faux pas* could create considerable
difficulties for us."[43] In November 1899, the *Reuters* general manager
for South Africa was judged too sympathetic to the Boers, and retired after twelve years at the post. His successor was, in the words of

Reuters historian Graham Storey, "an all-out enemy of Kruger, and was intolerant of even the slightest symptoms of sympathy with the Boers."[44]

The importance of the news agencies as channels for imperialist publicity was multiplied by the exclusive spheres of influence of the global cartel system. First, the system essentially eliminated competition with, and contradiction of, a semiofficial representation of events within the reserved territories. Second, the system interposed a government-friendly middleman (the national news agency) between the wholesaler of foreign intelligence (foreign news agencies) and the retailer (the press). Finally, the news exchange system of the alliance offered a cost-effective and virtually invisible means of distributing the official view abroad. Because each agency received much of its information unquestioningly from the others and forwarded it to their clients largely unaltered, allied agencies could become "Trojan horses" for foreign propaganda.

The cartel also became an instrument to be wielded in imperialist competition among the Great Powers. Just as an agency provided intelligence to the officials of its own country, so it might withhold or delay the transmission of vital political intelligence to the agency of a rival power. In 1884, for example, *Reuters* coverage of the London Conference on the Egyptian question, in which both British and French interests were at stake, was so insufficient that *Havas* had no choice but to deploy a special correspondent to London.[45] The same tactic was practiced by *Reuters* during the Anglo-French dispute at Fashoda in the summer of 1898. The *Havas* Cairo correspondent had traveled south to attempt to cover the standoff, but at Ouadi Alfa, he was politely detained by the British for two days before being informed by a British officer that he could not be allowed to continue south. "As I suppose that Ouadi Alfa has no special enchantment for you," the officer smiled, "I have arranged your return to Cairo." In consequence, France had to rely on *Reuters* for its news of the crisis.[46] In late September 1899, *Reuters* delayed in informing *Havas* of the arrival of Marchand's mission at Fashoda. When British spokesmen officially announced Delcassé's orders to Marchand to withdraw on 2 November 1899, *Reuters* was again late in informing *Havas*.

As a result of these and similar episodes, telegraphic news agencies and their news-exchange alliance increasingly became the subject of discussion, not always favorable, in magazines, editorial columns, and parliaments in the decades before the First World War. The same forces which had contributed to the rise of the "popular" press—education, literacy, broadened franchises, cheaper industrialized printing, and improved standards of living which generated greater disposable income and more leisure time—also contributed to a popularization of *politics*, and a growing interest in foreign affairs in broader sections of society. In the years around the turn of the century, a handful of crises sharpened the concern of *petit bourgeois* patriots with foreign affairs: in France, the Dreyfus Affair of 1894–1902 and the Fashoda Crisis of 1898; in Germany, the Naval Question of 1897 and the Algeçiras Conference in 1906; in the United States, the Spanish-American War of 1898; in Britain, the Boer War of 1899–1902. By the turn of the century, statesmen, diplomats, and a wider public of jingoists and nationalists began to call for the revision of the news agency cartel system.

Dependence upon the other agencies led to accusations that the foreign intelligence read at home was being "colored" by foreign powers, and especially by the British. The advantages of London— described by one contemporary analyst of the press as "the Hub of the Universe"[47]—had placed *Reuters* leagues ahead of its allies in terms of political importance, territorial scope, and telegraphic expenses. At the time of the earliest exchange agreements between the major telegraphic news agencies in 1859, Africa and Asia had been considered too inaccessible to become profitable or politically important, and were ignored. With the establishment of *Reuters* services there in the late 1860s, the cartel agreement of 1870 attributed the commercial exploitation of most of the future cable-heads on those continents (the British and Dutch colonies) to *Reuters*. British mastery of the seas and British control of strategic cable-heads consolidated London's position as the center of global communications: at the turn of the century, two-thirds of the world's cables were in English hands. Such advantages were of obvious significance to the telegraphic news agencies by the turn of the century. Important news from South America, from the Far East, and even from Tangiers was routed to London before reaching continental Europe. "Because of the English telegraphic equipment at all points of the world," remarked *Havas*, "London dominates all the agencies from on high."[48] Such domination did not sit well with the nationalists of other Powers. In America, the *Associated Press* was rebuked for its reliance upon the semiofficial cartel agencies, especially *Reuters*, for its main sources of foreign news.[49] Dependence upon *Reuters* for coverage of the Boer War provoked criticism of *Wolff* in the German press.[50] Nor was *Reuters* the only potential culprit. At the beginning of the Algeçiras Conference, *Wolff* had no representative at the summit, contenting itself with forwarding the reports of *Havas*; German editors protested violently, and the agency scrambled to provide coverage of its own.[51]

Such attacks inspired German competitors to *Wolff* who might operate outside the cartel's restrictions. The *Herold Depeschenbüro G.m.b.H.* was formed in 1894 to gather foreign news, but failed to achieve a meaningful breakthrough in Germany because it remained deprived of indispensable official connections.[52] In 1906, the Asher banking house put up 300,000 marks to found the *Deutsche Kabelgramm-Gesellschaft* to gather news from South and Central America, Morocco, Persia, and the Far East. Subsidized by the German Foreign Office to the tune of between fifty and one hundred thousand marks annually, its reliance upon journalistic dilettantes like consular officials or businessmen reduced the value of its material.[53] It was absorbed by a new conglomerate, the *Syndikat Deutscher Überseedienst,* whose backers—representatives of industry, commerce, shipping and banking, and the German Foreign Office—were resolved to make a "great pitch" for a worldwide German news service, but had no real plan or understanding of the legitimate needs of the press, and made little headway.[54]

Like *Wolff's* and the *Associated Press, Havas* also endured criticism from an increasingly anglophobic French press for its reliance upon *Reuters* during moments of Anglo-French imperial tension. Knowing that its reports were now under closer scrutiny, *Havas* had to maintain at least the appearance of independence, and issued instructions to its agents to present events from the French point of view.

> Your sources of information, . . . your French manner of seeing things, of asking questions, of reading press comment, will never be (our experience has shown this many a time) the way of an Englishman, or of another foreigner. Our newspapers no more than ourselves are not mistaken about this: and in important cases, we like to give the impression, and the demonstration as well, that we have services of our own, and that we are not only tributaries of foreign Agencies.[55]

But such efforts at "independence" from foreign allies, while politically important, were often in defiance of economic sense, as *Havas* itself ruefully admitted in 1909:

> Out of self-respect, for political reasons, or at least to defend ourselves against absurd accusations, we have . . . maintained our direct service [rather than relying on cheaper and faster services via London], throwing into the hamper every twenty-four hours telegrams which become of no use at all. This has cost us 100,000 francs at least, expenses at bottom without rhyme or reason.[56]

Imperialist tensions strained the cartel in other ways. The territorial monopolies of the cartel treaties allowed an agency to flood the overseas press within its "sphere" with news of its own country, to the exclusion of news of rival imperial powers. During times of diplomatic tension, tensions arose between the allied agencies over the territorial restrictions of the cartel system, such as those between *Reuters* and *Havas* when Britain and France vied for influence in the Near East in the 1870s. *Reuters* and *Havas* both had business in Egypt, a neutral territory. As Disraeli's purchase of the Suez Canal shares intensified British activity in Egypt after 1875, *Reuters* demanded that the Khedive increase his subscription to the British agency—at the expense of *Havas*.[57] As its finances crumbled, the Egyptian Government refused to pay its debts to the two agencies, knowing that if either one refused service to it, the other would be only too happy to step in.[58] Arguing that further disagreements in Egypt could only profit third parties, *Havas* pleaded with *Reuters* for an *entente*, but *Reuters* never agreed, until finally a revision of the treaty handed over the country entirely to the British agency.[59]

Egypt had been considered "neutral" territory in the cartel, but tensions also flared in the "reserved" territories as well. The *Reuters* representative at Constantinople in the 1870s was the wily and intriguing Bohemian exile, Dr. Sigmund Engländer. Keenly aware of the political nature of the telegraphic news enterprises, he began to distribute foreign news for free at Constantinople in the late 1870s, in order to compete with *Havas* and impress the British embassy.[60] According to the *Reuters-Havas* treaty of 1876, however, Turkey was *Havas* territory. *Havas* protested, calling Engländer's action "an act of gratuitous hostility."[61] Despite repeated pleas and even threats by *Havas*, however, Engländer's activity continued for months.[62] *Reuters* tried to disassociate itself from Engländer: like other imperialist ventures, the lead here appeared to be coming from "men on the spot."[63] A court of arbitration decided in favor of *Havas,* and ordered *Reuters* to withdraw from the field.[64] Despite this decision—indeed, despite repeated instructions from London—Engländer continued to violate the interagency treaty.[65] Only when Engländer left Turkey in the mid-1880s did the situation improve. His assistant later recalled:

> Although this service of telegrams was a restricted one, and entailed a loss financially, nevertheless, it proved of value as a means of propaganda besides enhancing our moral position and prestige in this part of the world. . . . Dr. Engländer was naturally proud of his achievements in that respect, especially after his successful struggle with headquarters in

London, convincing the latter of the utility and value to the Company of a service to Constantinople.[66]

Engländer's reports for the Turkish press were edited with a political agenda clearly in mind. But the "coloring" of news for export could also result from mere cost-cutting. *Reuters* news for Asia was primarily intended for consumption by Englishmen in India, and only incidentally routed east to Japan and China to recoup extra revenues. *Reuters* service for East Asia thus gave wide publicity to English developments, but seemed to set those of other nations aside.

In Germany, this English domination of overseas news dovetailed with mounting nationalist paranoia about Germany's "encirclement" and her deprivation of a world-power "place in the sun." Means had to be found to disseminate accurate information on German achievements or aspirations to foreign readers, in order to promote cultural hegemony, political awe, financial confidence, and commercial expansion. Nationalist pamphleteer Fritz Waltz charged *Reuters* and *Havas* with a conspiracy against German interests, advocating the establishment of a German news service independent of foreign agencies.[67] The Berlin *Neueste Nachrichten* called for the creation of a worldwide, rather than merely regional, German news service, by government subsidy if necessary.[68] The dramatic demonstration of German diplomatic isolation at the Algeçiras Conference over Morocco in 1906 inspired even more desperate calls for a modernization of German publicity campaigns abroad. Businessmen, colonial officials, and diplomats therefore pressed *Wolff* in Germany, and also *Havas* in France, to try to compete with *Reuters* in East Asia.

The directors of the agencies were willing to accommodate politically inspired revisions to the cartel system, and to deepen their involvement in foreign media markets, but only so long as someone else bore the costs. In response to mounting pressures from their official patrons and public opinion, the agencies punched loopholes into the territorial clauses of the cartel treaties. In 1898, as Great-Power tensions in the Far East, the Sudan, South Africa, and the Caribbean produced the worst professional and diplomatic strains yet endured by the European agencies, they began negotiations for a renewal of the cartel treaty. A secret note from the director of the Press Bureau of the *Wilhelmstraße* spelled out the mission of the *Wolff Bureau:* to broaden the service of German news to South America and the Far East—an objective clearly inspired by the expanding scope of German diplomacy.[69] After threatening to break off relations altogether if its demands were not met, *Wolff* achieved this objective in Article Fifteen of the new treaty:

> Given German interests in overseas countries, . . . the *Continental Telegraphen Compagnie* [*Wolff*] will have the right to telegraph to newspapers, to the exclusion of any agency and after having obtained the respective authorization of *Reuter's Telegram Company* and the *Agence Havas,* the news of the German Empire in the territories of China, Japan and South America. . . . If it is a question of a newspaper already subscribing to the service of *Reuter's Telegram Company* or the *Agence Havas,* the commission obtained by the *Continental Telegraphen Compagnie* should be paid to *Reuter's Telegram Company* or to the *Agence Havas.*[70]

The new clause was a naked attempt to transform news from a mere commodity to be sold for profit, into an instrument of power to be wielded explicitly and openly for political purposes.[71] And as early as the autumn of 1907, *Wolff* began to reassure the *Wilhelmstraße* that in negotiations for the renewal of the news agency alliance in 1909, it would clarify this loophole in the existing contract. But it cautiously reminded the *Wilhelmstraße* of the limits to which it was willing to modify the treaty. To date, German reports were almost never rejected by the partners of the cartel—even material distributed at the request of the German Foreign Office. Breaking up the monopolies of the allied agencies overseas might be possible, but would put an end to a collaboration which had afforded German publicity "the contribution of organizations which, over the course of fifty years, have developed gradually on the basis of real commercial and journalistic needs, and which are probably capable of making such a commanding influence in these areas effective for long time to come." Scaling the walls of Troy, in short, was pointless if one already had a Trojan horse. Direct competition with *Reuters* or *Havas* should be considered only "if a final attempt at an understanding with the two companies ultimately failed."[72]

Predictably, *Havas* opposed *Wolff's* suggestions to make Article Fifteen a permanent and routine feature of interagency relations. The "absolute lock-out" of the agencies from distributing dispatches in territories reserved to an associate was, in the eyes of *Havas,* "one of the capital conditions of our convention from its origin, and we hold that it is, as we see from experience, every day, for all parties, one of the reasons for the solidity of the Agency block." The demands of *Wolff* for a more regular service within the territories reserved to allies—"no doubt pushed by its Government"—would mean "the destruction of the very bases of our *entente.*"[73] But *Havas* had difficulty resisting Wolff's demands, for it was simultaneously besieged by *Reuters* for compensation for *Reuters* higher cable tolls (including many retransmissions via London of *Havas* news from *Havas* territories). The French found it impossible to create a united front against the Germans. *Havas* appealed to both allies for solidarity in the face of the public assaults on their credibility and the emergence everywhere of upstart competitors. But *Havas* found both allies astoundingly determined.

> Has *Reuters* seriously envisioned the possibility of a rupture? [*Havas* directors speculated.] Is it really prepared for one? In truth, this would surprise us. . . . At bottom, this would be veritable madness for everyone, something for the agencies analogous to the European war which should have exploded over Serbia. But it is nevertheless a hypothesis which is not to be ignored. . . .[74]

In the face of these tensions, *Havas* prepared itself for an honorable surrender:

> When a country has no army and no cannon, it should yield, even if its reasons are the best. In this case, the cannon and the armies are not the millions [of *Havas* francs in reserve], they are the telegraphic lines and cables. Sad to say, we do not have them, and we sink further and further in the rut.[75]

Havas therefore capitulated in the face of both the financial demands of *Reuters* and the political demands of *Wolff*. If a receiving agency refused to incorporate in its service certain dispatches of political importance to the sending agency, the sender had the right to *insist* that a certain quantity of such reports be distributed to the press within an ally's reserved territories. The volume of this special news was not to exceed one-fifth of the total service sent by the recipient to the territory in question. Unlike the routine services, these special dispatches would be distributed at the expense of the *sending* agency, not the *recipient*. Finally, a special signature word, *"Tractatus"*—Latin for "a handling"—would accompany all such reports to distinguish them as officially inspired. In practice, however, many editors were not informed of the significance of this signature, and the reading public certainly was not.

This clause represented two fundamental changes in the *modus operandi* of the cartel. First, it weakened the absolute lockout of the agencies from one another's territories. Second, it brought about a partial shift of costs of transmissions from the recipient to the sender. In most cases, these extra costs would be born by the sender's government. *Wolff's* directors attributed great significance to the concession. "Especially in times of political tension or aversion," recalled one director thirty years later, "this was the only possibility for the German government to reach the foreign public with its announcements."[76] In fact, however, the privilege was rarely necessary. With only the most trivial exceptions, the allied agencies distributed the entirety of the *Wolff* report to its overseas subscribers—even material inspired by the *Wilhelmstraße* which *Wolff* had tagged as *Tractatus* dispatches.[77] Swamped editors at agency headquarters only rarely had the time or the instructions to "kill" any but the most glaringly provocative of political dispatches.

The difficulty of establishing meaningful, systematic filters was not the only limitation upon telegraphic propaganda. Nationalists, colonial officials and diplomats assumed that extensive coverage of the accomplishments and activities of the nation would promote economic interest and political respect abroad: greater quantities of information on their pet policies, questions, or countries ought "naturally" to further their publicity goals. But as *Havas* explained to its allies in 1885, "Our role is not to impose upon the press interesting information about a fact which does not interest it."

> The Congress of Berlin on the Congo leaves the French press completely indifferent. This is so true that we have had to restrain considerably our service on this subject. . . . we have made great costs to be well informed, and we have sent to Berlin a special correspondent. . . . All this has been lost money, and we have had to recall our representative without awaiting the end of the Congress. . . . the French press will never have enough information on a criminal affair like the Troppmann affair—which is only in total a simple human interest story, without diplomatic bearing or any other—but it will content itself with three lines on the Congo. . . . By contrast, it would be a pleasure to receive a much more complete, much more nourished, much more . . . exciting service on the earthquakes in Spain. We should have veritably heart-rending details of this catastrophe, of such a nature to excite the whole public.[78]

The British Government seemed most sensitive to the limitations of an aggressive publicity policy, and the most reluctant to mix in private commercial endeavors to accomplish political ends. When *Reuters* requested a subsidy of the British Foreign Office in 1894, the British Permanent Undersecretary noted, "My own experience of attempts to influence opinion abroad on points on which it is excited, is that such attempts have very little success."[79] The Foreign Secretary was "very doubtful" about the proposal: "I do not believe that any statements of 'facts' will have much influence on . . . foreign opinion."[80] Ultimately, Lord Rosebery granted the subsidy, but his underlings remained skeptical of the outcome.

The expected limits to imperialist publicity were demonstrated in Canada. Though Canada was formally British territory, geography was destiny with respect to its foreign news. All contracts with the European agencies since 1870 had allotted all of North America, including Canada and the British Provinces, to the *Associated Press*.[81] In late 1906 and early 1907, however, Henry Collins, the agent responsible for establishing *Reuters* service to India, the Far East and Australia, visited New York to discuss Herbert de Reuter's plan for a *Reuters* service to and from Canada, largely for the sake of imperial prestige. *Associated Press* General Manager Melville Stone put up no opposition to the scheme, though he frankly declared the project unlikely to succeed, because wealthy Canadian papers already had their own foreign service from London, middle-sized papers were unwilling to take on new costs, and poor journals could not.[82]

Prominent Canadian politicians nevertheless expressed a lively interest in Collins' plan. The Governor General, Earl Grey, lamented the paucity of English news in the Canadian press, and requested to meet with Collins on several occasions to discuss Collins' progress.[83] Permanent Under-Secretary Pope was "most desirous" that Collins' mission "should prove to be a complete success."[84] The Military Secretary, Colonel Hanbury-Williams, was an old acquaintance of Collins from South Africa, affording Collins valuable introductions and bringing his mission to the attention of the Colonial Office.[85]

Collins himself concluded, however, that the "paucity of [British] cable intelligence" was due primarily to a "lack of interest in everything that is not Canadian or American."[86] In a letter to London, Collins outlined both the limitations to, and the stakes of, imperialist telegraphic publicity.

> If I have formed an opinion at all, it is that the feeling we seek to combat is already deep-seated, and that Canadians are unconscious of their tendency to welcome everything American. This does not necessarily imply disloyalty to the Crown, but I ask myself what will be the effect on the rising generation, and how could we look for their whole-hearted support if a crisis arose between us and the great Republic. . . . in Canada, as in Australia, there is a danger of drifting from the old country, and this is particularly the case in the Dominion, because it is inundated with American literature in the form of newspapers, magazines, &c., not to speak also of the facilities offered by the Railway and Telegraph Companies for rapid and cheap communication. . . . as regards the newspapers, from what I can learn, they are blissfully ignorant of their own defects, &

there appears to be no real desire on the part of any influential section to place more English or foreign news before their readers.[87]

Although Collins won over editors in Montreal, Ottawa, Winnipeg, Vancouver, and Victoria, his mission ended in disappointment. A Canadian newspaper summed up his dilemma in 1906:

Newspapers will pay for news which will interest their readers, but if a long dispatch be presented in a newspaper office every night dealing with subjects in which the readers of the newspaper have no interest, it will quickly find its way into the waste paper basket.[88]

In sum, by keeping favorable images of the empire in the cable news columns of the daily press, the agencies encouraged imperialist sentiment at home, in the colonies, and abroad. There were limits, however, to imperialist propaganda. Like all capitalist media organs, the telegraphic news agencies found themselves at the intersection of power, publicity, and profit. As such, the agencies were more than simply the dupes of imperialist interests. They often tried to have their relationship with imperialist interests both ways, one day exaggerating their abilities to influence public opinion in order to secure subsidies and privileges, the next denying their ability to effect real change in order to reduce effort, expense, or tensions with allies. Indeed, the economic realities of the news business and the aspirations of officials and nationalists often proved difficult to reconcile. Ultimately, three commercial factors accounted for the remarkable staying power and essentially static quality of the news agency alliance.

First, directors realized that imperialist competition would strain their alliance and entail outrageous costs. Second, despite occasional lapses in service—sometimes calculated, more often not—the actual distortion of the news in the hands of the allied agencies was minimal. The handful of harried editors of a global news service in the late nineteenth century were hardly capable of judicious, calculated selectivity as thousands of stories spilled, in no particular order, out of their tickers and across their desks. In practice, the agencies forwarded to their clients whatever was sent them by the foreign agencies, and passed on to their allies whatever was sent in by their own correspondents. Third, in all probability, a competing service in the "sphere" of an ally would have little impact on a press already satisfied with the existing service and unlikely to afford second and third services. Ultimately, thanks largely to the efforts of the telegraphic news agencies, news became a commodity whose market value was determined by the reading public itself. This fact determined the potentials and limitations of imperialist telegraphic publicity. For all the schemes of patriots and statesmen to open flows of subsidized news between the imperial metropoli and their colonial outposts or trading vassals, newspapers, as commercial enterprises, would only print items which their subscribers wanted or needed.

Yet one should not conclude from these caveats that the agencies played no part in the promotion of empire. Though they were unable to compel editors to print more imperialist publicity than was likely to interest subscribers, instructions from the telegraphic news agencies to their correspondents and to their editors severely limited the range of stories from which newspapers might choose in composing their columns. In this way, as the gatherers and gate-keepers of most overseas intelligence for press, commercial, financial, and even official circles throughout the late nineteenth century, the telegraphic news agencies of the nineteenth century became the indispensable "software of empire."

NOTES

1. Each of the European telegraphic news agencies was christened after its founder: Julius Reuter, Charles-Louis Havas, and Bernhard Wolff. To distinguish the agencies from their founders, I have italicized the names of all firms, including the *Associated Press*. There are a variety of spellings and abbreviations for the names of the three telegraphic news agencies. The most common seem to be: for *Reuter's Telegram Company*, the name "*Reuters*" with an "s" but without an apostrophe (the official name of the company since 1984); for the *Agence Havas*, simply "*Havas*;" and for *Wolff's Telegraphisches-Büro Continental Telegraphen-Compagnie*, "*Wolff*" without an "s."

2. For the early history of the *Agence Havas*, see Pierre Frédérix, *Un Siècle de Chasse aux Nouvelles de l'Agence d'Information Havas a l'Agence France-Presse (1837–1957)* (Paris: Flammarion, 1959) and Antoine Lefebure, *Havas: les arcanes de pouvoir* (Paris: B. Grasset, 1992). For *Reuters*, see Donald Read, *The Power of News: The History of Reuters, 1849–1989* (Oxford: Oxford University Press, 2000). For *Wolff's*, see Dieter Basse, *Wolff's Telegraphisches Bureau. Agenturpublizistik zwischen Politik und Wirtschaft* (München: K. G. Saur, 1991). For the Associated Press, see Richard Schwarzlose, *The Nation's Newsbrokers* (Evanston, Ill.: Northwestern University Press, 1989–90), 2 vols., and Menahem Blondheim, *News Over the Wires: The Telegraph and the Flow of Public Information in America, 1844–1897* (Cambridge: Harvard University Press, 1994).

3. Honoré de Balzac, *Revue Parisienne* no. 2 (25 August 1840), in *Oeuvres* (Paris: Michel Lévy Frères, 1869–76), vol. 23, 672. All translations are my own.

4. Copies of the *Reuters-Havas-Wolff* Treaty, 17 January 1870 may be found in the Reuters Archive (London) (hereafter R.A.), LN 446 (uncatalogued as of October 1996); Politisches Archiv des Auswärtigen Amtes (Bonn) (hereafter P.A./A.A.), Europa Generalia 86, Band 1 (National Archives microfilm reel T149 253). The map

mentioned in the introduction appears to have been lost or destroyed, but former directors of *Reuters* recalled having seen it before World War II (Jonathan Fenby, *The International News Services* (New York: Schocken Books, 1986), 252 n.). The *Associated Press* secured North America when it joined the alliance in 1875. Agreement between the *New York Associated Press* and *Havas-Reuters-Wolff,* 1 July 1870. R.A., 1/880234.

5. Treaty between *Havas* and *Reuters,* 20 May 1876. Archives nationales (Paris) (hereafter A.N.), 5AR 411.17, signed; R.A. 1/8818001, unsigned.

6. *Pall Mall Gazette,* 3 July 1895, quoted in Joseph J. Mathews, *Reporting the Wars* (Minneapolis: University of Minnesota Press, 1957), 129.

7. This afforded *Reuters* an important beat with the news of Kitchener's victory at Omdurman. See Graham Storey, *Reuters: The Story of a Century of News-Gathering* (New York: Greenwood Press, 1951/69), 97–98.

8. *Daily News,* 11 January 1898, quoted in Mathews, 129.

9. *Proceedings of the First National Newspaper Conference, Madison, July 29-August 1, 1912* (Madison, 1913), 46.

10. Reuter to Clarendon, 30 December 1857; Reuter to Clarendon, 29 January 1858; draft of reply, Clarendon to Reuter, 3 February 1858. Public Record Office, Kew Gardens (hereafter P.R.O.) FO/83/165; photocopy, R.A.

11. H. M. Collins, *From Pigeon Post to Wireless* (London: Hodder and Stoughton, Limited, 1925/79), 64–68.

12. Melville Stone, "The Associated Press. Fifth Paper: Its Work in War," *Century Magazine* 70 (1905): 505.

13. Storey, 35.

14. Llewellyn White and Robert D. Leigh, "The Growth of International Communications," in *Mass Communications,* ed., Wilbur Schramm (Urbana: University of Illinois Press, 1960), 73. Unlike overland telegraph networks, however, most cable companies were in *private* hands, and despite the international telegraph convention of 1874 establishing a special tariff for press dispatches, many transatlantic and cross-channel telegraph companies refused such rates to the cartel agencies. Likewise, while the Submarine Telegraph Company leased wires under the channel to British dailies, it refused to do so for the agencies.

15. *Reuters* shareholders in the nineteenth century enjoyed their last ten percent dividend in 1881; they would not regain that rate for another thirty years. Five per cent became the norm, and in 1882, 1884, and 1888, the company had to raid its reserves to pay this. See Storey, 105; Read, 74.

16. Quoted in Fenby, 37.

17. Read, 60, 63. For a description of the special service of news provided by *Reuters* to the Government of India during the Franco-Prussian War, see Read, 93.

18. Storey, 91.

19. Quoted in Read, 64.

20. It should not be thought, however, that *Reuters* got rich from these concessions. Dividends in 1911 and 1912 reached 10 percent, but fell to 7 percent in 1913, and were canceled in 1914 and 1915.

21. *Havas* to Rabanit, 31 December 1906, quoted in Tayeb Boutbouqalt, *Les agences mondiales d'information: Havas Maroc (1889–1940)* (Casablanca: Editions maghrébines, 1996), 61–62.

22. *Havas* was careful in the terms chosen to describe this support. "Do not speak of subsidies," it warned Rabanit on 1 July 1908. "It is a matter in the nature of a subscription to our services, subscription which should represent for us a commission and not a subsidy. This is not at all the same thing." Quoted in Boutbouqalt, 62.

23. Boutbouqalt, 72–73.

24. *Havas* to Rabanit (Havas/Tangiers), 26 January 1911. Quoted in Boutbouqalt, 71–72.

25. "[We draw] all your best attention to the word "subsidy" which you employ on numerous occasions," noted *Havas* to its agent at Rabat. "We ensure a service to the Residency, for which it pays us a sum "by the job," that is costs of transmission + commission. . . . Thus the word "subscription" should replace the word "subsidy", not only in your correspondence, but in your conversations with the Residency. The latter word could give rise to a misunderstanding the result of which could be, in certain cases, to alienate a part of our freedom. It should not at any price endanger us, the *Agence Havas* — which receives no subsidy—from being, at all points, absolutely independent." *Havas* to Guerard (Havas/Rabat). Quoted in Boutbouqalt, 83–84.

26. Report to *Reuters* Shareholders Assembly for 1913. Quoted in Friedrich Fuchs, "Agence Havas und das Reutersbureau" (Ph.D. Diss., Erlangen University, 1918), 55–56.

27. For an example of this argument, see the report of Charles Rouvier (head of the new *bureau de presse* of the Quai d'Orsay) for Premier Waddington, 16 November 1879. Archives diplomatiques du Ministère des affaires étrangères (Paris), papiers d'agents, Papiers Waddington, VI.

28. Concession granted to Baron de Reuter, 25 July 1872. Original in French, and translation, P.R.O./F.O. 60/405; R.A., photocopy.

29. P.R.O./F.O. 60/405, 406, and 407; R.A., photocopy.

30. Reuter to Lord Granville, 12 September 1872. P.R.O./F.O. 60/405; R.A., photocopy.

31. The British Government distrusted Reuter's plans for a railway network in northern Persia, more likely to serve Russian interests than British, and found Reuter an exasperating negotiator: "Baron Reuter is rather a difficult correspondent to deal with *as he pursues a regular plan of laying verbal traps for the Gvt. into which he tries to get them to entangle themselves.* He then writes to say that acting under the advice of this Gvt. he proposes to do so & so. He then goes a step further and says that he awaits the support of HMG for the steps which he has taken in pursuance of the policy he has undertaken to observe at their request & so on & so on." (Internal Minute from Tenterden, 12 October 1876. P.R.O./F.O. 60/407; R.A., photocopy. Emphasis in original.) For the end of the concession, see Collins, 191; Sir H. Drummond Wolff, *Rambling Recollections* (London: Macmillan and Co., 1908), vol. 2, 350.

32. Completed in 1869, this overland route was hampered by serious difficulties, and did not enter into operation until 1870. See Jorma Ahvenainen, *The Far Eastern Telegraphs: The History of Telegraphic Communication between the Far East, Europe and America before the First World War* (Helsinki: Suomalainen Tiedeakatemia, 1981), 16–17.

33. Collins, 57. In 1868 alone, the cable showed a profit of £29,744, almost one-fifth of the capital invested in the project. When the British Government nationalized telegraphy in 1870, the British General Post Office purchased Reuter's cable for £726,000—a price based on twenty years' profits, and more than five times its original cost of £153,000.

34. Erlanger and Reuter collaborated in raising capital for the French transatlantic cable to serve French interests and break the expensive monopoly of the Anglo-American company of Cyrus Field. See Alvin F. Harrow, *Old Wires and New Waves: The History of the Telegraph, Telephone and Wireless* (New York: D. Appleton-Century Company, Inc., 1936), 299; Read, 53.

35. Storey, 61.

36. Report of conversations with *Reuters* representative Dr. Sigmund Engländer by Foreign Office official "A.W.", 3 July 1894. P.R.O./HD 3/97; R.A., photocopy.

37. Collins, 301.

38. Storey, 70.

39. "Men of the Day. No. 55," *Vanity Fair* (14 December 1872).

40. See Francis Williams, *Transmitting World News: A Study of Communications and the Press* (Paris: UNESCO, 1953), 13.

41. *Havas* to Rabanit, 16 January 1911. Quoted in Boutbouqalt, 71.

42. *Havas* to *Reuters*, 30 April 1898. A.N., 5AR 66. *Havas* continued in another letter, "One speaks to us of 700,000 volunteers. We know all that the United States has great resources in men and in money; but 700,000 volunteers, like that, is all the same a great deal. It would be useful to present our recommendations below in order that we not be accused, the one and the others, of making journalism for stock-jobbing purposes [*à coup de grosse caisse*]. . . . The seriousness of our agencies does not lend itself to exaggerations. . . . All this is very embarrassing. We would like to see our service not depart from its character of authenticity that is natural to it." Quoted in Frédérix, 217.

43. *Havas* to Rabanit, 21 January 1907. Quoted in Boutbouqalt, 62.

44. Storey, 132.

45. *Havas* complained that *Reuters* had failed to signal the proposal of a conference at London in April. (*Havas* to *Reuters*, 23 April 1884.) Although *Reuters* coverage of the Conference for *Havas* was woefully inadequate, *Havas* coverage of the Paris end of the negotiations was so good that it was through *Havas* (and subsequently through *Reuters*) that the British government knew the responses of France to British demarches ten hours before Whitehall had received them. (Lebey to Herbert de Reuter, 2 May 1884.) Mercadier proved able to obtain "at London even from ministries and embassies information which you [*Reuters*] believe impossible to have." (Lebey to Reuter, 7 May 1884.) A.N., 5AR 64.

46. Frédérix, 219.

47. J. D. Symon, *The Press and its Story* (London: Seeley, Service and Co., 1914), 96.

48. *Havas* to Mercadier, 14 May 1909. "It is not the *Reuter Agency* in itself which dominates us," *Havas* observed, "it is *London*." 17 June 1909. A.N., 5AR 81.

49. "In Justice to the 'A.P.'," *Collier's* 53 (6 June 1914):16.

50. See Storey, 135.

51. Otto Groth, *Die Zeitung* (Mannheim: J. Bensheimer, 1928), vol. 1, 535.

52. See Ernst Hirsch to Otto Hammann, 21 August 1909. P.A./A.A., Europa Generalia 86, Band 16.

53. For the *Kabelgramm-Gesellschaft*, see Friedrich Fuchs, *Telegraphische Nachrichtenbüros. Eine Untersuchung über die Probleme des internationalen Nachrichtenwesens* (Berlin: D. Reimer-E. Vohsen, 1919), 89–90; Groth, vol. 1, 492.

54. Hammann to Regierungsrat Janzer (director of the Rheinischen Creditbank, Mannheim), 15 December 1916. Bundesarchiv Potsdam, A.A. Nr. 57.870, Transocean-Gesellschaft Allgemeines, Band 3.

55. Charles Houssaye to Collin-Delavaud (Havas/New York), 20 April 1914. A.N., 5AR 113.

56. Houssaye to Mercadier, 14 May 1909. A.N., 5AR 81.

57. *Havas* to *Reuters*, 2 February 1877. A.N., 5AR 63.

58. Edouard Lebey to Baron de Reuter, personal, 23 April 1878. A.N., 5AR 63.

59. Edouard Lebey to Baron de Reuter, confidential, 13 July 1878; *Havas* to

Baron de Reuter, 23 July 1878; 27 August 1878, *Havas* to *Reuters*; 25 October 1880, *Havas* to *Reuters*. A.N., 5AR 63.

60. *Havas* to *Reuters*, 3 August 1877. A.N., 5AR 63.

61. Ibid., 10 August 1877. A.N., 5AR 63.

62. Ibid., 25 October 1877. A.N., 5AR 63.

63. Ibid., 27 October 1877. A.N., 5AR 63.

64. "Sentence Arbitrale," 20 June 1879. R.A., 1/850738.

65. Engländer distributed news from London but also from Paris, Vienna, St. Petersburg, Alexandria, and even Turkey itself. Engländer employed a subterfuge to circumvent the prohibition against using news from non-British sources: he would send Turkish reports to *Reuters* at London, and then retransmit such news to Turkish clients, citing the British press as his source. See *Havas* to *Reuters*, 9 September 1879, 25 January 1881. A.N., 5AR 63.

66. W. H. G. Werndel to Managing Director, 21 February 1919. Quoted in "Sigismund Engländer—Rough Notes," R.A., database.

67. In Ausland-Deutschen, *Die Presse und die deutsche Weltpolitik* (Zurich: Zürcher and Furrer, 1906).

68. *Berliner Neueste Nachrichten*, 1 August 1905.

69. Secret Note by Hammann, 21 March 1898. P.A./A.A., Europa Generalia No. 86, Band 8.

70. A.N., 5AR 411.22. R.A., 1/863819; 1/871551; 1/8818803. P.A./A.A. Europa Generalia No. 86 No. 1, Band 8.

71. See Terhi Rantanen, "Foreign News in Imperial Russia: The Relationship between International and Russian News Agencies, 1856–1914," *Annales Academiae Scientarum Fennicae. Dissertationes Humanum Litterarym* 58 (Helsinki, 1990), 46.

72. Mantler to Hammann, 19 September 1907. P.A./A.A., Europa Generalia 86, Band 14.

73. *Havas* to Mercadier (*Havas*/London), 18 May 1908. A.N., 5AR 81.

74. Houssaye to Mercadier, 14 May 1909. 5AR 81.

75. Ibid., 17 June 1909. 5AR 81.

76. Hermann Diez, *Zeitungswissenschaft*, Jahrg. 1938, Nr. 1 (1 January 1938), 37. For their parts, *Reuters* and *Havas* felt they had spared themselves direct competition with *Wolff* in their reserved territories. In many ways, however, the compromise was actually *more* effective from the standpoint of propaganda than a direct distribution by the sending agency. On the one hand, inspired telegrams would be distributed by an innocuous allied agency, unlikely to arouse suspicion of foreign propaganda among any who did not know the significance of the *"Tractatus"* signature. On the other, *Wolff* was spared the costs of establishing a distributing network in the territories in question. See Mantler to Hammann, 16 September 1909. P.A./A.A., Europa Generalia 86, Band 16.

77. With the advent of the *Tractatus* privileges in 1910, *Wolff* had persuaded *Havas* to allow local resident representatives of *German* firms—Plaut in Buenos Aires, and Vorweck in Chile—to supervise *Havas* news material in South America. *Wolff* sent these agents copies of all telegrams which it sent to *Havas:* in the event of a suppression of news by *Havas,* they would be ready to distribute the material to the press. (Mantler to Legationsrat Esternaux, German Foreign Office, 29 July 1912 and 7 August 1912. P.A./A.A., Europa Generalia 86, Band 3, No. 2.) The Germans found, however, that this supervisory role was virtually unnecessary, as the French distributed almost everything sent to them. (Mantler to German Foreign Office, 27 August 1912. P.A./A.A., Europa Generalia 86, Band 3, No. 2.)

78. *Havas* to *Fabra*, 2 January 1885. A.N., 5AR 93.

79. T. H. Sanderson to Lord Rosebury, 6 July 1894. P.R.O./HD 3/97; R.A., photocopy.

80. Note of Lord Kimberley, 6 July 1894. P.R.O./HD 3/97; R.A., photocopy.

81. On 2 January 1894, Melville Stone concluded a five-year exclusive news exchange contract with W. C. Van Horne, president of the Canadian Pacific Railway Company, the dominant force in Canadian telegraphy which collected and distributed news for the press of Canada. The contract is reproduced in Associated Press (Illinois), *Second Annual Report* (1895), 125–27. The contract was extended in 1899, remaining in force until canceled by a six months notice by either party.

82. Collins (New York) to Herbert de Reuter, 4 November 1906. R.A., Sir Roderick Jones papers, Reuter's General, Pre-1915 (A) General (a) Box File 1.

83. Collins (Ottawa) to Herbert de Reuter, 18 November 1906, 22 November 1904. R.A., Jones papers.

84. Ibid., 26 November 1904. R.A., Jones papers.

85. Ibid., 2 December 1906. R.A., Jones papers.

86. Ibid., 26 November 1906. R.A., Jones papers.

87. Ibid., 18 November 1906. R.A., Jones papers.

88. "Canada and the Empire," Ottawa *Citizen*, 19 November 1906.

Imperial Self-Representation: Constructions of Empire in *Blackwood's Magazine,* 1880–1900

David Finkelstein

In a 1917 retrospective article commemorating the hundredth anniversary of *Blackwood's Magazine,* Charles Whibley declared: "Ever since 1817, when it came into being, it has held aloft the twin banners of sound criticism and Tory politics."[1] Past work on the magazine's history has concentrated on the truth or otherwise of this statement in relation to the magazine's mixture of fiction and literary criticism. Little attention has been paid as to whether such a statement equally applies to its representation of British activities overseas. This essay will address this issue, and examine in particular what views of the British Empire are evident in the magazine's pages in the last twenty years of the nineteenth century. It will also suggest how such images were constructed and shaped by editorial attitudes and policies, authorial interests, and general assumptions about implied audiences and readership responses.

As a recent study on India in the nineteenth century media has pointed out, media historians are prone to skipping over the Victorian empire, seemingly concluding that the mass media began with the first issue of the *Daily Mail* in 1896, and then subsequently exploded with the advent of cinema, radio, and television.[2] Nor can we look to colonial studies for insight into this topic. Media and colonial studies alike either ignore the Victorian press or isolate texts from their contexts. Examples of the latter are the frequent analyses of Joseph Conrad's *Heart of Darkness* that fail to account for its first appearance in 1899 as a serial in the very pro-empire monthly *Blackwood's Edinburgh Magazine.*[3]

Likewise ignored is the tradition throughout the century (prior to advancements in technology such as the telegraph that allowed for swift transmission of news) of including copies of articles from the colonies in the British press. This in turn was replicated by newspapers in India, for example, who repeatedly ran copies of articles from the *Times* as well as other British papers and periodicals. (The

Madras Male Asylum Herald in the 1840s, for one, often reprinted articles from *Blackwood's Edinburgh Magazine* and the *Edinburgh Review,* [Finkelstein and Peers, 14].)

Blackwood's Magazine is a particularly apposite journal for reviewing Imperial and colonial imagery in the nineteenth-century media. Founded in 1817 with the avowed intention of being a Tory alternative, "more nimble, more frequent, more familiar," to the Whig quarterly the *Edinburgh Review,* Blackwood's early on forged a reputation for itself as a journal aligned with radical conservative politics and power (Finkelstein, 1995, ix–x). Under the guidance first of John Blackwood (editor from 1845 to 1879), and then more significantly of William Blackwood III (editor from 1879 to 1912), "Maga" shifted ground to become identified as an official promulgator of conservative establishment views of the British imperial presence. Indeed, so strong was its identification as an essential part of the British colonial social life, found in every colonial backwater club and station, that George Orwell in the early 1940s was to scathingly characterise it as being read by "the 'service' middle classes," patriotic Colonel Blimps who "read Blackwood's Magazine and publicly thanked God [they] were 'not brainy.' "[4]

In the latter quarter of the nineteenth-century, the magazine's contents were strongly dictated by William Blackwood's and his editorial staff's personal tastes and political views. The Blackwood family had a strong personal interest in the workings of the empire: William's father and uncle had been a major and a colonel respectively in the East India Company; and two of William's brothers also served and died in India, one of them fighting in the Afghan war in 1880. Likewise, William's literary advisers and editorial staff were predominantly and staunchly Conservative and had connections with the Empire: Alexander Allardyce, for example, chief proof reader and assistant editor from 1879 to 1896, was a Scot with many years experience as journalist and newspaper editor in India and Sri Lanka, who espoused strong colonial interventionist policies and wrote over sixty articles on this subject for Maga during his tenure.

William Blackwood's main literary advisers included Sir Edward Hamley, best known for his command of the British interventionist campaign in Egypt in 1882, and a Conservative M.P. for Birkenhead from 1886 to 1992, Alexander Innes Shand, a Scottish lawyer and journalist, and Charles Whibley, another staunch conservative and prolific contributor to Maga until his death in 1930. Their views, and indeed even their leisure interests (William was a keen horse rider, fisher, and hunter, while A. Innes Shand was similarly described in the *Dictionary of National Biography* [1982] as a "fine rider, shot &

angler," p. 601), contributed to the development of Maga as an outlet for "hunting, shooting, fishing" stories and "colonial" fiction and travel pieces on the frontiers of Empire.

The early years of William Blackwood III's tenure as editor of the magazine were marked by a sense of complacency. Its solid profitability (the magazine produced a consistent and respectable profit of around £3700 a year from 1870 to 1880) initially assured the editor that all was well with its stance and readership.[5] "Maga was never going stronger or better than at present," William noted in the early 1880s, "this is the general opinion I have heard in many different quarters."[6] Even so, he admitted that careful monitoring was needed to maintain its position as a leading journal: "A careful study of Maga sales for past few years shows that, as I stated years ago, best to be hoped for with the severe competition is to keep up circulation."[7] This complacency was rudely disturbed by the emergence in March 1883 of the *National Review*, a monthly journal founded by Alfred Austin, coedited with the conservative journalist William J. Courthope, and published by the London firm W.H. Allen, that was to be "devoted to political and literary matters . . . [and] to be unashamedly committed to Tory principles."[8]

The idea for the *National Review* took shape in a conversation between Alfred Austin and Benjamin Disraeli shortly before the latter's death in 1881. The suggestion was for a philosophically consistent journal that would, in the words of Austin, promote Conservatism "by the demonstration that Conservatives have capacity, and not only political capacity, but capacity of the large and generous sort," and in so doing, "to go a long way towards converting people to Conservatism" (Sullivan, 242). Estimated sales of the journal during its first ten years were just under five thousand copies per month, comparing favorably with *Blackwood's Magazine* sales of just under fifty-three hundred copies a month. (Sales of the *National Review* were to rise after Leopold J. Maxse took over the editorship in 1893 to an average ten thousand copies per issue [Sullivan, 244].) Over the seventy-seven years of its existence, it gained a reputation for consistency and standing as a "long-lived, eloquent, and self-confident Tory spokesman" (Sullivan, 243). It also drew heavily on Blackwood's pool of contributors and political sources, including critic and academic George Saintsbury, essayist Sir Herbert Cowell, and Sir Stafford Henry Northcote (leader of the Conservative opposition in the House of Commons).

The arrival of the *National Review* represented a threat to Maga's self-perceived role in leading and reflecting nineteenth-century conservative, colonial, and High Tory political and social agendas, and helps partially to explain the nosedive in sales experienced by the magazine during the mid-1880s. Maga's sales, although in a downward trend dating back to 1860 (when sales averaged 7537 copies a month), declined even further in face of Austin's competition, moving from annual sales of 63,000 (or 5270 copies a month) in 1883 to 55,831 (or 4652 a month) by 1890. (Finkelstein, 2002, Appendix 2, 165–66)

From the mid-nineteenth century onwards, consensus within the firm, reinforced by a deliberate targeting of audiences after William Blackwood III took over in 1879, viewed its textual productions as speaking to and for a specific network of readers and opinion-makers in upper middle-class, military, colonial, and political circles. As one historian of the Conservative Party has observed, throughout much of its early history *Blackwood's Magazine* represented a specific High Tory Radical paternalist strand of the Conservative movement, one that ran both

> too far ahead and too far behind their times; ahead, in that their shadowy prevision of the welfare state and a planned economy would not be generally accepted even a hundred years later; behind, in that their views on such subjects as the Church were a reactionary as those of the Ultras.[9]

Thus while John Wilson and his Edinburgh cohorts in the 1820s and 1830s launched conservative attacks on radical literary movements (hitting out at targets as diverse as Wordsworth, Coleridge, and the "Spasmodic" school of poetry), others such as the economist David Robinson had produced powerful economic treatises that were taken up by John Maynard Keynes, among others, a century later.[10]

The arrival of the *National Review* threatened the monopoly *Blackwood's* believed it enjoyed in this area, encroaching on its target markets and audiences and poaching a significant proportion of the firm's established coterie of authors. The effect of this competition was a decided hardening and shifting in tone in the magazine to maintain a bedrock of loyal colonial and military audiences through essays and tales focused on Britain's overseas possessions and activities. Similarly there was a concentration in the firm's book publications on complementary niche markets. In the face of challenges such as Austin's journal, William quite consciously ventured into literary production that catered to markets he understood well.

In the 1880s and 1890s, William Blackwood III focused the magazine on maintaining its tradition of conservative formations, publishing polemical material from military, colonial, aristocratic, and opposition Tory figures such as Sir Theodore Martin, Sir Archibald

Alison, Gathorne Hardy (Secretary of State for India 1878–80), Lord Wolseley, Frederick Lugard (soldier and African administrator), Sir Edward Braddon (premier of Tasmania from 1894 to 1904), and Sir Henry Stafford Northcote (conservative MP for Exeter 1880–99, Governor-General of Australia 1903–07, and son of Sir Stafford Henry Northcote, a leader in the Conservative party). Lord John Manners and Lord Brabourne (member of the Tory opposition in the House of Lords 1880–85) were also mainstays of the firm's magazine and book lists (their importance to *Blackwood's* underlined in biographies subsequently commissioned from trusted Blackwoodian authors after their deaths).

The colonial market was one that other publishers had sought entry into since the early 1840s, when John Murray had begun Murray's Colonial and Home Library, aimed at selling cheap reprints at home and abroad.[11] Other publishers created journals targeting individuals with longstanding personal or family connections to the Empire. Eugenie Palmegiano has found in a study of the Victorian press and the Indian Revolt of 1857 that British journals like *Bentley's Miscellany*, *Blackwood's Edinburgh Magazine*, and *Fraser's* increasingly focused their attention on India (for example) with an eye to this market, while *Blackwood's* was especially persistent in appealing to those with an interest in the British empire in general and India in particular. Its regular inclusion of articles on India and other parts of the empire, as well as on the army, ensured that it was widely available in the libraries and messes of the British empire. In 1843 *Blackwood's* even launched a colonial edition, though it must be added that its market was smaller than it had anticipated. Its initial print run of one thousand copies per month was soon reduced to 350 and then killed off due to difficulties in marketing, shipping, and selling copies in the colonies (Finkelstein and Peers, 7–8).

An upsurge in the colonial book market in the 1880s, sparked in part by Macmillan's successful establishment of the Macmillan's Colonial Library in 1886, tied in with *Blackwood's* renewed commitment to reaching such audiences. Potential profits from such markets, as publishers soon realised, was huge. As Sir Walter Besant noted at the time, "largely as a result of British colonial policies, the readership of the English speaking world had expanded from 50,000 in 1830 to 120 million by the late 1890s."[12]

From 1894 onward, the firm began issuing novels in a Colonial Library series, taking sheets from the same print runs and producing separate cloth- and paper-bound editions to be sold in British colonies overseas at 2 shillings (cloth) and 1/6 (paper). The series continued through to the 1920s. Because of a long-standing policy

of gaining the most from texts commissioned or negotiated for publication by the firm, such works were often first serialized in the magazine and then reprinted in volume form. The firm thus committed
itself to recruiting and featuring colonial texts and authors for both
its magazine and its book lists, consolidating its reputation as a
major purveyor of British colonial imagery and views.

IMPERIAL IMAGERY

Blackwood's Magazine's place in maintaining a particular link to the
empire for the firm can be seen in the articles and stories it published during what many have characterized as the height of British
Imperial dominance, from the termination of the Afghan war in
1880 to the beginning of the Boer War in 1899. Of the just over two
thousand pieces published in the Magazine during this period, over
three hundred were exclusively set in or about the various British
imperial possession and colonies, India, Africa, Australia, Canada,
and Asia. Thus approximately fifteen percent concerned itself with
the work and play of the Empire Builder. If you included the various
political articles attacking Liberal policies on Foreign Affairs, which
accounted for approximately another five percent of Maga's contents, that meant at least twenty percent of Maga was devoted to the
Empire, its problems, its colonisers, and its indigenous people, as
well as to the standard smoking room anecdote of strange and amazing occurrences while out in the colonial jungle.

Invariably, the Empire as seen in these pieces was part of a disordered universe which was being put right by British skill, technology,
and moral superiority. Its political articles argued consistently for an
expansionist foreign policy, suggesting that only strong, forceful occupation of places like Afghanistan (in the early 1880s), Egypt in
1882, and African colonies in the 1890s, would allow good sound
government to prevail. More important, Maga's editorials argued,
it was Britain's duty as a ruling power to do so. As Herbert Cowell
commented in the closing piece of the March 1880 issue, "We are
not in India merely to be safe. Our mission there is to govern and
command, or we have no business there at all."[13]

In keeping with this, a common theme in Maga's articles toward
the turn of the century was how to avoid losing prestige in Europe
through actions undertaken in the colonies. An example of this
thinking affecting the presentation of other issues can be seen in
the many pieces from 1880 to 1900 on Irish Home Rule, a particular
bugbear of the features in Maga. In the run up to the 1880 General

Election, for example, several articles ran in Maga linking Glad-stone's espousal of Irish Home Rule with concurrent concerns over Russian incursions into British-controlled Afghanistan, suggesting such positions were tantamount to a foreign policy that threatened the foundation of British imperial rule and overseas standing. "The Crisis abroad," thundered a typical political editorial published in the April 1880 issue, "is the most momentous upon which the world has entered since Waterloo. The Crisis at home—the General Elec-tion—is equally momentous, as it is about to decide the Foreign Pol-icy, and with it the fortunes, of the British Empire."[14] By December 1880 the tone had not modified, with an editorially sanctioned blast from Henry Stafford Northcote exclaiming,

> It is painful for an Englishman to have to censure the foreign policy of his own Government; far rather would we pray for a time when, under the simple watchword of "Our country's honour and interests," Liberal and Tory might unite in the determination to prefer their fatherland to their party. But so long as, for the sake of driving a political foe from office, the Radical party does not scruple to sacrifice their country's wel-fare on the altar of faction, so long will the Tories use every legitimate method to prevent the abrogation of the position their ancestors have built up for the empire.[15]

Throughout the late nineteenth century, Maga's editorials consis-tently argued that a failure to maintain a strong presence and rule over its colonies would lead to disastrous consequences and loss of face in Europe and at home. Thus in Maga's pages, the colonies were viewed in context of power struggles against Russia in Afghani-stan, or France in Fashoda and Egypt, or Germany in Southern Af-rica. While altruistic activities, such as Christian conversion, had its place in colonization, a more significant factor was commercial gains to be made.

Even in articles about nature and travel in the far-flung outposts of empire, there was an underlying presumption about the commer-cial potentials available and the benefits of imposing British rule to achieve this. As noted in a typical interjection in a travelogue ac-count of touring Lake Nyassa, "If we wish to benefit Africa,—disregarding for the moment the benefits which may accrue to our own pocket and trade in the process—the first step is to introduce some settled law and order."[16] Similarly an article in 1890 on the wonders of deep-sea fishing off the South African coast, concludes by asking whether such natural riches cannot be exploited by the enterprising British. Perhaps an aquarium, or better yet an organized fishing industry, for "in the race for diamonds and gold in South Africa, may it not be suggested that the wealth of the seas is now being most unaccountably neglected. Yet there it lies in masses all round the coasts, ready at hand for those who wish, with little trouble, to take and utilise."[17]

While Maga's pages extolled the Empire's natural resources as ripe for commercial exploitation, it also offered visions of the colonies as a sportsman's paradise, a site where British men could do battle with nature and inevitably come out the winner. Maga's readers were warned in 1894 that big-game hunting in the colonies, for example, required a strength of character forged by hours of exposure in the colonial mountains and jungles: "It is needless to go in for the sport in earnest," readers were told,

> unless you have all the qualities that go to make a man, with others that are undefinable into the bargain. Courage, coolness, and indomitable patience are, of course, indispensable; and of course, also, the sportsman will last all the longer if he be blessed with an iron constitution, and lungs that can breathe poison without sensible injury. For the sport is often so identified with suffering, that it is next to impossible for the uninitiated to distinguish the one from the other.[18]

Nevertheless, such feats were also viewed in a rather blasé manner, as John Cecil Russell pointed out in a piece describing the thrill of chasing wild bison in their natural habitat. After describing the chase in detail, he records with relish the inevitable moment of satisfaction when, after dropping the quarry in its tracks, his guide rushed "at the mighty fallen, sprang upon the heaving side, and seizing a horn, plunged the knife in his throat. What a moment of satisfaction!" After satisfying this blood lust, and measuring the beast, Russell nonchalantly sits down to a spot of tiffin, as if this was merely a country stroll through the park: "So much exertion deserved refreshment, which I took in biscuits and cold tea, just tempered from my pocket flask."[19]

NEW LITERARY ADVISER, NEW EMPHASIS

The recruitment in 1893 of David Storrar Meldrum as chief literary adviser (and eventually copartner from 1903 to 1910 with William Blackwood III and his two nephews), brought new sophistication to the colonial material featured in Maga. Meldrum's valuable role in convincing William Blackwood to publish Joseph

Conrad's early work in *Blackwood's Magazine,* such as *Heart of Darkness* (1899) and *Lord Jim* (1902) is well known. Conrad was one of the many literary talents Meldrum was to champion for the firm's magazine and book list; others included Stephen Crane, the Australians Henry Lawson and Miles Franklin, and John Buchan. Meldrum was astute in gauging that the firm needed to recover its position as a leading publisher of the day by actively seeking out and developing new talent, rather than waiting for individuals to come to the firm. As early as May 1896, almost a full year before Edward Garnett is reputed to have suggested to Conrad that he submit material (in this case his short story "Karain: A Memory") for publication in *Blackwood's Magazine,*[20] Meldrum urged William Blackwood to consider Conrad's work as a potentially lucrative textual commodity. "What you write me about getting hold of a paying novelist," William responded, "is very much what we know, and have felt ourselves, and the difficulty is to spot the men who are just rising into a reputation, and whose work would be likely to carry large sales with it. . . . If you hear anything good about Joseph Conrad, will you kindly let me know. I have read none of his things. Is he not a Yankee author?"[21]

Meldrum was a sociable character and a member of the Garrick Club, the literary gentleman's club of London. He made contacts there and used it often as a base for social and business occasions. Thus we find Meldrum arranging lunches at the Garrick for prospective authors he hoped to entice into the circle of contributors to the firm's magazine and lists, or organizing dining parties for groups of "Blackwoodian" writers, either potential or actual, for whom he served as a social go-between. The "network" of writers that John Blackwood had encouraged in his time (and which William Blackwood III could only shyly attempt to emulate) was continued through Meldrum's contacts in appropriate literary circles. We can see this at work in Meldrum's bringing Conrad together with a wide variety of authors linked to the firm in one form or other, and the invisible network through which these contacts led to other friendships, links, and potential publications. Conrad was invited to lunch with Blackwood's "colonial" writers, such as the South African Douglas Blackburn (author of *Richard Hartley, Prospector,* a bestselling parodic riposte to H. Rider-Haggard's overblown visions of Africa such as *She*), as well as invited to attend late night dinners at the Garrick, such as the one in October 1900, where Conrad met Stephen Gwynn, a leading Irish novelist (and later nationalist MP for Galway City 1906–1918). Gwynn, an avid but oddly placed contributor to *Blackwood's Magazine* (a nationalist producing work for a conservative journal whose politics he did not agree with), returned

later with an introduction for Roger Casement, a fellow Irish nationalist with colonial credentials and a link to Conrad.

Roger Casement (1864–1916), British consular officer, reformer
and Irish nationalist leader, was knighted in 1911 for his efforts in
exposing Belgian colonial excesses in the Congo at the turn of the
century. (But was subsequently executed in controversial circumstances by the British in 1916 for war-time treason.) Conrad and
Casement first met in 1890, when Conrad arrived in the Matadi Station in the Congo to take command of a steamer for a Belgium commercial firm whose transport service Casement was responsible at
the time for co-ordinating.[22] Conrad resided with Casement during
the three weeks he was based at Matadi, and accompanied him on
expeditions to neighbouring villages to organize porters for the
company's caravans into the interior, incidents from which Conrad
drew heavily in *Heart of Darkness* nine years later, and which have
some to speculate that Casement was Conrad's inspiration for Kurtz
in *Heart of Darkness*.[23]

Casement's introduction to the editors who had supported Conrad's earlier literary endeavors came in 1905, when Stephen Gwynn
contacted William Blackwood III regarding a potential contributor
he felt sure would fit in well with past interests and published work
(such as Conrad's *Heart of Darkness* and Hugh Clifford's Malay
tales).[24] William responded enthusiastically, suggesting Casement
contribute something on his experiences in the Congo, and Casement sent in "The Careless Ethiopian," a sketch "avoiding the political aspects altogether of the existing Congo controversy, while
seeking to throw some light on the actual conditions of native life in
the interior."[25] Blackwood subsequently reviewed and returned the
piece, concluding that while he enjoyed his writing, "I have a feeling
that you could do better and I am reluctant for you to make your
debut in Maga with this paper."[26] Casement concurred, and while
promising to produce other work, never did, thus leaving unrealized
this potential link.

READERSHIP

As in the case of Casement, Maga's authors, both prospective and
actual, were drawn from linked colonial, military, and political circles and networks. Maga's readers were also drawn from these circles, a point many of Maga's authors seemed particularly conscious
of. In 1907, reminiscing about his connection with Maga, Conrad
wrote to his agent that "one was in decent company there and had

a good sort of public. There isn't a single club and messroom and man-of-war in the British Seas and Dominions which hasn't its copy of Maga."[27] That Conrad felt this way is interesting to note, considering that his novel *Heart of Darkness*, first serialised in Maga in early 1899, has often been taken as anti-imperialist in tone. Its readers, however, finding it alongside pieces on mountain exploration in the Canadian Rockies, the struggle between France and Great Britain for control of Nigeria, and a narrative of a Malaysian woman caring for her leprous husband, would not have seen it as anything less than the standard "Blackwoodian" imperial adventure anecdote.

Another writer used the colonial readership connection, and his own experience of finding Maga displayed and read in South African colonial clubs, to try to convince Alexander Allardyce to publish unchanged his piece on the Portuguese in East Africa in 1888. "The early portion of the article," J. E. C. Bodley wrote breathlessly, "is not only of importance to the British public, but will be read with the greatest interest throughout South Africa. The time-honoured cover of Maga was a very welcome sight to me not only on the tables of the Clubs at Capetown, Kimberley, Pretoria, but frequently also in remote stations & solitary Magistrates' residences, and great would be the disappointment of your Colonial readers if they found that I treated the Portuguese Question simply as a traveller up the East Coast" (Finkelstein, 1995, xiii).

William Blackwood was conscious of the colonial interest Maga attracted, and often took steps to avoid alienating this loyal public. In 1881, for example, we find him in a letter warning a writer to tone down the wording of a contemplated piece on military reforms in India, for

> The Magazine in India is very popular & carries considerable weight with the members of the old Indian armies whose claims Maga has always stood up for & I should not like to take any steps that might be prejudicial to them & destroy the influence of the the "old ship" out there without very careful consideration.[28]

Such editorial views of the invisible presence of the general Maga readership are intriguing and important in understanding the manner and reasons by which the magazine's contents were shaped and directed. Blackwood's caution was understandable, in light of the backlash the Magazine had suffered in a previous attempt to make Maga "controversial" with a serialized novel by George T. Chesney, a soldier and administrator of some renown in India. His best known work, *The Battle of Dorking*, was serialized in Maga 1871. In 1881 Maga serialized *The Private Secretary*, which featured its male protagonist seducing its unmarried heroine and making her his mistress. Maga's readers raised a storm and sales dropped overseas. Such degeneracy, according to various readers' letters, had no place in the comfortable drawing rooms of the British Empire. Blackwood tread warily after that, and fed his readers Conrad, Henry Newbolt, and Anthony Trollope instead.

Stephen Gwynn wrote in 1923 about the intangible network *Blackwood's Magazine* represented to him in terms of audience and contributors, consumers, and producers, noting,

> But certain publications have an atmosphere of their own, a personality which is not entirely the editor's, nor is it made by the readers, nor by the combined influence of all the customary writers. It results from all of these, and when I write, say for *Blackwood's Magazine*, I feel myself part of a society; I am affected by its tone, knowing in a general way what will interest it, what it will like and dislike. It does not get rid of me as the first audience; nothing by which I cannot interest myself thoroughly is going to interest this circle; but one writes there with a certain pleasure as one goes to a hospitable house.[29]

It was both Blackwood's strength and weakness that its name, its lists and its journal could evoke such specific identity among its contributors and readers. Under William Blackwood III, Maga became more closely identified as a journal of Empire, a strong promoter of colonial policies, and a conduit for works by colonial administrators and soldiers. Its identification with conservative administrative and foreign policies, and the colonial status quo, consolidated under his tenure, was carried on by successive editors right up until the journal's demise in 1980. The result was a particular worldview worthy of study for what it tells us about distinct British conservative responses to British Imperial aspirations and conditions.

NOTES

1. Charles Whibley, "A Retrospect," *Blackwood's Magazine* 201 (April 1917): 433.

2. David Finkelstein and Douglas Mark Peers, "'A Great System of Circulation': Introducing India into the Nineteenth-Century Media," *Negotiating India in the Nineteenth-Century Media*, eds., David Finkelstein and Douglas Mark Peers (Basingstoke: Macmillan Press, 2000), 5.

3. David Finkelstein, *An Index to Blackwood's Magazine, 1901–1980* (Aldershot: Scolar Press, 1995), *xiv.*

4. George Orwell, "Rudyard Kipling," *A Collection of Essays* (New York: Bantam Press, 1954), 128.

5. David Finkelstein, *The House of Blackwood: Author-Publisher Relations in the Victorian Era* (University Park: Pennsylvania State University Press, 2002), Appendix 2, 165–166.

6. Undated memorandum, MS. 30071, Blackwood Papers, National Library of Scotland.

7. Ibid.

8. Alvin Sullivan, ed., *British Literary Magazines: The Victorian and Edwardian Age, 1837–1913* (Westport, Conn.: Greenwood Press, 1984), 242.

9. Robert Blake, *The Conservative Party from Peel to Churchill* (London: Eyre and Spottiswood, 1970), 24.

10. For further information on the role of Blackwood's in shaping Tory economic policies, see Frank W. Fetter, "The Economic Articles in Blackwood's Edinburgh Magazine and their Authors 1817–1853," *Scottish Journal of Political Economy.* 7 (1960): 85–107; 213–31 and Salim Rashid, "David Robinson and the Tory Macroeconomics of Blackwood's Edinburgh Magazine," *History of Political Economy* 10 (1978): 259–70.

11. Simon Nowell-Smith, *International Copyright Law and the Publisher in the reign of Queen Victoria* (Oxford: Oxford University Press, 1968), 94. For more information on Murray's Colonial Library series, see Angus Fraser, "John Murray's Colonial and Home Library," *Papers of the Bibliographical Society of America* 91 (September 1997): 339–408, and Priya Joshi, "Culture and Consumption: Fiction, the Reading Public, and the British Novel in Colonial India," *Book History* 1 (1998): 206–7.

12. Quoted in Margaret Diane Stetz, "Sex, Lies, and Printed Cloth: Bookselling at the Bodley Head in the Eighteen-Nineties," *Victorian Studies* 35 (1991): 80–81.

13. Herbert Cowell, "The Opening of Parliament," *Blackwood's Magazine* 127 (March 1880): 405.

14. R. H. Patterson, "The Crisis Abroad," *Blackwood's Magazine* 127 (April 1880): 529.

15. Henry Stafford Northcote, "Paulo Paulo post futurum policy," *Blackwood's Magazine* 128 (December 1880): 774.

16. Frederick Dealtry Lugard, "A Glimpse of Lake Nyassa," *Blackwood's Magazine* 147 (January 1890): 27.

17. Walter B. Harris, "Sea Fishing at the Cape," *Blackwood's Magazine* 148 (November 1890): 635–36.

18. A. Innes Shand, "Big Game Shooting," *Blackwood's Magazine* 155 (April 1894): 582.

19. John Cecil Russell, "Bison Stalking in India," *Blackwood's Magazine.* 141 (June 1887): 795–806.

20. Quoted in William Blackburn, ed. *Joseph Conrad: Letters to William Blackwood and David S. Meldrum* (Durham, N.C.: Duke University Press, 1958), *xiv:* "And in April of 1897, when Conrad seemed at a loss to know what to do with his short story "Karain: A Memory," Garnett spoke with sudden inspiration and authority: it was "destined by Providence," he said, "for *Blackwood's Magazine.*"

21. William Blackwood III to David Storrar Meldrum, 27 May 1896, MS. 30392, 461–62, Blackwood Papers, National Library of Scotland.

22. Further information regarding Conrad and Casement is noted in Hunt Hawkins, "Joseph Conrad, Roger Casement and the Congo Reform Movement," *Journal of Modern Literature* 9 (1981–82): 65–80. Also, Jeffrey Meyers, "Conrad and Roger Casement," *Conradiana* 5 (1973): 64–69.

23. See for example, Jane Ford, "An African Encounter, A British Traitor, and *Heart of Darkness,*" *Conradiana* 27 (1995): 123–34, and Jeffrey Meyers, "Conrad and Roger Casement," *Conradiana* 5, no. 3 (1973): 64–69. I am indebted to Linda Dryden and Gene Moore for pointing out these sources to me.

24. Stephen Gwynn to William Blackwood III, 29 July 1905, MS. 30113, Blackwood Papers, National Library of Scotland.

25. Roger Casement to William Blackwood III, 5 September 1905, 22 September 1905, MS. 30111, Blackwood Papers, National Library of Scotland.

26. William Blackwood III to Roger Casement, 23 October 1905, MS. 30393, p. 231, Blackwood Papers, National Library of Scotland.

27. Frederick Karl and Laurence Davis, eds., *The Collected Letters of Joseph Conrad,* vol. 4: 1908–1911 (Cambridge: Cambridge University Press, 1990), 130.

28. Cited in Finkelstein, 1995, *xiii.*

29. Stephen Gwynn, *The Irish Statesman,* 10 November 1923, 279.

Selling the Mother Country to the Empire: The Imperial Press Conference of June 1909

J. Lee Thompson

Even more so than was usual in the period following 1906, when a Liberal landslide had swept the Unionists from office, the tumultuous year 1909 found Britain's major political parties at daggers drawn. Two intertwined controversies dominated the scene. The first was the Free Trade-Tariff Reform battle between the Liberal supporters of Lloyd George's high-tax "Peoples Budget" and Joseph Chamberlain's social imperialism based on preferential tariffs designed to link the empire and pay for social reforms. The second issue concerned the British navy and its new and expensive dreadnought-class battleships, vessels more heavily armored, faster and with more big guns than anything else afloat. Interparty warfare raged over how many such ships Britain needed and how they were to be paid for. The Unionist side supported a more rapid naval buildup than did the Liberal Government, citing the dire threat of a new German fleet being built across the North Sea. "We Want Eight and We Won't Wait" was the battle cry in the Unionist press. In June of 1909, however, a three-week spell of quiet cooperation fell over Britain and a political truce was declared. The event that elicited this temporary calm in the Edwardian storm was the Imperial Press Conference, an overlooked, yet important event, both to the history of Edwardian journalism and efforts to promote imperial unity.[1]

During this interlude, the Liberal lambs lay down with the Unionist lions in the interest of imperial cooperation and defense. Both sides hosted and propagandized a group of fifty-four imperial newspaper editors and proprietors in the hope that these emissaries of empire would return to rally their respective homelands around the mother country, particularly in support of her rivalry with Germany.[2] Whether much, or any, headway was made in this direction is debatable and needs further analysis and study; nevertheless, the Imperial Press Conference represented a noteworthy episode of cooperation among Britain's divided ruling class and demonstrates that both sides, Liberal and Unionist, realized the potential of the press to influence public opinion and imperial unity.

The Imperial Press Conference was the brainchild of the journalist and publicist Harry Brittain.[3] A 1907 trip across Canada for the Board of Trade made him aware of the great ignorance of the United Kingdom in the Dominion and of Canada in Britain. Discussions of the subject with Earl Grey, the Governor-General, further inspired Brittain to hatch a plan to bolster colonial support with a meeting in London. There, at the heart of the empire, the men who directed the leading colonial journals were to be briefed on imperial concerns by private and public men of influence, irrespective of party. This was needed, Brittain and others believed, as a curative for the failure of the 1907 London Colonial Conference, during which the visiting premiers failed to make headway towards either closer imperial unity or planning a shared defense.[4] Lord Grey told Brittain "if you can pull this off it will . . . do more for the empire than any form of conference which has yet taken place."[5]

Once back in England, Brittain lined up an impressive list of supporters, who lent their names and opened their pocketbooks to his scheme. Among the leaders of the press, Lord Burnham, proprietor of the *Daily Telegraph*, accepted the Presidency of the effort, with Sir Arthur Pearson, owner of the *Daily Express* and *Standard* as Chairman of the Executive Committee. The most powerful press lord of the era, and perhaps of all time, Lord Northcliffe, acted as Hon. Treasurer and was a member of the Executive Committee.[6] Brittain headed an Imperial Press Conference office, set up at the Savoy Hotel to organize the event. He and his press allies (in the Liberal and Unionist camps) convinced members of the government and leaders of the opposition to cooperate in the effort. The invitation sent to the imperial journalists called for them to stay eight or ten days in London with a similar period then to be spent touring Britain. "We feel," read the invitation, "that we have much to learn from our colleagues of our great Sister Nations, and we also believe that during their stay we may be able to show them some aspects of Britain, both at work and at play, which will greatly interest them. We further feel that, whilst learning to know one another better, we shall make some small return for that thorough hospitality which so many of us have enjoyed on our journeys through Greater Britain."[7]

The preparations for the conference did not proceed without controversy, in the main a by-product of the Tariff Reform-Free Trade battle. Both sides feared the conference would further the aims of the opposition. Liberals criticized the event as merely a platform to promote Tariff Reform, while at the same time Unionist partisans complained that it would be too much under Liberal control. Leo Maxse, editor of the *National Review* and a staunch advocate of national defense and Tariff Reform, feared the conference would fall too much under the Liberal influence of what he called "Spender and Co." He wrote to Northcliffe that it seemed rather ludicrous that J. A. Spender's *Westminster Gazette* should be allowed to 'posture as the Press of England.'[8] He complained that nothing controversial would be allowed and that the meetings and tours would be "sterilized." In Maxse's view, given the nature of the naval threat from Germany, the conference should be given more "useful" work in that direction. As Maxse feared, the conference was "sterilized" of fiscal questions, including Tariff Reform; however, discussions of imperial defense and unity proceeded.

Brittain was forced to deny accusations that the meeting was some sort of a "Tariff Reform plot," declaring the event "non-party."[9] Northcliffe, who would have been perfectly happy to see the meeting push Tariff Reform, also defended the gathering against accusations that it was "political." He wrote to Sir John Hanbury-Williams, Lord Grey's military secretary, that such charges were ridiculous, that most of the delegates were, unfortunately, Free Traders. The receptions given, he explained, would be "National" and irrespective of party. The aim was for the colonial editors to learn something of England, about which they knew as little as English editors did of the colonies. This was especially true of Canada, considered the key to any plan of imperial cooperation, where rumors abounded that Northcliffe was "up to something" with the conference.[10]

Geoffrey Robinson (later Dawson), editor of the Johannesburg *Star* and future editor of *The Times* in London, had sent Northcliffe his ideas on improving what he called the "rotten" news from England to the colonies. In his view, criticism of the dominions received too much space. To mute this he suggested an "Amalgamated Imperial Press Agency" to supply news in place of the existing agencies, such as Reuters.[11] The Imperial Press Conference, he went on, represented a good opportunity to get something done and he told Northcliffe that there was talk that he might be one of the South African delegates—which proved correct. The owner of the *Daily Mail* replied, "Curiously enough the matter concerning which you wrote to me . . . is one to which I gave a great deal of attention while in Canada. When you come to London I propose going into it. It will at any case be brought up at the Imperial Press Conference, where no agencies are to be represented at all, fortunately. The state of affairs in Canada is worse than in South Africa."[12] Northcliffe complained to Lord Grey that the Australian delegates were largely tied to a cable trust of very wealthy owners whose objective was to prevent new papers and that "those who hope to link the Empire are baffled at every turn."[13] He went on that the "only independent gentleman coming is Thomas Temperley [Editor of the *Richmond River Times*] whom I managed to get put in at the last moment."

In the days before the conference opened, the *Daily Mail* boomed the visiting journalists and the importance of the event. Flattering profiles of many of the delegates appeared which declared the Australian newspapermen "the greatest political force in the Commonwealth" because no orator could reach the vastnesses of the Continent as could their papers.[14] On the other hand, Canadian journalists, the *Daily Mail* reported, were hampered in their influence because of the larger numbers of rival journals and the mixed views of the population. The paper also warned of the evil influence of the United States in the style and make up of Canadian papers and also of an over-reliance on the United States' Associated Press news service because of the heavy expense of international cable services. The two greatest questions to be debated, said the *Daily Mail,* would be the creation of a "great imperial news agency" and the reduction of the present exorbitant cable rates.[15]

Brittain asked the Peninsular and Oriental Steamship Line to subsidize the fares of the representatives arriving from Australia, New Zealand, and India. When the P&O failed to make concessions, an alternative plan was hatched which brought the journalists across Canada, where the Canadian Railway offered reduced rates. This continent-wide leg of the journey served to give the newspapermen a close look at another part of the empire most had never visited. Lord Grey reported to Brittain that the journalists had thoroughly enjoyed their travels across the Dominion. The visit, he went on, had "pricked their desire for accelerated S. S. [steamship] service and cheaper cables." Grey commented that he would be "greatly disappointed if the work of your conference does not lead to important results. Cheap talk across the seas is an imperial necessity and ought to be provided at cost."[16]

On the evening of 5 June 1909, delegates from Canada (including a member of the French-Canadian Press), Australia, New Zealand, South Africa (including two representatives of the Afrikaans' press), Burma, Ceylon, the Straits Settlements of Malaya and India gathered at the Shepherd's Bush Exhibition Hall in London for the opening of the Imperial Press Conference. Aimed very much at the self-governing white dominions, the sole representative of the native press at the conference was Surendranath Banerjee, of *The Bengalee*, a member of the Indian National Congress and an advocate, noted the *Daily Mail*, of "India for the Indians."[17] Lord Rosebery, a former Liberal Prime Minister and the most noted orator of his time, began the event with an inspirational dinner address. Equal parts flattery and admonition, the speech welcomed home the colonial representatives (who were joined in the hall by six hundred British colleagues) to the heart of the British empire. With an impressive fireworks display resounding outside the hall to punctuate his remarks, Rosebery told the journalists that he believed theirs was a meeting of "vast importance" because, unlike the transient politicians he was used to speaking to, good newspapers "should be eternal; and the power of a great newspaper, with the double function of guiding and embodying the public opinion of the province over which it exerts an influence is immeasurably greater than that of any statesman could be."[18] The Earl went on that during their visit the representatives would see "an ancient and stately civilization . . . embodied in our old abbeys and cathedrals . . . in the ancient colleges of Oxford and Cambridge . . . you will see the little villages clustered about the heaven-directed spires . . . and you will see the ancient mother of all Parliaments." Besides these symbols of antiquity and tradition, said Rosebery, the journalists would also inspect the "teeming communities which represent the manufactures, the industry, the alertness of commercial life in Britain. And last of all, surrounding all and guarding it, you will see a . . . prodigious, but always inadequate armada. All of these, gentleman, are yours as much as ours. Your possessions, your pride, your home."

Moving on to the goals of the conference, Rosebery declared himself happy that improving imperial communications was to be discussed. However, in his opinion, imperial defense was the most vital topic on the agenda. Though Europe seemed peaceful and without "questions of friction," the former Prime Minister warned that never before in the history of the world was there "so threatening and overpowering a preparation for war. This is the sign which I regard as the most ominous. For forty years it has been a platitude to say that all of Europe is an armed camp. . . . And now what do we see? . . . nations preparing new armaments." Without mentioning Germany by name, he continued, "They cannot, indeed, arm any more men upon land, so they have to seek new armaments upon the sea, piling up this enormous preparation as if for some approaching Armageddon." He asked the visitors to "compare carefully the armaments of Europe with our preparations to meet them, and give your impressions to the Empire in return . . . I think it may be your duty to take back to your young dominions across the seas this message and this impression: that some personal duty for national defence rests on every man and citizen of the Empire." Rosebery ended as he began, welcoming home the delegates to "the home of your language, your liberties and your race . . . the source of your parliaments, your free institutions and of this immeasurable Empire."

After this riveting performance, the *Daily Mail* praised Rosebery, dubbing him the "Orator of the Empire."[19] J. A. Spender, who had helped plan the opening night, called Rosebery's speech the "most extraordinary performance by a public man" he had ever witnessed.[20] John Evelyn Wrench, editor of Northcliffe's *Overseas Daily Mail*, recalled that "Rosebery made the best speech I ever heard. . . . What an orator he is. If only there were something behind such eloquence." Nevertheless, Wrench was moved. He believed that the conference was "going to be the turning point in the history of the Imperial relationship." [21] Others, including the Liberal journalist W. T. Stead of the *Review of Reviews,* were less impressed, asserting in print that Rosebery had greatly exaggerated the German peril. Over the following days, the delegates and members of the British press attended panel sessions on the interrelated topics of imperial communications and security, particularly focusing on the question of the Dominion share of the naval defense of the empire.

The first business meeting, on imperial cable communications, was held at the Foreign Office and chaired by Lord Crewe, the Colonial Secretary. Sydney Buxton, the Postmaster-General, led the discussion of cable news services and press intercommunication across the empire. High cable rates, it was argued, impaired press discussion of imperial affairs and often led to misunderstandings between the Dominions and Britain. Out of this a Cable Committee was appointed to look into the matter and to report back on methods of facilitating cheaper communications. Buxton and this group later met with the Prime Minister, Herbert Asquith, and Colonel Seeley, the Under-Secretary at the Colonial Office, to discuss the issue. These efforts resulted in rate reductions, one of the solid accomplishments of the conference. The cost per word of a telegram from Britain to Australia was soon after reduced from 1s to 9d and two years later the rate for trans-Atlantic messages was halved for non-urgent telegrams.[22] On the first afternoon, those members from the Commons and Lords with journalistic or writing experience hosted a reception in Westminster Hall. Attendees from the Unionist camp included Lords Curzon, Cromer, and Milner, former imperial proconsuls in India, Egypt, and South Africa, respectively. Liberals including Sir Charles Dilke, T. P. O'Connor, and Winston Churchill joined them.[23]

Sir Edward Grey, the Foreign Secretary, and Reginald McKenna, the First Lord of the Admiralty, led the second day's session on the navy and imperial defense. Grey echoed Rosebery's remarks, telling the delegates that "we are in comparatively calm weather, not in stormy weather; but the extensive expenditure on armaments makes the weather sultry. The seriousness of that expenditure cannot be overrated." The *Daily Mail* praised the Foreign Secretary for backing up Rosebery's remarks, which, it noted; some had criticized for painting "too dark a picture" of the European situation.[24] McKenna stressed the need to keep Britain's navy strong enough to "keep open the highroad of the seas."[25] This session was not without incident as Lord Charles Beresford, the great naval rival and enemy of the First Sea Lord, Sir John Fisher, attacked Fisher's leadership and questioned British naval policy in the face of the German peril. Northcliffe, who was present, warned McKenna that the Germans, as he had seen for himself on a recent Continental tour, were "getting more and more into their heads the idea that the need of a strong navy is merely a Tory political device."[26] The *Daily Mail* called for "One Fleet, One Army, One People" and declared that "for the first time in history Britons beyond the seas realize and understand that the menace of the future is no dream of disordered brains—no figment of rival politicians—but a stern and pressing reality."[27]

In between business sessions during the first week, the imperial delegates were feted in London and the countryside. They were presented to Edward VII and attended a garden party at Marlborough House hosted by the Prince of Wales. On 8 June the colonial editors lunched at Sutton Place, Northcliffe's Tudor country home near Guildford in Surrey. While preparing for the event, the press lord told Wrench that he agreed with him, that there was "a waking up in England in many directions."[28] A special train took the journalists, including Geoffrey Robinson who commented on the "glorious weather," from Waterloo to Worplesdon. The rest of the trip to Sutton Place for the afternoon was made in a fleet of Standard automobiles. The company of journalists and notables listened attentively to Northcliffe's descriptions of German industrial might. Each factory chimney, he warned, was a "gun aimed at England." J. L. Garvin, the editor of Northcliffe's *Observer*, recorded that his colonial colleagues were noticeably impressed "and some depressed" by the disclosures.[29]

The day after the visit to Sutton Place, the third conference session turned to the army side of imperial defense in a meeting chaired by Arthur Balfour, Unionist Leader and former Prime Minister. The War Secretary, R. B. Haldane, and the old soldier Lord Roberts of Kandahar, the President of the National Service League, were also on the panel. Balfour declared that "no one can speak of Imperial Defence without a note of anxiety—not panic." In his view "Local defence must be subordinate to Imperial defence. The individual parts of the Empire never can be saved, never can be powerful, never can be strong if their defence is only local." If there was to be an Armageddon, warned Balfour, it would occur in the "German Ocean, the Channel, the neighborhood of these islands." He believed the national spirit would be equal to any challenge, but added, "we must give the national spirit a chance" (Hardman, 51).

War Secretary Haldane recognized the gravity of the situation which had been pointed out by Rosebery, Grey, and Balfour; however, he saw the threat further in the future and asked for time, stating that in "twenty years, if matters developed as they seemed likely to develop, the British Empire, in military and naval strength might tranquilly face comparison with any state in the world." In the meantime, he asked the Dominions to build a Home Defense as Britain had done with the Territorials. Lord Roberts was less optimistic, telling the delegates that at his advanced age he wished Britain's plans for defense would be in place rather "in twenty months than twenty years."[30] Roberts sensed serious danger ahead and worried that the public was not awake to it. His National Service League calls for compulsory military training, he explained, were not militarism, but prudent preparation. That afternoon, following a reception at the Mansion House, the delegates drove to the House of Commons for tea with Arthur Henderson MP and other Labour Party members.[31]

The following day's luncheon at the Constitutional Club was also presided over by Balfour. Lord Esher, the confidant of the King and a power behind the scenes in this period, had advised Balfour that a "note that wants striking hard is that Great Britain is the heritage of these people as well as ours. Not only the abbeys and churches and old domains, but the honour of England and her sea Dominions. Relatively we grow weaker, and they grow stronger, as their population and wealth increase . . . is it not time for them to consider what sacrifices they are ready to make? . . . it should not be beyond their wit and ours to discover a practical method by which the burden of Empire can be apportioned."[32] Concerning a shared imperial defense, Balfour told the delegates that as far as he had seen, "not a jarring note has been sounded." He went on that

If that doctrine . . . finds, as I am convinced it will find, ready acceptance among all classes of our fellow countrymen in every part of the world, will not the Press have been the greatest and the most effective conceivable agent for laying deep and solid the foundations of that unity which is our business to create out of the scattered and disparate fragments of this world-wide Empire? . . .

It is our business to see that this great and new experiment shall in our hands succeed . . . and it is on your cooperation and the assistance of the enlightened organs of public opinion that I would most rely for creating that public opinion which is the very basis of the whole fabric . . . what we want is for every part of the Empire . . . thoroughly to understand the conditions involved in Imperial defence, and then they ought to understand the sacrifices which each part of the Empire is making in that common cause . . .[33]

All the debates on naval affairs reflected the conflict between the Dominion desire for their naval forces to be stationed in local waters, and the British Admiralty's wish to have complete strategic control. This, and the amount of financial contribution the Dominions were to make, would continue to be points of contention until 1914. E. S. Cunningham, of the Melbourne *Argus*, spoke at the conference in favor of sharing some of the burden of imperial defense, but dwelt on the importance of building an Australian navy to secure its own frontiers. The Canadian position that two fleets, one for each of her coasts, were needed, was supported by J. S. Brierly of the Montreal *Daily Herald*. Canada was willing to share imperial duties, said Brierly, but would not simply hand over direct control of money or ships or troops. This stand was tempered by J. A. MacDonald, of the Toronto *Globe*, who called for the Canadian fleet to be "an integral part of the imperial navy" and to pass under Admiralty control in time of war (Hardman, 170, 176, 183).

To see Britain's armed forces firsthand, the delegates visited Aldershot, where they witnessed an impressive sham battle by the army. That evening the Government officially welcomed the journalists at a banquet held in the Grafton Galleries, where the Prime Minister was the chief speaker. Asquith acknowledged the significance and importance of the visit, declaring that in an Empire such as Britain's there was a sense of interdependence, almost of partnership, between the government and the press which was "the most potent, the most flexible, the most-trustworthy auxiliary which . . . Government in every country could possess." The press, he declared, was the "daily interpreter and mouthpiece of the tastes, the interests, the ideas—one might go farther and say the passions and the caprices—of the . . . people . . . as a dominant force in the formation of public opinion." This was particularly true between sessions of Parliament when, said the Prime Minister, "the Press is the only authentic mirror and reflection of the public opinion of the time."[34]

Seeing the Army in action and being flattered by the Prime Minister were both very impressive; however, from a propaganda point of view, the high point of the Imperial Press Conference was the 12 June review of the Home and Atlantic fleets at Spithead arranged by Sir John Fisher. The admiral, dressed in mufti, wandered among the delegates and their wives on the Admiralty tug *Volcano*, pointing out the various ships.[35] Wrench, also along for the trip down eighteen miles of warships, recorded that it was a "wonderful sight and made me realise what British seapower is."[36] The fleet included seven revolutionary dreadnought-class ships which, noted Wrench, were "so far the only ones afloat." Tea was laid out for the editors on the original *Dreadnought*, from which the company watched destroyers practice firing torpedoes. Fisher reported to Lord Esher that the "swarm of destroyers" had a very near miss with several passenger steamers and yachts. During this episode the delegate from the *Toronto Globe* seized the First Sea Lord by the arm and told him, "Sir, I see the glint of battle in your eye!"[37] Not to be outdone by the army's histrionics, Fisher also arranged for the party to witness a mock hostile landing on Whale Island, the property of the naval Gunnery School.

The conferees spent the following week touring England and Scotland, where, the *Daily Mail* reported, the delegates had their "First Taste of Haggis."[38] On a more serious note, the colonials inspected the industrial might of the country at Sheffield and Manchester where they toured the vast Vickers and Maxim arms establishments. At Windsor Castle, in an impressive ceremony, Edward VII presented colors to 108 new Territorial Force detachments. Lord Curzon, Chancellor of Oxford University, addressed the delegates at a luncheon at All Souls, but Brittain failed to persuade Curzon to confer degrees on several delegates. Glasgow University (of which Curzon was also Chancellor) did award honorary Doctor of Laws degrees to six of the journalists. The travelers returned for a final session in London on 26 June, chaired by Lord Esher, which revisited the question of what role the colonies would play in imperial defense. Esher called for a truly "imperial" navy to harness the "patriotic impulse" of the Dominions. Such a navy, he said, would not only engage and destroy the enemy in time of war, but also be responsible for defending the coasts of the empire, protecting its trade and policing the seas in times of peace.[39] A farewell reception was held at the Waldorf that evening.

When Fisher sent Northcliffe congratulations on the success of the conference, the press lord called it "one of the most important gatherings that has ever taken place in England," while he downplayed his own role.[40] The *Daily Mail* hailed the gathering as a "fresh advance" and a "brilliant success" during which both Britain and the Dominions had learned much about the other. The paper congratulated the conference for building a "great and non-partisan force" for "closer cooperation and better understanding between the separate parts of the Empire." At the same time it repeated Beresford's warning: "We Are Not Prepared."[41]

Others did not agree in the nonpartisan appraisal of the conference. In his *Review of Reviews,* W. T. Stead criticized the Tariff Reform forces and Lord Beresford's attacks on the navy for attempting to give a false impression that the British at home had "taken their place among the dying nations of the world." He went on that "We were supposed to be decadent if not dead and the only hope was to hoist the white flag of protection" as Joseph Chamberlain wished. "No wonder that our colonial guests were amazed almost beyond power of utterance when they found the heart of the Empire still sound and Britain throbbing with lusty life." Those who for "party purposes" had "vilified their Motherland in the hearing of all her children" were advised "henceforth to have the decency to shut up."[42]

The feelings of the delegates towards increased cooperation with Britain, and the tension between a growing colonial nationalism and imperial unity, were reflected during the meeting. On the opening day J. W. Kirwan, editor of the *Miner,* a leading paper of western Australia, took the podium for the visitors. Kirwan spoke of the growing "spirit and pride" associated with being an Australian, New Zealander, or Canadian, but also noted a change "slowly but surely tending towards a period of nations in alliance." He went on to predict that the relationship in "the future would be something grander and greater than it had been in the past."[43] At a banquet given a week later by the Corporation of Glasgow for the visiting journalists, P. D. Ross, editor of the *Ottawa Journal,* linked his strong Canadian patriotism to "the fervent hope that the future of Canada would be part of the future of Great Britain." Ross forecast that Britain and the Dominions would some day be "partners in a political alliance" (Hardman, 103). Even the former Boer enemy present was moved to comment on the subject. Charles Fichardt, editor of the Bloemfontein *Friend,* had been a captain of the southern Boer commandoes. At a banquet in Sheffield Fichardt pledged that when times of trouble came "there will speak for England on the wild and lonely veldt the unerring rifle of the Boer."[44]

To continue the work begun in London and to "tackle this Press cable-rate business thoroughly," Northcliffe suggested to Brittain that it would be a good idea to establish a "permanent Imperial Press Council" with a paid secretary.[45] Otherwise, he was "afraid that your splendid work may be wasted when the conference evaporates." Should Brittain accept the job, which in Northcliffe's estimation would take "at least several years work," the press lord pledged his willingness to contribute towards the salary. From this suggestion grew the Empire Press Union (later the Commonwealth Press Union), organized by Brittain, who became EPU secretary at the London headquarters in Fleet Street. The stated aims were to improve cable distribution of·news throughout the Empire and to provide a permanent base for representatives of newspapers published in the British Empire.[46] The EPU, which would later describe itself as a "progressive movement towards the unity of the Empire," also played an important propaganda role in the First World War.[47] In addition to the creation of the EPU and the strides made in imperial communications, such as the lowering of cable rates, the meeting is also of interest as at least a partial admission by the Liberal Government of the international dangers trumpeted by the Unionists and their press supporters, which the Liberals most often labeled, at least publicly, as "scaremongering." Even though it did not share the Unionist dream of a united Empire, by staging the impressive demonstrations at Aldershot and Spithead, the Government made clear to the visitors the size and cost of Britain's defense establishment and the need for assistance from the Empire to keep it up to the international mark.

Besides a heightened sense of the requirements and urgency of imperial defense, there is little doubt that the press delegates returned home with a greater awareness of their ties to each other and the mother country. They forged valuable bonds both with fellow journalists and government figures in Britain. A. F. MacDonald, of the *Halifax Daily Echo*, commented that "we met as strangers, we parted as friends." To MacDonald, the Imperial Press Conference symbolized the "Unity of the Empire, and the solidarity of the race which spreads its roots and branches to the far ends of the earth." Stanley Reed, the representative of *The Times* of India, described the conference as "enormously valuable" and "a really big thing." He went on that "we have laid the foundations for imperial defense" and aided the recognition that such an effort was "not inconsistent with the growth of nationalities." Reed returned to India prepared to defend the mother country against those who did "immense mischief" by declaring Britain decadent. The meeting's true value, he believed, would lie in the "work of the fifty-one missionaries of empire which will be diffused over the globe." P. D. Ross, of the *Ottawa Evening Journal,* commented "I am safe in saying that every man of us has come back a stronger imperialist than he was before, if he was one—and if he was not, he was probably converted. We were made to realize both England's strength and England's need."[48]

Despite such encouraging statements, those, such as Wrench and Northcliffe, who expected truly great things from the Imperial Press Conference remained disappointed in the degree of actual cooperation that would take place in the following years. Though the Empire Press Union would do valuable work, no imperial news agency, free of previous "vested interests," was constructed. At the 1911 Imperial Conference of Prime Ministers, the politicians remained unable to reach any substantial agreement, making no more real progress towards imperial unity and cooperation than had their predecessors. A second Imperial Press Conference, tentatively scheduled for 1912, was delayed and then finally cancelled by the Great War.

Some have credited the 1909 meeting for stimulating the contribution the Empire made in the 1914–18 struggle. Lord Milner, after the war, called the Imperial Press Conference a "landmark in history" at which "imperial questions were thoroughly discussed and a community of ideas established, to which I attribute in a great degree the marvelous way in which the Empire pulled together when the hour of trial came."[49] Millions from the empire, white and "coloured," fought in the conflict. Perhaps the closest thing to unified imperial government that the British Empire ever experienced came in the meetings of the Imperial War Cabinets from 1917. However, this link, which some hoped to continue, did not last beyond the war and would be discarded by both sides, as were other emergency measures. When the delegates convened at the Second Imperial Press Conference in 1920 they faced a drastically different world and Empire than had their brethren in 1909. By the time Empire answered Britain's call once again in 1939, promises of independence, rather than ties to a faraway mother country, were the primary motivating factors.

NOTES

1. This is equally true of the biographies of the politicians and press figures involved, the accounts of the political press in those years and the studies of imperial defense in the Edwardian period. For example, in *The Rise and Fall of the Political*

Press in Britain, vol. 2, *The Twentieth Century* (Chapel Hill: University of North Carolina Press, 1984) Stephen Koss makes only one brief reference (238) to the conference. In *Journalists for Empire: The Imperial Debate in the Edwardian Stately Press* (New York: Greenwood Press, 1991), James Startt briefly (180–83) considers the imperial communications aspect of the conference. More recently, Andrew S. Thompson, in *Imperial Britain: The Empire in British Politics c. 1880–1932* (London: Longman, 2000) has placed more emphasis on the importance of the meeting.

2. For the names of the delegates and the publications represented, see Thomas Hardman, *A Parliament of the Press: The First Imperial Press Conference* (London: Constable, 1909), 4–5.

3. Brittain was on the management staff of the *Standard* and a Conservative MP from 1918 to 1929.

4. In this failure, the conference joined its predecessors in 1887, 1897, and 1902. See John Kendle, *The Colonial and Imperial Conferences 1887–1911* (London: Macmillan, 1967).

5. Sir Harry Brittain, *Pilgrims and Pioneers* (London: Hodder and Stoughton, 1946), 198.

6. Burnham's role was limited by his advanced age and poor eyesight. Brittain also enlisted, among other press figures, Sir George Newnes, Robert Donald, editor of the *Daily Chronicle*, and Fabian Ware, editor of the *Morning Post*. Brittain to Northcliffe, 24 January 1908, Northcliffe Additional Manuscripts (afterwards NADM), 62165, British Library (afterwards BL).

7. Hardman, *Parliament of the Press*, 3.

8. Maxse to Northcliffe, 26 May 1909, NADM, 62175, BL.

9. In the *Newspaper Press Directory*, n.d., NADM, 62166, BL.

10. Northcliffe to Hanbury-Williams, n.d., NADM, 62302, BL. From early in 1909 Northcliffe, who owned *The Times*, the *Daily Mail*, and the *Observer*, among many other newspapers, was actively involved in shaping the conference. Several visits to Canada had alerted the press lord to the need for improved circulation of news in the empire and he corresponded with a variety of imperial journalists on this problem. Northcliffe's support for Tariff Reform waxed and waned. He was particurlay unhappy with the proposed taxes on food, which he dubbed "stomach taxes" first in his London *Evening News*. Little work has been done to determine even a rough estimate of colonial support for the two sides in the controversy. It is most likely that it follows a rough parallel with the political parties in England; however, even conservatives in the Dominions could be staunch guardians of their own colonial rights and not many were eager to sign on to Chamberlain's plan.

11. 18 January 1909, NADM, 62244, BL. Robinson was a member of Lord Milner's South African "kindergarten" of administrators. An avid imperialist, his views were very sympathetic to Northcliffe's and went far towards gaining him the editor's chair at *The Times* in London within a few years' time. For the news agencies question, see Donald Read, "The Relationship of Reuters and other News Agencies with the British Press, 1858–1984: Service at Cost or Business for Profit?" in Peter Catterall, Colin Seymour-Ure and Adrian Smith, eds., *Northcliffe's Legacy* (London: Macmillan, 2000).

12. 23 March 1909, NADM, 62244, BL.

13. Northcliffe to Grey, nd, NADM, 62155, BL.

14. *Daily Mail*, 3 June 1909.

15. Ibid., 4 June 1909.

16. Grey to Brittain, 19 May 1909, 0021, Brittain Papers, British Library of Economic and Political Science.

17. An eloquent spokesman for his cause, Banerjee recognized that he was attending a "non-controversial Conference" and did not openly criticize British policy in India. In fact, he decried, as the actions of anarchists, violent protests in his native land. See Hardman, *Parliament of the Press*, 164. W. T. Stead, editor of the *Review of Reviews*, acknowledged that the presence of the Dominion delegates had done much to "quicken the sense of the unity of the Empire," but he noted that this was only as far as "the white skinned races" were concerned, complaining that the conference had failed to address the "deeper trouble involved in the collision of the white and coloured races of the Empire." "The Editors of the Empire At Home," *The Contemporary Review* (July 1909), 48.

18. Rosebery's address is reproduced in Hardman, *Parliament of the Press*, 10–14. According to one account, Rosebery tried to escape this duty and "had almost to be brought up to London by force." Reginald Pound and Geoffrey Harmsworth, *Northcliffe* (London: Cassell, 1959), 369.

19. *Daily Mail*, 7 June 1909.

20. Quoted in Thompson, *Imperial Britain*, 76.

21. 5 June entry, Wrench Diary, Wrench Additional Manuscripts (afterwards WAM), 59569, BL. Rosebery has been called the political "Flying Dutchman" of his time because of his refusal, after one unhappy term of service as Premier in the 1890s, to lead the so-called Liberal Imperialist faction in his party, or some other centrist coalition. This despite repeated entreaties from many suitors, including Northcliffe in 1903. For this see J. Lee Thompson, *Northcliffe: Press Baron in Politics, 1865–1922* (London: John Murray, 2000).

22. Thompson, *Imperial Britain*, 78. The reduction in the trans-Atlantic rate came in part as a result of the efforts of the Empire Press Union.

23. It appears that Churchill's compatriot in planning the "New Liberalism," David Lloyd George, did not meet with the journalists.

24. *Daily Mail*, 9 June 1909.

25. Hardman, *Parliament of the Press*, 48.

26. Northcliffe to McKenna, 17 June 1909, NADM, 61257, BL.

27. *Daily Mail*, 10 June 1909.

28. Wrench Diary, WAM, 59569, BL.

29. Pound and Harmsworth, *Northcliffe*, 369. The delegates also attended functions at the country homes of Lords Burnham and Desborough, among others.

30. Hardman, *Parliament of the Press*, 51.

31. While their husbands and fathers were occupied at the Mansion House, Lady Northcliffe was among the hostesses for a wives and daughters luncheon at the Hyde Park Hotel sponsored by the Victoria League. The delegates were also given memberships in many organizations and clubs, including the Royal Colonial Institute, the Bath Club, the Savage Club, the Consitutional Club, the National Liberal Club, the Press Club, and the Walton Heath Golf Club.

32. Maurice Brett, *The Journals and Letters of Reginald, Viscount Esher*, vol. 2 (London: Ivor Nicholson and Watson, 1934), 392.

33. Hardman, *Parliament of the Press*, 58.

34. Ibid., p. 64. Asquith's praise here for the Press is more than a little disingenuous. He was heartily disdainful of the political press of both parties. The Northcliffe papers, which attacked his "wait and see" policies incessantly, were a continual object of his ire. However, he also looked down on the Liberal press, once describing it as being "written by ninnies for ninnies."

35. Brittain, *Pilgrims and Pioneers*, 208.

36. 12 June entry, Wrench Diary, WAM, 59569, BL.

37. Arthur J. Marder, *Fear God and Dread Nought: the Correspondence of Lord Fisher of Kilverston*, vol 2., (London: Jonathan Cape, 1956), 252.

38. *Daily Mail*, 24 June 1909.

39. Hardman, *Parliament of the Press*, 230.

40. Pound and Harmsworth, *Northcliffe*, 369.

41. *Daily Mail*, 28 June 1909.

42. *Review of Reviews*, 1 July 1909.

43. Hardman, *Parliament of the Press*, 44.

44. Quoted in Thompson, *Imperial Britain*, 30.

45. 12 June 1909, NADM, 62166, BL.

46. 19 July 1909, NADM, 62166, BL. Northcliffe agreed to become its Hon. Treasurer. The Commonwealth Press Union continues in operation today.

47. Thompson, *Imperial Britain*, 62.

48. Harry Brittain, "The First Imperial Press Conference," NADM, 62166, f. 52.

49. "Memorandum of Association of the Commonwealth Press Union," Brittain Papers, 0001, British Library of Economic and Political Science.

Constructing South Africa in the British Press, 1890–92: The *Pall Mall Gazette,* the *Daily Graphic,* and *The Times*

DOROTHY O. HELLY AND HELEN CALLAWAY

IN THE PREFACE TO HIS COLLECTION OF NEWSPAPER ARTICLES REPORTING from South Africa, Edmund Garrett called the 1890s "this African decade." During this period, South Africa more than any other colonial region captured the news in all sectors of the British press. The discovery of diamonds in Cape Colony in 1867 and, more recently, gold in the Transvaal represented a saga of untold riches, as did the promise of even greater wealth in the vast territory farther north, then popularly known as Mashonaland and soon to become Rhodesia, staked out by Cecil Rhodes for his newly chartered British South Africa Company. Contentious politics flaring between British mining interests and Dutch Boer farmers in the Transvaal touched a patriotic nerve, while the romance of the "frontier," with its exotic wild animals for hunting, caught the spirit of masculine adventure. All of these aspects created a continuous flow of news capturing the interest and emotions of readers throughout late-Victorian society.

Three series of articles in the British press at the beginning of the decade helped construct South Africa in the public imagination. While varying in style and coverage, the three accounts—running in the *Pall Mall Gazette* (and its weekly *Budget*) in 1890, the *Daily Graphic* (and weekly *Graphic*) in 1891–92, and *The Times* in 1892—were all written from a metropolitan perspective that assumed the primacy of Britain's imperial interests in the region and viewed southern Africa as a vivid landscape with an economic potential bordering on the mythical. These newspapers reached a wide range of readers, including the relatively small group of sophisticated intellectuals who followed the social and political comment of the *Pall Mall Gazette,* the newly educated masses who enjoyed the entertaining, richly illustrated presentations of the *Daily Graphic,* and the more exclusive ruling circles who looked to *The Times* for trustworthy political and

125

economic information. Two of these writers, the young Cambridge graduate Edmund Garrett and the experienced woman journalist Flora Shaw, wrote anonymously as Special Correspondents, while the articles of the third, the high-profile politician Lord Randolph Churchill, appeared in the *Daily Graphic* over his signature and were well advertised in advance.

These writers used their own vivid observations of people and places to construct the reality of South Africa for their readers at home, but they looked at the passing scene through the lenses of an imperial worldview and its value system. Their texts—similar to travelogues, missionary tracts, and fiction of the period—used the images, stereotypes, rhetorical strategies, and narrative devices of a powerful discursive formation projecting the ideology of empire in relation to specific historical locations. They drew on already established modes which formatted ways of seeing and understanding the colonies in the attempt to justify Britain's late-nineteenth century drive for domination in southern Africa.[1] In specific terms, these writers examined the political relations between Briton and Boer in the British colonies and Boer republics of the region, the investment potential of the diamond and gold-mining industries, African labor, or the "native question," as it affected politics and the economy, and the prospects for British emigration and the consolidation of the Empire. Though these accounts varied in detail, and did not always agree, at a key historical moment in South Africa's development, they transmitted to British readers of all social classes enduring patterns of political awareness and patriotic response that would serve to interpret the electrifying events that surrounded the raid by Dr. Jameson, the British South Africa Company's administrator in Rhodesia, into the Dutch republic of the Transvaal at the end of 1895 and the political tensions that led up to the Anglo-Boer war in 1899.

THE NEWSPAPERS, THEIR EDITORS AND WRITERS

The first series, seventeen letters appearing between January and July 1890 in the *Pall Mall Gazette,* was commissioned by W. T. Stead, its resourceful editor. In 1889, Stead, a keen observer of developments in South Africa, met the charismatic diamond magnate Cecil Rhodes in London when he was seeking a royal charter for his new British South Africa company to bolster its claims to mining concessions in Matabeleland and Mashonaland. Impressed by Rhodes's expectation of new mineral prospects in this area, and by his vision of a British Empire of self-governing colonies spread across the globe, Stead recognized the growing attraction for his readers of news about this region. When Edmund Garrett, a young member of his staff, was diagnosed with incipient tuberculosis, Stead arranged for him to go to South Africa to report on current conditions while improving his health.

The *Pall Mall Gazette*, mouthpiece of the zealous social reformer W. T. Stead since 1883 and the Radical voice of independent Liberalism, had become one of the new "penny" papers of London.[2] During the 1880s, the rapid growth of the telegraph with its speedy transmission of news, the typewriter, the telephone, and electric power were changing the face of newspaper operations. New, cheaper journals began to compete with the older London dailies by reaching out to the potentially vast new readership created by the Education Act of 1870 and the later introduction of compulsory schooling. In this fiercely-competitive arena, Stead improvised changes in style to attract new readers, using bolder headlines and larger print, and making use of the "interview," already widely employed in America but less so in Britain. He set a new standard for sensational writing and created "scoops" whenever he could.[3] Circulation of the four-page evening newspaper had risen from over eight thousand, when Stead took over, to its peak of more than twelve hundred two years later during his exposure of child prostitution in London, before beginning to drop. By 1889, Stead adopted a new six-page format but circulation continued to fall, and at the end of the year he left the paper to launch the new *Review of Reviews* (Whyte, I: 288). His assistant, E. T. Cook, became editor and published Garrett's reports (Koss, 322–25).

Sailing for South Africa in November 1889, Edmund Garrett (1865–1907) shared the reformist political views and enthusiasm for empire of both Stead and Cook. He had grown up among a family of strong-minded women who flaunted Victorian gender prescriptions. His half sister Rhoda Garrett and his cousin Agnes had established a successful home-decorating business which, like that of William Morris, promoted contemporary arts and crafts. His cousin Millicent Garrett Fawcett became a recognized leader in the women's suffrage campaign. On his South African trip, Garrett traveled light, mixed with people across the diverse political and ethnic spectrum, and prepared thoughtful reports on the unique issues facing "political, social and financial South Africa." Back in London, Garrett revised his letters for a *Pall Mall Gazette "Extra,"* glowingly entitled *In Afrikanderland and the Land of Ophir,* requiring a second edition within the year.[4] Twenty years later, Alfred Milner, High Commissioner in

South Africa from 1897 to 1905, praised these reports as "still the best description of South Africa in that momentous phase of its development."[5] In 1895, Garrett returned to South Africa where he played an important role in its politics as editor of the *Cape Times*, the leading English newspaper of the region, during the turbulent period of the Jameson Raid and from 1898 as a member of the Cape parliament through the years of the Anglo-Boer war.[6] He never recovered full health, and died in his early forties.

Quite different from the unknown journalist Garrett, Lord Randolph Churchill (1849–95) had long commanded press attention as a mercurial Conservative politician who had briefly become Chancellor of the Exchequer and Leader of the House of Commons in the mid-1880s. In 1891, his proposal to lead a full-scale expedition to the "gold fields" of Mashonaland raised speculation that at forty-two he was planning to use his travels to regain a central role in contemporary politics.[7] He was also seeking to improve his ill-health and replenish his finances. Though inexperienced as a journalist, Churchill had no hesitation in accepting the lucrative offer of two thousand guineas to write twenty articles for the *Daily Graphic*, the first illustrated morning penny paper which had made its appearance only a year earlier as an offshoot of a twenty-year-old weekly journal, *The Graphic*.[8] Reaching out to the newly literate masses, the newspaper claimed a long list of notable contributors and a readership of half a million.

Churchill's interest in South Africa grew out of conversations with Cecil Rhodes, now premier of the Cape Colony. Inspired by the idea of checking out the gold fields in South Africa, he set up a family-controlled syndicate to finance investments in the Transvaal and Mashonaland and looked forward to some big-game hunting. To his constituents in Paddington and the public at large, he emphasized his desire to see for himself whether Mashonaland might offer an attractive area for State-aided emigration. Lord Randolph did not travel light. He took along an American mining engineer used by the Rothschilds, a former Horse Guardsman as companion and secretary, and a personal physician.[9] He also employed a former royal artillery officer who was an accomplished artist, Captain (soon to be Major) George Edward Giles, to organize his elaborate expedition and provide sketches for the *Daily Graphic*.[10]

Treated royally by his hosts everywhere, Churchill reciprocated by writing disgruntled comments about shipboard food, the inadequacies of Government House at the Cape, and Boer accommodations. His biographers have agreed that Churchill was characterized all his life by both his charm and his appalling rudeness. In print, this latter behavior generated furious letters of response, published in the *Daily Graphic* and in other newspapers in London and South Africa. Though other journalists might criticize his letters as "dull and entirely lacking in perception and political shrewdness" (B. Roberts, 47–50), the London newspaper-reading public greatly enjoyed the unfolding drama, enhanced considerably by Major Giles's vivid sketches of South African personalities, horse-drawn carriages struggling in the rugged landscape, and hunters stalking wild animals, very often placed on the front page of the *Daily Graphic* as well as illustrating the pages of his letters.[11] These illustrations appeared again when Churchill published his letters in 1892 as *Men, Mines and Animals in South Africa*, omitting only his most outrageous comments. Three years later, Lord Randolph Churchill died of the syphilis that had caused his ill-health, but his South African gold-mining investment enabled his estate to pay off his outstanding debts.

At the other end of the scale from the penny *Daily Graphic* with its vast popular readership, *The Times* honored its tradition as a leading morning paper newspaper that had reached politically and financially sophisticated readers for over a century. In the early 1890s, it was struggling to reverse the losses in circulation and the legal debt incurred when incriminating letters the newspaper had published purportedly by the Irish nationalist leader, Charles Parnell, were later exposed as forgeries.[12] While modern scholars assess the newspaper's falling circulation as due primarily to its use of outdated machinery, its methods of distribution, and its holding its price to three-pence when other leading dailies charged a penny, contemporary management at *The Times* saw the problem as one of putting the scandal behind them and increasing their falling circulation by better news outreach in Europe and around the world. The conservatism and vested interests of its chief proprietor John Walter III, grandson of the founder, and his sons Arthur and Geoffrey, blocked any radical changes in the mode of producing the paper or its format. John Walter's political conservatism was also behind the decision to attack the Liberals' Home Rule policy and to publish the Parnell Letters. His editor, G. E. Buckle, appointed to that position in 1884 when he was twenty-four, was of a similar temperament.

The new element at *The Times* in 1890 was C. F. Moberly Bell, recalled to the Manager's Office from Egypt, where he had served for many years as the paper's correspondent. He brought enormous energy and fresh ideas to Printing House Square. As his administrative province extended to hiring as well as paying foreign correspondents and his daily routine included lunch with the Walters, Bell soon secured a major voice in policy decisions. In response to the decline in circulation (from over sixty thousand in the late 1870s to around forty thousand in 1891) and to reassert the newspaper's reputation for comprehensive and accurate news, Moberly Bell suggested ways of broadening its coverage beyond the British Isles.[13] He hired the experienced diplomat Donald MacKenzie Wallace, a friend of the Prince of Wales, as Foreign Editor in 1891, and pushed to appoint a Colonial Editor. Bell had a person in mind whom he had met in Egypt and whose journalism he admired, but this was *Miss* Flora Shaw. He knew *The Times* directorate held highly conservative views on gender, and supported an antisuffrage position. Not above using a strategy of subterfuge, however, he asked her to send in a sample piece using initials instead of her first name. Her explanation of the fiscal situation in Egypt won warm praise from proprietor and editor, and by November she was contributing a fortnightly column on "The Colonies."

Flora Shaw (1852–1929) came from a prominent Anglo-Irish family with connections in high military and political circles. Her writings included children's novels, travel literature, short stories, and essays before she turned to political journalism. Her first newspaper story, published in the *Pall Mall Gazette,* benefited from Stead's willingness to encourage women in this profession. From him she learned about the potential power of the press to influence politics by shaping public opinion. In 1889, Stead introduced her to Cecil Rhodes, with whom she discussed the future of the British Empire and his plans for expanding its realm over much of southern Africa.

In the early winter of 1892, the stress of Shaw's multiple journalist commitments—to the *Manchester Guardian,* the *Review of Reviews,* as well as *The Times*—so strained her health that she suffered a near fatal bout of influenza.[14] To help her slow recovery, Bell arranged for her to go to South Africa to write a few articles on Cape politics. She was fully aware that only the sex barrier prevented her from becoming Colonial Editor. Once in Cape Town she seized the opportunity to undertake a major reporting project by traveling to the interior. When Bell's cable arrived discouraging this move, she had already embarked on her journey. Her lucid analysis of political and economic issues in a series of eight long "Letters" brought immediate and immense success. Finally forced to acknowledge her unusual ability, the directorate of *The Times* sent her on to report from Australia and welcomed her back in July 1893 with a contract appointing her to the permanent staff at £800 a year. She became the highest paid woman in British journalism. Her articles published between July and October 1892 appeared in 1893 as a book with the modest title, *Letters from South Africa*.[15] Shaw continued as Colonial Editor for *The Times* until September 1900.

COVERING SOUTH AFRICA

In 1890 the British empire in southern Africa consisted of two British colonies, the Cape and Natal, and directly under the Governor of the Cape Colony, who was also the British High Commissioner for South Africa, the three African territories of Basutoland, Swaziland, and the Bechuanaland Protectorate. The region also included two Boer republics, the Orange Free State and the South African Republic (the Transvaal), the German protectorate in Southwest Africa, the Portuguese colonies of Angola and Mozambique, on the west and east sides of southern Africa, and the ill-defined territory of Matabeleland and Mashonaland, over which Chief Lobengula had a nominal control that he was rapidly losing to Rhodes's British South Africa Company, with its new royal charter. The Company had negotiated treaty rights to minerals and economic development. By its charter it was granted administrative rights, including the right to set up a police force, and its "pioneers" had begun trekking from the Cape into Mashonaland.

In the preface to his book in 1891, Edmund Garrett acknowledged the growing imperial interest in the region, announcing that his object had been to give readers "the sort of current conversance with the ideas and the affairs of that part of the world which in this African decade is demanded even at suburban dinner-tables. . . ." The journalists who wrote about South Africa in 1890–92 primarily configured it in terms of contrasts between the Boers and the British. Explicit in these comparisons was the question of the future of British imperial power. Beyond this political equation, they focused on Africans in terms of their sheer numbers and the growing European need to employ African labor. Critical to these assessments were the economic prospects of the diamond and gold mining industries. Although the three journalists we compare did not report on exactly the same areas, each did visit Cape Town and Kimberley in the Cape Colony and Johannesburg and Pretoria in the Transvaal. Without traveling to Mashonaland, which he called "Zambesia" or the mythical "Land of Ophir," Garrett gathered information from local sources to write two letters declaring it one of nature's "rare storehouses of mineral wealth." Churchill, on the other hand, took his heavily laden expedition through Bechuanaland to the pioneer forts of Mashonaland and devoted fourteen of his eighteen letters to this region north of the Transvaal.[16] In contrast to Garrett's rosy forecasts, repeating the optimistic reports of the day, Lord Randolph concluded with a negative assessment of the mineral prospects of this northern region, as confirmed by his mining engineer and other men whom he met in the field. Besides dashing hopes for the fabled gold of the region, Churchill actively discouraged Englishmen at home seeking to emigrate to take advantage of the agricultural opportunities Rhodes had promoted in this "Promised Land." Shaw did not visit Mashonaland and wisely refrained from reporting hearsay about conditions there.

Within the settled colonies and republics, Shaw travelled more extensively than her two predecessors. In two separate trips out of Cape Town, she visited, first, Kimberley, Johannesburg, and Pretoria, as well as Bloemfontein in the Orange Free State, and the "Native Reserve" of Basutoland. Her second trip took her to King William's Town in the Eastern Cape and to Natal. Appearing in *The Times* six months after the publication of Churchill's pessimistic views about the prospects of gold and agriculture in Mashonaland, Shaw's letters, in striking contrast, were confidently optimistic about the mining and agricultural potential in the already settled regions of South Africa. Garrett and Churchill had also been sanguine about economic development in the settled regions of South Africa, but Shaw, supporting her views with up-to-date statistics and selected models, projected unfailing enthusiasm about the economic progress being made.[17]

After rapid train journeys up to the Transvaal borders, all three writers experienced the discomforts of bumpy coach rides pulled along by a dozen horses or mules on rutted, muddy pathways, giving them added cause to urge the importance of a continuous railway system (and a related customs union) for a prosperous South Africa. All made a point of meeting President Kruger of the Transvaal, who in his person represented the character of the stout patriarchal Boer and the implacable need to factor the Transvaal Boers into the political equation of British imperial power in South Africa. Visiting the friendlier Boer president of the Orange Free State, Shaw expounded the thorny problems still besetting railway cooperation and a customs union in the region.

INSCRIBING INEQUALITIES

In their journalism, Garrett, Churchill, and Shaw all used the dominant imperial discourse inscribing "race," gender, and class hierarchies. They called the British Empire the greatest empire the world had known, and laid its success to the inherent superiority of the British as a governing "race." Like their contemporaries, they used "race" to denote loosely nationality and ethnicity—referring variously to the English, Boer, European, Irish, African, Kaffir or Basuto "races." Without confronting their ambivalence, they treated "race" as constituted by immutable differences while continuously urging a policy of educating and assimilating "racial others" to the ways of British civilization, defined in this context as a willingness to submit to discipline, to engage in hard work, and to develop desires for material goods.[18]

Observing the landscape on the train from Cape Town to Kimberley, Flora Shaw selected sequences of images that served as powerful metaphors of time and motion to construct racial identities. She glimpsed a "wretched hut" in the middle of desert waste, an image indicating a "native inhabitant" gaining a poor subsistence from the soil and conveying to readers the timeless indigenous African out of history or progress.[19] Next she described a trekking Boer family in a wagon of household goods drawn by sixteen pairs of oxen, with children trailing a little behind, and a herd of cattle alternately moving and grazing—a scene which located Dutch Africans in a slow-moving past. In contrast, Shaw associated train travel with Englishmen hurrying "as fast as steam and electricity can take you" to reach the mining centers, exemplifying energetic capitalist entrepreneurs shaping the future (*TT*, 22 July 1892).

Visiting a "native kraal," Garrett wrote of its friendly hospitality and kindliness toward age and childhood. Yet, he felt compelled to continue, "the squalor, alive with vermin—the body, horribly scarred and seamed, of an old crone bent double with laborious motherhood—the half-articulate animalism of the whole scene— these stuck in a pigeon-hole of my memory next to that which holds the pleasanter sights of Kafir service on Africander farms or in the Kimberley compounds" (*PMG*, 14 May 1890). Failing to recognize that these Africans had already been displaced from their traditional location and culture, Garrett uses the familiar description of their "animality" as a defining characteristic, contrasting those in the "native kraal" with those being assimilated to the work requirements of "civilized" society.[20]

While Shaw observed the occupants of the African soil from a train, and Garrett made a point of visiting African dwellings, Churchill was quite content to relay standard colonial views of Africans as "idle and insolent." He added to these his personal observations on Africans as untrustworthy and unpredictable servants. He made one exception, which in the discourse of the day attested to his own superiority as a master, for his faithful servant Tiriki, "as good a specimen of the savage as could be met with, quite intelligent, always cheerful, and willing to work" (*DG*, 13 Jan. 1892).[21]

Garrett endorsed the Boer patriarchal view of Africans as "children to be treated kindly, educated firmly—but always, at bottom, children" (*PMG*, 14 May 1890). Shaw, in contrast, praised the views of the British Resident Commissioner in Basutoland: "The system upon which he has worked rejects alike the theory that treats the native as a child irresponsible for his acts and dispossessed of personal rights and the theory which accepts him as a man and a brother equal in all things to his white neighbour. It deals with him as a man fully responsible for his acts, behind the white man in civilisation, but subject to precisely the same laws of development" (*TT*, 2 Sept. 1892). Yet Shaw called the population on the partially-protected native territories the "wild races" and wrote of "barbaric Pondoland, where the ruling chief, Sigean, roasted his stepmother the other day, and habitually fastens offenders against his sovereign pleasure into ant-heaps to be eaten alive . . ." (*TT*, 3 Oct. 1892). Her reference to hearsay cannibalism and spectacular brutality shows her use of stereotypes as a familiar strategy of colonial discourse in the way analyzed by Homi Bhabha, as "a form of knowledge and identification that vacillates between what is always 'in place', already known, and something that must be anxiously repeated."[22]

These press accounts of the early 1890s, including those of Shaw, presented South Africa as predominantly a male world. Garrett wrote as a serious, unassuming but personable young man, informal in tone, and not infrequently, self-deprecating. His literary style reflected his recent university education, dotted with allusions to literature, familiar Latin tags, and exhortations to the "gentle reader." Lord Randolph Churchill used his well-established public and political persona to sell his signed letters to the *Daily Graphic,* and felt free to express his aristocratic disdain, to repeat local hearsay, and to indulge in off-hand, disparaging remarks. Unlike Garrett and Shaw, he showed little thoughtfulness about the political implications of what he wrote; he was at his most earnest when describing the joys of big-game hunting and admiring the vistas of great open spaces.[23]

Displaying male misogyny, both Garrett and Churchill wrote of the "causal" connection they understood to exist between mining for diamonds and women. Garrett announced that it was women's desire for diamonds that created the industry, while Churchill declared that a diamond was only "a tiny crystal to be used for the gratification of female vanity in imitation of a lust for personal adornment essentially barbaric if not altogether savage." He went on to remark that since diamonds were not used to adorn only "the beautiful, the virtuous, and the young," for which he could see some justification, he had come "coldly to the conclusion that, whatever may be the origin of man, woman is descended from an ape" (*DG*, 20 July 1891). His flippant remark brought down outrage and indignation upon his head from other newspapers—"quite serious journals denounced Churchill as an unutterable cad" (B. Roberts, 30–31)—but not the *Daily Graphic*, whose editors apparently also found it amusing.[24]

Flora Shaw, as a woman journalist and *The Times* "Special Correspondent," carefully used the impersonal tone of that newspaper, by default a male voice, brisk and business-like, building rational arguments and making judicious assessments. She engaged readers with graphic descriptions of the scenes she experienced—there were no sketches of what she saw in *The Times*—and, after concentrated information collecting, she presented clear explanations addressing the issues of imperial politics and the long-run investment prospects. Her reporting was called "remarkable" by her employers and those who praised the newspaper for publishing them.[25] Her eight letters presented a well-honed set of descriptions of what she observed and trenchant analyses of the major political and economic issues of imperial concern in South Africa.

CONTEMPORARY POLITICS

The Transvaal, annexed by Britain in 1877, regained its independence as a republic in 1881 after the Boers had defeated British troops at Majuba Hill.[26] President Kruger was responsible for the London Convention in 1884 which restored to the Transvaal the official name of the South African Republic. But that Convention continued to limit its full independence by giving the Imperial Government the right to approve any treaties the South African Republic concluded with any state other than the Orange Free State. In 1886, the discovery of gold brought new prosperity to the republic, rapidly attracting external mining capital and a steady influx of *uitlanders* (foreigners—Englishmen, Americans, Germans, Australians, men from the Cape and Natal), whose numbers threatened to overwhelm the adult male Boers. Their presence in Johannesburg exacerbated the ongoing tensions between British and Boers in terms of British imperial power in the region and its political future. President Kruger, as a child of original *trekboers*, embodied their spirit of fierce independence and continued in office for four five-year terms from 1883. Both Garrett and Shaw interviewed him at his home, where he conducted public business, and wrote sympatheti-cally of his concern to attach Swaziland to the Transvaal. In contrast, Churchill met Kruger only briefly, when he was presiding over the Transvaal parliament, the *Volksraad*. Lord Randolph acknowledged the President's considerable power over his countrymen while deni-grating his high-handed political tactics.

Garrett admired the Cape Boers for their success as fruit farmers and wine-growers and reported with approval their contentment to live under the British flag so long as they were allowed a free hand ("home rule") over their African laborers. The Boers of the Trans-vaal, however, he sharply criticized as "a case of arrested develop-ment," describing their "intensely narrow Calvinism, . . . utter illiteracy, [and] the bucolic grossness of the men." The Transvaal Boer was "lazy, . . . not caring while he can live on his cattle, to turn the rich soil at his feet, or to supply the markets that are springing up before him" (*PMG*, 3 March 1890). Noting the steady inflow of Englishmen and other foreigners to the mining industry, he was san-guine that in time their influence might be expected to temper the less liberal nature of the Boer Government for he assumed they would enter into the politics of the country with their votes. But, in fact, the franchise for the Johannesburg *uitlanders* became an in-creasingly tense political issue in the 1890s.

Churchill's depiction of the Boers of the Transvaal reinforced Garrett's observations and endorsed the contemporary stereotype which cast them as "dirty," lacking in intelligence, inefficient, unfair to the *uitlanders* in terms of heavy and arbitrary taxation of the exter-nally capitalized mining industry, engaging in corrupt political and monopolistic practices. He summed up their character as marked by "fanaticism . . . ignorance, and selfishness." His interests as a "sportsman" led him to complain of what he had heard of their in-discriminate slaughter of every kind of wild animal, while he ex-pressed a traditional English humanitarian concern about the failure of their justice system to punish any Boer who injured or killed an African (*DG*, 27 July; 3, 17, 24, 31 Aug. 1891).

Unlike her predecessors, Shaw had been writing about politics in South Africa—in her "Colonies" column in *The Times*—for two years before she arrived there. She quickly took stock of the political situa-tion at the Cape, finding that Boer farmers and their political party, the Afrikaner Bond led by Jan Hofmeyr, were now willing to support Rhodes's ideas for a united South Africa (connected by railways and a customs union, and expanding northward toward the Zambesi

River) if in turn he and his coalition government agreed to limit the franchise of the ever-increasing population of Africans and "Cape coloreds" in the colony. Rhodes had previously explained to her that he saw the issue not as "Dutch *versus* English" or "native *versus* white," but as "civilization *versus* barbarism." As he reiterated on her arrival, the policy of his government was to make sure that the "savages" who outnumbered them did not gain a voting power that would allow them to decide policies affecting the fate of the "civilized" whites in the colony.[27]

Like Garrett, but emphasizing the English language generally introduced by the *uitlanders,* Shaw looked to the eventual "Englishing" of the Transvaal. She understood that the "Old Transvaal" of the Grand Trek, which had fought fiercely for their independence did not like it. But she believed she saw a "New Transvaal" developing, one that would combine Boer ownership and cultivation of the land with English as the language of mining and trade and even diplomacy. She also remarked on the unfair tax burden placed by the current Boer government on the mining interest, which had no political voice. She acknowledged that the "Old Transvaal . . . feel the danger that they may be stifled out of their national existence," but she, like Garrett, explicitly predicted a future in which the Transvaal Boers would make the necessary accommodation with the new economic order. As the war at the end of the decade would demonstrate, their predictions, just as much as Churchill's outright dismissal of the Boers as an unprogressive people, failed to assess the depth of the republican Boer concern for their independent national existence.

Garrett's interview with "Oom Paul" on his *stoep* in Pretoria at 6:00 on a January morning in 1890 focused on the "Swaziland Question" at Kruger's insistence. The president assured Garrett that if Britain allowed Swaziland to be placed under the Transvaal, then the Transvaal would join the customs union and cooperate with the British colonies to create a railway link across South Africa. Garrett summed up his own views, "Oom Paul is a bad enemy, as we have learnt to our cost. He has proved to us of late that he can also be a leal [loyal] friend" (*PMG,* 24 Feb. 1890). Garrett believed that Kruger was ready to honor this kind of agreement, but when the Imperial Government, through its High Commissioner, Sir Henry Loch, proposed a very similar one later that spring, the *Volksraad* proved unwilling to accept it. When Churchill was introduced to Kruger a year later, during a session of the *Volksraad* in 1891, he described him as so "extremely gracious and genial" that it was possible to understand his great influence over his countrymen. He could not resist, however, going on to caricature the members of the legislative chambers, repeating several anecdotes about them, including a story that Kruger generally got his way by threatening to reduce the salaries of those who disagreed with him (*DG*, 24 Aug. 1891).[28] Lord Randolph's knowledge of parliamentary politics in Britain gave him no useful insights into the workings of the political system in Pretoria.

Like Garrett two years earlier, Shaw found Kruger willing to speak to her at home at 6:30 in the morning but only on the topic of Transvaal's rights to Swaziland. And like Garrett, she took his points seriously and declared that she saw no threat to the British empire in South Africa in acceding to his wishes, seeing no danger if the Transvaal gained an exit to the sea where the British navy was already supreme. It was her assessment that South Africa had reached the stage when "the steam engine has become a more effective instrument of empire than the cannon" (*TT*, 12 Aug. 1892).[29]

THE LABOR QUESTION

All three journalists described in some detail the methods by which the mining industry confined African labor within high-walled compounds, focusing on the efforts of the diamond industry in Kimberley to guard against theft. Garrett declared that during the term of their contract, African laborers were "practically prisoners." He was ambivalent, however, for he accepted the colonial view of illicit diamond smuggling as immoral as well as criminal, while expressing disgust at the humiliating body searches Africans had to undergo every day and before leaving the compound. He characterized new African laborers as "raw savages" and accepted the industry view that they could not be depended upon for jobs requiring "skill and trust," which required white laborers (*PMG*, 19 March 1890). Both Garrett and Churchill reacted with strong distaste in describing these intimate body searches, and agreed, as Churchill put it, that "White men would never submit to such a process, but the native sustains the indignity with cheerful equanimity, considering the high wages which he earns" (*DG*, 20 July 1891). Shaw was clearly not invited to view these strip searches, but she did remark on the high level of compound surveillance that allowed an African laborer to speak to a visiting wife or family member only through a grating and only in the presence of an overseer. Yet, unlike Garrett's view of it as a prison, she actually called the compound a "monastery of labour," one that was very effective for the diamond industry, though not applicable, she concluded, on a wider scale (*TT*, 28 July 1892).

Garrett made various observations on labor conditions in the mines and on the farms, but never took up "the labor question" as a general issue for South African development. Churchill focused on the opportunities for British labor, emphasizing the high salaries emigrants could earn as supervisors in the mining industries. He also wrote of the opportunities that existed for energetic farmers who, unlike the Transvaal Boers, were willing to supply the market in the growing mining cities. Of emigration to cultivate or prospect in Mashonaland, however, he had only discouraging remarks to make. Shaw, however, explicitly analyzed South African labor requirements, skilled and unskilled, as a key element in the economic expansion of the whole region. While she also encouraged entrepreneurial white emigrants, she emphasized that Africans would be critical to the labor needs of material development: "manual labour, and manual labour in large quantities, is absolutely essential to success." With the needs of both farming and industry in mind, she praised the Native Reserve system in Basutoland, where Imperial control supported missionary and educational efforts to instill those wants of "civilization" that only individual labor for wages could supply. She argued for the end to community land tenure in order to convert all South African land to individual landholding, with the expectation that a landless population would become a disciplined labor force. She proclaimed that "philanthropists, practical politicians, and native leaders unite heartily in the endeavour to induce the native masses to become labouring masses . . ." (*TT*, 20 Sept. 1892).

ECONOMIC DEVELOPMENT

Garrett expressed the fundamental imperialist assumption that "European civilisation has shrunk the earth, and cannot afford to allow so big a piece of its surface to go to waste. Europe, therefore, must *exploiter* Africa" (*PMG*, 14 May 1890). All three writers saw the diamond industry in Kimberley as an inexhaustible source of wealth and reported that the Transvaal gold-mining industry was beginning to resolve its technological and financial problems with new deep-level shafts. They cited the main obstacles to economic growth as political: the delay in rail construction, the high taxes on mining, and the government's creation of a dynamite monopoly. They reported opportunities to meet the growing demand for market pro-

duce in the mining cities that was not being met by the cattle-raising
Dutch farmers. Only Shaw, however, used these observations to offer
a comprehensive analysis of South Africa's economic needs and future development. While Garrett speculated on a growing unity between Boers and Britons, he acknowledged the problems of
culturally backward Boers and "savage" Africans. Churchill allowed
his criticism of things South African and his pessimism about Mashonaland to permeate his letters (*DG*, 17 Dec. 1891; 12 Jan. 1892). In
striking contrast, Shaw expressed a buoyant optimism, underpinned
by statistics: "Everything that is written of the material resources of
this astonishing country must read like exaggeration, and yet exaggeration is hardly possible. The fertility of the soil is no less amazing
that the mineral wealth." Of the Transvaal, she proclaimed, "this is
a country in the making . . . the creation of an enormously rich province in South Africa. . . . The natural wealth is Dutch, the energy to
develop it is English, the profits of the whole will be South African"
(*TT*, 8, 12 Aug. 1892).

CONCLUSION

In the first three years of the 1890s, these three series of letters in
the English press helped to construct and reinforce a familiar image
of "South Africa" for British newspaper readers, its possibilities for
investment wealth, its labor problems, its "native question" as it im-
pinged on imperial development, the tensions that existed between
Briton and Boer, and the possible political solutions that might be
found to bind the region under British rule. This composite view
of "South Africa" held out opportunities for English emigration to
rapidly developing areas like Kimberley and Johannesburg, if not yet
farther north in Mashonaland. Behind the excitement in the British
press about South Africa's potential development within the empire,
shaped by projected stereotypes and assumptions, loomed the powerful figure of the visionary Cecil Rhodes and his plans to expand
British rule over Africa as far as it was possible. While Churchill and
Shaw alluded to his central role in pushing for a united South Africa, Garrett in 1890 specifically called him "the necessary man":
"Power is his idol: creative power, efficient energy, control over men
and things in the mass. In the British Empire he recognises the most
perfect and far-reaching machine for this purpose which the world
has yet seen, and the Empire, accordingly, is his religion" (*PMG*, 14
May 1890).
Garrett's observation on the 1890s as "this African decade" for

Britain proved more prescient than might have been predicted at the time. Both Garrett and Shaw continued to interact with Rhodes and, as journalists, played active roles in the dramatic unfolding of events as the politics of mistrust between the British and the Boers led almost inexorably to war in 1899. During this decade of high-handed imperialism which ended in a colonial war of vast cost in lives to both sides, these press reports by Garrett, Churchill, and Shaw provided an early framework for metropolitan readers to assess Britain's critical political and economic interests in South Africa as part of the empire and to interpret later developments with a heightened patriotic fervor.

NOTES

1. Since the generally acknowledged foundational text of Edward W. Said's *Orientalism* (London: Vintage Press, 1978), sophisticated analyses of colonial discourses have been carried out mainly in literary and cultural studies, but also in anthropology and history. In his recent study of exploration and empire, Felix Driver warns against the type of postcolonial criticism that gives way "to an essentialized model of 'colonial discourse' which obscures the heterogeneous, contingent and conflictual character of imperial projects." He advises that texts be located historically and analysed not only as texts but also with attention to the ways they were produced and consumed. *Geography Militant: Cultures of Exploration and Empire* (Oxford: Blackwell, 2001), 8.

2. Stephen Koss, *The Rise and Fall of the Political Press in Britain* (London: Fontana Press, 1990), 229–30; Frederic Whyte, *The Life of W. T. Stead* (New York: Garland Publishing, 1971), vol. 1, 68–69.

3. Raymond L. Schultz, *Crusader in Babylon: W. T. Stead and the Pall Mall Gazette* (Lincoln: University of Nebraska Press, 1972), xiv–xvi. For the earlier use of the interview by Edmund Yates, see Joel H. Wiener, "Edmund Yates: The Gossip as Editor," in *Innovators and Preachers: The Role of the Editor in Victorian England*, ed. Joel H. Wiener (Westport, Conn.: Greenwood Press, 1985), 260.

4. F. Edmund Garrett, *In Afrikanderland and the Land of Ophir, being Notes and Sketches in Political, Social, and Financial South Africa* (London: Pall Mall Gazette, 1891).

5. "Fydell Edmund Garrett," by "AAM" [Viscount Alfred Milner], *Dictionary of National Biography, Second Supplement*, vol. 1, January 1901–December 1911, ed. Sir Sidney Lee (London, reprint, 1920), 83–84.

6. See E. T. Cook, *Edmund Garrett, a Memoir* (London: Edwin Arnold, 1909) and Gerald Shaw, *The Garrett Papers* (Cape Town: Van Riebeeck Society, 1984).

7. Brian Roberts, *Churchills in Africa* (London: Hamish Hamilton, 1970), 3–86, and R. F. Foster, *Lord Randolph Churchill* (Oxford: Clarendon Press, 1981), esp. ch. 1 and 372–74.

8. This description is from the "Preliminary Number of the *Daily Graphic*,"published with the Christmas number of the *Graphic*, December 1889. The editorial staff shared many of the imperialist views expressed by Churchill. The new journal's racial attitudes were clear in its first number, 4 January 1890, with an illustrated

"letter" from "Buccra" in Jamaica, a lampoon on black Jamaicans "mimicking" their white betters at a Christmas ball. The editorial enthusiasm for empire was evident in the build-up to the publication of Churchill's letters, including a story about Mashonaland, entitled "The New El Dorado," 25 April 1891. The writer here lifted material verbatim, without acknowledgement, from an article by Flora Shaw on "The British South Africa Company" in the *Fortnightly Review* for November 1889.

9. The American, Henry Cleveland Perkins, the aide-de-camp Captain Gwynydd Williams, and Dr. Hugh Rayner, a surgeon of the Grenadier Guards. Roberts, 14–15 and Foster, 372.

10. The British press described Giles, who had seen service at the Cape and in Basutoland, as "a master of all the wrinkles of South African travel." Roberts, 14, 344. Compare the views of an experienced local man hired to accompany Churchill and Alfred Beit, South African born Percy Fitzpatrick, who disliked Churchill's "arrogance" and reported on the trip for the *Cape Argus* and the Johannesburg *Star*, his letters being reprinted in book form in 1892. "Intending pioneers and explorers could learn a great deal by studying the list of those things making up the 'absolute necessary' in expeditions such as Lord Randolph's and others. They would at least know in future what not to bring." J. Percy Fitzpatrick, *Through Mashonaland with Pick and Pen*, ed. A. P. Cartwright (Johannesburg: Argus Printing and Publishing Company, 1892; rev. ed. 1973), 27.

11. Roberts (47–50) cites press criticism in the *Spectator*, the *Speaker*, and the *St. James's Gazette* as well as in the *Cape Argus*, the Johannesburg *Star*, and the Pretoria *De Volksstem*. Churchill was also parodied in a popular skit at the Gaiety Theater in London. For the letters generated by Churchill's criticism of a new army rifle, which he tested at Fort Tuli in Mashonaland, see the *Daily Graphic*, 15, 16, 17, and 19 September 1891. For a full front-page illustration, see the lions in the *Daily Graphic*, 19 October 1891.

12. *The History of The Times*, vol. 2, *The Tradition Established, 1841–1884* (London: The Times, 1939), Introduction, *v–x*.

13. For Moberly Bell and *The Times* see E. H. C. Moberly Bell, *The Life and Letters of C. F. Moberly Bell* (London: Richard Press, 1927), and *The History of The Times*, vol. 3, *The Twentieth Century Test, 1884–1912* (London, 1947).

14. The press carried daily reports on the influenza epidemic, which claimed the life of the son of the Prince of Wales on the eve of his wedding. *Daily Graphic*, 15 January 1892, 5.

15. Her authorship, unlike that of the other two South African journalists, remained anonymous.

16. Though commissioned and presumably paid for twenty letters, Churchill supplied only eighteen, and one consisted of the journal entries of Dr. Rayner (*Daily Graphic*, 28 September 1891). The newspaper used various means to spread its coverage out: by bold-face, front-page advertising of the series beginning 7 April 1891; by printing separate letters from Major Giles before and after the series began, and after Churchill's first letter (22 June 1891); and by printing each of the remaining seventeen in two halves on 34 separate days. The "concluding" letter, so titled, appeared on 12 and 13 January 1892. Brian Roberts relied on Churchill's book for his discussion of the contents of these letters and does not comment on this discrepancy.

17. Despite the forged Parnell letters, *The Times* maintained its reputation in political and financial circles. Shaw's optimism about economic development in South Africa, therefore, carried considerable weight. Widespread notice of her letters included the *World*, which "quotes your opinions about the mining in a series

of important articles lately appearing in the Times." Louise Shaw to Flora Shaw, 11 August 1892, Shaw Papers, Rhodes House Library, Oxford.

18. For example, Garrett used the term "lazy" to describe the "uncivilized" African native and the Transvaal Boer. *Pall Mall Gazette,* 3 March 1890, and 14 May 1890.

19. See Johannes Fabian's cogent analysis of the time warp in typical anthropological accounts, *Time and the Other* (New York: Columbia University Press, 1983) and Sidonie Smith's discussion of women travelers and perceived space and time in train travel, *Moving Lives: Twentieth Century Women's Travel Writing* (Minneapolis and London: University of Minnesota Press, 2001), 128–31.

20. For this type of writing, see David Spurr's analysis of "Debasement" as a rhetorical strategy in colonial discourses, *The Rhetoric of Empire. Colonial Discourse in Journalism, Travel Writing, and Imperial Administration* (Durham, N.C.: Duke University Press, 1993), 76–91.

21. The letter was illustrated by a drawing of Tiriki with the caption: "He entered my service stark naked, but at his departure had accumulated an extraordinarily varied wardrobe. Every cast off pair of trousers, drawers, boots, and shoes, every coat and waistcoat thrown aside had been carefully collected by him. . . ."

22. Homi K. Bhabha, "The Other Question: Stereotype, discrimination and the discourse of colonialism," in *The Location of Culture* (London: Routledge, 1994), 66.

23. Besides the enjoyment of the "kill," Churchill wrote of the study of "Nature" and the profound knowledge gained from sport. *Daily Graphic,* 12 October; 7 December 1891. Joined by the African hunter Hans Lee and his African servant, called the "Baboon," Churchill filled many of his letters with their joint exploits. See, for example, 19 and 20 October 1891.

24. The *Daily Graphic,* in response to the furor, simply reprinted the equally misogynistic comments of Augustus Sala in the *Sunday Times.* See *Daily Graphic,* 27 July 1891, 5.

25. ". . . never have I so often heard the term 'Remarkable' applied so generally & by so many different sorts of people as to your letters." C. F. Moberly Bell to Flora Shaw, 12 August 1892, Manager's Letterbook 6/57–58, *The Times* Record Office.

26. For the material in this paragraph, see chap. 6, "Great Britain and the Afrikaner Republics, 1870–1899," by Leonard Thompson, in *The Oxford History of South Africa,* vol. II: *South Africa 1870–1966,* ed. Monica Wilson and Leonard Thompson (Oxford: Clarendon Press, 1971).

27. "The Franchise Question at the Cape," *The Times,* 7 June 1892. When the Opposition demanded at the opening of the Cape parliament early in July to know how *The Times* knew about the proposed Government franchise bill before they received it, a local newspaper observed that this had been achieved "by the exercise of journalistic smartness on the part of a *Times* correspondent now in Cape Town . . . [and was] the most interesting production on South Africa which has seen the light since Mr. Garrett's remarkable survey of the position. . . ." *Cape Argus,* Weekly Edition, 6 July 1892. For Shaw's earlier remarks on this political issue, see "The Colonies," *The Times,* 31 August 1891.

28. The Dutch press in Pretoria called his remarks "hasty and ill-tempered." A cartoon appeared in a Pretoria shop window showing Kruger kicking Churchill out of the Transvaal; and an angry crowd in Pretoria "paraded an effigy of Lord Randolph through the town." The South African press elsewhere also reported on this reception of Churchill's published letters. See Roberts, 52, 346, and between 50 and 51 for the cartoon.

29. Sir Henry Loch, Governor of the Cape Colony and High Commissioner in South Africa, reported to the Colonial Secretary in London: ". . . the accredited representative of the Times newspaper, Miss Shaw . . . saw Kruger & I understand interviewed him for more than a hour . . . I understand Kruger rather suspects she is a man in female garb-." Sir Henry B. Loch to Lord Knutsford, Cape Town, 5 July 1892, "Private." Loch Muniments, Scottish Record Office, Edinburgh.

Part 2

Sites of Fracture:
Resistance and Autonomy
in Imperial Representations

Objects and the Press: Images of China in Nineteenth-Century Britain

Catherine Pagani

THE NINETEENTH CENTURY WITNESSED TWO DRAMATIC ENCOUNTERS between the British and the Chinese: the Opium War of 1839–42 and the Arrow War of 1856–60. China was no match for Britain's military superiority and these attacks devastated the Chinese. For the British, these victories were timely and highly significant: the earlier humiliating diplomatic failures under the embassies to China of Lord Macartney in 1793 and Lord Amhert in 1816 had not been forgotten and remained deeply rooted in the British consciousness.

These conflicts also served to intensify an already strong and longstanding British interest in China, a nation with whom Britain had been trading officially since the founding of the Honourable East India Company in 1600. The public could satisfy its craving for information on the empire at the center of these hostilities through the illustrated articles on Chinese culture and social customs that were carried in the popular press alongside accounts of British progress against the Chinese in the war, and in the exhibitions of Chinese material culture that appeared in London. China thus was presented both verbally and visually, placing this foreign culture prominently in the British imagination.

The writings concerning China and the Chinese found in newspapers, such as the *Illustrated London News*, offer a means of exploring British attitudes regarding the Chinese at a time when the social and political relationships between the two empires were changing. Throughout this period, the general discourses on the conflicts may be seen as colonial in nature as they functioned as one means of representing "otherness," particularly in their portrayal of the Chinese as a race of "unenlightened savages." As such, these writings reflected the imperialistic attitudes and feelings of cultural superiority that came with Britain's growing military and political dominance over the Chinese. The discourses concerning Chinese objects, however, reveal that these attitudes were highly complex, presenting

147

contradictory and conflicting views. Chinese material culture was portrayed in two ways: as something desirable and worthy of admiration, and as symbolic representations of power and dominance through their association with a people defeated;[1] when compared to British art and technology, Chinese art objects acted as foils to British achievements and were used to support British notions of progress. The situation was thus one in which the lure of the beautiful, the exotic, and the pleasurable competed with imperialism and jingoistic pride. These writings on art therefore reveal not only the varied cultural identity that the British constructed of the Chinese, but also the identity that the British desired for themselves.

This essay explores the nature of this shift in attitudes by examining the manner in which Chinese material culture was displayed and discussed in exhibitions that took place between two pivotal events in Sino-British relations: the Opium War, which ended in 1842, and the conquest of Beijing by Franco-British forces in 1860. Notable among them were Nathan Dunn's "The Chinese Collection," first exhibited in 1842; the exhibition of the Chinese junk, *Keying*, in 1848; displays of Chinese goods at the Great International Exhibition of 1851; and the collection of J. L. Negroni, a captain with the French army whose collection, acquired during the sack of Beijing in 1860, was exhibited in London in 1865.

For the British, the Opium War of 1839–42 was not only a conflict regarding trade disputes but was a means of asserting cultural dominance after the failure of the embassies first under Lord Macartney (1737–1806) in 1792–93 and then under Lord Amherst (1773–1857) in 1816. Problems in the China trade had been ongoing for more than half a century. England had begun formal trade with China in 1600 when the Honourable East India Company was granted its charter by Elizabeth I, and by the early eighteenth century, regular trade passed between the two nations. However, while the British had acquired a taste for Chinese products, most notably tea, the Chinese found that England had little to offer them. As a result, by the early eighteenth century, trade flowed overwhelmingly in favor of the Chinese. As trade tensions mounted, the British redressed this imbalance by supplying the Chinese with opium, grown in the British-controlled areas of India, and soon the habit touched all levels of Chinese society. Imperial edicts against the importation and growing of opium were ineffective and the both the trade and the habit continued to grow.

In 1839, the Emperor appointed Lin Zexu (1785–1850) as Imperial High Commissioner at Canton (Guangzhou) to deal with the opium situation. Lin's orders to stop the smuggling of opium were ignored by the foreign dealers; in one final attempt to control the situation, Lin cut off the food and water supplies to the foreign factories and destroyed twenty thousand chests of opium. In retaliation, on 3 November 1839, the English declared war. The Chinese were no match for Britain's military might and the British won handily. The war ended on 29 August 1842 with the signing of the Treaty of Nanjing: among the twelve articles, the Chinese were forced to cede Hong Kong to England, open Canton and four other ports for trade, and pay over twenty-one million dollars in silver to the British to cover in part the value of the destroyed opium.

Under the conditions of the Treaty of 1842, the British were now in control of the trade. In that year, feelings of cultural and economic superiority were high; and China's now-subordinate status was the subject of the lengthy satirical poem entitled "The Chinese War," published first in *The Comic Album* of 1842 and excerpted later that year with an illustration in a book review for the *Illustrated London News*. The poem begins: "Every one's heard of the Chinese nation / The people of which declare / That several years before Creation/ Their ancestors were settled there!" The poem continues with a long account of the effects of opium smoking and of the ensuing war. The concluding lines tell of England's new position in the China trade:

> With this nation so deluded
> Peace is happily concluded:
> Let us now no longer teaze
> The unfortunate Chinese.
> We are ready to befriend them;
> Cotton night-gowns we will send them;
> For their use we will import
> Articles of every sort . . .
> Everything, in fact, to please
> And enlighten the Chinese,
> England, this time forth supplies them.
> Only just to civilize them.[2]

According to this poem, these "[a]rticles of every sort," which included razor-strappers, stockings, pomatum, and wigs, had the ability to transform and enrich Chinese culture by virtue of their British origins alone regardless of their actual usefulness to the Chinese. Just one week before the review of the *Comic Album* appeared in the *Illustrated London News*, a similar opinion was expressed in the newspaper's pages reporting the end of the war. This "large family of the human race" was now about to enter into a "mutual" trade and diplomatic intercourse in which Britain's commercial influence would be "almost as enormous and unequalled as the most ample imagination could desire."[3]

Coinciding with China's prominence in the popular press owing to British involvement in the Opium War, were a number of important exhibitions in London of Chinese material culture. Chinese objects were nothing new in Britain: beginning in the seventeenth century, trade in Chinese goods was a regular occurrence; however, these objects were different and carried with them new significance. These were presented as items for display, not as trade commodities for private consumption, and were of interest both for their intrinsic value as examples of Chinese material culture and also for what they could reveal about Chinese culture as a whole.

On 23 June 1842, the "Chinese Collection," the largest and most comprehensive assemblage of Chinese artifacts of the day, opened in London to great popular acclaim (fig. 18). The Collection's more than thirteen hundred artifacts amassed by the merchant Nathan

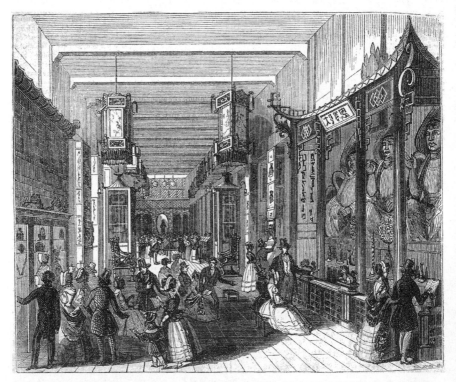

Figure 18. "A Chinese Collection, Hyde Park," *Illustrated London News*, **6 August 1842, p. 204.**

Dunn (1782–1844) during his twelve years in the China trade prior to his retirement in 1830[4] ranged from paintings and porcelains to costumes and Buddhist sculpture, and contrasted sharply with earlier exhibitions of the 1830s that consisted of small, isolated displays of widely varying Asian artifacts.[5] The exhibition hall was a grand building resembling a Chinese residence painted in "gold and bright colours, its roof and veranda turned up at the corners, painted green, and supported on columns of red with dragon-shaped brackets—a novel and striking object, and not inelegant."[6] Dunn's collection was first shown in Philadelphia in late 1838, and its catalogue, entitled *Ten Thousand Chinese Things* (with the Chinese characters *wan tangrenwu* included), sold approximately fifty thousand copies. In London, its curator and co-proprietor, William B. Langdon, enlarged the catalogue to include contributions by noted specialists on China;[7] owing to the collection's popularity, more than three hundred thousand catalogues (of which there were several editions between 1842 and 1844) were sold.[8] Shortly after Dunn's death in 1844, the collection toured England before being returned to the United States where it was shown at P. T. Barnum's Broadway Museum in New York. Eventually much of what was left of the collection was sold at auction in 1851.[9] While in London, however, the exhibition received extensive coverage in the popular press, particularly the *Illustrated London News*.

In presenting Dunn's collection in London at this time, William B. Langdon was taking advantage of the unprecedented interest in China generated by Britain's involvement with China in the Opium War. He writes in his introduction to the catalogue, "At no period in the history of the world, has the attention of civilised nations been so fully directed towards China, its early history, and modern position, as at the present moment."[10] The Chinese Collection was the perfect resource for anyone who sought information on China: through a single visit to the collection, it was claimed, the viewer would obtain a better understanding of the Chinese than through books alone, for a single artifact "will illustrate whole pages of written description"[11] resulting in "a more definite and permanent idea of these Tartar-governed millions than volumes of ordinary details."[12] In short, this collection was designed to educate "by *things* rather than words."[13]

According to the contemporary press accounts, the collection appeared to have met its educational objectives. The *Illustrated London News* praised Langdon's exhibition, claiming that collection's comprehensiveness allowed the viewing public to

analyse the mental and moral qualities of the Chinese, and gather some
knowledge of their idols, their temples, their pagodas, their bridges,
their arts, their sciences, their manufactures, their fancies, their par-
lours, their drawing rooms. . . . Here we have, not one object, but thousands; not a single discovery, but an empire with all its variety of light
and shade, its experience, [and] its mind.[14]

The *Spectator* provided a similar assessment. Here was a display that
allowed the viewer to see a broad sampling of Chinese life and culture:

At any time, such a museum as this, giving an insight into the habits and
arts of life of a people of whom we know so little, would be interesting;
but at the present juncture it is most especially so. A few hours spent in
studying the contents of this collection, with the aid of the descriptive
catalogue, which is full of information, much of it original, will possess
the visitor with an idea of the Chinese almost as complete and vivid as
could be formed by a voyage to China.[15]

The Chinese Collection was promoted as an objective and balanced look at Chinese culture through its large selection of Chinese
artifacts. Newspaper advertisements for the exhibition promised the
viewing public an understanding of the entire Chinese population
("more than three hundred million Chinese") through its assemblage of natural history specimens and "miscellaneous curiosities."[16] Objects, it was said in the catalogue, by their very nature are
free of the biases found in texts alone for they are "visible and tangible, and, therefore, cannot be easily misunderstood."[17] Efforts were
made to "narrate nothing but facts, and thus to impart correct information" by carefully avoiding "[a]ll fiction and romance."[18] This
was a remarkable collection in the scope and quantity of the artifacts
and in the information contained in its catalogue; the Chinese Collection was certainly the most diverse display of Chinese items thus
seen in London.

But while on the surface it appeared that the emphasis of the exhibition was to showcase "the beauty, rarity, novelty, and extreme singularity" of the "leading objects of curiosity, taste, and skill in the
Chinese world,"[19] a deeper reading reveals that Langdon was also
carefully positioning the exhibition to fit within the larger British
social and cultural scene by appealing to the dominant imperialist
sentiments of the day. He took advantage of the current high interest in China and the Victorian fascination with the exotic, while at
the same time catering to cultural misperceptions and stereotypes
fueled by the euphoria brought on by a victory in the Opium War.

It is not surprising to find a section of the exhibition and catalogue devoted to opium smoking and the "opium debauchee" (Langdon, 78). Furthermore, neither the catalogue nor the newspapers referred to the items in the Chinese Collection as "art." These "objects," "wonders," "curiosities" and "specimens" were thus automatically given a subordinate status in the British world of art.

Following the success of Dunn's Chinese Collection came other exhibitions of Chinese material culture, although none were to be as comprehensive. [20] The exhibitions of the late 1840s were much narrower in scope, and could not offer "at one view an epitome of Chinese life and character, arts and manufacture, scenery and natural productions"[21] as the Chinese Collection had; they instead tended to focus more on the exotic and sensationalistic aspects of Chinese culture. The displays and the discourses associated with them highlighted the differences between the British and the Chinese and made a clear distinction between the ingenious "Us" and the curious and inferior "Other."

Growing frustrations with the China trade contributed to these attitudes. The signing of the Treaty of Nanjing at the conclusion of the Opium War did not end the trade disputes. The treaty gave diplomatic equality to British and Chinese officials and was designed to facilitate trade between the nations. In reality, however, the British soon found that the situation had changed very little. Most frustrating was the difficulty they had in contacting the Governor-General of Canton, Ye Mingchen (governed from 1848–58) with whom the foreign countries had to deal. Ye simply refused to meet any of the foreign envoys.

In addition, the public also had access to first-hand accounts by recent travellers to China. Colorful and timely, these eyewitness descriptions could not but affect the popular perception of the Chinese. Prominent among these writers was Sir Robert Fortune (1813–80), first sent to China as the Botanical Collector to the Royal Horticultural Society. In 1848, he made a second journey, on behalf of the British East India Company, in which he collected tea plants to be introduced into India. In his 1847 work, *Three Years' Wandering in the Northern Provinces of China*, he described China as no longer the "enchanted fairy-land" she once had been, and the Chinese as a "lazy" and "stupid . . . lawless race" that was "filled with the most conceited notions of their own importance and power."[22]

It was at this time that Britons witnessed the arrival and display of the Chinese junk, *Keying*, in March 1848 (fig. 19). *Keying*, named for Qiying (spelled at the time Kiying), the chief Manchu negotiator of the Treaty of Nanjing, was hailed in the press as "the first ship con-

Figure 19. "The Chinese Junk 'Keying'," *Illustrated London News*, 1 April 1848, p. 220.

structed by the Chinese which has ever reached Europe."[23] The junk was purchased in Canton, arriving in Hong Kong on 19 October 1846. While in Hong Kong, she was fitted for a special exhibition of artifacts, likely influenced by Dunn's well-known and popular collection. She set sail from Hong Kong Harbour on 6 December with a crew of thirty Chinese and twelve Englishmen, travelled around the Cape of Good Hope (most likely the first Chinese junk to do so) where *Keying* successfully weathered a hurricane, and continued on her way to London. However, the winds and currents took her instead toward the United States and *Keying* landed in New York where she was greeted by a "general display of flags and saluting from the large assembly of shipping in the harbour."[24]

Much excitement was created by the visit of *Keying* and she was made open for view by the public; it was reported that "for a succession of days subsequent to her arrival, as many as seven thousand to eight thousand persons daily went on board."[25] *Keying* spent a brief period in Boston before setting for London, crossing the Atlantic in a remarkable twenty-one days. In London, she was repainted, and was then placed on display "for exhibition to the sight-loving Londoners."[26] Unusual in form and bright in color, including two large painted eyes on the bow of the junk, *Keying* immediately became a popular attraction.

Keying's appeal, however, went beyond her striking appearance. As the first sailing vessel from distant China to reach England, she was unlike anything that the British public had ever seen. Here was an object that was both exotic and rare. At the same time, as a tangible example of Chinese ship-building—a technology with which Britons were well acquainted—*Keying* was not completely unfamiliar. In this capacity she served as the perfect point of comparison between Chinese and British technological and cultural achievements.

Keying's arrival was timely as well. Her obvious practical function met with the approval of a Britain now enjoying the benefits of a modern industrial age. At a time when feats of technology and engineering instilled a belief in progress among the Victorians, *Keying* stood apart from other imported (and decorative) objects that had little utilitarian value. However, discourses in the popular press show conflicting feelings regarding the vessel. On the one hand, *Keying* was admired for her unusual looks and for her ability to travel several thousand miles under adverse conditions to reach England; on the other hand, because she looked nothing like a "real" (i.e., British) ship, she was considered to be more an oddity than an item worthy of serious consideration. As a reporter for the *Illustrated London News* wrote, *Keying* "promises to be one of the most popular exhibitions of our metropolis for some time to come; it is, certainly, one of the most rational objects of curiosity which has ever been brought to our shores."[27] Thus *Keying*, regardless of the obvious technological merits that made her "rational," ultimately was regarded as a mere "curiosity."

More important, however, in this age of industry and empire, the discourses of the period show that *Keying* served to emphasize British cultural and technological superiority over the Chinese by highlighting the striking differences between Chinese and British shipbuilding (the British methods were, of course, considered to be far superior). *Keying*, as such, represented Chinese culture; and as a foil to British culture, she contributed to the identity the British were constructing of themselves.

The shape and construction of the junk offered an opportunity to point out the backwardness of the Chinese in the area of naval technology. A writer in *The Examiner* mocked China's long history of shipbuilding and the overall lack of technical know-how:

Talk of the wisdom of our ancestors! Here is an example of the shipbuilding wisdom and skill of the ancestors of the Chinese, which may have dated from the earliest ages of the world. Certainly never before did so unwieldy and misshapen a vessel traverse the Indian and Atlantic oceans; and the underwriters, if there were to be found men bold enough to insure a craft of this build, had great need of the pious invocation which is appended to the bills of lading in use amongst Christian nations.[28]

Thus, "[t]he primitive build, and still more primitive contrivances for handling this specimen of Chinese naval architecture, are in themselves worth all the money and time that must be expended in paying it a visit."[29] The following month, a writer for *The Examiner* made rather stinging remarks directed at *Keying*'s appearance: "If there be any one thing in the world that it is not at all like, that thing is a ship of any kind." He continued:

> So narrow, so long, so grotesque, so low in the middle, so high at each end (like a China pen-tray), with no rigging, with nowhere to go aloft, with mats for sails, great warped cigars for masts, gaudy dragons and sea monsters disporting themselves from stem to stern, and, on the stern, a gigantic cock of impossible aspect, defying the work (as well he may) to produce his equal.[30]

The newspaper also used this opportunity to supply a contrast between the British and the Chinese:

> The crew of Chinamen aboard the Keying devoutly believed that their good ship would arrive quite safe . . . if they only tied red rags enough upon the mast, rudder, and cable. . . .
>
> It is pleasant . . . to think that WE trust no red rags in storms, and burn no joss-sticks before idols; that WE never grope our way by the aid of conventional eyes which have no sight in them; and that, in our civilisation, we sacrifice absurd forms to substantial facts. The ignorant crew of the Keying refused to enter upon the ship's books, until "a considerable amount of silvered paper, tin-foil, and joss-sticks" had been laid in, by the owners, for the purposes of their worship; but OUR seamen—far less our bishops, priests, and deacons—never stand out upon points of silvered paper and tin-foil, or the lighting up of joss-sticks upon altars! Christianity is not Chin-Teeism; and therein all significant quarrels as to means, are lost sight of in remembrance of the end.[31]

These sentiments were echoed in the *Illustrated London News*. Upon viewing the junk, the visitor is "struck with her very rude construction. . . . The whole of the work is of the roughest kind. . . . Hundreds of European ships, with all their elegance of form and beauty, and lightness of rigging, have been repeatedly before the Chinese, without their appearing conscious of the superiority, or desirous of imitating it" owing to the "unconquerable prejudice, and utter contempt for everything foreign" on the part of the Chinese.[32]

Even the tale surrounding Keying's acquisition was related with an emphasis on the triumph of British cunning over the Chinese. The junk had been purchased by "a few enterprising Englishmen" (Captain Charles A. Kellett; S. Revett, the Second Mate; T. A. Lane; and Douglas Lapraik) who resorted to a number of strategies to obtain *Keying* as Chinese law prohibited foreigners from owning a Chinese-made vessel. The destination of the ship was kept secret and the buyers "were likewise compelled to adopt various disguises to enable them to penetrate the interior of the country, and effect the purchase of the vessel."[33] Such a story added to *Keying*'s prestige as she was an object acquired by surreptious means; it also served to present subtlely the message that British cunning was not limited to matters of war alone. *Keying* thus functioned simultaneously as a rare curiosity from a far-off land, and as (prominent) tangible evidence of overall British cultural preeminence and advancement that began with victory in the Opium War. Such attitudes would dominate the exhibition discourse of the 1850s.

The Chinese junk *Keying* was still in London in 1851 when the Great International Exhibition (Great Exhibition of the Works of Industry of All Nations) opened on 1 May at the Crystal Palace in Hyde Park. This was the exhibition of exhibitions, designed to showcase advances in technology and science as well as the arts; notions of progress and ingenuity were of primary importance and imperial achievement was celebrated to its fullest.[34] Chinese material culture, which up until this time had enjoyed a certain amount of prestige particularly when compared to the Chinese themselves, began to suffer in the context of the Great Exhibition. Trade with China had slowed and Britain had come to rely less and less on Chinese goods. Very few Chinese items were shown at the exhibition and even less was written about them: in the numerous pages comprising the various exhibition supplements to the *Illustrated London News*, they hardly received a mention.[35]

Although the Chinese objects were considered intriguing, overall they were deemed less than extraordinary. Carved nested ivory balls and little else caught the attention of the observer for the *Illustrated London News:*

> The Chinese have long been famous for their caprices of invention, and whimsicalities of workmanship, over each article of which the greater portion of the lives of several artisans appear to have been expended. We find exhibited here some of their celebrated ivory balls, richly carved

outside and containing another, a size less, inside, richly carved also, with open-work . . . to show you that there are balls within balls to the extend of twenty or more.[36]

The discourses also tended to suggest a connection between these artifacts and the culture that produced them by implying that these arts were representative of Chinese national character. Their ability to create such intricate objects demonstrated that "the Chinese are capable of wasting any amount of time upon any triviality." However, this explanation was not fully satisfactory and the newspaper further suggested that the Chinese must have resorted to some sort of deception in making the nesting balls. The Chinese must have discovered "a certain ivory cement so strong as to be carved upon, and so exactly of the same colour of ivory as to be indistinguishable." These balls, it was speculated, were then made in two halves, which would "render the entire process easy in comparison, or . . . would rob it . . . of the greater part of its difficulty." While the writer had to admit that "we have never been able to detect the sign of a joint, and we never heard of one of their balls coming in two pieces, or even showing an artificial crack," he also pointed out that "if the world *must* have these toys," English artisans could substitute a "common penknife" and effect the same result in "a tenth, perhaps a hundredth of the time."

This quotation is interesting for the contradictions it presents, arguing both for and against ingenuity and skill, with the purpose of expressing British supremacy in all things, even carved nested ivory balls. It was not possible simply to acknowledge the workmanship of the Chinese: such an accomplishment could only have been the result of either wasting time or undetectable trickery. Even so, had they wanted to create such things, the British could have done it better, faster and with less effort, but chose not to as it was implied that these artists were engaged in far more lofty pursuits.

Much of the problem was that in the eyes of the British the Chinese had not progressed and did not meet British expectations. The victory in the Opium War and the subsequent opening of trade with the British, as reported by the *Illustrated London News* in 1842, would help the Chinese "break through the ignorance which for ages had enveloped them, . . . enjoy the freedom of a more expanded civilisation, and enter upon prospects immeasurably grander" to take advantage of the new opportunities given by "the new freedoms offered by British political and commercial influence."[37] China had failed to progress: her art offered nothing new and was not in keeping with the spirit of the Great Exhibition. "The expectations of a nation," concluded the papers, "have rarely been opened to more magnificent and glorious views."[38] It should be noted that the items selected for exhibition were not sent by the country of manufacture as the best they had to offer but were an odd assortment of objects gathered from various local private collections and were hardly representative of China's arts. That this escaped notice of reviewers in making their assessments merely shows a lack of both understanding or any desire to understand Chinese culture.

By the early 1850s, the excitement generated among the British by victory in the Opium War in 1842 was over and relations between the two nations were once again strained. In 1854, seeking to renegotiate the Treaty of Nanjing, the British presented a list of requests to the Chinese. Among them were that Britain be given access to the entire interior of China, or at least the coastal areas of Zhejiang province and the lower Yangzi River to Nanjing; that the opium trade be legalized; that the internal transit dues on foreign goods be abolished; that piracy be suppressed; that the British ambassador be given a residence in Beijing; and that in the case of any disputes, British rather than Chinese interpretations of the revised treaty were to be followed. In seeking these revisions, the British joined with the French and the Americans who were hoping to revise their own treaties with the Chinese.[39]

The foreigners were unsuccessful in pressing their claims, even after visits by envoys to Shanghai and Tianjin, and later threats of the use of force. By late 1856, tensions were high; finally it was the incident involving the lorcha *Arrow* at Canton, that prompted the British to take military action. On 8 October, the Chinese boarded the *Arrow* and arrested her Chinese crew, accusing them of piracy, and they lowered the flag. The vessel had been of Hong Kong registry; the captain was British, as was her flag. With protests unsuccessful, the British then bombarded Canton. By December, the situation had deteriorated further. British sailors had been killed, and in retaliation, the village responsible was burned by the British. The Chinese then set fire to the foreign "factories" (warehouses) at Canton where the foreigners lived. By July 1857, the British and French sent the Earl of Elgin and Baron Gros as high commissioners to settle the matter. Again, with their requests ignored, the forces sent an ultimatum on 24 December. Canton was bombarded and fell to the foreign forces on 29 December 1857. Canton would remain under foreign occupation until the signing of the Convention of Peking on 24 October 1860.

In March of 1858, the British and French troops sailed north, arriving at Tianjin in May. Joined by the Russians and the Americans, the four foreign groups succeeded in having their treaties signed. Included in the Treaty of Tianjin was the right to a diplomatic residence in Beijing and the opening of the Yangzi to trade. When the British and French returned in June 1859 to take up residence at the Chinese capital, they found that they were barred from the city. They returned in August accompanied by a strong contingent of troops that easily defeated the Chinese. The emperor fled the Summer Palace for his residence at Jehol, located some one hundred miles to the north. On 5 October, the joint British-French troops reached Beijing; on 7 October the French captured the Summer Palace and began their sack of the Yuanmingyuan and were soon joined by the British. The "Palace of the Yuen-ming-yuen, the Summer palace of the Emperor, the glory and boast of the Chinese Empire, was levelled to the ground" on 18 and 19 October 1860.[40] As reported in the press: "Thus it has been the destiny of England, directly and indirectly, to break down a governmental fabric which has so long mystified the European world, and to uncover to its own subjects its hollowness and its evils. We have in this matter taken on ourselves a great responsibility in its fullest and widest sense."[41] This was done in retaliation for the executions of several foreign prisoners by the Chinese.

Britain had expected full victory: "From the moment we first seriously entered into hostile collision with the Chinese empire, and brought the force of active and intrusive Western Civilisation to bear upon its mysterious and exclusive barbarism—using the word as we understand it—it was palpably obvious that the days of that obsolete sovereignty were numbered."[42] That success came on 24 October 1860 with the ratification of the Treaty of Tianjin and the Convention of Peking. In addition to the ratifications, the Chinese were also required to pay eight million taels in indemnity and cede the Kowloon peninsula to Hong Kong. The West's dominance of China was indisputable.

Few public exhibitions of Chinese art were staged in the years following the 1860 attack on Beijing. However, of particular interest were the objects taken from the Chinese emperor's Summer Palace on 18 and 19 October 1860, when Anglo-French troops under the commands of Sir James Hope Grant and General Cousin de Montauban seized the treasures of the Yuanmingyuan.[43] This "righteous retribution enacted by the allied armies of the foreigners"[44] resulted in the destruction by burning of the palace complex as well as the looting and breakage of the imperial treasures. "All night long," said the *Illustrated London News* in reporting the story, "the smoke and flames were rising up to heaven and obscuring the sky and stars."[45] Such an act "destroys the Emperor's prestige, and dissipates with a rude hand that halo of divinity with which he has always been surrounded in the imagination of the people."

In London, these treasures from the Yuanmingyuan were first exhibited at the International Exhibition of 1862. While items had been shown in Paris as early as April 1861 (these were presented to Napoleon III by the French soldiers),[46] the situation in London was different as few items made their way into the possession of the British crown. Because of auctions in Beijing and London,[47] most items were instead dispersed into a number of private hands.[48] When the Chinese Court was set up at the 1862 International Exhibition, a large proportion of the items consisted of the "spoils from Pekin,"[49] forcing the exhibition organizers to solicit assistance from British consuls in China. Among the items said to be from the Summer Palace was the skull of Confucius mounted as a drinking cup.[50]

A larger extensive exhibition was held in 1865 at the Crystal Palace, featuring the collection of J. L. de Negroni, an officer of the French army, who had accumulated a large number of objects while at the sacking of the Summer Palace (fig. 20). He spared no expense in acquiring these objects, and because he found them to be "in a number of different hands," he was obliged to purchase many from the soldiers, at great cost.[51] The artifacts included Chinese items such as a red lacquer cabinet and a carved stone grotto, as well as items of European manufacture consisting in part of elaborately jewelled clocks, some of which had ironically served as presentation gifts from the King of England to the Chinese emperor in the late eighteenth century.

In the 1860s, the focus on items taken from the Chinese emperor's palace and the new meanings ascribed to them gave the exhibitions a unique character quite different from earlier displays. Unlike the Chinese collection of 1842, in which the assemblage of objects was presented as a broad look at a foreign culture, or the display of *Keying* in 1848, where the ship represented the superiority of British know-how over that of the Chinese, the Yuanmingyuan[52] artifacts were not emblematic of China in general but rather stood specifically for the emperor himself, and with him, Chinese power. Thus, the presentations of these plundered objects made tangible the final British conquest over China. Even the European artifacts functioned within this interpretation: at one time presented to the Chinese court to gain much-desired imperial favor, they now were liberated from the possession of a ruler defeated, and returned home.

Thus, the significance of the Yuanmingyuan artifacts, and that which set them apart from Chinese material culture previously dis-

Figure 20. "The Chinese Exhibition at the Crystal Palace," *Illustrated London News,*
6 May 1865, p. 423.

played, lay in the fact that they were "loot": goods acquired as spoils
of war. These objects took on a number of meanings from the time
they were acquired by the Anglo-French forces to their eventual exhibition in London. James L. Hevia argues that these changing
meanings were disconnected from the objects' culture of origin and
were often ambiguous and contradictory: prized as treasures of a
ruler, ultimately they were devalued and labelled as "curiosities." In
the hands of the British, these objects became symbolic of the attitudes of colonizers to the colonized and of the ultimate triumph of
the British over the Chinese.

This paper has examined the changing British perceptions of
China as revealed through the discourses relating to exhibitions of
Chinese material culture found in the popular press between 1842
and 1865. This was a time of intense Sino-British interaction, from
the Opium War in 1842 to the destruction of the emperor's Summer
Palace outside of Beijing in 1860. This period was dominated by feel-

ings of jingoistic pride: the British soundly defeated the Chinese not once but twice and were, at last, in control of the trade between the two empires. To them, the Chinese were a curious race of unenlightened savages.

However, over this two-decade span, British attitudes toward the Chinese underwent a subtle development revealed in the discourses about Chinese art. As the economic, social, and military power shifted in favor of the British, exhibitions of material culture, too, changed in both the nature and content of their displays. What had been regarded in 1842 as "products of Chinese ingenuity" designed to introduce the viewer to the "habits and arts" of a people with whom the British had recently been at war, acquired new meanings two decades later. On display in 1865 were items forcibly taken from the imperial palace as a "solemn act of retribution." No longer art objects, these items—the "glory and boast of the Chinese empire" and representative of the Chinese emperor himself—now were in foreign hands. The British at last had achieved final satisfaction after the political humiliations over trade issues that dated back to the late eighteenth century.

This is not to suggest, however, that such attitudes represent a homogeneity of response to the Chinese. Throughout this period, these conflicting and contradictory attitudes were the result of the residual and emerging perceptions and stereotypes concerning the Chinese that came both from long-term British involvement in the China trade and the national identity that the British were constructing of themselves. At a time when Victorian England was enjoying an economic prosperity brought about by industrialization, technological innovations, and the satisfaction of an expanded empire, Chinese artifacts were presented simultaneously as exotic and unusual, and as products of a backward, barbarian culture. These strategies objectified Chinese "otherness"[53] and through them the Chinese and Chinese artifacts became inextricably linked. With their symbolic associations, these objects supported notions of British ingenuity; most important, they symbolized British cultural and moral superiority as much as, or perhaps more than, they represented Chinese culture.

NOTES

1. Recent reseach has examined the display of the art of other cultures to discuss the history of British imperialism and ideas concerning the colonial encounter.

See, for example, Annie E. Coombes, *Reinventing Africa: Museums, Material Culture and Popular Imagination* (New Haven: Yale University Press, 1994).

2. "The Chinese War," from *The Comic Album: A Book for Every Table* (London: Orr and Co., 1842), n.p.

3. *Illustrated London News*, 3 December 1842, 469.

4. Nathan Dunn and Company traded out of Canton and was one of few businesses that refused to participate in the opium trade. Francis Ross Carpenter, *The Old China Trade. Americans in Canton, 1784–1843* (New York: Coward, McCann and Geoghegan, 1976), 93.

5. These included a small temple containing Buddha figures, and an exhibition of seventy-eight life-sized figures of "the principal images of Hindu worship," cited in Richard D. Altick, *The Shows of London* (Cambridge: Harvard University Press, 1978), 292.

6. *The Spectator*, no. 730, 25 June 1842, 616. This building was located at Hyde Park Corner.

7. These included Sir John Francis Davis (1795–1890), Dr. Robert Morrison (1782–1834), Karl Gutzlaff (1803–51), and the eighteenth-century Jesuit missionary Jean-Joseph-Marie Amiot (1718–93).

8. Nathan Dunn, "Ten Thousand Chinese Things." *A Descriptive Catalogue of the Chinese Collection in Philadelphia with Miscellaneous Remarks Upon the Manners, Customs, Trade, and Government of the Celestial Empire* (Philadelphia: Printed for the Proprietor, 1839); and William B. Langdon published several editions over the next two years including *"Ten Thousand Chinese Things": A Descriptive Catalogue of the Chinese Collection, Now Exhibiting at St. George's Place, Hyde Park Coner, London, with Condensed Account of the Genius, Government, History, Literature, Agriculture, Arts, Trade, Manners, Customs and Social Life of the People of the Celestial Empire* (London: Printed for the Proprietor, 1842); the edition used in this study: *"Ten Thousand Chinese Things": A Descriptive Catalogue of the Chinese Collection, Now Exhibiting at St. George's Place, Hyde Park Coner; London, with Condensed Accounts of the Genius, Government, History, Literature, Agriculture, Arts, Trade, Manners, Customs, and Social Life of the People of the Celestial Empire* (London: Printed for the Proprietor, 1843); and *Ten Thousand Things Relating to China and the Chinese; An Epitome of the Genius, Government, History, Literature, Agriculture, Arts, Trade, Manners, Customs, and Social Life of the People of the Celestial Empire, Together with a Synposis of the Chinese Collection* (London: To be had only at the Collection, Hyde Park Corner, 1842).

9. Jean Gordon Lee, "Introduction," in *Philadelphians and the China Trade* (Philadelphia: Philadelphia Museum of Art, 1984), 18; and Christie and Manson, London, *Catalogue of the Celebrated Assemblage Which Formed the Chinese Exhibition, Collected by the Late Nathan Dunn, Esq.* (10–14 December 1851).

10. Langdon, *"Ten Thousand Chinese Things"* (1843), 5.

11. Ibid., 3.

12. Ibid., 4.

13. Ibid., 14. Italics appear in the original text.

14. *Illustrated London News* 1, no. 13, 6 August 1842, 204–5. This passage was taken from various parts of Langdon's introduction to the catalogue of the collection, 13–14.

15. *The Spectator*, no. 730, 25 June 1842, 616.

16. *The Illustrated London News*, 30 July 1842, 191.

17. Langdon, *"Ten Thousand Chinese Things"* (1843), 14.

18. Ibid., 14.

19. Ibid., 12, 13, 15.

20. Other "Chinese Collections" followed, including one which advertised the display of a group of Chinese people in the *Illustrated London News* of 1851.

21. *The Spectator*, no. 730, 25 June 1842, 616.

22. Robert Fortune, *Three Years' Wanderings in the Northern Provinces of China, Including a Visit to the Tea, Silk, and Cotton Countries: with an Account of the Agriculture and Horticulture of the Chinese, New Plants, Etc.* (London: John Murray, 1847; reprinted New York: Garland Publishing, Inc., 1979), 2–8.

23. *Illustrated London News*, 1 April 1848, 220.

24. Ibid. and 222.

25. Ibid., 222.

26. Ibid.

27. Ibid., 20 May 1848, 332.

28. *The Examiner*, 20 May 1848, 333.

29. Ibid.

30. Ibid., 24 June 1848, 403.

31. Ibid.

32. *Illustrated London News*, 20 May 1848, 381.

33. Ibid., 1 April 1848, 220.

34. Industry and empire were presented at the Great Exhibition; for a full consideration of this exhibition, see "Imperial display," Paul Greenhalgh, *Ephemeral Vistas: The Expositions Universelles, Great Exhibitions and World's Fairs, 1851–1939* (Manchester: Manchester University Press, 1988), 52–81.

35. This situation was much different for India, the jewel of British colonial enterprise, which was provided with thirty-thousand square feet of exhibition space. Greenhalgh, 59.

36. *Illustrated London News*, 23 August 1851, 254. This is also found in John Tallis, *Tallis's History and Description of the Crystal Palace, and the Exhibition of the World's Industry in 1851*. 2 vols. (London: John Tallis and Co., 1851), 1: 113.

37. *Illustrated London News*, 1, no. 31, 3 December 1842, 469.

38. Ibid.

39. Americans had signed the Treaty of Wanghia; the French had signed the Treaty of Whampoa.

40. James, Lord Elgin, *Letters and Journals of James, Eighth Earl of Elgin*, ed., Theodore Warland (London: John Murray, 1872), 365.

41. *Illustrated London News*, 17 November 1860, 461.

42. Ibid.

43. James L. Hevia examines the multiple transformations and meanings of these objects as they passed from Chinese to European hands in his article, "Loot's Fate: The Economy of Plunder and The Moral Life of Objects 'From The Summer Palace of The Emperor of China,'" *History and Anthropology*, 6 (1994): 319–345.

44. *Illustrated London News*, 5 January 1861, 18.

45. Ibid.

46. These included military items such as swords, saddles, and "the Chinese emperor's war costume," as well as a model of a pagoda, a bronze bell and two *ruyi*, or sceptres. *Illustrated London News*, 13 April 1861, 334 and 339.

47. In Beijing, the spoils were put up for general auction on 10 October 1860 by order of Hope Grant with the proceeds of £26,000 to be divided among the British officers and the noncommissioned men and was likely held at the Tibetan Buddhist Western Yellow Temple (Xihuangsi) in Beijing.

48. In 1861 and 1862, the London auction house of Christie, Manson and Woods featured items labeled as coming from the Summer Palace. Hevia provides a com-

plete list of the London auctions of goods from the Summer Palace, pp. 341–42. Many other objects taken by the soldiers appeared on the European auction market: in Decemeber 1861, a "precious collection" of articles from the Yuanmingyuan were sold in Paris. *Catalogue d'une précieuse collection d'objets d'art et de curiosité de la Chine provenant du Palais d'été de Yuen-ming-yuen* (Paris: Imprimerie de Pillet fils anié, 5, rue des Grands Augustins, 1861).

49. *The Queen,* 18 January 1862, 398.

50. *International Exhibition of 1862. Illustrated Catalogue,* 4 vols. (London) 3: 43–44.

51. They were eventually set up in the Chinese Museum at Fontainebleau by the Empress Eugenie. See the catalogue, *Le Musée Chinois de l'Imperatrice Eugénie* (Paris: Réunion des Musées Nationaux, 1994).

52. This complex previously had been made known to the general public through a lengthy description with detailed illustrations in the popular press. See *Illustrated London News,* 27 April 1861, 390 and 410.

53. The notion of constructed positions of "otherness" is discussed in Lisa Lowe's *Critical Terrains: French and British Orientalisms* (Ithaca, N.Y.: Cornell University Press, 1991).

"True Englishwomen" and "Anglo-Indians": Gender, National Identity, and Feminism in the Victorian Women's Periodical Press

Denise P. Quirk

In 1867, THE *QUEEN, THE LADY'S NEWSPAPER*, A LONDON PUBLICATION, AN-
nounced that "considering . . . that there are few families indeed of
which some members are not in India, it is singular that there
should exist . . . so great ignorance with regard to that vast portion
of our empire." For those unable to gain "personal knowledge" of
India, the *Queen* would strive to supply it, stretching women's imaginations beyond domestic shores while reinforcing their Englishness.[1] Amid the articles and advice columns on English social,
cultural, and domestic life, the *Queen* both addressed Englishwomen
living throughout the empire and included articles on colonial people, places, societies, and cultures.

What I call a colonial circuitry of people, practices, and goods between Britain and India and the colonies provided a material and
discursive framework for Victorian patterns of national identity formation. The Victorian women's periodical press played an important role in this circuitry by creating a virtual community of
participants and readers that linked—and paradoxically distinguished—colonial society in India and Victorian society in England
as it produced a shared national (imperial) identity.[2] In the 1860s
and 1870s—that is, in the period between the Indian Mutiny and
the onset of British "high imperialism"—hundreds of articles on
the empire appeared in mainstream women's periodicals and wom-
en's rights journals.[3] The women's periodical press educated multiple female constituencies on their relationship to empire and to
colonized peoples and imperial products—women who would go to
India or other colonies to live, women who would go to visit, and
women who would never leave British shores but who would instead
receive and adapt the products and culture of empire to new performances of English womanhood.

167

Contradictions in English national identity resulted from shifting racial, cultural, and geographic boundaries in the 1860s and 1870s. Periodicals were performative sites in the formation of English and colonial "British" identities that were changing in this period because of the formalization of empire, contested theories of "race" circulating at the time of Darwin, the rise of new feminist claims about women's subjectivity, and shifts in consumer culture. A key tension formed around questions of authenticity and artifice, the "naturalness" of gender, and explicitly contextualized performances of national (imperial) identity.

India had changed hands from the East India Company to the British Crown in 1858, and a growing administrative and legal network increased the number of English people living in India, diversifying the colonial society of "Anglo-Indians," as Britons living in India were called. In the nineteenth century, the term *Anglo-Indian* referred to British people living in India, not to people of mixed Indian and British parentage. Increasingly toward the end of the century, *Anglo-Indian* was often reserved for British men who were in India as part of official society—that is, attached to the upper ranks of civil or military service—and by extension their families; thus, not all English people in India were considered Anglo-Indians, a term also marked by class.[4] In the 1860s and 1870s, as white Englishwomen began going to India in larger numbers than before, Anglo-Indian women's experiences and debates about Anglo-Indian identity became part of the colonial circuitry explored in the pages of the women's press.

In this chapter, I examine women's periodicals as performative artifacts; that is, I argue that Victorian notions of race, gender, and nation conceived of and transmitted through the periodical press produced performances of national identity for readers, rather than merely reflecting already existent ideologies.[5] The recurrent format combined with the serial nature of periodicals underscores the dual, and potentially subversive, ability of periodicals to offer readers both familiarity and change. Thus the format, content, and circulation of the periodical press allowed Victorian women to imagine themselves as part of a national community outside the confines of domestic space (and the shores of England) and as actors in historical time; new locations in time and space for women. Unlike the images in men's and boys' literature, those of empire in the women's press were more subtle and diffuse, yet nonetheless effective in (re)defining Englishwomen's national identity within what Mrinhalini Sinha has called an "imperial social formation."[6]

PERIODICALS, NATIONAL IDENTITY, AND FEMINISM

National identity in the representational economy of Victorian women's periodicals was constructed as a racialized identity through descriptions and illustrations of cultural artifacts and through narratives that ritualized social practices. Situated amid the *Queen*'s fashion plates in the 1860s and 1870s were illustrations of various regional, national, and racial "types." Differentiation of "race" in the accompanying text often turned as much on details of "costume" as on physical attributes.[7] The interest in costume in these ethnographic "scenes" cannot be reduced simply to the visual rhetoric of a fashion magazine. How these representations elided physical and cultural markers of national identity exemplifies the contested theories of Victorian racial discourse circulating at the time. Although Darwinian biologism was gaining ascendancy, cultural markers and allegiances were still considered "racial" determinants.[8] Because in the periodicals there were strong semiotic similarities among illustrations of idealized English life, examples of Parisian haute couture, and ethnic or racial "types," *English*women as representatives of nation and race, too, were acknowledged to be *in* costume, to be performing, even as their bodily features marked them as English.

The generic format of women's periodicals, with its juxtaposition of news and fiction, work and leisure, fashion and reform, produced further an English femininity that was once classifiable *and* variable—a woman could remake herself, and indeed was required to do so as she performed the different roles that headed the columns of the *Queen*: "housewife," "gardener," "society figure," "tourist," and "worker." The attention in the women's periodical press to the various roles women might be expected to play led as well to a concern about artificiality—the ability to put on a face, to play a part—and this concern with artifice versus "authenticity" was also reflected in and constituted by the women's press.[9] The very form and content of women's periodicals and thus their attempt to reach many types of women always included in their pages a deconstruction of the stereotype of the unified white, middle-class Victorian woman, even while they put forth a normative figure. As Margaret Beetham has argued in her study of nineteenth-century women's periodicals, "The 'domestic woman' of the magazine was both as central and as potentially unstable a figure as her counterpart, the self-made man."[10] Part of this instability, I contend, resulted from the appearance in the late 1850s of arguments for women's social, political, and economic rights in specialized periodicals written by and for women. Feminist editors and writers were able to appropriate images of English womanhood as they used the press to disseminate their ideas, at times strategically deploying dominant ideologies, at times resisting them, and at others reproducing them.

The emergence of a women's public culture in the 1850s and 1860s—signified most importantly by the beginning of a distinctly feminist press—was critical in the shaping not only of the women's movement but also of the broader imaginings of gender, race, and national identity. The contemporaneous occurrence of the British feminist campaign for a Married Women's Property Act in 1854 followed by the founding of a feminist press in 1856 and the Indian Mutiny of 1857–58 heightened the tensions around gender, class, and race in white, masculinist claims for imperial cultural authority. The feminist *English Woman's Journal*, founded in 1858, and its successors challenged not only the idea of "woman" but also the idea of "Englishness."[11] As Englishwomen began to make public claims for work, education, property, and suffrage rights, they called into question the naturalized conflation of women's "nature" with traditional women's roles. Adopting the masculine ideal of the "self-made" man popular at mid-century, feminists encouraged women to aspire to autonomy through the "self-help" model as presented in the feminist press and even created employment societies to provide women with opportunities to enact that model.[12] These images of "strong-minded" women challenged the predominant ideal of "domestic" Englishwomen exemplified by, among other cultural forms, the best-selling women's periodical of the 1850s, the *Englishwoman's Domestic Magazine*.[13] While historians of English feminism have discussed the political intentions of feminists to become enfranchised members of the nation, there has been little attention to the ways in which feminist cultural and social campaigns as produced and reported in the press reconfigured national identity as an effect, if not out of an explicit intent, of new gender performances and the deconstruction of naturalized understandings of gender and national identity.[14]

Representations featured in specialized periodicals of the women's rights movement and reprinted in the *Queen* and other mainstream women's periodicals further complicated redefinitions of British imperial identity. Images of "strong-minded" women appeared alongside discussions of goods and practices that were considered intrinsic to performing as "true Englishwomen" and "Anglo-Indian" women. In the 1860s and 1870s, then, women's periodicals informed women's expectations of and aspirations for roles as participants in domestic and colonial public and private spheres.[15]

COMMODITIES, RACE, AND IMPERIAL IDENTITIES

As the *Queen* led the way among women's periodicals in shifting the image of the ideal Englishwoman from "domestic manager" to "lady-at-leisure" in the 1860s and 1870s, women's periodicals increasingly positioned women as consumers of the empire, often of fashionable clothing and what were highlighted as "exotic" goods in the numerous advertisements for silks, Indian shawls, and porcelains. The women's periodical press thus incorporated readers at home into the imperial economy, as descriptions of foodstuffs, garments, rugs, and luxurious or necessary fabrics created greater demand for such goods. Articles on spectacles and exhibitions around England reinforced that demand. For example, an article in the *Queen* about the Indian department at the 1871 International Exhibition not only encouraged specular appreciation for the "beautiful or curious specimens" of "the gorgeousness of Oriental taste" but incited readers to regard the textiles on display as potential "useful and graceful additions" to English homes and wardrobes. India, the "noblest of our possessions" according to a writer in the *Queen*, could be brought home in the guise of transportable material possessions. But the empire's goods could not simply be added to the English lifestyle; for if they could, the naturalized impermeability of national identity would prove penetrable. Instead, noting that Indian shawls and scarves had become "familiar and popular," the writer assures readers that ". . . there is no good reason why other [things] should not be *adapted* to our use" (my emphasis).[16]

Women's periodicals not only presented the editors' and contributors' material on the empire to readers but also created a community of readers addressed by each other. The *Queen, Englishwoman's Domestic Magazine,* and the feminist *Englishwoman's Review* and *Victoria Magazine* were all available in India and various other parts of the empire, creating opportunities for readers to participate in British imperial culture. In various columns in the *Queen* and the *Englishwoman's Domestic Magazine,* readers swapped queries, recipes, advice, goods, and services, indicating that many readers had firsthand knowledge of colonial experience. Empire added an "exoticism" to the "Personal" column: in addition to items of concerts, university appointments, and publications at home and abroad, from India and Africa came accounts of interracial marriages, elephant acci-

dents, Anglo-Indian balls, railway wrecks, and boating mishaps.[17]
"Notes and Queries on Dress" and "The Tourist" columns in the
Queen often carried requests for advice on what clothing to pack for
visiting or taking up residence in India or the West Indies, indicating
how well traveled many of the readers were. The requests ranged
from interest in the appropriate type and weight of material for winter temperatures in northern Bengal or Madras to concern for dress
"suitable to wear at Calcutta for receiving calls, &c., before going up
the country to a station," implying that the writer fully expected
other readers not only to be familiar with the demands of climate
but also with the requirements of the social environment.[18] Women
readers and contributors supplied advice about what items were essential and information about where to purchase them and how
much to expect to pay. One enterprising reader suggested that
women who returned from India use their experience to establish
themselves as "buying agents" for women caught abroad without
"necessary" English goods.[19]

Representations of colonial life refigured performances of English national identity, and women's periodicals provided the means
for enacting new everyday practices. Articles such as an 1869 "Conversazione" in the *Englishwoman's Domestic Magazine* outlined the
ways to apportion "necessary" English materials within the 336-
pound baggage allotment permitted on the P&O steamer line that
transported most Englishwomen to India. Such articles detailed the
types and quantities of clothes to bring; what items could be bought
in India and what needed to be brought from England; what kinds
of luggage to use; what foods to bring for the voyage.[20] These elaborate lists and carefully plotted details signify that Englishwomen
could transport their cultural, material connection to their Englishness, to a racialized identity constructed through dress and food,
with them as they went out to the colonies. Women's periodicals
constructed the possibility that the fashionable middle-class white
Englishwomen was transferable to a colonial landscape; the *Queen*
and the *Englishwoman's Domestic* offered both instructions and, in
their dress patterns, the literal trappings for carrying out some of
those instructions.[21] Women were reminded that "It is most desirable to have things for India made in the latest fashion. The toilette
of new arrivals are eagerly scanned by old residents, and everybody
naturally likes to make a good first impression."[22] For further reference, these periodicals carried advertisements for the various versions of *Indian Outfits,* a popular manual for living in the colonies
produced and revised a dozen times from the 1860s into the twentieth century.[23] The expectations were that new arrivals in India would

be on display for their ability both to fit into British colonial society
with the appropriate trappings and to infuse that society with fresh
cultural materials and ideas from home.

Articles in the women's periodical press further conflated cultural
markers of national identity with race in their concern over the effect of climate and contact with "native" Indians on white Englishwomen in India. One writer, on meeting an Englishwoman who had
lived a few months in India, noted the "havoc" wrecked on her: "A
blooming and beauteous bride who arrives at Calcutta or Madras
with rosy cheeks and a rich supply of golden locks, will be converted
in a year or so into a melancholy object of contemplation—pale as
the lily or yellow as the buttercup, the rich tresses diminished to a
few corkscrew tendrils, . . . the rounded limbs metamorphosed into
drumsticks, decorated with festoons of limp flesh."[24] The writer deployed a common explanation that the climate was inhospitable to
the "English race," and his suggested cure was a visit to a British hill
station in India or to somewhere in Europe. It was not simply the
cooler climate of the hill stations or Europe that would presumably
restore his female friend, but the comforts of familiar cultural surroundings.

The suggestion that Englishwomen who languished in the dusty
plains stations where they were in close contact to "real" India could
be returned to the shining hair and rosy cheeks of English womanhood fits in with two contemporaneous Victorian notions of race.
One notion incorporated the racialized discourse of hair type and
skin color with belief in climatic determinism. The other notion that
was much in currency in the mid-nineteenth century, as George
Watson noted, was the belief that "race is more often a matter of
cultural affinity and allegiance."[25] Illustrations and descriptions of
colonial life in the Victorian women's press were thus bound up in
ideas that cultural practice defined race despite the circulating theories of scientific racism.

Bringing home materials from India suggests a similar transfer-
ability of "Anglo-Indian" identity; however, looking at these ex-
changes in the context of periodical articles on imperial goods, it is
evident that the cultural valences of goods from the empire worked
differently in the metropole. Nupur Chaudhuri has argued that the
"Exchange" columns of the *Queen* and the *Englishwoman's Domestic
Magazine* were a means by which Englishwomen returning from
India contributed to importing imperial culture into Britain, as well
as establishing "a mutually beneficial economic system outside the
mainstream economic structure" among memsahibs in India and
Englishwomen at home. She has tracked the introduction of Indian

jewelry and shawls into the wardrobes of the wealthy, as well as curry and rice into household of many classes, through the "Exchange" columns of these two journals from 1860 to 1876.[26] But what can also be seen in women's periodicals is that goods from India helped Anglo-Indian women back in England to maintain connections to their own experiences as "Anglo-Indians." At the same time, as Indian items became desirable markers of middle- and upper-class wealth and taste for Englishwomen at home who could afford to purchase them, imperial goods also worked to display returning Anglo-Indian women's experience, riches, and worldliness, providing these women with cultural capital as privileged "Englishwomen" when they returned to England.

ENGLISHNESS, GENDER, AND IMPERIAL ENCOUNTERS

These cultural signifiers of Englishness featured as well in fictional narratives, news reports, and letters about Anglo-Indians in the women's press. Women's periodicals, however, also circulated images of Englishwomen in India and in England whose interest in the empire was not defined by consumerism or attachment to a male colonial figure. The women's periodical press often reprinted articles on Englishwomen's efforts to improve domestic and imperial social conditions. The intertextual dialogue of mainstream women's and feminist periodicals thus complicated the formation of imperial identities as it offered alternative scripts for the gender performance expected from Englishwomen in India.

Images of Anglo-Indians already in the cultural imaginary had been shaped in large part by George Atkinson in his 1859 book of caricatures, *Curry and Rice,* and by Florence Marryat in her 1868 memoir, *Gup: Sketches of Anglo-Indian Life and Character.* Each of these books of "sketches" depicted the various "types" present in colonial society—colonial officer, local magistrate, clergymen, planter, and their wives—in satiric terms. Anglo-Indian women were usually sketched as having become vain, frivolous, and indolent from life in India. These caricatures appeared after the Indian Mutiny, which had shaken the early nineteenth-century British belief in Anglicizing Indians through the introduction of English ways, and there was a concerted effort, often with guidelines for Englishwomen gleaned from the pages of the women's press, to widen the distance between English and Indian societies, even as projects to educate a male Indian middle class for the civil service were to continue.

Significant in this regard is a serialized fictional account of English life in India published in the *Englishwoman's Domestic Magazine* that presented a more complex—and ambivalent—depiction of Anglo-Indian society than the books of caricatures, suggesting that views of Anglo-Indian society in the cultural imaginary of the 1860s and 1870s were shifting. The protagonist is a clergyman's daughter whose marriage to an English aristocrat is thwarted by the man's father and who is sent off to India to live with an uncle until she finds a more suitable husband. Her voyage preparation includes so much clothing that she declares, "One might have fancies that I was bound for a barbarous land where European clothing was unprocurable."[27] On the voyage out, a "radical" military officer provides her and readers with details of history and geography and stands in counterpoint to the other passengers. The protagonist is tormented by the boorish wife of a lower military officer who inundates her with Anglo-Indian vocabulary and snobberies, and she is subjected to snubs by higher officers when her status as a relative of a tea planter, rather than of a civil service or military officer, is revealed. Yet all is well when she is warmly greeted by her good-hearted uncle who treats his Indian workers well and hires for them a visiting doctor and resident schoolmaster. The uncle is considered "clever" in his business dealings but also sensitive to his position as a subject of the ruling nation: "[H]e was not one of those who systematically run down and abuse the natives. . . . He was always ready to make allowances for a conquered race at variance with their conquerors on every essential point." The uncle notes that missionaries and the British government of India fear full-scale English colonization because "[w]ith all their assumed arrogance and self-assurance, they know right well that if ever an English public is constituted in Bengal, the reign of incompetency and favouritism will come to an end. And then what is to become of them and theirs?"[28] In this tale, readers are thus given a familiar picture of the hierarchies of colonial society and a critique of those hierarchies.

In 1868, the feminist *Englishwoman's Review* featured a review essay that contrasted Florence Marryat's *Gup* to Mary Carpenter's *Six Months in India*. Mary Carpenter was a reformer of female prisons and ragged schools in England who turned her attention to Indian women's education. Carpenter's visits to India in 1866 and 1875 captured the attention of both the feminist and women's press, as empire loomed increasingly larger in the cultural imaginary.[29] *Six Months in India*, a chronicle of Carpenter's 1866 trip, includes a critique of Anglo-Indian life and suggestions for ways that Englishwomen might involve themselves in Indian society. The reviewer in the *Englishwoman's Review* uses Carpenter's book to refute Marryat's

caricature of Anglo-Indian women as being representative of their
"nature." Carpenter, the reviewer claims, offers a reformist view that
Englishwomen in India could engage themselves by taking up teaching or nursing, or at least could do their part to resist the prejudices
of Anglo-Indian society.[30]

The women's and feminist press also reported on imperial encounters between Englishwomen and Indians in England that were
part of the colonial circuitry. In November 1870, the *Victoria Magazine* reported extensively on the visit to England of Keshub Chunder
Sen, a leader of the progressive Brahmo Samaj movement in India.
Some historians, including Barbara Ramusack and Antoinette Burton, have suggested that the reforms of Indian women's education
initiated by Keshub Chunder Sen and carried out by Mary Carpenter and other British feminists simply replaced one patriarchal system with another and shored up white women's privilege in the
empire.[31] What is missing in this assessment, however, is an acknowl-
edgment that although the alliance of English feminists and male
Indian reformers did not subvert imperial ideology (especially since
this alliance was enacted within a gender and racial order that at
times elevated English feminine gender because of its visible but
"unmarked" whiteness over Indian masculinity), the very reportage
of that alliance in the women's press did suggest possible transgressions of imperial ideology: indeed such transgressions did occur.
These possibilities were shaped in part through feminists' trans-
gressive gender performance as they involved themselves in imperial
practices and with colonized peoples (other than servants) without
the mediation of British men.[32]

The web of context within which mid-Victorian feminist activities
were represented in the women's periodical press produced what
anthropologists John and Jean Comaroff call "ambiguous processes" consisting of "continuous activity—activity that, because it is
always a product of complex experience and contradictory conditions, simultaneously reproduces *and* transforms the world."[33] Such
potential transformations were made visible by the frequent accounts in the *Victoria Magazine, Englishwoman's Review,* and *Queen* of
the National Indian Association (NIA), founded in 1870 in Bristol
by Mary Carpenter, at Keshub Chunder Sen's suggestion, to encourage knowledge of India in England. The NIA's domestic goal was to
"promote friendly intercourse with native gentlemen now in England, and to introduce them to a knowledge of such institutions in
our country as may benefit theirs."[34] By the late 1870s, the NIA was
also supporting Indian women who came to study in England. Accounts of the proceedings of the association prompted letters from

readers of both the women's and feminist press expressing a growing desire for becoming "better acquainted with India" and learning "something of [India's] real condition."[35] In these accounts,
however, feminists were also presented as encouraging readers to
grant Indian visitors access to information about England, particularly about English home life, thus opening a channel for Indians to
gain knowledge of imperial metropolitan society.[36] Suggestions for
such cultural exchange were contrary to the advice often given to
wives of colonial agents elsewhere in the women's press to uphold
"their husbands' [imperial] interests in the subcontinent" by creating what Nupur Chaudhuri terms "an ethnocentric 'home' environment" and maintaining a social distance from "real" India.[37] The
feminist interventions in imperial encounters in England thus traversed the gap that Anglo-Indians so carefully maintained between
Indians and English people in India.[38]

Despite the *Queen*'s seeming endorsement of the NIA's domestic
work, other accounts in the *Queen* exhibit tension about the potential disruptions of the imperial social order because of women's entrance into public culture and the effect calls for cultural exchange
might have in India. In 1871, the *Queen* paraphrased two letters published in the Anglo-Indian *Homeward Mail* on "English Ladies in
India" signed by "One of Them." The *Queen* commented that the
writer "complains" that while her girlhood companions "in the
West advance and improve," Anglo-Indians "stand still or fall back."
She claims that it was "a rare thing" to find an Englishwoman in
India "who has cared to interest herself in the history, past or present, of the country"; unlike women in England involved in the wom-
en's movement, "[g]enerations of Englishwomen leave the country
without showing any feeling or sympathy for their sex." Thus, the
Queen notes, the writer encourages women in India to take up "en-
deavours for the benefit of native women" rather than rely on prejudices.[39] Recommendations by Englishwomen in India that they
become involved with Indian women (beyond their children's
nurses), as we have seen, would have been at odds with official and
customary relations between Anglo-Indian women and Indians. The
Queen's excerpt tries to resolve this tension through a slippage between the need for Englishwomen in India to pursue the Victorian
ideals of self-improvement commensurate with that of their sisters
back home and the idea that this self-improvement includes reform
work on behalf of Indian women.[40]

Such slippage mirrors attempts in the mainstream women's press
to elide feminist activities in England aimed at educating and employing middle-class women with "respectable" philanthropic

schemes for the poor. This elision attempted to mitigate feminists' radical calls for social transformation by incorporating the new performance of middle-class women's public work into existing forms of domestic femininity. But although contemporaries and historians sometimes argue that feminist work *was* simply an outgrowth of charity work or concern for the poor, it is important to remember that middle-class mid-Victorian feminism ushered in the start of a women's public culture—largely institutionalized through the periodical press—in which (white) women spoke for themselves. The most vocal "women's-rights women" who were crossing gender boundaries by making themselves seen and heard through claims to cultural authority in the periodical press and through public performances of "self-help" autonomy in the streets, on the speaking platform, and in the workplace could not be integrated into existing gender schemes; these women were often criticized as being unnaturally "strong-minded," even "epicene."[41]

Perhaps most interesting in this light is the *Queen*'s selective paraphrase of these letters. In the *Homeward Mail*, the "English Lady in India" spells out her concern that women in England "are growing stronger, nobler, more intellectual, more fitted to take rank intellectually, side by side with men," while Anglo-Indian women are left in stasis. The original letter notes further: "[O]ur contemporaries in England, who are now intelligent and highly educated woman, tak[e] interest in matters far above the ordinary domestic interests of women, and [are] able to discuss politics and other questions of weight and interest with an intelligence and observation that show them to be well informed." The writer goes on, admonishing Englishwomen in India for not "car[ing] to inform themselves on the subject of political interest that is before their very eyes."[42] The *Queen*'s paraphrase omits the writer's original call for Anglo-Indian women's greater participation in imperial *politics,* thus suppressing a radical suggestion that Anglo-Indian women cross the boundaries of acceptable gender and racial norms as they were being constructed by the British in England and India.

A fictional tale in the feminist *Victoria Magazine* challenged the boundaries of Anglo-Indian society outright, and, significantly, featured a character who commented on women's rights activities in England. The first-person narrator of "A Story of Anglo-Indian Life at Ahmedabad" decries Anglo-Indians' tendency to "caricature the people a good deal" and the "habit in India to speak disparagingly of the natives, even when in your heart you question the fitness and justice of the prevailing contemptuous estimate of the Hindus' moral and intellectual worth."[43] While the tale deploys some conventional Victorian attitudes toward "native" Indians, the narrator and her party "set about educating ourselves and each other on Indian matters" despite her hosts's derision, and her nuanced descriptions and characterizations refute the negative generalizations used in much writing about India at the time (E. L., 402). Her party stays in the "traveler's bungalow" rather than in the Anglo-Indian hotel and shops in the "native bazaar." The narrator describes in detail the workings of Anglo-Indian society and criticizes the imperial notions that the English must keep their distance from the "native" Indian population (E. L., 407). At one point, an Anglo-Indian character mentions that she has heard "dreadful" news from home: "The way some women have gone in for politics since we left England is quite absurd—ridiculous." The first-person narrator, who is cheerfully described to the Anglo-Indian woman by a companion as "a rabid woman's-rights woman," comes out as the hero of the story as her party moves throughout Anglo-Indian society, constantly pushing the boundaries of what their Anglo-Indian companions deemed appropriate speech and practice.[44]

The writer of "English Ladies in India," among other correspondents and contributors to the women's press, demanded that Anglo-Indian women's performance of femininity include "taking an interest in politics," or educating Indian women for "India's future welfare." Such demands blurred middle-class divisions between public and private spheres seen in typical constructions of idealized Englishwomen. Because of the frequent accounts of feminist activities, women's reform efforts could be construed not only as philanthropic extensions of women's domesticity, but also possibly as "women's-rights," women's "self-help," or "strong-minded" reform efforts. The gender and class order in England and that being established in India as a naturalized colonial manifestation of English national identity was thus threatened.[45]

ANGLO-INDIANS: A DIFFERENT SPECIES?

The ongoing effects of such a juxtaposition of gender performances in the women's and feminist press called into question not only the merits of Anglo-Indian society but also the very meanings of "Englishwoman" and "Anglo-Indian." Throughout the 1870s, articles focusing on which performances of gender and national identity were deemed appropriate in the colonial setting began to be inflected by Darwinism. In 1877, a debate in the pages of the *Queen* exhibited concern over social mixing that echoed fears of racial mixing and was conceptualized in terms of whether Anglo-Indians represented a different "species."[46] At stake in this discussion was the performance of national identity that relied on English gender order, and the effect on Britons' Englishness by life in colonial society.

A letter in the *Queen* in July 1877 noted that since many men sent out to India were younger than those in the past, they arrived without having had "social education in England." They were likely to marry an equally inexperienced partner, and they thus, the writer claims, "see the things from an Anglo-Indian—as opposed to an English—point of view." The writer asserted that unquestionably

> the English is the healthier, the better, and above all, the nobler point of view. Anglo-Indian society is at present in a transition state, and, like all transitions, combines many of the failings both of the old school (who made themselves as Indian as they could) and the new, who try and make themselves in some ways as English, only they do not exactly hit the right way; no doubt they soon will. Meanwhile they remain, and are only, Anglo-Indians.[47]

What then did it mean to "remain" an Anglo-Indian? Here the opposition between *Anglo-Indian* and *English* as well as the slippery use of *Indian* suggest that "Anglo-Indian" was a colonial identity under construction. Spatially and temporally liminal, this colonial identity was not "English"—and not "Indian" in either the sense of an older pattern of English people "going native" ("the old school" "made themselves as Indian as they could") or in the sense of being representative of indigenous culture. In many articles in the women's press, as in the general press, the interpellation *Indian* for Britons suggested the power dynamics in the colonial domination and appropriation of a territory that gives races, or tribes, or nations their names. In the wake of the 1876 formalization of empire as Queen Victoria was named Empress of India, *Anglo-Indian* increasingly referred to members of British official society.[48] Significantly, despite having no official power, wives, daughters, and sisters of British officers embraced the terms *Anglo-Indian* and *Indian*, including a writer in this debate who, because of her location, signed herself "An Indian Lady."

A letter from "An Indian Lady" emphasized that the contingency of being an "Anglo-Indian" meant relocating some familiar social performances to a colonial setting, so that young people's ability to take on "Anglo-Indian" ways may be to the good: "they adapt themselves to the ways best suited to the country, and make themselves at

home in it, as much as is possible to do in a land of exile." Those
who come out at a later age, she continues, "with genuine English
as opposed to Anglo-Indian tastes and views, cannot settle down or
reconcile themselves to circumstances in the same way: they are always pining for home, their clubs, and their daily papers, and English pursuits, and can never get over their contempt for the
natives."[49]

"An Indian Lady's" narrative of Anglo-Indian women's interest
and involvement in European benevolent institutions as well as Indian education schemes also explores the role played by English national identity in the depiction of Anglo-Indian women's activities,
interests, and normative performance of English femininity. She
claims that her narrative proves that "the useful and busy lives led by
many Englishwomen in India" were not exceptional and that "the
proportion of English ladies in India who interest themselves in anything beyond their own household and domestic duties are [sic]
quite as large, if not larger, than among the same class in England."[50] These myriad activities mark Anglo-Indian women as "domestic" yet interested in "benevolent institutions"; there is no hint
of interest in transforming society or women's involvement in politics. She asserts "that the Anglo-Indian view of life can be quite as
healthy as the English, and that we in India are not a distinct species,
but true Englishwomen in the best sense of the term."[51] Another
correspondent seemingly defends this position, recuperating Anglo-
Indian women in familiar English domestic terms, yet the writer
highlights the separateness of British India from England: "It may
be that Anglo-Indian ladies seem vain and frivolous in society; the
peculiar conditions of their lives tend to make them so: but I believe
in no country in the world are to be found such devoted wives and
mothers in private life as these ladies."[52]

Anglo-Indian as a distinct colonial identity that signified *both* "Englishness" *and* "British Indianness" emerged in the 1860s to 1870s
"transitional" period of British imperial culture, influenced by constructions of national identity and gender performance in the wom-
en's periodical press. The emphasis on the questions of identity and
difference seen in the letters in the *Queen* was shaped in part by the
ways in which the women's and feminist press located readers' experience and expectations within a colonial circuit between England
and India. Women's identity in British imperial culture seemed tied
less to an overarching English national identity created through the
general press in the sense of Benedict Anderson's notion that the
nation is an "imagined community," than to specifically contextualized cultural practices circulated through the women's press.[53] Most

of the correspondents in the *Queen* lived mobile lives, uprooted with transfers from colonial post to colonial post; most went out to India with, usually, every intention of returning to England. The claim to the label of Anglo-Indian, however, seemed to return with them. The need to give a new label to English people living in India belies the sense of a fixed Englishness that was carried into the empire.

As the number of Britons in India increased and their individual stays of residence grew longer, colonial social practices became constitutive of boundaries between not just ruler and ruled but also of distinctions within white British colonial society. Numerous studies of the makeup of Indian colonial society give testimony to the phenomenon articulated by Anne Laura Stoler in which "[t]he markers of European identity and the criteria for community membership no longer appear as fixed but emerge as a more obviously fluid, permeable, and historically disputed terrain. The colonial politics of exclusion was contingent on constructing categories. . . . What mattered was not only one's physical properties but who counted as 'European' and by what measure."[54] Building on Stoler's idea of contingent "measures" of Europeanness, I would argue that a crucial measure in the British case was gender performance, particularly for women, whose membership in the nation before women's suffrage and married women's property rights was more social and cultural than political or legal. I suggest further that the "measures" of British imperial community created in women's periodicals through the juxtapositions of representations of empire and of feminist textual and material practices and performances shifted the negotiation of this kind of culturally racialized national identity back to the metropole. Real and imagined boundaries were thus constituted *between* white English identity in the colonies and that at home, as well within Victorian society in England. What resulted, then, was a narrower range of colonial feminine performance that both reinforced Anglo-Indians as a distinct group and, despite the ascendance of biological racism, secured cultural signifiers and national allegiance as potent markers of racialized national identity that could be transferred to the colonies. That is, as English people went out to India and returned, their experiences as "Anglo-Indians," as Britons in India, made legible the white Englishness that was to become the cornerstone of imperial and national identity. The colonial circuitry of people and goods between India and England depicted in the women's press served to suture notions of imperial "Britishness" and national "Englishness" as they made that very suturing visible.

NOTES

I would like to acknowledge my thanks to John Gillis, Bonnie Smith and the members of the Rutgers University European History Seminar, Joy Dixon, and especially Hilary Mason; and to Lisa Merrill whose continuing support, sound advice, and exemplary scholarship inspire every word.

1. "Education of Women in India," *Queen*, 12 October 1867. The *Queen* was founded in 1861 by Samuel and Isabella Beeton, who described it as "not merely a newspaper, though in one shape or other it will contain whatever in the way of news is likely to interest its reader." "Conversazione," *Englishwoman's Domestic Magazine*, September 1861, 264. In 1863, the *Queen* was sold to Harold Cox and merged with *The Lady's Newspaper*. See J. Watkins, "Editing a 'Class' Journal: Four Decades of *The Queen*," *Innovators and Preachers: The Role of the Editor in Victorian England*, ed. Joel Wiener (Westport, Conn.: Greenwood Press, 1985), 186.

2. "Virtual community" is a gloss on Benedict Anderson, *Imagined Communities*, rev. ed. (London: Verso, 1991).

3. This estimate is based on my survey of *Englishwomen's Domestic Magazine*, *Queen*, *Ladies' Treasury*, *Woman's Opinion*, *English Woman's Journal*, *Englishwoman's Review*, *Victoria Magazine*, *Alexandra Magazine*, *Kettledrum*, *Lady's Own Paper*, *Women and Work*, *Work and Leisure*, and *Women's Suffrage Journal*, as part of my research for my dissertation, "The Empire of Opinion: Gender, Feminism and Cultural Authority in Victorian Britain" (in progress).

4. Here I am using "Anglo-Indian" in the nineteenth-century sense, to denote British representatives in India; not until the twentieth century did it refer to people of mixed race. Henry Yule and A. C. Burnell, *Hobson-Jobson*, ed. William Crooke (London: J. Murray, 1903; London: Routledge and Kegan Paul, 1968), 44–45. See also Mrinhalini Sinha, *Colonial Masculinity: The "Manly Englishman" and the "Effeminate Bengali" in the Late Nineteenth Century* (Manchester: Manchester University Press, 1995), 18–19.

5. On theorizing performativity and the performance of everyday life, see Judith Butler, *Gender Trouble* (New York: Routledge, 1990), and *Bodies That Matter* (New York: Routledge, 1994); Michel de Certeau, *The Practice of Everyday Life*, trans. Stephen Rendall (Berkeley and Los Angeles: University of California Press, 1984); Erving Goffman, *The Presentation of Self in Everyday Life* (New York: Anchor, 1959); Della Pollock, ed. *Exceptional Spaces: Essays in Performance and History* (Chapel Hill: University of North Carolina Press, 1998).

6. Sinha, 2. Although recent studies have explored popular culture targeted at male readers and spectators, there are no comparable studies that explore the representations of empire directed toward women; see, for example, John Mackenzie, *Propaganda and Empire* (Manchester: Manchester University Press, 1984), and John Mackenzie, ed., *Imperialism and Popular Culture* (Manchester: Manchester University Press, 1986). Book-length studies of women's periodicals, most notably Margaret Beetham's excellent *"Magazine of Her Own?: Domesticity and Desire in the Woman's Magazine, 1800–1914* (London: Routledge, 1996), do not take into account the effect of either imperialism or feminism in the pages of women's magazines; see also Cynthia White, *Women's Magazines, 1693–1968* (London: Michael Joseph, 1970), and Ros Ballaster, Margaret Beetham, Elizabeth Frazer, and Sandra Hebron, *Women's Worlds: Ideology, Femininity and the Women's Magazine* (London: Macmillan, 1991). Beetham's contribution in this volume and her article "The Reinvention of the English Domestic Woman: Class and 'Race' in the 1890s' Woman's Magazine," *Women's Studies International Forum* 21 (May–June 1998), do focus on imperialism.

7. For example, "Syrian Women," *Queen*, 20 May 1871; "Roumanian Ladies," *Queen*, 17 February 1877, 111; "Women in Turkey," *Queen*, 17 February 1877, 177; "A Coptic Wedding," *Queen*, 6 January 1877; "Oriental Ladies," *Queen*, 23 December 1877.

8. On the complicity of culture in racializing discourse see Robert Young, *Colonial Desire: Hybridity in Theory, Culture and Race* (New York: Routledge, 1995).

9. As Margaret Homans has recently suggested, everyday events and rituals in mid-Victorian England were profoundly staged and consciously designed; women were taught to perform their domestic roles beyond the typical way in which Victorian women learned to be "true" women or subordinated wives. She argues, then, that the resulting "artificiality," the attention to surface and the visible, came to stand for what was argued as natural and authentic. *Royal Representations: Queen Victoria and British Culture, 1837–1876* (Chicago: University of Chicago Press, 1998), 25.

10. Beetham, 59.

11. The *English Woman's Journal* was founded by Barbara Leigh Smith and Bessie Rayner Parkes and edited by Parkes and Matilda Hays. It has its origins in the *Waverley*, which Parkes, Leigh Smith, and Hays began writing for in 1856. The definitive article on the *EJW* to date is Jane Rendall, "'A Moral Engine'? Feminism, Liberalism and the *English Woman's Journal*," in *Equal or Different: Women's Politics 1800–1914*, ed. Jane Rendall (London: Basil Blackwell, 1987), 112–38. I am indebted to Jane for graciously entertaining an early exposition of my views of the *EWJ* and her willingness to share her enthusiasm, ideas, and archival material on Parkes. Successors to the *English Woman's Journal* were the *Victoria Magazine*, the *Alexandra Magazine*, and the *Englishwoman's Review*. Appearing quarterly, then monthly, from 1866 through 1910, the *Englishwoman's Review* became an important vehicle of the women's movement. While it has been treated in historical literature as if it follows the *English Woman's Journal* ideologically, it took a much more conservative turn under the editorship of Jessie Boucherett. The *Alexandra Magazine* was Parkes's short-lived (1864–65) successor to the *English Woman's Journal*. A monthly edited by Emily Faithfull, the *Victoria* was modeled on *Macmillan's Magazine* and *Cornhill Magazine*. Emily Davies, Family Chronicle, March 1863, Davies Collection, Girton College, Cambridge.

12. Samuel Smiles, *Self-Help* (London: J. Murray, 1859); on some of the effects of this concept in the imperial "civilizing mission," see Michael Adas, *Machines as the Measure of Men: Science, Technology, and Ideologies of Western Dominance* (Ithaca: Cornell University Press, 1989).

13. The *Englishwoman's Domestic Magazine* was founded by Samuel and Isabella Beeton in 1852. A two-penny monthly, its circulation more or less remained stable throughout the run; in 1862, it claimed a readership of sixty thousand. Richard D. Altick, *The English Common Reader: "Social History of the Mass Reading Public, 1800–1900* (Chicago: University of Chicago Press, 1957), appendix b. See also H. Montgomery Hyde, *Mr. and Mrs. Beeton* (London: George G. Harrap, 1951).

14. I develop this analysis of the mid-Victorian women's movement in "The Empire of Opinion." These same historians of English feminism also tend to see the mid-Victorians feminists as being interested only in "practical" work, a characterization I challenge. See, for example, Philippa Levine, *Victorian Feminism 1850–1900* (London: Hutchison, 1987); Jane Rendall, *The Origins of Modern Feminism: Women in Britain, France and the United States* (New York: Shocken, 1984); and Antoinette Burton, *Burdens of History: British Feminists, Indian Women, and Imperial Culture, 1865–1915* (Chapel Hill: University of North Carolina Press, 1994); Barbara Caine, *English Feminism, 1780–1980* (New York: Oxford University Press, 1998).

15. The editors of the *Queen* stated that "women's rights" was a subject about which they would "carefully note the discussions which appear in relation to it"; Rev. of *The Englishwoman's Review: A Journal of Woman's Work, Queen,* 17 November 1866, 347.

16. "Indian Textile Fabrics in the International Exhibition," *Queen,* 9 September 1871, 162.

17. "Personal," *Queen,* 2 September 1871, 157.

18. "A.B.C.," "Notes and Queries on Dress: Northern Bengal," *Queen,* 5 January 1871, 7; "The Tourist: Bungalows," *Queen,* 24 November 1875, 360.

19. Punjaub, "The Work-Table: Remunerative Employment for Ladies: Lady Agents for India," *Queen,* 24 November 1877, 345.

20. "Conversazione: Hints for India," *Englishwoman's Domestic Magazine,* March 1869, 168. See also "Indian Outfits, Wedding Trousseaux, and Baby Linen," *Englishwoman's Domestic Magazine,* February 1870; Viatrix, "An Outfit for India," *Queen,* 17 November 1866, 355; "Outfit for Central India," *Queen,* 19 August 1871; "Indian Outfit," *Queen,* 31 October 1871, 259.

21. "Conversazione," *Englishwoman's Domestic Magazine,* January 1872, 64.

22. "Dress for India," *Queen,* 3 September 1870, 161.

23. "Conversazione," *Englishwoman's Domestic Magazine,* May 1868, 278; "Indian Outfits," *Englishwoman's Domestic Magazine,* July 1869, 56. See, for example, Maude Bradshaw, *Indian Outfits* (London, 1876); *Indian Outfits: A Short Sketch of the Requirements of the Voyage to, and Residence in, the Presidencies* (London, 1882).

24. "Yankee Ladies," *Queen,* 26 August 1865, 140–41.

25. George Watson, *The English Ideology: Studies in the Language of Victorian Politics* (London: Allen Lane, 1973), 200, quoted in Jennifer DeVere Brody, *Impossible Purities: Blackness, Femininity, and Victorian Culture* (Durham, N.C.: Duke University Press, 1998), 156.

26. Nupur Chaudhuri, "Shawls, Jewelry, Curry, and Rice in Victorian Britain," in *Western Women and Imperialism: Complicity and Resistance,* ed. Nupur Chaudhuri and Margaret Strobel (Bloomington: Indiana University Press, 1992), 232.

27. "Thrice Wedded and Never a Wife," *Englishwoman's Domestic Magazine,* March 1874, 124. The serialized tale ran from late 1873 to early 1875.

28. Ibid., June 1874, 291 and 294.

29. "Education of Women in India," *Queen,* 13 April 1867, 295; "Education in India," *Queen,* 12 October 1867, 271; "Social Science at Belfast: Miss Carpenter's "Address on 'Female Education in India,'" *Englishwoman's Review,* October 1867, 316–20; Rev. of *Six Months in India,* by Mary Carpenter, *Victoria Magazine* 10 (April 1868): 573; Mary Carpenter, "Female Education in India," *Queen,* 11 April 1877.

30. Mary Carpenter, *Six Months in India* (London: Longmans, Green, 1868); Mrs. Bayle Bernard, "The Position of Women in India," *Englishwoman's Review,* July 1868, 471–82.

31. Barbara Ramusack, "Cultural Missionaries, Maternal Imperialists, Feminist Allies: British Women Activists in India, 1865–1945," in *Western Women and Imperialism,* 123; Burton, *Burdens of History.*

32. See for example, Deirdre David, *Rule Britannia: Women, Empire, and Victorian Writing* (Ithaca, N.Y.: Cornell University Press, 1995), 119–30.

33. John and Jean Comaroff, *Ethnography and the Historical Imagination* (Boulder, Colo.: Westview Press, 1992), 38. Arguably in this case, feminists aided in the establishment of the Indian National Congress: the Society for Aiding Social Progress in India, formed in London by Elizabeth Manning, included Indian men on its executive committee from its inception. At least one initial and continuing member, Da-

dabhai Nairoji, was later a founding member of the Indian National Congress. Committee Book 3, Indian Association collection, Bristol and London, Eur. MSS F1471, OIOC, British Library.

34. "Farewell Soirée for Baboo Keshub Chunder Sen," *Victoria Magazine* 15 (October 1870): 579; "Social Reform in India," *Englishwoman's Review,* October 1871, 289–92. "The Indian Association," *Englishwoman's Review,* April 1871, 85, 87–88. In this and other articles, readers were encouraged to go to India, if properly trained, as teachers and medical practitioners. See, for example, "Medical Education of Women in India," *Victoria Magazine* 16 (April 1871): 563–64; "Hospital in Bhopal," *Victoria Magazine* 32 (April 1879): 401.

35. Untitled, *Queen,* 16 September 1871, 177.

36. In some ways, this channel disrupted, if not reversed, the assumption of a one-directional "production of certain kinds of knowledge" between England and India that Thomas Richards has argued "was in fact constitutive of the extension of certain forms of power," and some historians have asserted lay behind feminist interest in India. Thomas Richards, "Archive and Utopia," *Representations* 37 (Winter 1992): 105; see, for example Burton, *Burdens of History,* 100.

37. Chaudhuri, "Shawls," 242. Chaudhuri explores this idea further in "Memsahibs and Their Servants in Nineteenth-Century India," *Women's History Review* 3, no. 4 (1994): 549–62.

38. "Events of the Quarter: Social Reform in India," *Englishwoman's Review,* October 1871, 290.

39. "Gazette des Dames," *Queen,* 7 October 1871, 224.

40. This is the predominant reading Burton, *Burdens of History,* gives of articles on Indian women in the *Englishwoman's Review.* Burton revises her thesis somewhat in *At the Heart of the Empire* (Berkeley: University of California Press, 1998). My conclusions rest on an analysis not only of those articles but also on the context of those articles and their interrelationship with the issues and operations of the feminist press within the women's press. In "The Empire of Opinion," I contend that a focus on the effects of the intertextual dialogue produced in the press and less on the presumed intentionality of the feminists writing in the press may yield a richer and more fruitful understanding of the place of feminism in Victorian domestic and imperial culture. In exploring the more complex relationships among Englishwomen and Indians, I have been influenced by Kumkum Sangari and Sudesh Vaid, eds., *Recasting Women: Essays in Indian Colonial History* (New Brunswick: Rutgers University Press, 1990); Inderpal Grewal, *Home and Harem: Nation, Gender, Empire, and the Cultures of Travel* (London: University of Leicester Press, 1996); and Kumari Jayawardena, *The White Woman's Other Burden* (New York: Routledge, 1996).

41. Eliza Lynn Linton, "Epicene Women," *Saturday Review* (1868); reprinted in Eliza Lynn Linton, *The Girl of the Period and Other Social Essays* (London: R. Bentley, 1883).

42. "English Ladies in India (By One of Them)," *Homeward Mail* [Allahabad], 23 September 1871, 1069.

43. E. L., "A Story of Anglo-Indian Life at Ahmedabad," Part 2, *Victoria Magazine* 29 (September 1877): 401; the story ran from August to October. The narrative continues in "At Bombay: Sequel to a Story of Anglo-Indian Life," *Victoria Magazine* 30, running from November 1877 to January 1878.

44. E. L., "A Story of Anglo-Indian Life at Ahmedabad," Part 3, *Victoria Magazine* 29 (October 1877): 490.

45. Margaret Macmillan notes categorically, "They [women] were not expected to take too close an interest in India; that would have been unseemly. They did not

carry out charitable works among the Indians because that was the sort of thing missionaries—generally regarded with some disdain—did. And the Indians themselves might get upset, which was the last thing the Raj wanted." *Women of the Raj* (London: Thames and Hudson, 1988), 113.

46. The debate runs in "The Boudoir" column of the *Queen* from June through September 1877. The "species" quote is from An Indian Lady, "Anglo-Indians," *Queen*, 21 July 1877, 55.

47. The Writer of the Article, "Anglo-Indian Society," *Queen*, 7 July 1877, 6.

48. David Cannadine, "The Context, Performance and Meaning of Ritual: The British Monarchy and the 'Invention of Tradition,' c. 1820–1977," in *The Invention of Tradition,* ed. Eric Hobsbawm and Terence Ranger (Cambridge: Cambridge University Press, 1983), 101–164.

49. An Indian Lady, "Anglo-Indians," *Queen*, 21 July 1877, 54.

50. Ibid., *Queen*, 23 June 1877, 459.

51. Ibid., *Queen*, 21 July 1877, 55.

52. The Exile (India), *Queen*, 1 September 1877, 143.

53. In "Empire of Opinion," I directly engage with Anderson's idea of the nation as an "imagined community" in the context of British imperialism, exploring how in the Victorian period women were included (and excluded) from that community, how gender (imbricated with class and race) plays out in the textual and material processes that create the imagined community of the nation, and how Victorian feminism and the women's press affected the conception of nation and empire.

54. Anne Laura Stoler, "Carnal Knowledge and Imperial Power," in *Feminism & History,* ed. Joan Scott (New York: Oxford University Press, 1998), 211, 212; see also Stoler, *Race and the Education of Desire: Foucault's* History of Sexuality *and the Colonial Order of Things* (Durham, N.C.: Duke University Press, 1995). Thanks to Dwight Conquergood for helping me refine my interpretation of the cultural work performed by women's periodicals in light of Stoler's arguments.

The Empire Writes Back: Native Informant Discourse in the Victorian Press

Julie F. Codell

> It is in the emergence of the interstices—the overlap and dis-
> placement of domains of difference—that the intersubjective
> and collective experiences of *nationness*, community interest, or
> cultural value are negotiated. . . . How are subjects formed 'in-
> between', or in excess of, the sum of the 'parts' of difference
> (usually intoned as race/class/gender, etc.)? How do strategies
> of representation or empowerment come to be formulated in
> the competing claims of communities where, despite shared his-
> tories of deprivation and discrimination, the exchange of values,
> meanings and priorities may not always be collaborative and dia-
> logical, but may be profoundly antagonistic, conflictual and even
> incommensurable?
>
> —Homi K. Bhabha, *The Location of Culture*

NATIVE INFORMANCY AND MULTIPLE IDENTITIES

MUCH COLONIAL AND POSTCOLONIAL THEORIZING IS ROOTED IN THE
assumption that the Other was denied the opportunity to speak but
was instead "spoken for" by the colonizer. However, at the turn of
the last century leaders of colonized countries in the British Empire
published essays in periodicals,[1] had their lives described in biographies, their bodies represented in photographs and their public
speeches published, sometimes in England, sometimes in their native countries. Between 1840 and 1901 there were over one hundred
articles by sixty authors from India, Afghanistan, Iran, Egypt, China,
Japan, Turkey, Armenia, Sudan, and South Africa—both Zulu and
Boer. While not all these countries were British colonies, they all felt
the effects of British imperialism.

The discourses of native informants bring into question our assumed ideas about national identity, "Englishness," and the content
of "Victorian" culture. Intervening in always already Orientalist discourses and desiring to reach a British audience, these authors
carved out a language of rationality, resistance, and authority. As na-

tive informants—aristocratic or bourgeois elites—they appropriated and deployed European political and social rhetoric to seek approval and cooperation from their British readers to affect policy changes. Sometimes in conflict with indigenous subaltern forces, they often represented their "people" in Orientalist terms as anti-progressive, ignorant, and superstitious. However, they were just as often sympathetic to subaltern resistance and used this real and imagined threat to construct their own subjectivities between Anglicized hegemony and indigenous subalternity.

"Native informant" has often been applied pejoratively to those who sided with the colonizer and failed to identify with subaltern interests. Gayatri Spivak presents the dilemma of the native informant "treated as the objective evidence of the founding of so-called sciences like ethnography, ethno-linguistics, comparative religion, and so on" who "seems not to have a problematic self . . . the self of the Other is authentic without a problem, naturally available to all kinds of complications" (Spivak, 1990, 66). Native informants writing in the British press spoke their identities as deeply problematic, complex, and hybrid.

As Mrinalini Sinha and others have argued, colonizer and colonized were both unstable terms defining heterogeneous groups constructed out of the historical "uneven and contradictory intersections of various axes of power" (colonial, national, both colonizer and colonized) and subject to changing material conditions (Sinha, 1). Intersections of economic, political, social, and gendered values and forces were uneven and groups aligned differently depending on circumstances. For example, British-educated Indians, once considered the bulwark of colonial administrative policy in the first half of the nineteenth century, were decentered after the 1857 Mutiny or War of Independence, as British policy moved from "anglicism" to Orientalism, and the Indian elite moved from collaboration to resistance (Sinha, 4–6). In establishing a social and political site for themselves, elite native informants intervened in the discourse of Orientalism, applying Orientalist stereotypes to the British themselves and de-racializing concepts of culture and progress.

Authors understood their task as educating the British about what was "real" about their cultures, e.g., "The real status of women in Islam," "Some real tiger stories." Authors spoke for their countries and offered "native" perspectives, e.g., "A Moslem view of Abdul Hamid and the Powers," "Some Indian suggestions for India," "A Chinese view of railways in China," "A Japanese view of new Japan." Essays were long and complex, and some were even serialized: "Memoirs of a Soudanese soldier" had four installments in 1896 in the *Cornhill Magazine*, and Feringee Furaree's travel notes appeared in four installments in the *Dublin University Magazine* in the 1840s.

Who were these authors and native informants? They included the Khedive of Egypt, Maharajah Sayaji Rao of Baroda, the Prime Minister of Hyderabad Salar Jung, and the Zulu King Cetywayo who nearly defeated the British but received a hero's welcome when he came to England. Some authors had troubled relations with the British: Hilmi Abbas, Pasha of Egypt, later sided with the Turks in World War I and was deposed by the British after the war. Some were advocates of pan-Islam and virulent nationalists and anti-imperialists (Jamal al-Din al-Afghani and Ahmed Arabi Pasha). Most were moderately or harshly critical of British imperialism (Syed Ameer Ali), and several loved Britain (Cornelia Sorabji). One author, Dadabhai Naoroji, was the first Indian elected to Parliament in 1892.[2] A vast majority, including the nationalists, were English-educated barristers and jurists (Ameer Ali, Sorabji, Sir Mancherjee Merwanjee Bhownaggree, Sir Hury Singh Gour, Bishen Narayan Dar, Romesh Chunder Dutt). Many of these authors became national leaders later in the twentieth century and entered the *DNB* and *Who Was Who*, in both British and colonial versions. Few were women, but one, Cornelia Sorabji, graduate of Oxford's Somerville College, was a jurist, prolific author, and Anglophile.

In short, these authors were well-to-do, Anglicized, and well educated, but just as likely to criticize the British as to praise them. Few were as syncophantic as Prince Ranjitsinhji who praised British physical prowess in his article on the universality of cricket in the pro-Empire periodical *Blackwood's Magazine*.[3] Many spoke on behalf of both sides simultaneously: Protap Chunder Mozoomdar, newspaper editor and apologist for British rule, defended Hindus as both manly and spiritual, anticipated the disappearance of caste as Indians became educated, hoped that more temperate Christians would become accepted by Hindus, and praised England for the "freedom of public opinion."[4] He sought a "providential union" (1000) between Britain and India to eliminate Indian famines of the body and of the soul, the latter caused by European hostility to Indians despite Indian reverence for the Queen they call "Mother" (999).

Many authors combined perspectives and roles as intermediaries, arguing for new directions and greater autonomy under British imperial administration and defending their countries as manageable and progressive. They saw the British from a native perspective, but they also saw themselves through British eyes. They applied oriental stereotypes to the British. But they also measured their native cultures by European standards and values derived from their English educations. As Gauri Viswanathan demonstrates, native education became a site for "representations of Western literary knowledge as objective, universal, and rational" through a "structural congruence between Christianity and English literature."[5] British administrators insisted that English literature taught empirical thinking from evidence, and contrasted English "rationalism" to Oriental "despotism," underscoring presumptions about British authority and claimed cultural superiority. Through literature, the English represented themselves "as benign, disinterested, detached, impartial, and judicious" (Viswanathan, 125). The downside was the fear that Indians would interpret this as irreligion, a loss compensated by British claims to reinforce Christian beliefs and "to penetrate the mysteries of the natural and phenomenal world" (Viswanathan, 126). Student-written exams in missionary institutions were on such ideological topics as the disadvantage of caste, falsehood in the Hindu Shastras, or the merits of Christianity and demerits of Hinduism (Viswanathan, 127):

> The strategy of locating authority in English texts all but effaced the often sordid history of colonialist expropriation, material exploitation, and class and race oppression behind European world dominance. Making the Englishman known to the natives through the products of his mental labor removed him from the plane of ongoing colonialist activity—of commercial operations, military expansion, administration of territories—and deactualized and diffused his material presence in the process. . . . His material reality as subjugator and alien ruler was dissolved in his mental output. . . . The split between the material and the cultural practices of colonialism is nowhere sharper than in the progressive rarefaction of the rapacious, exploitative, and ruthless actor of history into the reflective subject of literature.[6]

This reflective "subject of literature" and its enlightenment self-representation created roles that native informants also claimed to inhabit and which they performed in the press. It also created opportunities to critique British rule. In an article in *Nineteenth Century and After* in Feb. 1901, Sayaji Rao Gaekwar, Maharajah of Baroda, presented himself as an enlightened synthesis of British and Indian.[7] His home was part English house, part Indian palace.[8] He assured his English readers of his fiscal responsibility (maharajas were considered flagrant spenders) and of his knowledge of European culture. He detailed his average day: Hindu devotions blended with readings from Herbert Spencer, Gibbons, Greek and Roman history, philosophy, Bryce's *Democracy*, Mill, Tocqueville, Shakespeare, and Bentham, a reading list fit for any English gentleman (216). Even his meals combined European and Indian dishes while maintaining a "European character" (216) in materials and manner of serving. Time with his wife and children punctuated his long hours of administrative work, demonstrating his adherence to domestic life, the work ethic, and utilitarianism ("pleasure . . . pains"): "Business has become a passion to me, and my work for the people a real pleasure; so I have spent more personal pains than, strictly speaking, I need have done" (217). He also commented on his subjects' religious "ritualistic and narrow point of view" which perpetuated their "prejudices and sentiments" from which he distanced himself, proclaiming that the most important religion they could have is "the love of their country" (218). His advocacy of domesticity, nationalism, and progress—all Victorian articles of faith—were appeals to his British readers.

Sayaji Rao's resistance was in the form of a reversed Orientalism. Citing the cliché that India is mysterious and irrational, he reascribed these attributes to the British government: "India is said to be land of anomalies, inconsistencies, and surprises. . . . nowhere is the truth of this remark more forcibly brought home than in the dealings of the British Government with Native States" (220). He did not need British "intervention," since his own extensive program of reform was based on English models of administration, public education, and philanthropy. Flattering his British readers by appealing to their Enlightenment rationalism, he also "irrationalized" the British government in India as feudal and hysterical (220–21), a common strategy among colonial authors.

Finally, he commended England for granting self-government to Australia and hoped this would also be granted to India; he was certainly aware of the dual categories of colonies and their different treatment by the British, differences he strategically elided in his request for independence (224). He further praised his British readers for their "high moral condition and greater strength of character" but rooted British character in education rather than in race to argue that such traits could be found among Indians. His arguments rested on Enlightenment principles—as a very progressive reformer of Baroda, he argued that Baroda was a model of modern civilization and that by Britain's own colonial logic, it warranted independence. Sayaji Rao presented/performed himself as the best of both worlds, exemplifying English culture, while also resisting Britain's imperial domination in defense of a rational and reformist India.

Like Maharaja Sayaji Rao, other Indian authors critiqued imperial policies and proposed changes. In addition to policy recommendations, most focused on two other topics: women, who became the sign of civilizing "progress" both for Britons and for colonized peoples; and the defense of Islam, as demonized then as it still is today. These three topics were not discrete but overlapped in many ways— the reiterated defense of Islam was that Islamic women were better off than British women and had more rights regarding property, divorce, and even education. Comments on issues relating to imperial policy, such as the gold standard or the cow agitation, often contained explanations of Hindu or Muslim religious beliefs.

DE-NATURALIZING THE UNIVERSAL: HISTORY AND PLACE

The three topics I focus on were hotly debated in the British and in the Indian press. I would argue that the overarching intention of the colonized authors in the Victorian press was to re-inscribe particular situations and historical circumstances onto British policies. Most authors sought to inform British readers of the material conditions of native populations, to de-universalize, de-naturalize, localize, and historicize British and native laws and policies. In this way they hoped to make policies and laws accessible to debates for or against their applicability to particular historical and cultural situations and locales. They wrote to the British public in order to de-textualize British rule and turn its political and legal acts and ideologies back into a discourse in which they had a voice. Textualization under colonial rule privileged writing as the force that "produced consequences of domination" (Mani, "Production," 122), a force in which colonized authors participated. Furthermore, they wrote to influence policies through readers whom they addressed directly in the belief that they would support their views.

These authors' effectiveness depended on their claim to authority as "insiders." Employing Foucault's notion of "the rituals of speaking," Linda Alcoff points out that the author's location "within a social space including the persons involved in, acting upon, and/or affected by the words" contextualizes meaning.[9] This location implies the author's authority and whether that author is heard; it is part of a network of "connections and relations of involvement between the utterance/text and other utterances and texts as well as the material practices in the relevant environment" (Alcoff, 12). The intellectual space Indian authors inhabited permitted them to quote English jurists and authors and range freely through political and literary texts in support of their arguments. Romesh Chunder Dutt quotes Sir Henry Brackenbury, military member of the Council of the Viceroy of India, because his "is a stronger argument than mine, and it is urged by a high authority who has a claim to be heard"; his voice "will no doubt appeal strongly to the minds of all thoughtful Englishmen" who would then agree to help resolve the famine that is the subject of Dutt's 1897 *Fortnightly Review* essay.[10]

As Alcoff argues, these rituals "are constitutive of meaning" within the larger space of the "discursive context," which makes meaning "plural and shifting" (Alcoff, 12) within the parameters of each periodical's readership and political alignments into which these authors fit. But, as many scholars of the Victorian periodical press have pointed out, the press is a site both for validation and for a permitted oppositional discourse on a wide range of topics, making it also a safe place for colonial resistance and accommodation. Indian authors' accommodations to periodicals' readers and ideologies were articulated in the same logic as other essays in these periodicals—factual evidence, historical narrative, enlightenment rationalism, and rhetorical sophistication—techniques and rhetorical rituals that also constructed these authors' authority.

Political instabilities among colonized people and among European nations empowered native informants' truth claims for their assertions, and gave weight to their recommendations as a means of protecting the Empire, making them invaluable allies of the British. These authors reinforced their authority by pointing out the Empire's continually recurring rebellions: the shooting of British officers, secret practices of sati and child marriage despite government bans, rioting peasants, and the publication of seditious newspapers. Public outcries and demonstrations from the 1806 uprising in Madras over British interference in religious practices, to the increase in sati in Bengal after the ban in 1839, or the Bengalese protests over the Age of Consent Act of 1891 offered opportunities for informants to strengthen their arguments that their insights were vital to the successful persistance of the British Empire because the Empire was precariously poised among natives always about to rebel.[11] Sometimes authors alluded to the 1857 Indian Rebellion that haunted the British as much as its remembrance empowered Indians. Shoshee Chunder Dutt, named in the beginning of the essay and with "Justice of the Peace, Calcutta," in the byline to present his authority from the beginning, rather than at the end of the essay where most signatures appeared in periodical essays, begins his essay in *Fraser's* in 1876 dramatically by stating, "We are not Russophobists."[12] He blamed the 1857 Mutiny/Rebellion on a combination of "the instigation of Russian spies," and "the bad estimation in which the British Government was then, *as it is yet*, held by the natives for diverse reasons, one of the most prominent of them being the irritating system of taxation which it has enforced" (302; italics mine). The past rebellion foreshadows other rebellions to come, if British policies do not change, especially "unjust and oppressive" taxation that was arbitrary and unmerciful, terms the British applied to Asians (319).

But Dutt also addressed his readers as potentially just and empathetic, the typical rhetoric of this claim to authority. This appeal even allowed him to speak for the English, as well as for the Indians: "The real wish of the English people—the people of England—is to do justice to India. This wish ought not to be allowed to be strangled by the governing class in India, who can consider no question apart from class interest, who in all their acts are assiduous to ignore the people of India" (324). Dutt pitted ordinary people, British and Indian, against their politicians, appealing to their class hostilities to offer a transnational bond that superceded class or national interests.

Internecine European competition and antagonisms were another threat informants could cite to sustain the authority of their warnings. A. S. Ghosh, writing on financial relations between England and India (*Westminster Review*, 1897), insisted, "I write as a friend and not as a foe. . . . none has it nearer to his heart than I have the desire for a more equitable, and therefore a more permanent union between England and India," but he concluded his essay with foreboding threats of European rivalries:

> The Cossack, the Teuton, the Frank, and their attendant jackals, may indeed stand on guard over one another . . . but if there be any common feeling in which they participate, it is the hatred of England, or any common purpose in which they would fain co-operate, it is to bring about the downfall of England. . . . the days of adversity must inevitably come, as it has come to other great nations; and England would do well to profit by their example, and strengthen the foundations of her Empire—while there is yet time.[13]

Finally, authors were located in their own social, caste, national, and political ideologies. Authors openly debated issues with each other such as the Armenian question, argued from the Armenian side (e.g., Mihran Sévasly, *New Review*, 1889) and the Turkish side (e.g., Ghulam-us-Saqlain, *Nineteenth Century*, 1895). Hindus and Muslims disagreed. Maharajahs defended the landed aristocracy against middle-class jurists and journalists who sided with peasants on issues of taxation, land ownership, and famine relief.[14]

REVISING IMPERIAL POLICIES:
POLITICS, ORDER, AND RESISTANCE

Native informants offered suggestions and revisions of British imperial policies. Uma Sankar Misra in 1889 in a thoroughly anglophile voice, quoted Viceroy Dufferin on the gradual increase in civic freedoms and the "natural" tendencies of Indian "educated classes" to be closer to Britain and refers to Dufferin's "principle of the survival of the fittest."[15] Admitting that democracy comes gradually to most countries like India with centuries of despotism, Misra proceeded to point out Dufferin's objections to the Indian Congress: that India is not ready for democracy due to its "microscopic minority" (Dufferin's phrases) of educated "men of Western culture and Western thought" who could not control the "credulous and ignorant masses," (94–95). Misra agreed with these objections and concerns, arguing that sanitation and social reforms should precede political change. He criticized the Congress for publishing inflammatory pamphlets because these "place us in an ugly light before the civilized world, where we are striving hard to take up a position" to fulfill "the many blessings which British rule in India has brought" (95). Misra unhesitatingly claimed "it is England which has made us what we are" (95). However, despite his anglophilia, he recommended a national representative body, while condemning the violence of "the rabble" and "tribal and racial jealousies." Rather than dismantle the Congress, Misra hoped to encourage it "to receive the support of the people and retain at the same time the good-will of the Government"—to appease Indians and British both (96).

Other authors also advocated Indian representation within the British Raj. Oday Pertap Singh, Raja of Bhinga, in 1894 on the cow agitation addressed conflicts between Hindus and Muslims over a Muslim cow sacrifice.[16] Singh praised the British government for its handling of sedition and refusal to pit Hindu against Muslim in any "Machiavellian" scheme. Going further than Misra in his criticisms, he attacked the British for *not* encouraging loyalty among Indians serving in the military and civil service (669). He argued for an association of landed aristocracy and gentry against "power-seeking" arrivistes and politicos "who morally, socially, and politically are quite unfit to be our masters" (671). He pleaded for better selections of Indians in government while praising "the peace we enjoy under the British rule" (672).

M. M. Bhownaggree, an Indian lawyer and politician, calls for the repeal of the Free Press laws on the part of the British government, "our Indian Administration."[17] His criticism is that Indians adopting British ways agitate for freedoms and become seditious (304). He ascribed political agitation in India to young men trying to apply British "freedoms" to India. Unlike the earlier generation of Anglophiles who were "reasonable and respectful" (308), young agitators lack "moderation and common sense" (309). Orientalizing the "Anglophobe" agitators, he insisted that reason and order were nonetheless "prominent traits in the character of the better classes of the Indian people," and only those who dwell in the "darkness of the purdah and the superstitious worship of earthly deities" blame England for keeping India from "a lusty national manhood," needed to become a modern nation (309). He cited the Indian Mutiny/Rebellion of 1857 to impress his readers with the urgency of the problem and blamed "a few designing and ambitious" Britons for provoking the agitators (306). Yet he assured his British readers that seditionists represent a fraction of Indian subjects provoked by journalists "of a very low type . . . ignorant men" (312). Bhownaggree blamed both British and Indian participants for agitation.

Bhownaggree similarly criticized the Indian National Congress for failing to appreciate "the systems of dispensing justice, of imparting instruction, and of relieving sickness, which *we* have established all over India" (311). His "we" is British, but he urged Britain to control its own officers' "mean prejudice against colour," estranging Indians and "South African and other Colonies" (306). He distinguished between "true" and "false" Britons (307), as he divided Indians, yoking the "fanaticism of the lower orders of Moslems" and "the Poona Brahmin's unreasoning hatred of the British suzerainty of India," on the one hand, against educated, reasonable Indians, on the other hand (305). He warned and assured Britons at the same time, strategies that validated insider information through which these authors perform their loyalty and promise to sustain British rule, suggesting the urgency of heeding their advice.

These Anglophiles recommend representation by Indians and defend Indian "character" against orientalizing stereotypes. Those more critical of the British went further to attack empire through its own ironies and contradictions. Among the most direct and outspoken critics of British foreign policy was Jamal-al-Din al-Afghani, a lifelong critic and protestor of British rule. His "Reign of Terror in Persia" in *The Contemporary Review* in 1892 was so extreme that the essay was foreworded by Reverend H. R. Howeis who legitimized Afghani as "the eminent Oriental statesman, scholar, orator, and reformer" who traveled "throughout Europe in order to acquire the elements of our civilisation . . . to adapt the modern idea to the needs of Asiatics."[18] Identifying "England's Imperial interests . . . with the safety and independence of Persia," Rev. Howeis authorized Afghani's truth claims that the Shah was conducting a reign of terror against Persians and failing to keep promises he made to the British.

Afghani's rhetoric exploited his identifications with his British readers. He appealed to British class identity by attacking the illiterate lower class administrators put in place by the Shah. He also appealed to British colonial and commercial interests by describing a country laid waste in agriculture and unmined resources because of the Shah's cruelties (239, 245). Requesting English help, he calls his readers "you law-abiding English" (242), hoping they would be touched by the moral of his story, or by the consequences of ignoring him—the loss of English prestige. He played on the British claim that empire's purpose was to civilize, not to profiteer (245): "Persia still waits for a message at this crisis. But you are afraid of your pockets. The bank interest might go down if any rumour of disagreement between the Shah's Ministers and your diplomatists at Teheran got wind. . . . England, so ready to help Garibaldi—so willing to sacrifice untold wealth in order to put down the slave trade. Yet England refuses a word of remonstrance or advice" (247). Then, turning 180 degrees, Afghani claimed that "so great is still the prestige of England" (247) that the Shah would cave in to English demands "which would cost no ships, no money, and would not really endanger your banking or your trade; a word from a free, powerful people on behalf of a beleaguered and enslaved, but noble, active minded, and capable people" (248).

Afghani flattered and criticized by turns to stir up what he and many authors projected onto their readers: self-images as well-meaning, moral, and lawful to affect reform, inflating British belief in their own idealism as reformist and evangelical. But he also insisted that Persians, too, were noble, intelligent, and capable of self-governance, were Britain to withdraw support from the Shah.

Muhammad 'Abd al Halim Pasha (Halim Pasha), exiled from Egypt to Constantinople as his right of succession was usurped by Tewfik, argued in September 1885 in *Nineteenth Century* on behalf of the Egyptian subalterns whose farming lands were taken by the current Khedive.[19] Halim's most striking rhetoric was employed against his two English critics, Sir Julian Goldsmid and Edward Dicey. He attacked Goldsmid as ignorant of Egypt and a puppet of the Khedive, and Dicey as infatuated with privilege. He calls these two critics "literary" and implies that what they write is fiction (485): "Fully conscious of my inferiority as a writer to the accomplished authors who have assailed me, I shall attempt to answer them, encouraged by the thought that having only simple truths to tell I may not need literary training such as theirs to fulfil my tasks." He pits his truthfulness against their "literary" skill, a subtle poisoning of the well (485).

Halim undercut Dicey's presumed authority: "He has been to Egypt, and is well-acquainted with Shepheard's Hotel, the Government Offices and Consulates in Cairo, the banking houses of Alexandria, and, for aught I know to the contrary, the Pyramids and the Second Cataract," hardly a deep knowledge of the country and its people (487). He tied Dicey to money and "other circumstances attaching to his relations to Egypt, upon which it is necessary to enter," an insinuation as suggestive and damaging as any correction of Dicey's factual errors (488). Dicey's "infatuation" with privilege entitle him "to the eminent place he holds as an authority on Egyptian affairs" (487), in Halim's sarcastic phrase. He invoked an English authority, Mackenzie Wallace, to attack Dicey (488). Enamored, seduced, treacherous, instinctual, irrational, self-contradictory, aggressive, attracted to a despotic and greedy Khedive, lying, puerile, fanciful, and ingenuous—Dicey and Goldsmid were thoroughly orientalized by Halim. He, on the other hand, represented himself as truthful, enlightened, factual, and logical, presenting statistical data of the Khedive's income, while advocating for local traditions and political representation (490–92). Halim was an Enlightenment construct, a British ideal who appealed to the idealist ideologies of Empire, as did many other writers—the desire to do good and "civilize" others, the expressed distaste for personal gain from empire, the desire to appear factual and empirical (488–89). He also appealed to the notion that the British had a moral obligation to improve the life of the indigenous who "are entitled to be relieved" from poverty and despotism (486).

Syed Ameer Ali, Indian jurist (called to the bar in England) and Islamic leader, was one of most prolific writers among native informants. In "Some Indian Suggestions for India" (1880, *Nineteenth Century*), he sided with the new liberal government and called for the government to abandon indirect taxes on cotton that benefit the rich. He promised that his suggestions will help English ascertain "genuine Indian public opinion."[20] He asked his British readers to imagine how Indians "live from hand to mouth" within a system of informers that maintains English inaccessibility to Indians through corruption and easily bribed "informers and unpaid assessors" (964). Ameer Ali argued from statistics to expose the misuse of figures, errors, and false budget estimates of Sir John Strachey. He criticized Strachey's excessive military spending and cited the *Bombay Review*'s call for an investigation of Afghan War expenses because of Britain's "desire to slur over hard facts," such as India's tremendous debt caused by being charged for the War's costs (965–66).

Above all, Ameer Ali appealed to the "earnest people in England" to understand consequences of export duty on rice as beneficial only to "speculators and traders" (966–67). He opposed direct taxation and called for the re-imposition of tax duty consistent with free trade and which will not harm the poor (967). He claimed that equal pay is "a principle of political economy," appealing to the "dismal science" from which the British argued their own economic principles at home (970). He called for more education for Indians, who were "as efficient as any ordinary European official" and have "personal integrity" with which they can "discharge of public duties, and the grasp of administrative details," being "not inferior in the smallest degree to any foreigner" (971). He openly questioned English integrity; he suggested their prejudice and ignorance resulted in "frequent miscarriages of justice," while "the judicial capacity of the Indians is universally admitted" (971).

Ameer Ali offered suggestions from the dual perspective of the native informant—advice that would ensure British rule, and advice the neglect of which would provoke rebellion. As a native informant he refused to reinforce British orientalizing, but insisted that, "the Ryots [peasants] as a rule are not so 'child-like' as they are occasionally represented to be. Child-like Ryots are as difficult to find in India as elsewhere" (977). The Government's support of landowners failed to hear "the voice of the Ryot," a failure that may lead to "some revolting deed of agrarian violence" (977). His most emphatic remarks criticized British justice, the very thing Britons thought they brought to their supposedly chaotic or autocratic colonies: "In no country in the world, perhaps, is justice taxed so heavily as in India." For good measure, he reminded his British readers of agrarian riots in the past (974): if the government wanted to "strengthen its hold on the affections of the people," it needs to relax the harsh land tax and stop taking farms for debt (975).

His authority lay in his claims "to represent the views of the Indian nation without regard to the interest of any class or creed" and his promise to deal "only with matters on which there is a consensus of opinion among the people of India" in hopes of "evoking the sympathy of the British public" (978). Thus Ameer Ali could claim to assist the British in avoiding disaster, while also severely criticizing their policies and practices. He praised his readers while condemning their leaders and thus found a path for the mutual collusion of Indian and British publics against politicians.

Ameer Ali often suggested new economic and political measures. In "The Rupee and the Ruin of India" (1893), he argued that the bimetallism of the gold standard for the pound and the silver for the rupee is destroying India for the majority of Indians, both urban and rural, and for Anglo-Indians whose standard of living is also declining. If Anglo-Indians left, they could be replaced by Indians, "but whether that will be for the advantage of the State is a matter for question. To my mind it will be an evil day for India when, from a permanent reduction in the emoluments of officers in the civil and military employ of Government, the agency which has been the making of India is either withdrawn or its efficiency impaired."[21] The revaluation of the rupee, then, would guarantee the continuation of British rule! His essay included charts of annual income for farmers and urban professionals (517), and he laments the inability of Indians and English alike to send their sons to English public school "to acquire that training, discipline, and culture which are conspicuous by their absence from the educational institutions of this country" (519).

Ameer Ali spoke both on behalf of beleaguered Indians and in support of British Rule: "Not even the wildest Home-ruler would suggest that cutting India adrift from England, even if it were possible, would be for the benefit of this country" (520). But "even if it were possible" is a provocative phrase, implying an option that is threateningly subtextual and always present. He also evoked the constant anxieties of European competition: if the Dutch "could devise a means for the protection of its colonies . . . surely it is possible for the talented men at the helm here and in England to find a remedy for the evil" (524). In his rhetorically strategic native informancy, he challenged England's own Enlightenment values; the fluctuating rupee postponed projects, such as sewage, irrigation, and railways, upon which the British justified their imperial claims of improving India (523). Ameer Ali claimed that if his suggestions were taken, "the country's progress and prosperity during the next twenty years will be such as has never before been recorded in the annals of Indian history" (524).

"The Grievances of India" was signed "A Hindu," and has been ascribed by the *Wellesley Index* to Romesh Chunder Dutt. Dutt was an Indian civil servant, Baroda Minister of Finance, 1904–6, member of the Royal Society of Literature and the Royal Asiatic Society, and a barrister.[22] Startlingly hostile, Dutt called Lord Clive "an unscrupulous forger," Warren Hastings, "a noted villain," and Lord Dalhou-

sie, "the very incarnation of injustice."[23] Dutt cited Parliamentary
debate, speeches, and inconsistencies in Britain's application of its
own laws to condemn Britain as utterly failing to bring some justice
to India: lack of habeas corpus, no fair trials for deposed princes, no
procedures for petitioning Parliament, excessive taxes in India for
salt and for wars outside its borders despite laws against charging
India for such wars, and prohibition of Indians from military careers
and civil service. The civil service, Dutt insisted, was open to Indians
in theory only, as it required training in England, which caused Hindus to lose caste, and even when they went to England, they failed
to obtain civil service appointments (330–31).

Underlying these unfair practices is his assertion of the English
hostility toward Indians: "A native is a liar; perjury is habitual to him;
morality he has not; bigotry and ignorance are his strongholds"
(327). He believed that if civil service exams were truly open, Indians "would pass in considerable numbers" (331). Like so many
other Indian authors, Dutt advocated representative government for
India. He argued that this institution took a long time to develop
even in England, not because of a "natural" progression or development but because it was "the desire of the oligarchy to withhold"
representative government (336). And he believed the Government,
carrying out its own oligarchic desires, "has no intention to give us
natives of India any share" because it believes that representation
"is an institution foreign to the Asiatics," which Dutt denied (336).
He advocated for the new rising educated classes tempted to join
England's enemies and rivals, Russia, America, and Germany; it was,
therefore, he argued, in England's best interest to assimilate Indians
into Raj government (341).

Employing the double-edged arguments of native informancy to
both threaten and defend empire, he claimed that English rule had
not "been actually productive of the good ascribed to it," and the
native press "is honestly working to check this indifference, and to
expose *from loyal motives*, all the abuses that constantly crop up. The
time cannot be distant where our educated youths will come forward
to vindicate their rights. . . . The present position of England is far
from firm and secure" (340–41; italics mine). The Queen's 1859
proclamation was "notorious now for being more a dead letter than
anything else" in the opinion of "all the inhabitants of India" (341).

These authors share rhetorical strategies despite their political
differences: they openly attack bad policies and offer suggestions
they expect their readers to support; they threaten rebellion implicitly or explicitly if their suggestions are not taken seriously; they
speak as authorities who, existing in both worlds, claim to know the

English character at its best and worst, and they write to educate their readers about the "native" character which they portray as reasonable and complex. They Orientalize incompetent British administrators, but treat their readers as enlightened, empathetic, and engaged, to provoke them to support their suggestions for new imperial policies. Threatening and cajoling, they secure a positional authority through a mixture of enlightenment ideals (factual evidence—charts, statistics; legalistic arguments; appeals of justice) and native knowledge of religions, customs, and, above all, popular reactions to policies.

Bodies of Women: Signs of Civilization

As Antoinette Burton in *Burdens of History* points out, the secular work of British feminism and female emancipation was "frequently undertaken in the name of Indian women"[24] (2), giving British women an active role in Empire and aligning them with hegemonic imperial policies. British feminists attacked the zanana, purdah, sati, child marriage, and abusive widowhood: "Oriental womanhood as a trope for sexual difference, primitive society, and colonial backwardness was certainly not limited to British feminist writing. . . . rhetoric about Indian women's condition . . . was no less crucial to notions of British cultural superiority and to rationales for the British imperial presence in India" (7). Essays by Indian men in the press were equally adamant whether defending the elevated role of women in Islamic society against British charges that Islam kept women uneducated and helpless, or advocating for the end of sati and child marriages through British legislation and intervention.

Sati and child marriage had been the subject of laws (1829 and 1891, respectively) that banned these practices and provoked resistance, public demonstrations, and incendiary writings on all sides—reformist, traditionalist, liberal, religious, legal, social, political, British, Indian, Hindu, Muslim. As Dagmar Engels points out, "In British India some of the most emotionally-charged conflicts between colonised and coloniser were about the control of female sexuality."[25] The issues debated in the late Victorian press regarding sati and child marriage overlapped with issues of religious tolerance for Hindus and Muslims.

As Lata Mani and Jyotsna Singh point out, sati women did not speak on their own behalf but were vociferously spoken for by British and Indian men; press articles on sati were almost exclusively written by men.[26] Even more insidious, as Engels points out, native informants' testimony was manipulated and appropriated by British authorities. Statements made by pandits about child marriage or sati were often tentative, the pandits refusing to speak as ultimate authorities. British administrators, however, took the statements they preferred and textualised them, as Lata Mani describes the process using Paul Ricoeur's term: "discourse is realised temporally, it has a subject who speaks, 'a world which it claims to describe, to express or to represent,'" while textualisation, "results in the fixation of meaning, its dissociation from any authorial intention, the display of non-ostensive references and a universal range of addressees. . . . Opinions pronounced on particular cases became rules applicable to all cases." These textualizations allowed British officials to interpret statements about customs and religious texts "in ways that both reflected and did not reflect the intention of pundits" (Mani, 121–22, citing Ricoeur, 531).[27]

Interestingly, the subjects of purdah and sati were more sensational than widespread, as Engels points out in the case of purdah.[28] As Janaki Nair argues, the zenana, too, was "confined to certain classes and regions" that had experienced Muslim influence, yet the zenana, like sati and purdah, became "representative" of Indian culture, inscribed as superstitious and idolatrous.[29] These practices, despite their generally restricted application in India, became textual signs of the "barbarism" of Indian culture, and their reform became a sign of British evangelical sanctimoniousness and moral superiority. According to Partha Chatterjee, the reform of these practices "was not so much about the specific condition of women within a determinate set of social relations as it was about the political encounter between a colonial state and the supposed 'tradition' of a conquered people."[30] Writers on all sides treated these practices as "a problem of Indian tradition," not as a problem regarding social change for women *per se*, in order to pursue "the nationalist project of rationalizing and reforming the traditional culture of their people" without simply imitating the West (623). Male writers on these subjects wrote, in Chatterjee's view, in "the seeming absence of any autonomous struggle by women themselves for equality and freedom" (631). They argued for the superiority of Eastern spirituality over Western materiality and maintained that gender difference distinguished Indian from European cultures (Chatterjee, 623, 627).

Whether defending their own cultures on the grounds that Islamic women were treated as well as, or even better than, English women, or calling for reformism from British sources, these male essayists all assumed that woman was a measure of their nation's civilization and progress. They appropriated a British measure of progress and either advocated for the rights of women or defended their cultures as already advanced in the treatment of women. Cornelia Sorabji's essays are moderate in tone, though her own legal work was assertive and truly influential in assisting purdah women. Sorabji was a barrister, educated at Somerville College, Oxford, and the first woman admitted to the Deccan College, Poona. She was finally called to the bar in 1923 (women were not eligible until 1919) and spent her last years residing in England.[31] Her 1898 essay on women and the law in India is a compelling comparison between India and Britain and between legal theory and practice. Noting that women in India had considerable property rights that far surpassed property rights for women in Britain until the 1882 Women's Property Act, Sorabji argues that purdah keeps Indian women from claiming their property rights, since they cannot argue their cases in court. Sorabji recommends women as land agents and legal pleaders to help purdah women, "orthodox and unenlightened," plead in court. Praising those in Oxford and London who helped her in her career, she also insisted that women lawyers are trained in India and permitted to practice in many places (865–66). Working within purdah for the emancipation of purdah women, Sorabji was yet uncompromising about women's right to work. An Anglophile who settled in England at the end of her life, she pleaded the Indian woman's case before the English public and in the English press, as well as in Indian courts.

Syed Ameer Ali on "The real status of women in Islam" in *The Nineteenth Century*, 1891, responded to an attack on Islam's treatment of women by Annie Reichardt in June 1891.[32] Ameer Ali carefully interpreted passages from the Koran and the history of Jewish and Christian treatment of women to trace "the existing aversion to Islam" to Pope Gregory and the Crusades.[33] Ameer Ali demonstrated that Reichardt's "vaunted 'Old Covenant'" treated women like chattel: the ban on women in the clergy, the Church Fathers' hostile writings against women as "the devil's gateway," and the violence inflicted on women during the so-called chivalric period (389–90). He described widespread polygamy among Christians, including the clergy and Charlemagne (390) in contrast to Mohammed's attempt to change deep-seated cultural practices hostile to women (391). Ameer Ali contrasts Mohammed's attempts to alter cultural practices gradually with the behavior of Christian missionaries, hysterically and irrationally "unhinging people's minds by announcing the immediate advent of the 'Kingdom of Heaven'" (391). He turned Oriental stereotypes against the English and constructs an Enlightenment Mohammed; the hysterical Reichardt who is ignorant of the Koran contrasts with the culturally sensitive, rational Prophet who worked to improve women's rights and status against centuries-old practices. Mohammed revised divorce laws, discouraged polygamy, and argued for the emancipation of slaves, including concubines, and the property rights of women even after marriage (392–94). Ameer Ali insisted Islamic women were as advanced as European ones; their marriages are civic, not religious, guaranteeing their property rights under law and allowing them to keep money earned as their own (398). His major strategy is to move Islam from a theology to an historical set of practices, opening up options for change in defiance of the essentialized "medievalism" projected by Western Orientalists (399).[34]

Hindus also defended themselves on women's issues. Protap Chunder Mozoomdar, writing in 1900, insists that Hindus no longer support the seclusion of women, that "at last a hundred thousand Hindu girls attend public schools," while Calcutta University has about three dozen lady graduates," and women are "poets . . . novelists, . . . doctors, . . . even strong supporters of the Women's Suffrage Movement!"[35] In his view, all this and other benefits of education and technology resulted from British rule in which "uprightness and truthfulness. . . . have silently spread a higher ideal of personal and public life," eliminating corruption and promoting religious tolerance through British "non-religious rule. . . . non-sectarian policy" (993).

Some reformers felt the British were essential for change. T. Vijaya-Raghavan on Hindu marriage customs and British law in *The National Review* of 1891 praised the British for ending sati and working to end child marriages. But he also argued that these reforms made amends for "the crimes that stained the honor of the early Proconsuls, Clive and Warren Hastings."[36] Raghavan praised British reforms to "eradicate the evils of Indian society, evils that were a blot upon humanity and civilization" (80). But his intention was also to give British readers "a correct account . . . of the present situation, and in showing that the time has come for legislation on the social question" (81). Like many Indian authors, he insisted on the distinction between religious text (the Veda that does not sanction child marriages) and the historical practice, based on fears of concubinage of Hindu women by Muslim conquerors (82–83). He also proposed measures to change the practices (84–85).

His central plea was for immediate legislation in agreement with the reform party within: "You may preach and write, and quote lengthy extracts from Macaulay and Spenser to prove that reform must come only from within. . . . but the facts of history go to show that reform has never proved successful in India, until brought about by the strong arm of Government" (85). As a subject of the Crown, he appealed for change lest "the dignity of the British Empire will be irretrievably lost" (86). Raghavan addressed his readers "as Englishman [sic], as Christians" (86). In conclusion he cited Indian and English medical sources and Indian reformers to encourage the British to recognize Indian support of the Age of Consent legislation for "your suffering sisters" as a "duty which you possess by right of conquest, nay, by a holier name, by your religion. Amen" (90).

Other authors urged British intervention, as well. Devendra N. Das, writing about the extraordinary cruelties suffered by Hindu widows in his 1886 article in *The Nineteenth Century,* described their suffering in great detail to foreground dramatically the need for British intervention. Das argued that the British abolition of sati was only half a solution. As a result of British influences, especially "the benign influence of English education," Hindus are "awakening to the horrors of their vicious system." They need the English to continue "the steady infusion of the spirit of European culture and refinement" to "bring about the elevation of Hindu women and further the progress of the country at large."[37]

Taking the opposite view, Nanda Lal Ghosh argued that changes must come from within and that the Government cannot interfere with religious practices if "unasked."[38] He cited Indian-generated decrees to improve the conditions of widows and denied enforced widowhood is a legal practice, although it is widespread as a religious practice. He presented "Indian" arguments against re-marriage, such as social ostracism of families who lose caste (363). Ghosh argued that widows and their families deserve government protection as persecuted minorities (363–64) and that infant marriages violate Brahmanic law that stipulates that marriage must follow education (366). Ghosh separated custom from religious edicts, but acknowledged that social and political spheres are interdependent and that social change must precede "political advancement," but only if Indians are allowed "constitutional freedom in their domestic life" (366–68). He concluded that the despotism of Brahmins and tyrannies of fathers and husbands were worse than "the imaginary despotism of the British nation." He admonished Indians to attend to social change instead of "political agitation and speculations" against the British who "will guide, protect, and watch" India (368).

Hury Singh Gour, barrister and author, took the English to task in 1891 for criticizing Indian home life while being completely ignorant of it. He offered to compare "Indian home life as seen and led

by the present writer . . . and the English home life of which only
the superficial aspect is portrayed in English novels," thus turning
the tables on the nature of mutual representation and playing with
notions of authoritative sources of information on both sides.[39] He
glorified and idealized Indian marriage, arguing that the remarriage
of widows would "defeat the very purpose for which a Hindu mar-
ries," a marriage of utter devotion and faithfulness (503). Thus the
prohibition against widows' remarriage was not the result of "irrational custom," but of faithfulness to one's spouse, especially the husband's religious needs served by his wife, which guarantees he will
treat her well (504). The Englishmen, on the contrary, were
"strangely lacking in sentiment" and an Englishman "seeks for a
wife through the columns of a morning newspaper," treating wives
as replaceable like bargains (505). Despite "much to reform in
India," its home life does not need "Western propagandism" (506).

Many authors, however, felt that without British intervention,
child marriages would not end. In 1890 Rukhmabai[40] condemned
the practice as the cause of injustices and a form of slavery that has
"proved fatal not only to individuals, families, and communities, but
to the whole Hindu race," and for which "it is the duty of every
thoughtful patriot to agitate for its abolition."[41] Wedding expenses
often landed fathers in debtors' prisons, and socially ostracized families for failure to participate, ruining Hindus "morally and physi-
cally" (268), an argument the British used as well (264–65). She
argued that child marriage enslaved the girl to her mother-in-law
and often to a cruel husband. Rukhmabai described child marriage
from the perspective of women's rights; for her, the only salvation
was intervention by "the British Government."

THE COMPLEXITIES OF ISLAM: HISTORY V. THEOLOGY

Clearly, discussions about women's status involved "correcting"
British stereotypes about Hindus and Muslims, and as Chatherjee
notes, women's issues were elided into nationalistic arguments in
support of Islam as historical, pluralistic, and "progressive." These
arguments are evident in Rafiüddin Ahmad's 1898 article in *The
Nineteenth Century* on the significance of the Battle of Omdurman.
Ahmad was a barrister-at-law, the Minister for Education in Bombay
(1928–32), and a founder of All India Muslim League in 1906. His
vocabulary of "progress" (688) embraced Victorian hegemony, and
his arguments were both *native* and *informant*. First he argued that
the British view of the battle as a victory of Christianity over Islam is

incorrect. The Sudanese Mahdi was not the representative of Pan-Islam and he "had no political recognition whatever in the Musselman world. He was an avowed rebel to the Governments of Egypt and Turkey."[42] Furthermore, British forces included Egyptian Muslims, not just British soldiers (689). Ahmad praised the Dervishes' devotion and courage, and in their honor he even quoted Tennyson's "Charge of the Light Brigade," using the English poet laureate to commemorate Dervishes who fought against the British at Omdurman and who twenty years earlier killed Gordon (689)! Ahmad reminded the English of their earlier defeat and argued that if properly armed, the Dervishes might have won at Omdurman, not unlike the Afridis who inflicted extensive casualties on the British before being defeated (691).

The lesson Ahmad drew is complex. One part is that Islamic armies need to modernize in arms and in discipline (692). Ahmad's second lesson is even more disturbing to British equilibrium. Acknowledging that the victory at Omdurman "makes England the complete mistress of the Nile," he pointed out that, thanks to English railways, telegraph, language, and commerce, all of Islam from India to Egypt is united, "between the Nile and the Niger . . . Khartûm and Zanzibar, through Uganda and British East Africa," as "Great Britain once more comes into contact with several millions of the followers of the Prophet" (692–93). After all, Ahmad argued, the "Pan-Islamic revival has suffered nothing by the fall of Khartûm; if anything, it has profited by it" (694). Turkey for twenty-five years desired "to open the whole of the Sûdán for purposes of commerce," and the British also assisted Egypt's access to the Sudan. British victory is re-defined as a victory for Islam for whom the "inaccessible" Sudan is now accessible (695). He advised the British to be careful about what form of government they inflict, especially upon Arabs, "the most orthodox and the most warlike of all the Musselman races" (693). They should not start a mission school in Khartoum, for example. Upsetting Arabs would leave an opportunity for Russia and France, ready for "taking advantage of the difficulties of England in the Dark Continent," he warned (693).

Ahmad played the cards of inter-European competition, as well as the threats to English power from a united Islam. English domination required the cooperation of Islam: "if England is to remain a great Asiatic power, and if she is to have a great African Empire, the loyal attachment and the cordial support of the Mûslims are to her an absolute necessity" (696). England cannot rule without Islamic cooperation, modernization, and sustained cultural integrity. Ahmad warned of future internecine conflict among Muslim states that the British would have to arbitrate, and suggested a Muslim international arbitration committee of the ablest Islamic jurists independent of their countries' governments (694), a plan like that proposed by Russia which Ahmad condemned as "impracticable" but of which mere mention reminded his English readers of the threat of Russia in the region. He appealed to the British as peacemakers.[43]

Clearly the meanings of Islam were as political as they were historical or theological. In *The Nineteenth Century* in 1897, Ahmad warns: "The riot in Calcutta was not unlike other riots which almost annually take place in India owing to trifling causes."[44] But he also insists that sedition, "in the real sense of the word, hardly exists in India. There is no desire among any community in India to get rid of British rule. What reasonable people want is the mending and not the ending of the Queen's government" (498). Ahmad argued for the loyalty of Muslims of India to the Crown, their "unabated confidence in the British rule . . . a kind of legitimate pride with their English fellow citizens in the greatness and prosperity of that empire" (499).

Riza Ahmed's description of the Caliphate of Egypt in his 1896 article in *The Contemporary Review* argues for an inherent democracy in Islam. Ahmed was a Turkish journalist in Paris. He describes the Caliph's "real tradition," serving at the disposal and approval of the people.[45] He even claims "that Islam knew how to determine and regulate the rights and duties of the sovereign, even before England essayed the task" (207). He insists Islam is without caste and that the mosque serves as a meeting place "for public deliberation on the affairs of the country" as well as for prayers (207). Islam helps promote civic participation: "Monarch and private subject, linked together by a common faith, worked together for a common interest. . . . the object of all was the pursuit of truth and justice" without clerical domination" (207). In short, "Arab civilisation was simply the scene of the progress of individuals" (208). Quoting Mohammed's dictum that it is right to overthrow a tyrant, he argues that Islamic citizens "have a civil duty . . . of controlling the conduct of Caesar," a statement that could apply to the British, as well as to the Caliphate (209).

But Ameer Ali in "A cry from the Indian Mohammedans" argued that Britons abuse Muslims. He criticized the government's oversensitivity: "An honest criticism is often construed into a hostile attack," making even "legitimate" comments on policy appear to be cases of "disloyalty."[46] The British are, he argued, no closer to understanding Muslims then they were fifty years ago, and seem unconcerned that fifty million "homogenous" Muslims with a common language and religion are "discontented . . . a matter for the serious consideration of the administrator of Indian policy" (194). He used "their" to refer to Muslims and thus speaks from an "English" positional superiority, to use Edward Said's phrase.[47] His topic is the dramatic decline in Muslim government jobs. Throughout he quoted Dr. Hunter, an English "authority," in support of his claims for the loss of Muslim jobs due to broken treaties and agreements which have devastated Muslim families: "The decadence of many leading families is due to the great social upheaval which ensued after the mutiny" (196). Lands handed down for generations were taken away because deeds, deteriorated by insects and time, could no longer be found to prove ownership. Hundreds of families were ruined and the great system of Muslim education destroyed, as even Hunter describes (197–98). Hindus began replacing Muslims in 1828, reducing Muslims to 1/7 and after 1880 to 1/10 of the work force.[48] In good Enlightenment fashion he included tables and statistics, derived from British sources, to prove his case (203–4).

Ameer Ali, like his compatriot authors, balanced his unrelenting criticism with praise for those English who were "large-minded, far seeing statesman of the type of the Marquis of Wellesley and the Marquis of Hastings" (205). He strategically employed the power of threats: "There is every danger if the feeling of discontent be allowed to grow chronic" and engender "an active feeling of disaffection" (205), further aggravated by British failure to understand and uphold Muslim laws (206). Given that religious intolerance was considered the ostensible cause of the 1857 Mutiny/Rebellion, Ameer Ali's remarks were indeed foreboding, but he insisted that Muslims wanted unity under British rule and desired to study "English language and literature" from which they were now barred by British-caused poverty destroying the Muslim middleclass, "the backbone of a nation" who lacked an education plan like that provided for Eurasians (210). To justify his recommendations, Ali insisted that his advice fulfilled the dreams of Empire: "The regeneration of India now depends on the spread of English education and the diffusion of Western ideas" especially if natives were really to have a part in their government as the British promised (211). Again he separated the British into good and bad: "The administration of justice is the strongest and most favorable feature of the British Government," despite its lapse during the last thirty years (213).

Throughout his criticisms, Ameer Ali proclaimed his loyalty: "No one can attach greater importance to the permanence of the British rule in India than myself, for I believe that upon it depends for a long time to come the well-being and progress of the country" (214). Out of this loyalty, he hoped to evoke "the interest of the English people" to help Muslims by "assisting the statesmen" to benefit the disenfranchised fifty million (a threatening number, to be sure) "'with great traditions but without a career'" and to replace British "mistaken sentimentalism, mixed with contemptuous regard for popular feeling" with his suggestions (215).[49]

Dominant rhetorical strategies among these authors were to make Islam historical and malleable, and not essential or medieval. They argued for the civility and modernity of Islam and represented Hindus and Moslems as rational, explicable, historical, learned, and thus "civilized" according to Europeans' own Enlightenment measures. Such reversed identities were deployed by almost all of these authors.[50]

CONCLUSION IN THEORY: WRITING CO-HISTORY

> . . . there is a prevailing trend for the language of dominated cultures to accommodate to the demands and concepts of the dominating culture. . . . How such new and alien concepts actually reorganise indigenous practices, and the kinds of resistance they meet, are clearly important questions for investigation . . . we must not suppose that the process of linguistic accommodation takes place mechanically or without resistance, or that where it is successful it produces a homogeneous result. But "resistance" is itself a sign of unequal power.
> —Talal Asad and John Dixon, "Translating Europe's Others," *Europe and its Others*

Those who accommodate to the language of the colonizer are often in a state of resisting, even when complying, as many of these essays demonstrate. The ability to play on British anxieties about its European competitors, as well as the dangers of ignoring the "insider" information that native informants offer, were ways in which authors resisted, even when advocating for, British intervention. It is precisely because they acquired the use of English, and acquired it so well, that these authors could also acquire the privilege to appear in the press and advocate their positions. As Asad and Dixon argue, the style of representations of the "Other" depends on the training and expectations of readers and authors, driven by a desire to appear logical within the systematic concepts in which they organize their expressions (176). The use of Enlightenment assumptions that authors applied to their own people while applying Orientalizing stereotypes to the British demonstrates these authors' recognition of their readers' expectations and ideologies.

But as Simon Gikandi demonstrates, colonized writers who wrote back to British defenders of Englishness and its civilizing authority did not write as simple reflexes or reactions: they wrote "not only as a direct rebuttal . . . to the doctrine of inalienable empire—and white supremacy—but also as a subtle affiliation with the culture that colonialism had created."[51] The authors I have examined were both resistant to, and affiliated with, their British colonizers; the affiliation afforded them the power to express their views and gain a place in the press to address British readers. And in this endeavour they are not simply "fixed in zones of dependency and peripherality, stigmatized in the designation of underdeveloped, less-developed, developing states," as Said claims.[52] Instead, they speak from a center they have acquired by their "subtle affiliation," to use Gikandi's phrase. Whether or not they constitute the role of *interlocateur valable*, caught in conflict and compliant as Said defines such an interlocutor, they are certainly not the silent "native intellectual" who resists any cooperation that Franz Fanon describes (cited in Said, 210). And they are not Said's antiseptic or domesticated interlocutor, either, who is finally allowed "inside" (210).

These authors resist any simple definitions or roles, but instead inhabit a complex set of selves and a range of opinions and authorities. In Laurel Brake's formation study of *The Nineteenth Century*, where a majority of these essays appeared, she argues that the periodical intended to be a site of "divergent positions on questions of philosophy, theology and science" and "to exploit the revelations of signature" that underscored diversity and authority.[53] Interestingly, the signatures of the "Other" were as authoritative as they were diverse—Pashas, Rajahs, barristers, diplomats. These authors were a subset of insiders and expressed opposition and the criticism of empire within the hegemony of British doubts about empire at the time expressed in *The Nineteenth Century* by such authorities as Gladstone.[54] These informant essays were thus "in the discourse" as British foreign policy in the last quarter of the century became dominated by doubt and hesitancy, self-questionings about the extent of British intervention in native customs, laws, practices, carving out a space for native agency to balance British intervention. To gain the empathy of British readers, these authors advocated uplift, reform, progress, moral virtue, representation, and rationalism. Their identities as "Other" joined them to an intermediate identity of English enlightenment and a revised native representation as un-Oriental and unsubaltern.

Perhaps these authors wrote for the same reason Fanon wrote, in
Said's view: "to force the European metropolis to think its history
together with the history of colonies awakening from the cruel stupor
and abused immobility of imperial dominion" (Said, 223). They offered a co-history, along with their resistance and the seduction of
their insider, "secret" knowledge. Their writings were essays of
agency and urgency. The authors' agency was in collusion with the
readers' agency—goaded to urge England to save the Persians, end
infant marriages and eternal widowhood, or provide a banking system to hedge against famines in India. The reader became a force
for imperial administration as these authors encouraged readers to
perceive the empire as discursive not as textual which it was for most
English readers, to see native people not only as palpable, human,
suffering, but also as civilized, educated, and reformist.

Ann Parry compellingly argues for the press as a "process without
an individual subject" (101), derived from Foucault's recognition
that a discourse "regulates the reader's access to knowledge and . . .
provides that reader with a social location and a sense of his [sic]
country's history and national superiority."[55] Parry's model of a
"composite text" built of "a complex process of collation and dis-
continuity" is exemplified by these essays in which discourses of colonialism and Orientalism become convoluted, folded back upon
themselves, and turned upside down.[56] Native informancy held out
a promise to British readers of change within the system and a bulwark against more violent resistance that was becoming increasingly
visible throughout the Empire. In this way the press helped promote
the move toward a modern Empire and a new colonized Other, both
advocated in these essays, regardless of authors' proximity to or distance from British imperial policies. These essays also exemplify
Bakhtin's dialogic, multivoiced literature and offer up articulate recommendations for colonial administration—when to intervene,
when to watch, whom to protect—by those who possessed crucial
knowledges as intermediaries, mediators, informants, and loyal non-
subalterns, hybrid, and enlightened.

The mediating role of the press was exercised here too. Between
violent sedition and utter Anglicization lay a range of native infor-
mancies by which British hegemony could effect reform and progress to sustain the myth of the civilizing effect of Empire. Whatever
the authors' views on this civilizing force, they readily appealed to it
and its formation of English national identity to substantiate their
own agendas in their own countries, as they represented their societies as post-Enlightenment rather than medieval, law-abiding rather

than chaotic, rational rather than superstitious, and discursive rather than inscrutably silent.

NOTES

1. Essays appeared in *The Nineteenth-Century, Fraser's, Fortnightly Review, Temple Bar, Cornhill Magazine, Ainsworth's Magazine, Dublin University Magazine, National Review, Westminster Review, Macmillan's, Dark Blue, New Monthly Magazine, Scottish Review, Blackwood's, New Review, Longman's Review, Contemporary Review,* as well as in missionary and women's periodicals.

2. See Antoinette Burton, "Tongues Untied: Lord Salisbury's 'Black Man' and the Boundaries of Imperial Democracy," *Comparative Study of Society and History* (2000): 632–61, for an excellent study of Naoroji's campaign in 1892.

3. Nawangar, Maharaja Shri Ranjitsinhji Vibhaji, "Cricket and the Victorian Era," *Blackwood's Magazine*, 162 (July 1897): 1–16.

4. Mozoomdar, Protap Chunder, "Present-day progress in India," *The Nineteenth Century*, 48 (December 1900), 998.

5. Gauri Viswanathan, "Currying Favor: The Politics of British Educational and Cultural Policy in India, 1813–54," *Dangerous Liaisons: Gender, Nation, and Postcolonial Perspectives*, eds. A. McClintock, A. Mufti, and E. Shohat (Minneapolis: University of Minnesota Press, 1997), 121.

6. Viswanathan, 127–28.

7. Julie F. Codell, "Resistance and Performance: Native Informant Discourse in the Biographies of Maharaja Sayaji Rao III of Baroda," *Orientalism Transposed: The Impact of the Colonies on British Culture*, eds. Julie F. Codell and Dianne Sachko Macleod (Aldershot: Ashgate, 1998), 13–45.

8. Sayaji Rao Gaekwar, "My Ways and Days in Europe and in India," *The Nineteenth Century and After* 49 (February 1901): 215.

9. Linda Alcoff, "The Problem of Speaking for Others," *Cultural Critique* 12 (Winter 1991): 12.

10. Romesh Chunder Dutt, "Famines in India and their remedy," *Fortnightly Review,* 68 o.s., 62 n.s. (August 1897): 205 (signed "A Hindu," ascribed by *Wellesley Index*).

11. See Ainslie T. Embree, "Comment: Widows as Cultural Symbols," *Sati, the Blessing and the Curse*, ed. John Stratton Hawley (Oxford: Oxford University Press, 1994), 154, and Engels, 1983.

12. Dutt (or Datt), Shoshee Chunder, Raî Báhádur, (or Sasi Chandra), "Taxation in India," *Fraser's*, 94 o.s., 14 n.s. (September 1876): 302.

13. A. Sarathkumar Ghosh, "The financial relation between England and India," *Westminster Review,* 148 (October 1897): 412.

14. Odai Partab Singh, Rajah of Bhinga, "The decay of landed aristocracy in India," *The Nineteenth Century* 31 (May 1892): 830–38, who did not believe democracy would work in India, wrote on the landed aristocracy; Syed Ameer Ali, "The Life Problem of Bengal," *The Nineteenth Century* 14 (September 1883): 421–40, or A. S. Ghosh, "A Remedy for Indian Famines," *Contemporary Review* 72 (August 1897): 268–71, both of whom argued for representation and on behalf of peasants.

15. Uma Sankar Misra, "Lord Dufferin and the Indian National Congress," *Westminster Review* 132 (July 1889): 93.

16. Odai Partab Singh, Rajah of Bhinga, "The cow agitation, or the mutiny-plasm in England," *The Nineteenth Century* 35 (April 1894): 667.

17. Mancherjee Merwanjee Bhownaggree, "The present agitation in India and the vernacular press," *Fortnightly Review*, 68 o.s., 62 n.s. (August 1897): 305.

18. Jamal al-Din al-Afghani, "The Reign of Terror in Persia," *Contemporary Review* 61 (February 1892): 238.

19. Muhammad 'Abd al Halim Pasha, "A reply to my critics," *The Nineteenth Century* 18 (September 1885): 486–87.

20. Syed Ameer Ali, "Some Indian suggestions for India," *The Nineteenth Century* 7 (June 1880): 963.

21. Syed Ameer Ali, "The rupee and the ruin of India," *The Nineteenth Century* 33 (March 1893): 523.

22. Antoinette Burton, *At the Heart of the Empire: Indians and the Colonial Encounter in Late-Victorian Britain* (Berkeley and Los Angeles: University of California Press, 1998), 47–49.

23. Romesh Chunder Dutt, "The grievances of India," *Dark Blue* 3 (May 1872): 328 (signed "A Hindu," ascribed by *Wellesley Index*).

24. Antoinette Burton, *Burdens of History: British Feminists, Indian Women, and Imperial Culture, 1865–1915* (Chapel Hill: University of North Carolina Press, 1994), 2.

25. Dagmar Engels, "The Age of Consent Act of 1891: Colonial Ideology in Bengal," *South Asia Research* 3 (1983): 107.

26. Lata Mani, "The Production of an Official Discourse on *Sati* in Early Nine-teenth-Century Bengal," *Europe and its Others*, ed. Francis Barker, 2 vols. (Colchester: University of Essex, 1979), 1: 117; and Joytsna G. Singh, *Colonial Narratives, Cultural Dialogues: "Discoveries" of India in the Language of Colonialism* (London: Routledge, 1996), 98–100.

27. Paul Ricoeur, "The Model of the Text: Meaningful Action Considered as a Text," *Social Research* 38 (1971): 529–62.

28. Dagmar Engels, "The Limits of Gender Ideology: Bengali Women, the Colonial State, and the Private Sphere, 1890–1930," *Women's Studies International Forum* 12 (1989): 425–37. Geraldine Forbes in "Women and Modernity: The Issue of Child Marriage in India," *Women's Studies International Quarterly* 1 (1979): 409, points out that child marriage was widespread in the nineteenth century. Engels (1989) writes that purdah "was in fact rigidly practised only by a minority of women" (425), although what the qualifier "rigidly" means in this context is unclear, and her assertion is certainly debatable.

29. Janaki Nair, "Uncovering the Zenana: Visions of Indian Womanhood in Englishwomen's Writings, 1813–1940," *Journal of Women's History* 2 (Spring 1990): 11, 17.

30. Partha Chatterjee, "Colonialism, Nationalism and Colonialized Women: The Contest in India," *American Ethnologist* 16 (November 1989): 623.

31. Meredith Borthwick, *The Changing Role of Women in Bengal, 1849–1905* (Princeton: Princeton University Press, 1984), 21, 329; see also A. Burton, *At the Heart*, 110–51, on Sorabji.

32. Annie Reichardt, "Mohammedan Women," *The Nineteenth Century* 20 (June 1891): 941–52.

33. Syed Ameer Ali, "The real status of women in Islam," *The Nineteenth Century* 20 (September 1891): 387.

34. Ameer Ali's strategies are repeated in his other essays on women, such as "The Influence of Women in India," *The Nineteenth Century*, 1899.

35. Protap Chunder Mozoomdar, "Present-day progress in India," *The Nineteenth Century* 48 (December 1900): 994.

36. T. Vijaya-Raghavan, "Hindu marriage customs and British law," *National Review* 17 (March 1891): 80.

37. Devendra N. Das, "The Hindu widow," *The Nineteenth Century* 20 (September 1886): 373.

38. Nanda Ghosh, "Social reforms in India," *National Review* 8 (November 1886): 361.

39. Hury Singh Gour, "Hindu theory of marriage," *National Review* 18 (December 1891): 502.

40. I suspect this author is really Pandita Ramabai, an advocate of women's rights. See Borthwick, 237, 277, 291, 339, 341; Burton, *At the Heart*, 72–109, on Ramabai.

41. Rukhmabai, "Indian child marriages: an appeal to the British government," *New Review* 3 (September 1890): 263.

42. Maulvi Rafiüddin Ahmad, "The Battle of Omdurman and the Mussulman World" *The Nineteenth Century* 44 (October 1898): 688–89.

43. In an essay in 1895 in *The Nineteenth Century* Ahmad also speaks as an insider—"I have resided too long in Stainboul to believe any such twaddle" (159; twaddle is a very "English" colloquialism), Ahmad offers "a Moslem view of the question before the British public" with the help of the journal's editor (156). He reminds the British public how strategic Turkey is to the protection of India from Russia (164).

44. Maulvi Rafiüddin Ahmad, "India II: Is the British 'Raj' in danger?" *The Nineteenth Century* 42 (September 1897): 497.

45. Riza Ahmed, "The Caliph and his duties," *Contemporary Review* 17 (September 1896): 206.

46. Syed Ameer Ali, "A cry from the Indian Mohammedans," *The Nineteenth Century* 12 (August 1882): 193.

47. Edward Said, *Orientalism* (New York: Vintage Books, 1979), 7.

48. "Of the foreign office's 54 workers, only one was Muslim; Finance of Revenue had 75 employees but no Muslims; the Accountant General in Bengal had 181 employees, but no Muslims; the Board of Revenue's 113 employees included only one Muslim (Ameer Ali, "A Cry from the Indian Mohammedans," 202).

49. Ameer Ali uses these strategies in most of his essays. In "Islam and its Critics," *The Nineteenth Century* 38 (September 1895): 361–80 and in "Islam and Canon MacColl," *The Nineteenth Century* 38 (November 1895): 778–85, he characterized his antagonist as a fanatic whose "seeds of dissension and discord, encourage discontent and agitation," and "murderous reprisals," portraying the clergyman as hysterical and diabolical ("Islam and Canon MacColl," 783). In "Islam and Canon MacColl" Ameer Ali historicized Islamic law, describing centuries of commentaries and changing practices in post-Koranic texts over the centuries, and pointed out the existence of precedence in Islam law that is also fundamental to English law (779–80). He cited English jurists to support his views (i.e., Neill, Baillie, 780) to argue for Turkish civility toward Christians in its law courts (Harris in *Blackwood's*, October 1895, 782), and to offer a proper interpretation of misquoted Arabic legal terms both misunderstood (Hamilton) and correctly understood (Baillie, 783) by English authors.

50. See, for example, Barakatüllah on differences between Sufi and Islam: Mohammad Barakatüllah, "Islam and Soofeeism," *Westminster Review* 144 (December 1895): 674–78.

51. Simon Gikandi. *Maps of Englishness: Writing Identity in the Culture of Colonialism* (New York: Columbia University Press, 1996), *xiv.*

52. Edward Said, "Representing the Colonized: Anthropology's Interlocutors," *Critical Inquiry* 15 (Winter 1989): 207.

53. Laurel Brake, *Subjugated Knowledges: Journalism, Gender and Literature in the Nineteenth Century* (London: Macmillan, 1994), 51–52.

54. Brake, 60–61. See also Brake, "Theories of Formation: The Nineteenth Century: Vol. I, No. I, March 1877, Monthly. 2/6," *Victorian Periodicals Review* 25 (1992): 16–21.

55. Ann Parry, "Theories of Formation: *Macmillan's Magazine:* Vol. 1, November 1859. Monthly. 1/0," *Victorian Periodicals Review* 26 (1993): 101–2.

56. As Rosalie O'Hanlon suggests, the categories of "British" and "colonial" need each other for mutually defining identities ever unstable and in process; see O'Hanlon, Rosalind, "Recovering the Subject: Subaltern Studies and Histories of Resistance in Colonial South Asia," *Modern Asian Studies* 22 (1988): 189–224.

History by Installment: The Australian Centenary and the *Picturesque Atlas of Australasia,* 1886–1888

Tony Hughes-d'Aeth

On the 26th of January 1888 Australia celebrated its centenary of settlement. That day marked the passing of one hundred years since a fleet of British naval vessels bearing a cargo of 756 convicted criminals landed on the shores of New South Wales. In a period obsessed with origins, the founding moment of Australia's colonization was deeply problematic. The 1880s, nevertheless, were boom years for much of colonial Australia, still riding the wave of a gold-based prosperity that had emerged in the 1850s. The colonies were inching towards federation, although the eventual form this would take was still a matter of considerable debate. Despite a nascent nationalism expressed most famously in the pages of the Sydney *Bulletin,* the overwhelming sentiment was still in favor of the British Empire, a fact underscored by the deployment of a contingent of New South Wales soldiers to fight in the Sudan in 1886. Large-scale celebrations, moreover, took place throughout the colonies in 1887 in honor of Queen Victoria's jubilee. The centenary of 1888 attempted to marry an allegiance to empire with a commitment to a nation that had not yet come into existence. Unfortunately, it proved difficult to divorce the occasion of Australia's founding (as a prison) from the sensation of triumph that the centenary was designed to evoke.

The ambivalence of the Australian centenary, however, did not deter the Picturesque Atlas Publishing Company from undertaking the largest publication project ever attempted in the Australian colonies. The publication was called the *Picturesque Atlas of Australasia* and was sold by subscription to over fifty-thousand people, roughly 1.3 percent of the population. It was the biggest of several centennial publications, and shared with its rivals a periodical format, emerging in parts between 1886 and 1888.[1] The resulting work is a rich case study of the manner in which the Australian colonial press

219

embodied the mixed allegiances to British and Australian systems of social identity. The identity issues are particularly highlighted by the representation of history in the *Atlas*. The centennial occasion created an environment of celebration and the desire to mark achievement and progress, but at the same time uncovered feelings of inadequacy based around Australia's position far from the center of the empire on which it depended for many aspects of its survival.

This essay explores the way that the *Atlas* sought to celebrate the history of a country that held deep concerns about the status of its historical experience. In this way the Australian experience replicates the anxieties, and resultant compensations of exuberant confidence, of other settler colonies. To read the *Atlas* is to explore the problematics of colonial history and the difficulties associated with telling and showing a national story beneath an imperial umbrella. The narrative of Australian history in the *Atlas* reveals the strains and contradictions within this project. Moreover, as an illustrated publication, the makers of the *Atlas* were also confronted with the task of representing this history visually. The strategies of visualisation that underpin the illustrations are an important aspect of the way the *Atlas* appealed to its readership. Once again, the *Atlas* is representative here of broader cultural trends and desires. Its pictures combine the practices of history, memory, visuality, and materiality to produce an image-world that expresses the desire of colonial readers for historical justification and to mask the ambivalences of their condition.

THE AUSTRALIAN CENTENARY

The event that more than any other shaped the *Atlas* was the centenary of European settlement in Australia, marking the hundred-year anniversary of the landing of Arthur Phillip and his cargo of convicts at Sydney Cove on 26 January 1788. In its promotional literature, the *Atlas* was put forward as a kind of centennial progress report, a snapshot of Australia on its hundredth birthday. It was an unashamedly celebratory publication, a work designed to capitalize on the percolating sentiments of Australian patriotism that the centennial occasion was expected to generate. The Australian centenary of 1888, however, was a vexed event. It was not just that the people of the Australian colonies were unsure about how to celebrate the occasion, but that there was, according to Maya Tucker, considerable "confusion amongst the public as to what was actually being celebrated on 26 January."[2] Tucker paints a picture of celebrations that were alternatively grandiose and abortive, spasmodic and banal. There were statues and yachting regattas, speeches and public dinners. What, after all, did the centenary mean in a loose collection of colonies habitually accustomed to looking "home" more than at each other? Responses ranged, according to Graeme Davison, between "optimistic and pessimistic, committed and apathetic."[3] The very idea of a "national" day of centennial celebration, as opposed to the various colony-based "foundation," "separation," and "settlement" days, was itself novel, and its success rested primarily on the industry and efforts of grass roots lobbying by groups such as the Australian Natives Association and committed federationists like Sir Henry Parkes and Alfred Deakin. Reactions to the event also varied according to social position and geography. While the governors and premiers of the various colonies were shipped in luxury to Sydney to wine and dine at the expense of its debt-laden taxpayers, there was little in terms of symbolism around which popular sentiment could congeal. The jubilation of booming Melbourne was balanced by the relative quiet of a recessed Adelaide.[4] Celebrations in Hobart, Perth, Brisbane, and regional Australia were respectful if, on the whole, rather subdued. New South Wales, which as the first colony to be settled saw itself as the obvious epicenter of centennial celebration, was beset by spiralling public debt and was enduring a series of austerity budgets.

Yet the problems of New South Wales were more than financial. Celebrating the centenary meant remembering the occasion of its settlement and the sting of its penal past. It was an issue that would resurface a century later when the Australian Bicentennial Authority, "refused to support the First Fleet Re-enactment project because it focused on the convict past."[5] In the mid-1880s, however, the prosperity of convict-free Victoria ensured there was a good deal to celebrate in that colony and, more important, the means with which to do so. Melbourne's Centennial International Exhibition, which ran from August 1888 to February 1889, was as much an advertisement of Victoria's material wealth as a commemoration of one hundred years of European settlement on the Australian continent. In the acerbic pages of the Sydney *Bulletin*, however, a sniping anti-centenary campaign continued from at least the middle of 1886. "There are," it suggests, "most excellent reasons why this so-called centenary should not be celebrated at all."[6] For the *Bulletin*, 26 January 1788 was not a day of glorious inception, but "the day we were lagged."

Despite the derision of the *Bulletin*, the centenary remained important not just as a backward-looking gesture toward the mother country, but as an event which lent substantial impetus to the process of colonial federation. As the *Sydney Morning Herald* announced: " "Nation" is a big word to use . . . though it is rather the symbol of what shall be than the expression of what is, still, if ever there was a time when it was fitting to use the word it is now."[7] While many agreed in principle to federation, and found its various arguments in relation to tariffs, infrastructure, defense, and immigration compelling, the details were proving difficult to resolve. Thus the centenary, particularly in New South Wales, presented itself as a public policy conundrum. It was an event that could neither be avoided nor satisfactorily embraced by all sides. Added to this was the embarrassment that the colony of New South Wales was quite simply too poor to afford its own birthday party, a position highlighted by the fact that the "Centennial" exhibition was being held in Melbourne in the rival colony of Victoria, which was still many years short of its century.

It is with a faint note of perversity, then, that in this climate of equivocation, restraint, and ambiguity, the Picturesque Atlas Publishing Co. launched a publishing project of unprecedented grandeur in Sydney. The significance of this context was not lost on the promoters of the *Atlas*. In August of 1886, leading *Atlas* artist (and recent resident of Victoria) Julian Ashton addressed the topic of the approaching centenary in a speech to assembled political dignitaries on the occasion of the visit of the newly appointed Governor, Lord Carrington, to the *Atlas* factory in Wynyard Square. "New South Wales," he announced, "was approaching a memorable time in her history, namely, her hundredth birthday," and while "her infancy was over . . . she was too young to go without a birthday present to mark the event."[8] Yet who would provide such a gift? Who would step forward and provide a present worthy of this historic occasion? These were the questions implicit in Ashton's address. And if the questions were implicit then the answer certainly was not. "If the Government should unwisely decide to hold no commemoration of this important period in our history, but to leave the matter in private hands," then, Ashton had no doubt that, "amongst all the schemes proposed for the celebration of our centenary, that for magnitude of design, for the effect it would produce upon the outside world, as to our resources, or for the impetus it would give to all matters pertaining to art in the colonies, none could compare with such a publication as the "Picturesque Atlas of Australasia," the last number of which would be completed about the year 1888" (*Herald*, 24 August 1886).

There is a certain suggestiveness in the idea that the Australian centenary was to find its apotheosis in paper. Indeed, the *Atlas* accomplished in paper many of the aims that rival centennial schemes (monuments, exhibitions, statues, parks, pantheons) had proposed to be conducted in stone, steel, and glass. The imposing large-scale format of the *Atlas* gave to it a monumental quality. W. B. Dalley, the Attorney-General of New South Wales called the *Atlas* a "beautiful memorial" (*Herald*, 24 August 1886), while the Melbourne *Age*, whose support for the *Atlas* was not without reservation, also found it to be a "striking monument."[9] Its range of chapters, moreover, which would cover history, geography, art, and the sciences, had the compendious and displayable qualities of an exhibition, while its numerous historical portraits would serve the purpose of the historical pantheon proposed by Henry Parkes as the centerpiece of Centennial Park. The *Atlas* therefore united within the dimensions of a single project, the virtues of the monument, the colonial exhibition, and the historical pantheon. It combined permanence with public profile, grandeur with accessibility, and a singularity of presence with the totality of its purview. Although based in Sydney, by using contributors from across the colonies, it enfranchised colonists in a way that other centennial functions could not. The *Atlas* thus put itself forward as a genuinely "national" undertaking, enacting in its pages a federation that was proving elusive in the world of colonial politics.

Telling Australian History

The same anxieties that mark the *Atlas* as a historical product also permeate the attempts within the work to render a history of Australia. The matter can be approached in two ways, internationally and (proto)nationally. In the first instance, the historical dimension of the *Atlas* might be seen as part of the international genres, well-established by the late nineteenth century, of popular illustrated history and regional description. The leading publishing house in these genres was undoubtedly Cassell, which had in the 1870s published *Picturesque Europe* (1876–79), *Picturesque Canada* (1882–84) and *Picturesque America* (1872–74), as well as historical works like *Cassell's History of India* (1876–77). Illustrated "part-issues" were a particular specialty of the Cassell company. These were lengthy publications issued in serial form, which were also often sold as bound editions following the completion of the serial issue. Another practice employed frequently by Cassell's, particularly in relation to its part-issues, was the tying of popular works to topical occasions, and in particular the commemorative publication. As Simon Nowell-Smith, historian of the Cassell house, remarks: "Not an international event of any significance was allowed to pass without a part-issue explaining its historical setting."[10] The *Atlas* draws on these generic forms but also hybridizes them in ways that reveal the specificities of its production in Australia at the time of the centenary. Cast as a "picturesque" descriptive compendium, the *Atlas* is weighed down by a compulsion toward the telling of history. The *Atlas* was far more historically focused than the picturesque works about Europe and North America, which are predominantly descriptive and touristic. The historical bent of the *Atlas* is indicative of the nascent nationalism of the Australian colonies in the 1880s that was coalescing through narrative, if not through institutions.

Writers in the *Atlas*, engaged in the ideological labor of formulating a viable national narrative, faced several difficulties. A key problem was that of settling on a point of departure, a point at which Australian history could be said to commence. Certainly there was no suggestion of locating the origins of Australian history within the experience and lifeways of the indigenous owners. Co-opting Aboriginality into Australian history was a twentieth-century development. To the extent that Aboriginal Australians appeared in the *Atlas* it was largely in terms of the "natural history" of the continent. The human history of Australia was, by assumption, generated by European contact and the earliest beginnings of Australian history in the *Atlas* are located in the early encounters by Dutch and Portuguese navigators, and most notably the British adventurer and pirate William Dampier. Attractive in terms of antiquity, these encounters are ultimately rejected as the "true" beginning of Australia because they do not lead directly to colonization by Britain. Far more significant than these "blind, stumbling discoveries" (3)[11], was the systematic exploration of the east coast of Australia by James Cook. It is Cook who is selected as the hero of the historical narrative of the *Atlas* and it is his noble countenance that stares out of the finely textured engraving in the frontispiece (fig. 21), "the finest engraving of Captain Cook in existence."[12] Cook's much-vaunted bravery and ultimate sacrifice make him an ideal metonym for a heroic national identity.[13] The "Captain Cook" chapter, written by historian and headmaster of Melbourne's Carlton College Alexander Sutherland, neatly enfolds several representational layers in the *Atlas*. His story, like the nation he is now claimed to have founded, is one of spectacular success from humble beginnings: "No one would have prophesied in James Cook's early youth, that he was destined to fill so prominent a place in the list of the world's great men" (7). Suther-

**Figure 21. "James Cook," frontispiece of *Picturesque Atlas
of Australasia*, edited by Andrew Garran. 3 vols. (Sydney:
The Picturesque Atlas Publishing Company, 1886–1888).**

land's focus on Cook was appreciated by the local press who reviewed the *Atlas*. The *Daily Telegraph* praised Sutherland for "the
most admirable ingenuity displayed in wrapping up so many important circumstances in a single chapter" (14 August 1886). "To us,"
continued the *Telegraph*, "the landing of the circumnavigator and
his party on the shores of Botany Bay, often as we have read of it,
and stale as it may seem, is ever a pleasant yarn." It was "an account
so light and flowing that no one would say that it was really overbur-
dened with solid fact." Cook's story follows the poetics of populist
history, which is based on the imperative to tell the good story, the
one that speaks warmly to the idea one has of oneself. A story which
says, *this is your story*. It is the kind of history Greg Dening calls "political parable" where "to be a cliché is a virtue," a history "directed
at evoking mythical metonymies, likenesses that are seen immedi-

ately to be true and are sustaining not because they are new, but because they are old."[14]

For all the celebration of Cook, it was an inescapable fact that an additional eighteen years separated the voyage of the *Endeavour* in 1770 from the arrival of the First Fleet that signalled the beginning of European occupation of Australia.[15] The centenary marked this latter event and it was this occasion to which the *Atlas* was tethered. Ordinarily, one might have thought that some pride of place would have been accorded to the leader of that first expedition. However, although a portrait of "Captain Arthur Phillip" (16) is duly included among the *Atlas*'s gallery of notable figures, and while his accomplishments are politely acknowledged, there is no attempt to elevate Phillip to the position of founding patriarch. The "stain" of the convict system tended to render any attempt to talk about the moment of first settlement, including Phillip's role, abortive. The writers of the *Atlas* were acutely aware of this problem at the heart of the history of the European in Australia. "The early history of colonisation in Australia," noted Frank Donohue, has "been blackened by a record of tyranny on the one hand and criminality on the other, over which it is best that we should draw a veil of discreet silence, and pass on to a more inviting chapter in our national story" (771). Reviews of the *Atlas* also emphasize the need for discretion in dealing with the convict past. "In the third chapter," writes the *Daily Telegraph* in its review of the first part of the *Atlas*, "the question of the early settlement is handled so delicately that the pages are unstained by a single word that might mar for one moment the pleasure of the most susceptible of readers" (14 August 1886).

Convict heritage is no longer a matter of shame in Australia, rather a matter of pride. In the 1880s, however, it constituted the central dilemma for the formation of a localized identity. The dilemma was made pressing because of a nationalist ideology founded on a doctrine of origins that was tied to a broader demand in nineteenth-century epistemology to know the origin of things, the moment in which the present was ultimately sourced. Historians of late nineteenth-century Australia, like Alexander Sutherland, George Barton, and William Traill writing for the *Atlas*, were caught between the demand to celebrate a true beginning and a need to suppress the truth of this beginning.[16] How does one Other one's origin? This is the persistent difficulty of Australian centennial histories like the *Atlas*. That the *Atlas* does produce a celebratory history of Australia is the result of a number of strategies which had the effect of affirming Australian identity against an ambivalent sense of the past.

If the convict system contributed to a sense of what Reekie and

Whitlock have called Australia's "uncertain beginnings" then this problem can also be seen to shape the themes that dominate the historical narratives of the *Atlas*.[17] Indeed, despite the "delicacy" of Sutherland and Barton, a story emerges of the opening years of the colony that is shot through with episodes that do not seem to fit easily within the narrative of social ascent that provided the framework for centennial celebrations. Criminality, famine, disease, insurrection, traffic in spirits, despotism, *de facto* martial law, mismanagement, labor shortages, and arrested development all emerge in one way or another in the *Atlas's* histories of early settlement. The response of writers to the encroachment of unsavory events is to mobilize the transformative narrative of progress. "For more than half a century," writes Sutherland of the early colonies, "their progress had been a slow and generally a painful one" (35). Yet the crucial point is that progress always remains immanent in these events, because Australia in the 1880s was the living proof of this outcome.[18]

Again there is both a general and a local explanation for the progressivism of the historical narratives in the *Atlas*. In the broadest sense, history moves, and it moves forward. Historical subjects—people, institutions, nations—are impelled forward by the narratives of history, against a graduated calendar that measures the passing of time. "Progress" writes de Certeau, is the "motto" of history.[19] This was never more so than in the nineteenth century when, according to historians such as Peter J. Bowler and A. Dwight Culler, progress was integral to the various forms of historical explanation that emerged.[20] It was not just that the past became fascinating to the Victorians, though this certainly happened, it was that the past began to speak through a diverse array of knowledges. The sciences, for instance, became historicized in such a way that "a particular theory of human progress soon came to depend for its conceptual foundations upon a compatible interpretation of the origin of mankind, and hence of the history of life on earth" (Bowler, 192). History was part of a grand, if at times conflicted, teleology.

The metrical occasion of the Australian centenary bore the burden of this teleological drive. The *Atlas*, as a centennial publication, carries the cargo of progress in the form of its histories. The sense of brevity that assailed nineteenth-century Australian historians was compensated for by an emphasis on rapidity. Indeed, the principal theme of the history in the *Atlas*, the engine that drives all other gears and mechanisms, was the astonishing rate of progress in the Australasian colonies. In the period of economic prosperity succeeding the discovery of gold, "progress" wrote Geoffrey Blainey, "was an incantation more than a word."[21] It was the same engine that drove the ephemeral majesty of the colonial exhibitions. "The Centennial Exhibition held in Melbourne in 1888," wrote Frank Donohue for the *Atlas*, "was not only a notable witness to Australian progress in the past, but a gage of prosperity in the future, and a landmark in its history from which the past as well as the years that are to come will be measured" (793). Melbourne in particular was felt to embody this breathtaking acceleration. The people of Melbourne, according to Graeme Davison, had always been enamoured with the rapidity of their city's growth, "but in the 1880s growth became an obsession," and by the end of this decade "the city was intoxicated with the idea of growth for growth's sake."[22] Melbourne's transformation from a series of small huts on the bank of the Yarra to a bustling modern city within the ambit of living memory occasioned reveries. E. E. Morris, in his "Editor's Note" to a rival publication of the *Atlas*—*Cassell's Picturesque Australasia*—reflects upon his supervising an examination in the Wilson Hall, at Melbourne University. "It is difficult," he remarked, thinking of the young scholars before him, "to conceive a greater contrast to a corroboree of aborigines, such as men now living have often witnessed on this very spot" (Morris, vol. 4, 296). The transformative power of civilization suffuses the *Atlas* and is inevitably accompanied by a rhetoric of wonder, which lends to even the most material events an element of the miraculous. "Not even the most sanguine of prophets," wrote James Smith of the growth of Melbourne, "could then have anticipated what those thirteen huts were to grow to, but there are men still living who have watched the development" (254).

Historiographers of nineteenth-century Australia have noted that the form of progress that gained ascendancy in the latter half of the century was based almost entirely around materialism and the generation of wealth, and it is certainly wealth that ties together the success narratives in the *Atlas*. "Australia," announced Andrew Garran in his Editor's preface, "beginning as a prison, discovered in time that it was a splendid wool farm, and, when that industry had been established on secure foundations, it made the further discovery that underneath the grass lay a magnificent gold mine . . . from that moment forth its material resources have been steadily developed" (iv). Wealth creation becomes a way of talking about not only Australasia as a whole, but each colony, each city and town, each port and branch of railroad, and each industry and institution. In the logic of the *Atlas*, wealth also became a marker of other forms of moral and civil ascent within Australia. Playing on the quantitative certainty of money, "wealth" was used to denote progress along less tangible avenues of achievement: "And side by side with its increase in wealth has been its advancement socially, intellectually and politically" (iv). William Traill, writing of Queensland in the *Atlas*, spoke of the "thousand and one industries that attest the prosperity and vitality of this favoured colony" (410). Money leant its measurability to history, thereby helping to authenticate the cumulative premise of the centenary.

Showing Australian History

The *Atlas* publicity clearly conceives of the work as performing at two levels, in words and pictures. "The writers have kept on their even course," explained the *Daily Telegraph*, "picking and choosing from a large mass of material as the interest of the narrative demanded, and only here and there casting the lightest possible allusions to the presence of brush and palette" (14 August 1886). The use of pictures was also seen as a way of enfranchising the entire family unit, with pictures allowing children to participate in each monthly part: "We venture to say that each part of "Picturesque Australasia" will be read and read again, and that by the time the next monthly part is issued the grown up people in subscribing households will be as familiar with the letterpress as their children will be familiar with the illustrations." Illustration, however, was not just a matter for children. The act of seeing was a major ingredient in the Victorian pursuit of knowledge and a central drive behind the explosion of illustrated publications in the nineteenth century. Visuality was equally important in colonial Australia. A diorama of Captain Cook's landing at Botany Bay was reportedly the most popular exhibit at the Melbourne Centennial Exhibition, and the popularity of cycloramas and panoramas in the nineteenth century in portraying everything from the Burke and Wills expedition to scenes from *Uncle Tom's Cabin* further attest to a desire for consuming events visually.[23]

Like the written chapters, the historical pictures in the *Atlas* display a need to validate the historical present and are subject to even stronger codes of "discretion" in terms of what was depicted. The issue of pictorial discretion is highlighted by the absence of any pictures of convicts in the *Atlas* chapters devoted to settlement in New South Wales. Indeed, there are no pictures which even hint at the presence of the convict system. A glance across the pictures of this chapter devoted to the beginnings of settlement yields no sign of the *raison d'être* of that settlement.[24] There is, however, evidence that at a certain stage of the planning of the *Atlas*, convict images were going to be included. In Macleod's "Sketch Notebook" dating from approximately May of 1886 there is a jotted list of the proposed illus-trations for the first section of the *Atlas*.[25] Being quite close to the point of publication, there is a high degree of correspondence be-tween the illustrations that actually appear in the *Atlas*. Included in the list, however, is the title "Convicts Fishing." Certainly, there is no such picture in the *Atlas*, and in fact a dark bracket drawn around this title in Macleod's book indicates that its inclusion was already under question. Indeed, additional notation in the notebook ap-pears to suggest that this picture might be replaced with another showing a "spray of or bundle of food—to represent food—vignettes, fish, berries." In the printed version of the *Atlas* it is the food vignette that appears and not the illustration of the convicts fishing. Such pictures provide an interesting study in metonymy and memory, where pictures of fish stand for the people who caught them and pictures of native fauna (cockatoos and black swans) take the place of pictures of native people.

There is a further metonymy involving the French navigator, La Perouse, whose ships entered Port Jackson shortly after the arrival of the First Fleet. In the *Atlas* there are pictures not only of La Perouse, but also of his doomed ships, the relics eventually recovered, and the monument erected to the man in Sydney. The elevation of La Perouse seems to be at the expense of Phillip and was consonant with the state of affairs in New South Wales at this time, where no monument to Phillip had been built.[26] Nor indeed was there any concerted push to have one built to mark the passing of the hun-dred years since he led the First Fleet into Port Jackson. Phillip is portrayed in the *Atlas*, but without any signs of his actual job—the supervision of a penal settlement. His role either fades into that of Cook, where he rather awkwardly replays the drama of discovery, or he is given a supporting role in another play based around his meet-ing with La Perouse: the meeting of civilized enemies in a savage land. The effort expended in authenticating the La Perouse episode is commensurate with the effort made in silencing Phillip and the day-to-day relationships of custody, conflict, and commerce in the colonies. These picturesque dramas are allowed to stand for the more pervasive forms of interpersonal contact in the colony based around the structures of incarceration and the troubled boundaries of contact with the aboriginal owners.

While some illustrations were motivated by evasion, others were designed to articulate in a positive way the historical experiences of the Australian colonies. A popular method of making history visible in the *Atlas* was to draw a picture of its events and the historical chap-ters have extensive recourse to these illustrated restagings. These illustrations are not, of course, real-time sketches of events unfolding, but engraved simulacra of historical events. There was a consciousness of this distinction in the *Daily Telegraph's* review (14 August 1886). In a discussion of the pictures in the first part, the reviewer (p. 9) points out certain inconsistencies between the picture (fig. 22) and the story of "Tasman's Carpenter Landing":

The carpenter, with his long curls and shaved chin, though he looks somewhat perplexed, bears no traces of his recent battle with the surf.

TASMAN'S CARPENTER LANDING.

Figure 22. "Tasman's Carpenter Landing." In *Picturesque Atlas of Australasia*, edited by Andrew Garran. 3 vols. (Sydney: The Picturesque Atlas Publishing Company, 1886–1888), p. 3.

We fear either that Mr. M'Leod, to whose vivid imagination we are indebted for this decidedly stylish carpenter, has flattered the original, or else the yarn itself is a little out of joint. But that is not to the point. What is more important is the very pretty, romantic and generally intelligent picture.

As the reviewer understands, whether the picture matches the story is not the point. The point is that the story is "very pretty," and more important, picturable. Moreover, the fact that such pictures were artists' impressions about what a particular historical event *must have looked like* carries with it a presumption that such grand events must have been in some sense *watched.* No one saw Torres seeing Cape York, yet on the first page of the *Atlas* there is a picture of "Torres Sighting Cape York" (1). When the Cape York tribes drove the Dutch crew of the *Duyfhen* back from their shores in 1606, who was there to watch it happen from the outside? Certainly not Frederic Schell, the American artist who sketched this drawing and was employed as pictorial editor by the Atlas company. Nevertheless, Schell's "The "Duyfhen" in the Gulf of Carpenteria" (2), a picture of "awful serenity" according to the *Telegraph*, is seen from the solid, third-person vantage of the historical observer. Such pictures have a quality that is both histrionic and iconographic. They have the effect of reducing history to a select group of seminal, displayable moments.

As a result of such picturing practices it would be difficult, for instance, to imagine the settlement of Australia without seeing a ship. In one way or another, ships find their way into many of the illustrations in the opening chapters of the *Atlas*. They are the sign of European arrival. In pictures such as "Captain Cook Proclaiming New South Wales a British Possession" (8), "The First Fleet Entering Botany Bay," and "Captain Phillip's First Sight of Port Jackson," they signify not only the arrival of European people, but the coming of history onto the timeless Australian shore. But as icons, the trope that underwrites such pictures is not arrival but birth, the wondrous birth of a British colony. These quaint engravings with their sailing ships, long boats, oarsmen and soldiers, union jacks and gum trees, and naked, bemused aboriginal people are the file footage of the rebirth of Britain in the antipodes. Birth-pictures are also coupled with growth-pictures, sets of pictures that show the rapid transformation of cities over time. By producing a snapshot of a place from an earlier point in time, the *Atlas* conveys the idea of historical growth. "Sydney Cove, August 20, 1788" (17), "Newcastle in 1829" (101), and "Queen-street, Brisbane, in 1860" (357) are all pictures which, in displaying the past, congratulate the present on its progress. This display of growth is still more explicit in the "Descriptive Sketch of South Australia" where an illustration of "Port Adelaide in 1840" (442) is paired with another of "Port Adelaide in 1888." These illustrations provide a visual index for the success narratives in the written text. Like baby photos, they invite from the latter-day colonist of the 1880s a feeling of parental pride—which reverses the ancestral relationship of colonist to land. The colonist is not the child of the colony, but rather the colony is a child that is growing up under the admiring eyes of the colonist.

A second visual strategy by which the *Atlas* displays its history, was the use of portraits. Portraits helped to negotiate between the programmatic certainty of national birth and the colorful banality of the "picturesque episode." As wealth ensured the measurability of history, so portraits provided to history an indisputable, unique, and personalized visibility. Portraits are the most prevalent form of historical image in the *Atlas* and it is through them that the *Atlas* gains its greatest purchase in history. The earliest illustrated weekly in Australia, as Elizabeth Webby has pointed out, was *Heads of the People* published in Sydney between 1847 and 1848.[27] "These illustrated mini-biographies," explains Webby, were also "a popular feature of many later journals," including the *Bulletin*, who published in its early issues a "portrait gallery of Australian celebrities."[28] Indeed, at the time of the publication of the *Atlas*, the "representative life" was a powerful historical unit.[29] One book, *Australian Men of Mark* (1888), put itself forward as "an historico-biographical record" of the growth and progress of the Australasian colonies. It combined a brief curriculum vitae with a full-page portrait of each subject. The premise of the book was that by selecting "representative careers from every walk of Colonial life," it was possible to generate "a thoroughly complete reproduction of our social and political conditions at this important epoch in Australian history." There was a powerful belief in the ability of these lives to tell the story of the society *en masse.*

> Treated in this way, the memoir of a prominent politician becomes a history of the national events in which he took part, and of the public business of the people who confide to him the trust of their political representation.
> The biography of the founder of a flourishing industry will present the record of that particular department of the industrial or trading interest.
> The life-story of the successful emigrant reproduces the difficulties

and hardships of early settlement, and the labours of pioneer enterprise, traced through the circumstances and period in which the subject lived.[30]

It was a representative democracy of life-stories, although the suffrage was hardly universal. The book covers "all classes of prominent colonial men," but necessarily excludes all those who were neither men nor "prominent." Like an antipodean update of Carlyle's "Great Men," a century of history was condensed in the lives of a few.[31] This prevalence of portraits in the *Atlas* is at odds with its generational partners in Europe and America. In the *Atlas*, the demands of a visible history of great men were superimposed on the concerns of the picturesque compendium.

Gerard Curtis has written on the increasing importance, towards the end of the nineteenth century, of frontispiece portraits in Victorian fiction. He suggests that, "for the Victorians the 'art of seeing' meant a dramatic rise in the use of frontispiece portraits—reflecting a desire to observe the ultimate voice of creation and an almost biblical belief in a connection between fiction, a nonfictive voice, and a real world."[32] The facial image in a novel's frontispiece became the icon of creation. In the *Atlas*, a similar process appears to be at work from the point of view of history. The creationary aura that surrounds Cook's frontispiece portrait filters into other figures represented in the *Atlas*, into the reverends and rear admirals, governors and pioneers. However, if, as John Tagg has claimed, the portrait is "a sign whose purpose is both the description of an individual and the inscription of social identity," then social identity had a relatively limited purview within the *Atlas*.[33] The exclusively male portraits in the *Atlas* hardwire the template of masculine achievement into its image bank. While the faces represented are historically diverse, from William Dampier to the current Victorian Governor (and vocal *Atlas* supporter), Henry Loch, what they share is the status that is embodied in the fact of their being in a portrait. A portrait does two things. Firstly, it individuates a subject as a distinct social entity. Secondly, it renders a subject according to a code which acknowledges this subject's place in the public order.[34] A small profile of the Tasmanian Aboriginal woman "Truganini" is, ironically, the only female portrait in the Australian chapters of the *Atlas*. Her inclusion is not, however, an attempt at either gender or racial equity but the result of a different visual imperative. While the other portraits are included so that the colonists can look upon the face, as it were, of creation, the portrait of Truganini is reproduced as the "last of her race." Not the face of creation but the face of disappearance.

These issues of presence and absence are at the heart of the *Atlas's* third visual strategy for the display of history, the depiction of monuments. Collectively, the historical portraits and re-enacted scenes develop for Australian nationalist history a mnemonic system which places valued historical events under the visual badge of its relevant portrait or scene. However, while portraits and historical re-enactments were ways of illustrating the birth of the Australian colonies, other images appear to signal a demand for more concrete traces of colonial birth; for some way of marking the authenticity of Australasia's origins as a newly defined branch of European civilisation. Such a desire gives sense to the repetition of pictures of monuments in the *Atlas*, including statues, obelisks, marked trees, historical buildings, and grave sites. This category of image is significant because the lack of human monuments had traditionally featured as a prominent entry in Australia's catalogue of absences. Certainly, the editor of the *Atlas* Andrew Garran attached significance to this fact: "Australia has no part in the early history of the human race or in the development of its civilisation; it contains no traces of ever having been the seat of empire—no ruins, no mounds to indicate that it was the dwelling-place, in the far past, of industrious and fertile populations" (iii). This conviction that Australia lacked historical credentials was an issue in the narrativity of the continent. Explorers and travellers, for instance, often fantasized about the resemblance of rocky outcrops to ruined castles.[35] Frederick Sinnett lamented that no novelist could rely on the castles and manor houses to torment or extricate their characters in Australian novels. "We are quite debarred," he wrote, "from all interest to be extracted from any kind of archaeological accessories."[36] Later in the century, a spate of popular novels were produced about so-called "lost civilisations" in the Australian interior.[37] Such romantic projections should not be dismissed as idle meanderings of the colonial mind, but symptomatic of a firmly entrenched collective belief in the essential emptiness of Australia. It is a belief that in legal discourse found expression in the doctrine of *terra nullius*. And as nature abhors a vacuum, the colonists of Australia felt duty-bound to fill the continental void with civilization.

Moreover, the monuments that litter the pages of the *Atlas* set up a contrast between the permanence of colonial history and the transience of aboriginal presence. In the mind of colonial Australia, according to Tom Griffiths, one of the chief sins of the Aborigines was that they "had failed to sign history."[38] And it was a failure to "sign" in a number of senses. It was a failure to provide the continent with a legible cultural *signature*, no spectacular defining icons of its uniqueness that could be co-opted in the colonial acquisition of place. It was also a failure to provide *signals* which would adequately reference aboriginal land use practices, means of communication, and social networks. All these appeared, as Andrew Garran notes, as a dreary blank: "Australia, though populated for centuries, was a blank in history until discovered by Europeans" (iii). But above all it was a failure on the part of the Aboriginal people of Australia to provide architectural monuments which would serve as signs of their pastness. It was a peculiar form of regret that among the ongoing ruination which colonization wrought on Australian indigenous cultures, there were no ruins to mark their passing.

The *Atlas* uses these various visual strategies (re-enactments, portraits, and monuments) in combination to produce a visible, showable history. Schell's sketch of the "Burial of Captain Cook's Remains at Sea" is given a permanence by the inclusion of a second sketch of a stone obelisk marking the place "Where Cook Was Killed" (fig. 23), hovering just above the principal engraving. In "Early Settlement," a portrait of "Captain Arthur Phillip" (16) is combined with a facsimile of Governor Hunter's sketch of "Sydney Cove, August 20, 1788" (17) and a third engraving of "The First Landing Place, Botany Bay" (16) adapted "from a recent sketch" and overlaid with the image of harvested grain that represent the dividend of the colonial project. The pictures, working together, replicate the textual narrative of colonial success and visually imbue this story with location, personality, and purpose. A similar suite of images is found in "Historical Sketch of New South Wales," and are used to display the history of the wool industry pioneered by John Macarthur. Firstly, "Macarthur's Homestead, Camden" with its inset merino ram, then "The Cow Pastures, Camden Park," and finally "Macarthur's Tomb at Camden." The pictures invite a minipilgrimage of the eye through the sacred sites of this industry and the man who is remembered for bringing it into being.

The Atlas as Communicative Act

The reflections in this essay have proceeded on the assumption that the readership of the *Atlas* was essentially Australian. And indeed it is safe to say that this was the case. It was, after all, the prospect of readerly demand in Australia that prompted the Atlas Company to set up a factory in Sydney, and it was in the Australian colonies that its extraordinary marketing effort was concentrated. What is interesting, however, is how often the prospect of an over-

Figure 23. "Where Cook Was Killed" and "Burial of
Captain Cook's Remains at Sea," in *Picturesque Atlas of
Australasia*, edited by Andrew Garran. 3 vols. (Sydney: The
Picturesque Atlas Publishing Company, 1886–1888), p. 10.

seas audience was voiced in the publicity rhetoric of the *Atlas*. There
was a fascination with the idea that this would not simply be a publication that would be sold in Australia, but that it was going to be
"world-wide" in its distribution. The *Atlas*, on this view, was imagined as an elaborate exercise in regional promotion. E. E. Morris,
editor of the rival publication *Cassell's Picturesque Australasia*, specifically addressed the issue of readership. "Those who have been connected with its preparation," wrote Miller in his "Editor's Note,"
"have striven for a double object—to make Australasia better known
to those who live at a distance, and to enable each colony to know
its neighbours better." The editor of the *Atlas*, Andrew Garran, tack-

les the issue of readership in his preface with more circumspection, writing that the *Atlas* "tells the story of the great southern land in all its different subdivisions," and how it would, "by the aid of pen and pencil, show, to all who wish to know, how Australia presents itself" (iv). Garran's emphasis is on the presentation of Australia, how it appears in the eyes of those who seek to see it. This viewing universe is more explicitly invoked in the publicity blurbs on the dust jackets of the *Atlas* parts:

> The paramount object of the publishers is to carry out this most important object in a manner to secure the hearty response of the great English-speaking communities throughout the globe; also to give the world the best delineation of the Australasian colonies, and the everyday life of their people.[39]

The "English-speaking communities" whose attention was the "paramount object" of the *Atlas* makers, locate Australian history, and by extension Australian identity, firmly within a discourse of race. *Atlas* contributor Alexander Sutherland foregrounded this aspect in his own work of centennial history, *Victoria and its Metropolis* (1888). Victoria's history was valuable as part of an articulation of the "process by which the English-speaking race has encompassed the world." The histories of the "daughter-states" were thus important because they constituted "the records of the race" (Sutherland, v).

The paradox of the *Atlas* is that while the readership was predominantly local, the reader who is addressed is often an outsider. In other words, the voice that the local population wished to hear was the voice that spoke outside. In interpolating an external audience, the *Atlas* in its public voice, its "preface" voice, used this externality to establish the legitimacy of its story. It was only in telling the story to another—a significant Euro-American other—that the story of selfhood could be satisfactorily enacted. This somewhat complicates the position that Australian history was simply a chapter within the broader history of the British "race," by attempting to delineate a subject position that was both within and outside that broader narrative.

Roland Barthes has suggested that history is hysterical, because "it is constituted only if we consider it, only if we look at it—and in order to look at it, we must be excluded from it." The *Atlas* could not be regarded as a hysterical publication, but it does display in its attempt to create an Australian history something of this ambivalence that Barthes's aphorism distils. The historians and illustrators of the *Atlas* were seeking to create a history of Australia which could be claimed by readers as a suitable validation of their society at a moment (the centenary) that demanded that validation. They avoid the hysteria of a self-removing historical gaze by positing an external historical audience for whom the stories of material success and illustrations of societal birth would be intelligible and appreciated. Nevertheless, while the voice is directed outward, the representation of history in the *Atlas* is beset with preoccupations about origins and futures that are particularly those of colonial Australia and relate to uncertainties about the bases of social identity. The use of Aboriginal people, for instance, as a submerged point of reference in the success narratives and portraits of great men points to a validation of identity based on a colonial logic of succession. Similarly, the materialist emphasis of the narratives and the recurrent illustration of monuments in the pictures reveal an insistent need to affirm the solidity of Australian historical experience. Equally, the need to be "discreet" about origins while at the same time loudly proclaiming the outcome of these origins is a distinctive problem of nineteenth-century Australian historiography. These concerns about convict origins, brevity of history, a sense of impermanence, and cultural authenticity are those of the real, rather than the notional, readership.

NOTES

1. Other notable centennial publications include E. E. Morris, ed., *Cassell's Picturesque Australasia* (London: Cassell, 1887–1889), Alexander Sutherland, ed., *Victoria and its Metropolis: Past and Present* (Melbourne: McCarron, Bird, 1888) and W. Frederic Morrison, ed., *The Aldine Centennial History of New South Wales* (Sydney: Aldine Pub. Co., 1888).

2. Maya Tucker, "Centennial Celebrations 1888," *Australia, 1888* 7 (April 1981): 12. I am indebted to Tucker's insightful and detailed account of these celebrations. Particularly useful is the way that Tucker's article explores differing reactions to the centenary throughout the Australian colonies.

3. Graeme Davison, "Historic Time and Everyday Time," *Australia, 1888* 7 (April 1981): 7.

4. Jenny Lee and Charles Fahey, "A boom for whom? Some developments in the Australian labour market, 1870–1891," in *Pastiche I: Reflections on Nineteenth-Century Australia*, eds. Penny Russell and Richard White (Sydney: Allen & Unwin, 1994), 162–84.

5. George Shaw, "Bicentennial Writing: Revealing the Ash in the Australian Soul," *1888 and All That: New Views of Australia's Past*, ed. George Shaw (St. Lucia: University of Queensland Press, 1988), 3.

6. "A.D. 1888—The Proposed Australian Centenary," *Bulletin*, 11 September 1886, 4.

7. 31 January 1888, quoted in Luke Trainor, *British Imperialism and Australian Nationalism* (Melbourne: Cambridge University Press), 73.

8. Speech reported in "The Picturesque Atlas Publishing Company," *Sydney Morning Herald*, 24 August 1886, 5.

9. "The Picturesque Atlas of Australasia," *Age* [Melbourne], 2 April 1887, 13.

10. Simon Nowell-Smith, *The House of Cassell* (London: Cassell, 1958), 102.

11. Parenthetical numbers designate pages in the *Atlas.*

12. *Daily Telegraph,* 14 August 1886, 9. The report notes that "the engraving itself was executed on steel-plate in New York, and cost £100."

13. For a useful discussion of the place of Cook in Australian (both indigenous and nonindigenous) social memory, see Chris Healy, *From the Ruins of Colonialism: History as Social Memory* (Cambridge: Cambridge University Press, 1997) 16–72.

14. Greg Dening, "A Poetics of History," *Performances* (Melbourne: Melbourne University Press, 1996), 52.

15. "The confusion of Cook with Australian destiny, still an article of faith in our nationalist historiography, makes it impossible to criticise one without bringing into question the other." Paul Carter, "Strange Seas of Thought," *The Australian's Review of Books* June 1998, 20. Ron Dunphy, moreover, suggests that Cook, not Phillip, was the icon of the centenary. *Australians 1888*, 24, marginal notes.

16. Michel Foucault argues that the nineteenth century's obsession with history, "its concern to historicize everything, to write a general history of everything" was prompted by a new consciousness of the radical historicity of humankind itself, the fact of its own temporal modality. *The Order of Things: an Archaeology of the Human Sciences* (1970; reprint, New York: Vintage Books, 1994), 370.

17. Gillian Whitlock and Gail Reekie, eds., *Uncertain Beginnings: Debates in Australian Studies* (St. Lucia: Queensland University Press, 1993).

18. The idea of narrative immanence is developed in the separate work of Paul Ricouer and Hayden White. Ricouer argues that narratives are re-read in light of their endings in order to trace the seeds of a meaning that was immanent. *Time and Narrative*, 2 vols., trans. Kathleen McLaughlin and David Pellauer. (1983; reprint, Chicago: University of Chicago Press, 1984), 1: 65–68. White suggests that the end of a story inflects retrospectively every event within that story with the moral force of its finality. "The Value of Narrativity in the Representation of Reality," *The Content of the Form: Narrative Discourse and Historical Representation* (Baltimore: Johns Hopkins University Press, 1987), 1–25.

19. Michel de Certeau, *The Writing of History*, trans. Tom Conley. (New York: Columbia University Press, 1988), 5.

20. A. Dwight Culler, *The Victorian Mirror of History* (New Haven: Yale University Press, 1985); Peter J. Bowler, *The Invention of Progress: the Victorian and the Past* (Oxford: Basil Blackwell, 1989).

21. Geoffrey Blainey, *A Land Half Won* (Melbourne: Macmillan, 1980), 289.

22. Graeme Davison, *The Rise and Fall of Marvellous Melbourne* (Melbourne: Melbourne University Press, 1978), 72. For other descriptions of the booming of Melbourne in the 1880s, see Stuart Macintyre, *A Colonial Liberalism: The Lost World of Three Victorian Visionaries* (Oxford: Oxford University Press, 1991), 169–71; and Ambrose Pratt, *David Syme: The Father of Protection in Australia* (London: Ward Lock, 1908), 197–203.

23. Graeme Davison, et al., eds., *Australians, 1888* (Sydney: Fairfax, Syme and Weldon, 1987), 24. Also, M. Askew and B. Hubber, "The Colonial Reader Observed: Reading in its Colonial Context," *The Book in Australia: Essays Towards a Cultural & Social History*, eds., D. H. Borchardt & W. Kirsop, Historical Bibliography Monograph No. 16 (Melbourne: Australian Reference Publications, 1988), 110–38.

24. The avoidance was certainly not based on an aversion to criminality per se. In a later chapter on New Caledonia, for instance, there are illustrations of "A Prison Interior," "Convicts Making Roads," "Convicts Washing Clothes," and "A Convict

Prison" (700–701). The depravities of the French criminals on Australia's Pacific doorstep are decried extensively. The irony of this indignation might well have amused French authorities.

25. William Macleod, Sketch Notebook, c. May 1886, ML A2147, Item 1, Mitchell Library, State Library of New South Wales, 25–26.

26. Tom Griffiths, "Past Silences: Aborigines and Convicts in Our History Making," *Pastiche I: Reflections on Nineteenth-Century Australia*, eds. Penny Russell and Richard White (Sydney: Allen and Unwin, 1989), 17–23. For a sympathetic account of the role of Phillips, see Robert Hughes, *The Fatal Shore: a History of the Transportation of Convicts to Australia* (London: Collins, Harvill, 1987), 67–108.

27. Elizabeth Webby, "Journals in the Nineteenth Century," *The Book in Australia*, eds. D. H. Borchardt and W. Kirspop (Melbourne: Australian Reference Publications, 1988), 63.

28. The *Illustrated Sydney News* also included portraits as part of its regular format under such titles as "Our Portrait Gallery" over its entire lifetime, from the 1850s to the 1890s.

29. "You can never understand a man's conduct or calculate his future actions half so well, unless you have that key to his character which is furnished in his countenance and aspect." "History's Telescope," *The Leader: a Political and Literary Review* 4, no. 287 (22 September 1855): 914.

30. *Australian Men of Mark*, 2 vols. (Sydney and Melbourne: Charles F. Maxwell, 1888), no pagination.

31. "For, as I take it, Universal History, the history of what man has accomplished in this world, it at bottom the History of the Greatest Men who have worked here ... the soul of the whole world's history, it may justly be considered, were the history of these." Thomas Carlyle, "On Heroes, Hero-Worship, and the Heroic in History," *Thomas Carlyle's Works*, Standard Ed. 18 vols. (London: Chapman and Hall, 1913), 4:1.

32. Gerard Curtis, "Dickens in the Visual Market," *Literature in the Marketplace: Nineteenth-Century Publishing and Reading Practices*, eds. John O. Jordan and Robert L. Patten (Cambridge: Cambridge University Press, 1995), 242.

33. John Tagg, *The Burden of Representation: Essays on Photographies and Histories* (London: Mcmillan, 1988), 37. Richard Brilliant suggests that "portraits exist at the interface between art and social life." *Portraiture* (London: Reaktion Books, 1991), 11.

34. Suren Lalvani has written that "the portrait as record registers both social situatedness and cultural intentionality which, communicated by way of the disposition and display of the represented body, always occurs within a particular ideological form." "Photography, Epistemology, and the Body," *Cultural Studies* 7 (1993): 448.

35. Simon Ryan, *The Cartographic Eye: How Explorers Saw Australia* (Melbourne: Cambridge University Press, 1996), 76–83.

36. Frederick Sinnett, *The Fiction Fields of Australia*, ed. Cecil Hadgraft (1856; reprint, St. Lucia: University of Queensland, 1966), 23.

37. Robert Dixon, *Writing the Colonial Adventure: Race, Gender and Nation in Anglo-Australian Popular Fiction, 1825–1914* (Cambridge: Cambridge University Press, 1995), 62–81; John Docker, *The Nervous Nineties: Australian Cultural Life in the 1890s* (Oxford: Oxford University Press, 1991), 199–232; J. J. Healy, "The Lemurian Nineties," *Australian Literary Studies* 8 (1978): 307–16.

38. Griffiths, "A Natural Myth-maker," *The Australian's Review of Books*, June 1997, 15. Also, Griffiths, *Hunters and Collectors: The Antiquarian Imagination in Australia* (Melbourne: Cambridge University Press, 1996), 14.

39. Dust-jacket, *Atlas* part-issues 1886–88.

Welsh Missionary Journalism in India, 1880–1947

Aled Jones

A CONTINUOUS STREAM OF PERIODICAL WRITING, OFFICIAL REPORTS AND travellers' tales flowed from the Christian missionaries who left Wales for India between 1840 and the mid-1960s. But while these narratives may have seeped into the Nonconformist imagination, and generated funds to finance further missionary activity, it is evident that the Welsh missionary presence in India has never fully reentered the mainstream of what constitutes British postcolonial history in Wales. Little is known about the majority of these missionaries, especially so the women, and few have speculated on how their participation as members of both a religious, and a cultural, and linguistic minority within the colonial expansion of the British Empire might be interpreted. Though they left their home country voluntarily, with enthusiasm, high expectations and the support of their religious constituency, history has effectively turned them into exiles. Yet, they were collectively involved in what Nigel Jenkins has recently termed "the biggest overseas venture ever sustained by the Welsh."[1] This paper intends to throw some additional light on aspects of their "multiple identities," to explore some of the ways in which their work was received by their fellow Welsh Nonconformists, and to address the politically fraught question of how this missionary activity might be situated in the history of modern Wales. Evidence will be drawn primarily from missionary journalism, those news reports, essays in reflection, ethnographic accounts, and items of travel writing where missionary self-representation was at its least mediated and its most beguiling.

The mission was organized by the Presbyterian Church of Wales, originally known as the Welsh Calvinistic Methodists, Wales's largest, most powerful Nonconformist denomination, and was concentrated in a divided region that sat astride the frontier between Assam and Eastern Bengal, which in 1947 was to become the international border separating India from East Pakistan.[2] Relatively small in scale—

rarely were there more than fifty missionary workers in the field at any one time—it employed only a tiny portion of the ten thousand or so British missionaries who were on active service abroad in 1900. While other missionaries from Wales were at work in various parts of the world, including France, the islands of the Pacific, the Caribbean, parts of western and southern Africa, and China, those in northeast India formed the largest, most continuous project funded and organized by any Welsh-based denomination. They included evangelical preachers, doctors, nurses, and teachers—and substantial numbers of them, constituting at times a clear majority, were lay women, mostly young and unmarried. Their legacy was complex. In the mission field, the effects of their presence were strikingly uneven, leaving a powerful religious mark on Mizoram and the Khasi Hills but making little impression on other areas of the field such as Sylhet. In Wales, too, the sounds of their evangelical fury have been strangely muted. In spite of the extraordinary richness of the primary and printed records that they bequeathed to the home church, their activities were, for much of the second half of the twentieth century, marginalized if not ignored.[3] This remarkable historiographical silence may primarily be attributed to the implicit rejection of British colonializm that defined postwar constructions of Welsh national identity. An acute unease with a history of participation in, or, to borrow from an Irish parallel, of "collaboration" with, British imperial expansion may have served as a powerful motive for avoiding the integration of Welsh missionary activity fully into the social and political—as distinct from the religious—history of modern Wales.[4] It is also worth noting that the history of the Welsh mission is to a considerable extent a history of educated and largely middle-class women and men. In a postwar historiography of the nineteenth and twentieth centuries dominated by the study of political, labor, and social institutions, the colonial, largely middle-class and female composition of the missionary cohort attracted the attention of few professional historians. Nor, one might add, did the necessity to engage with the evangelical and theological, rather than the political, dimension of Nonconformity appeal to a more secular generation of historians eager to emerge from the long shadow of nineteenth-century Methodism.[5]

Signs of change, however, have been evident for some time. Growing public and professional interest in the so-called "Welsh diaspora" has produced a number of important historical studies of the Welsh outside Wales, while the lives of women in the Welsh past have come under increasing scrutiny.[6] The theoretical landscape, too, has been transformed, principally by the debates on colonial and postcolonial experience that followed the publication of Edward Said's *Orientalism,* which point to new, more integrated and interdisciplinary avenues of investigation, different narrative strategies, and alternative forms of explanation.[7] These suggest a need not only to take into account both the subjectivities of those who ran the mission and those with whom they came into contact, but also the effects their writing may have had on those in Wales who read and discussed their journalism. More also needs to be learned about what occurred in practice in the "contact zones" where these groups met and interacted. For example, very little is known about Muslim or Hindu responses to the section of the mission that operated in what is now Bangladesh, while Assamese Christians may read the history of the mission very differently from those whom the Welsh tried but failed to convert.[8]

A study of missionary journalism forms an integral part of such a broader, multicentered project. In addition to its functions in constructing a Nonconformist sense of Welsh nationhood,[9] the missionary press remains a surprisingly little appreciated dimension of Welsh-language writing. Yet its reflections on an imperial Welsh cultural identity, and its analyses of the colonial social, religious, and political order, are of a kind not found elsewhere in the literature, and its many forays into travel writing are among the most distinctive and intriguing in the language. Colonial and religious discourses, as distinctive but closely related genres of Welsh writing, deserve to be subjected to far greater critical scrutiny and debate.

They also offer a noticeably different set of perspectives on a century of extraordinary change in Welsh society and politics. The period of the mission included the late nineteenth-century industrialization of Wales and its attendant population movements, the making of national institutions such as the University, the displacement of Liberalism by Labor, the growth of nationalism, particularly in Welsh-speaking Wales, the hemorrhaging effects of the interwar depression, and war. But running parallel to these narratives is another chronology, one that increasingly came to preoccupy Welsh-speaking Nonconformity, namely the fusion of an enthusiasm for converting others to a peculiarly Welsh form of Christian belief with the opportunities offered by the extension of British Imperial power. The Welsh Calvinistic Methodists had formed themselves into a separate connexion in 1811, and in September 1814 established their first home missionary society. Soon, they were writing missionary hymns and preparing to take their peculiarly Welsh bundle of theological beliefs out to the world. For the first twenty-five years, they gave their general support to the Foreign Mission Society of Great

Britain, though the distance between west Wales and London reduced its effectiveness, and the Society's use of English further
dampened Welsh Nonconformist enthusiasm for its activities. In
1840, the Calvinistic Methodists took their first independent steps by
launching a separate overseas missionary society. Their first missionary, Thomas Jones, from Aberriw, Montgomeryshire, was sent to the
Khasi Hills in Assam later that year, arriving there via Calcutta in
June 1841. William Lewis and his wife followed him there in 1843.
The field was chosen on the advice of Jacob Tomlin, a retired missionary from Malacca who had strayed into the Khasi Hills in the
1830s, through which David Scott, Agent to the Governor General
on the North East Frontier, had built a road from Sylhet to the Brah-
maputra Valley in 1826. In retirement in Bangor, north Wales, To-
malin reported to local Presbyterians how he had found in Khasia a
number of hill tribes, whom he described as demon worshippers or
animists in urgent need of redemption.[10] The early missionaries met
with very little success. Khasia had nominally been British territory
since 1833, and the adjacent Jaintia Hills since 1835, but both had
enjoyed considerable autonomy until the introduction of taxation
by the British authorities in Assam in 1860. Following rebellions between 1860 and 1863, the militarization of the hills and the removal
of local political control from Cherrapunji to Shillong in 1864,
Assam in 1874 became a separate Province under a Chief Commissioner, also based in Shillong.[11] According to Assam District Gazetteer B. C. Allen, the Welsh mission in the Khasi Hills made "very
little progress" during either the period of *de facto* native rule, or
during the political unrest and sporadic violence that accompanied
its erosion. Only around five hundred Khasis were converted in the
thirty years that followed Williams's arrival in 1841, but the extension of imperial control coupled with the growth of a medical mission, under the direction of Dr. Griffiths, led to greater success. The
Khasi Christian community grew from 1,796 in 1881 to 6,766 a decade later. By 1901 the figure had reached 15,937 and by 1905, the
year of the Welsh Revival, the missionaries had established a following of some 23,000 (Allen, vol. 10, 66). The Khasis were believed to
be "peculiarly susceptible" to the influences of the Welsh Christian
missionaries broadly for two reasons. Firstly, missionary medical services were deemed to be more effective than local practices, and,
while missionaries enforced sabbatarianism, prevented unrestricted
divorce, and banned drunkenness among their converts, there were
in Khasi social order "no ties of caste or social or family restrictions
to act as an obstacle to conversion" (Allen, vol. 10, 66). Further-

more, Christianity involved social mobility and the values of Western bourgeois respectability. In 1906, it was reported that

> now-a-days it is the correct thing in the Khasi and Jaintia Hills to be a Christian. Good houses, good clothes, cleanliness and prosperity are the outward and visible signs of the members of the church. The old Khasi religion is becoming a genuine paganism, a religion of the villages.[12]

Growth in the number of converts also followed closely an increase from the 1870s in educational provision. In 1873–74, the Welsh mission was responsible for seventy-three schools, attended by 1,666 pupils. By 1900–1901, that number had grown to 325 schools with 6,535 pupils, by which time it was estimated that 57 per 1000 of the population in the Hills were literate, a proportion higher than in any other district in the province of Assam. This was especially true in relation to women, of whom in 1901, 34 per 1000 could read and write, a figure seven times greater than in any other district in the province (Allen, vol. 10, 108).

In 1850, William Pryse, a new arrival, returned to the Sylheti plains to the south to resume Christian evangelical activity there. Though "universally esteemed" (the cost of his funeral was borne by Sylheti Hindus, who also opened a commemorative library[13]), Pryse was obliged to engage with Muslims and Hindus who were far more reluctant to abandon their belief systems and institutions, in part since, on social grounds, "the neophyte . . . has to abjure too much" (Allen, 2:90). The Sylheti mission was abandoned in the mid-1860s, but was restarted by John Pengwern Jones and his wife in November 1887. By 1905, there were only 394 native Christians in the district; Sylhet being deemed "too civilised to allow of conversion proceeding rapidly" (Allen, 2:90). Of these only 80 were associated with the Welsh mission, then based in Sylhet town, Karimganj and Maulavi Bazar (Allen, 2:90). Unlike in the Khasi Hills, educational provision for girls declined sharply in the opening years of the century (Allen, 2:264, 351). In 1897, the Welsh field was further extended to include the upland districts of Lushai (Mizoram) and Cachar, to continue work begun in 1894 by two English Baptist missionaries, J. H. Lorrain and F. W. Savidge. Again, movement here was slow, with only 683 native Christians reported in 1901.[14] However, by 1909, the mission field as a whole could count 9,569 communicants, with a total Sunday school attendance of twice that figure.[15] To put that in proportion, the population of the field at that time was about 3 million.

Themes of danger, hostility, and resistance from other religions constantly recur throughout the missionaries' reports. On Pengwern Jones's arrival in Sylhet in November 1887, for example, it was reported that a "Hindu missionary" had appeared in the town with the specific intention of obstructing his progress.[16] Farther north in the Khasi Hills, the formation in 1899 of the Seng Khasi signalled the renaissance of Khasi culture, religion, and identity. Today, while virtually all Mizos and Nagas are Christian, only 55 percent of the Khasis consider themselves to be so, and among those there is, and has long been, pressure to indigenize the Khasi Church.[17] It is worth recalling that virtually all its evangelical activity was conducted in indigenous languages. Missionaries were expected to become fluent in the language of their chosen field within three years of their appointment, or be held at their probationary salary until the final language examinations were successfully passed.[18] Furthermore, at least from the early 1920s, the Welsh were a minority within their own mission. In 1926, when 50 Welsh missionaries were active in the field, 45 Khasi ministers had been ordained in the period since 1895, and a further 36 indigenous preachers were actively engaged in evangelizing the Hills.[19]

Despite their relative success in the Hills, the experience of the Welsh mission, especially in the Sylhet region, was one where, as Anthony Copley has described of Bengal in general, "the exponents of a traditional Hinduism and Indian Islam . . . effectively . . . smothered an embattled Christianity."[20] While it was sharply divided by its religious as well as its physical and administrative topography, the mission field continued to encompass an unstable frontier region, and was to be divided and further weakened by Partition in 1947. Furthermore, evidence suggests that it was fragmented too by the agendas and personalities of the individual missionaries themselves. Despite the pervasive influence of the denomination's fundamental creed, and the *Rules* and administrative structures that guided the mission's general policy, individual missionaries did take initiatives, and were in numerous ways able to express their individuality. Some did so in what are for us today highly visible ways, particularly through their writing and lobbying. But fuller biographical accounts, noting areas of expertise and individual involvement in specific missionary projects, are needed before a history of the internal dynamics of the mission can be attempted. It would, for example, be useful to know whether individual Welsh Presbyterian missionaries were in touch with other Protestant missionaries deployed in the region in the same period. The C.M.S. mission had been active in Bengal at least since 1818,[21] and Welsh Anglicans appear to have strengthened their support for missionary activity in the 1890s,[22] the first separate Report of the C.M.S. in Wales being published in 1894.[23] The Baptist Missionary Society (B.M.S.), whose work in northeast India was strongly influenced by the Welsh mission in Khasia, did establish operational links with Welsh Presbyterians in Lushai (Mizoram), following which the Welsh in 1900 agreed to cede the southern area of the territory to the B.M.S. (Stanley, 1992, 271–73), but, other than that, little evidence has come to light that might indicate forms of collaboration between the Welsh and other Christian denominations. It would, of course, be unwise to discount the possibility that such links existed in the field.

It would similarly be a mistake to ignore the theological, institutional, and cultural specificity of this denomination.[24] While it is not necessary to accept Nicholas Thomas's view that "*only* localized theories and historically specific accounts can provide much insight into the varied articulations of colonising and counter-colonial representations and practices" (my italics; Thomas, 1994, ix), it is nevertheless instructive to identify the distinctive characteristics of particular institutions and the specific nature of their engagements with colonized peoples precisely in order to locate them as agents within the broader experience of colonization. Welsh Calvinistic Methodism may be distinguished from other forms of Christianity by its combination of a belief in election through God's Grace,[25] the morally purifying power of the Welsh language,[26] a socially conservative ethos that also stressed the importance of "obedience to established government," a revivalist style, and a highly structured internal organisation.[27]

Furthermore, it existed only in Wales, among Welsh émigrés abroad, and in its two missions, one in Brittany, the other in India. In the years that followed George Whitfield's death in 1770, only in Wales, via Howel Harris and the Trefeca group, did his brand of Calvinistic Methodism remain a real force.[28] The number of adherents in Wales rose from 163,158 in 1855 to a peak of 347,758 in 1906, in the immediate aftermath of the 1904–5 religious revival. By 1963, the figure had returned to the 1855 level.[29] But the church had been changing, particularly perhaps in the period of its most spectacular growth. The death in 1841 of John Elias, Calvinistic Methodism's conservative leader, had led to a period of relative liberalization that included the increasing involvement of Presbyterian ministers in local and national political activity. As a result, Calvinistic Methodism's political connections, its social networks, its newspaper and periodical press, its internal voluntary institutions that later included even its own health insurance society,[30] provided Wales not only with a highly effective group of intellectuals but also a powerful Liberal electoral machine, and an instrument of popular mobilization. The changing social and linguistic demography of Wales also forced sections of the church to reposition itself, notably in response to industrial in-migration and the subsequent growth of the English language. Inevitably, perhaps, in such time of change, concerns were expressed that the theological condition of the church was swiftly deteriorating. Referring to its origins in the late eighteenth and early nineteenth centuries, one critic scornfully observed in 1870 "(how) the mighty have fallen! The bones, with all their repulsive hideousness, are strewn about our feet as if they indicated the wreck of some mighty system, whose far-reaching influence enclosed Wales in its soft embrace."[31]

In the closing decades of the nineteenth century, some in the church saw the Indian mission as a means of revivifying Calvinistic Methodism as an evangelical creed. The church had over the years grown in part through a number of small revivals, which marked periods of intense though localized evangelical activity. The nationwide revival, led by Evan Roberts, in 1904–5 can be read in numerous ways, including as a symptom of a crisis within Welsh Nonconformity in the face of overwhelming social change and increasing secularisation. But the Evan Roberts revival also involved the Indian mission. Sidney Margaret Roberts, attending a service in Pariong, Khasia, in 1905 recalled how one member of the congregation, U. Ruton, had prayed aloud that "whilst Thou art blessing the people of Wales so much, do not send us away empty." She also reported the prevalence during those strange times of miraculous "visions and trances" and "ecstasies of delight." One prayer meeting in Mawphlang continued without interruption for ten days. Yet these supposed manifestations of the divine were confined to the hills, and although "the vast plains of Sylhet and Silchar (were) stretching forth their hands to Wales," they showed little enthusiasm for revivalist Christianity.[32] But successes in Khasia, where in 1906 missionaries reversed the usual funding course by raising 19,000 rupees to help defray the costs of the revival in Wales (*Report of the Foreign Mission,* 1910, xv) had other consequences, too, for the home church. Most important, a new generation of missionaries, captivated by the revival, came forward to volunteer for service. An article in *Y Gymraes* (*The Welshwoman*) in March 1909 attributed the departure of three young female missionaries for India to the spiritually purifying effects of the revival, while praising the "moral courage" of the denomination in confirming their confidence in women as agents of religious change.[33] Such forces enabled the frenzy of the Welsh revival to be continued in the mission field for another two to three years, when the number of adherents in the field rose from 22,500 in 1905 to 27,500 in 1907 (Jenkins, 274). Over a longer period of time, the number of Welsh Presbyterian chapels in Silchar and Sylhet grew from six in 1899 to sixty-three in 1941. In turn, the energy of the revival in India put pressure on the church at home to increase its home missionary efforts. The relationship between the home church and the mission was thus symbiotic, the mission field being an essential function of the church's operation. This was particularly true after 1891, when the church's Forward Movement was launched to extend its home evangelical activity.

Rules governing the appointment, training, conduct, and remuneration of missionaries were published by the church in 1870, and were updated in 1928.[34] Missionaries were to be "ambassadors for Christ," their purpose being "to produce and organise a new centre of light and power" (*General Regulations*, 1870, 38). While the work of the church provided the moral justification for travel and, in numerous cases, for long-term if not permanent settlement in the mission field, regular contact with the church at home remained essential. Missionaries were obliged to return on furlough for eighteen months after ten years abroad, or for two years after fifteen (*General Regulations*, 1870, 30–31).[35] Together, the rules conveyed the clear message that the mission was not for individualists, nor should they regard themselves as settlers, and that their work was to be subject to regulation and monitoring by the home church. But what is striking from even a cursory study of the mission is how much operational autonomy was in practice granted to the missionaries in the field. Given the distance and the costs of travel, this is hardly surprising. And while the disciplinary powers of the home church were on a number of occasions invoked, particularly during the first three decades, it became clear from the 1890s, and even more so after 1905, that those who wished to work in the field were often among the most dedicated, though not necessarily the most conservative and doctrinaire, exponents of the creed. Reports from the field frequently stressed the difficulty of the enterprise, and the pain and discomfort that missionaries endured in the name of their faith. In 1908, Elizabeth Williams wrote of the relief she felt when a villager fell ill, since only the prospect of visiting the sick could lift from her shoulders "*trymder yr unigrwydd llethol*" ("the weight of lethal loneliness").[36] Readers at home were constantly being reminded that their adversaries were not "pagan savages" but strong, confident, and highly motivated religious communities. Opposition to Protestant evangelicalism in Europe, they implied, was as nothing compared with the hostility of Islam and Hinduism to Christian missionary activity in India.[37] The missionaries projected themselves as being at the frontline of a religious war, the ferocity of which, they implied, the majority of church members at home had either forgotten or had never known.

While work in the zenanas appears to have remained a significant part of their conversion strategy until the 1930s, most missionaries were engaged in educational or medical work, or in the running of orphanages and homes for widows. Significantly, the style of teaching was adopted from the hugely successful Welsh system of circulating schools developed in eighteenth-century rural Wales by Griffith Jones, Llanddowror, the aim of which was to teach children and adults to read the Bible and the hymn book.[38] In the mission schools, children and adults thus received a "Christian training," but they did not necessarily become Christians as a consequence.[39] It is difficult to measure the impact of this process on the lives of those who were educated in this way, especially on the subsequent socioeconomic status of women, or on public life in general, through the creation of new elites. Moreover, it is evident that some at least of the resources for setting up Welsh mission schools came from local Muslim and Hindu benefactors, which tantalizingly implies that negotiations between missionaries and established religious communities over the delivery of services could prove to be successful and mutually beneficial. Evidence of practical co-operation of this kind strikingly contrasts with the dominant image of ceaseless conflict projected by the missionaries both in their formal reports to the home church in their journalism.[40] Medical work also ostensibly offered evangelical opportunities. On opening the mission hospital in Mawphlong in 1878, its manager, Dr. Griffiths, declared confidently that there was "no more effective means of destroying the superstitions of the people and to lead them to the Truth."[41] In 1928, Ceridwen Edwards, a missionary nurse, described how in the Habiganj mission hospital Hindu, Muslim and Christian women were

> brought together under one roof, and treated alike without distinction of caste or creed or social position. They lie side by side. . . . As we see first one prejudice and then another dropped, we realize that they are beginning to learn, perhaps unconsciously, the great lesson of the Fatherhood of God, and the Brotherhood of Man.[42]

She did not say whether the Habiganj hospital had the same separate, fee-paying wards exclusively for the use of European as did the mission hospital in Shillong,[43] but the possibility that it might undermines somewhat the strength of her insistence on equality of medical treatment as a cardinal and socially liberating Christian virtue.

It follows from what has been said so far that these missionaries were charged with two major responsibilities. One was to take Welsh Calvinistic Methodism to the Assamese and Bengalis; the other was not only to keep the Welsh informed of their activities, but also to do so in a fashion that both spurred the church to make greater missionary efforts at home and to attract sufficient voluntary donations to finance their work in the field. They carried out the second responsibility in a number of ways and by a variety of routes. Of particular interest are the more discursive and self-reflective forms of missionary writing, although the importance of other forms of report should not be minimized. It is important to recall that most written and oral communication with the home church was conducted in Welsh. This, of course, effectively excluded it from scrutiny by indigenous ministers, converts, or those who drew on missionary services. With the exception of the field journals, which were printed in English, or bilingually in English and Bengali, communication with the home church and its members was in Welsh and was intended to flow only in the one direction.

Transmission routes for these communications took a number of forms. Formal reports were submitted annually for publication in the *Report of the Foreign Mission*, but news also returned by means of letters, the contents of which at times filtered through to the newspaper press. News coverage of events in 1857 provides an interesting illustration of the way in which editors used missionaries effectively as foreign correspondents. The monthly denominational journal *Y Drysorfa* (The Treasury) included from 1847 a separate "missionary chronicle" section, *Y Cronicl Cenhadol* (Missionary Chronicle), a periodical within a periodical, where reports from the field were regularly printed alongside other religious news and comment. Lectures and sermons given by missionaries on furlough, with occasional visits by converts, were widely publicized, as were special chapel events. Touring exhibitions of Indian villages and bazaars were intended further to excite the sympathies of their audiences. These were augmented in the 1920s by missionary films, shown in schools and chapels, such as the one shot by Mostyn Lewis, son of the Liberal MP Sir Herbert Lewis, in 1928 (*Cenhadwr*, Rhagfyr 1928, 236). The conversion of chapels into cinemas, albeit temporarily, signified a huge, even a shocking, shift in Nonconformist cultural sensibilities. Obituaries in newspapers also provided opportunities for the work of missionaries to be constructed as heroic, and allowed the church to appeal for more volunteers.[44] The most ubiquitous form of communication, however, was the missionary periodical press. It is certainly the most accessible to us today, yet it remains a surprisingly underused historical resource.

The Welsh mission field created its own communications media. John Pengwern Jones launched the *Friend of Sylhet* and *The Friend of the Women of Bengal* in 1899, and Helen Rowlands started *The Link* in 1933. But the most important missionary periodical was without doubt *Y Cenhadwr* (The Missionary), published wholly in Welsh between 1922 and 1974, and aimed at a popular Welsh audience at home (fig. 24).[45] Initially edited by the Rev. J. Hughes Morris and published at monthly intervals from the denomination's own press at Caernarfon, north Wales, it printed a wide variety of articles, reports, essays, and photographs from the mission field. Missionaries contributed the vast majority of items. No circulation figures have as yet come to light, but it is known that the journal was distributed principally through the chapels and by subscription. As a propagandist text, whose purpose was to draw attention to the mission and to attract greater support for it, *Y Cenhadwr* is for a number of reasons a problematic source.[46] For one thing, the *General Regulations* of the mission had stipulated that "Nothing shall be printed at any of the Society's presses which has not the approval of the District Committee. And the Committee shall take precautions against the printing and publishing of political works calculated to interfere with the Society's usefulness" (*General Regulations*, 1870, 23). Clearly, the denomination was from the beginning aware of the political sensitivities of its missionary work, but it is difficult to judge the extent to which the choice of themes for articles, and their wording, was edited in the light of the above injunction.[47] What we can say, however, is that a disproportionate number of articles originate in Sylhet and Silchar, rather than in the Khasi Hills. In other words, they describe life and work in the most embattled section of the mission. Rather than describing success, their authors foreground the difficulties of the task, the personal struggle it involves, and the resistance they encounter. It is a moot point whether this was deliberate editorial policy aimed at generating a more sympathetic public response, or the consequence of the particular combination of gifted and prolific writers whose talents had led the mission leadership to station them in the most difficult areas of the field. An emphasis on the conversion, and subsequent isolation, of Muslims and higher-caste Hindus may also have embodied deep assumptions about the differential value placed upon the Christianising of powerful and "civilized" religious communities over "animist" tribal peoples. In 1895, Sylhet missionary Laura Evans excitedly reported that

Figure 24. The first issue of *Y Cenhadwr*, January 1922. Reprinted with the kind permission of the National Library of Wales.

*Brahmin a'i deulu o wraig a dwy eneth, wedi gadael tad, mam, brodyr a chwior-
ydd er mwyn ei enw Ef—ac wedi dyfod i geisio gorphwys eu heneidiau arno am
iachadwriaeth. Bydd clywed hyn yn llawenydd i lawer iawn yng Nghymru.*[48]

(A Brahmin, with his wife and two daughters, has left his father, mother,
brothers and sisters for His sake—and have come to try to rest their souls
on Him for salvation. This news will bring joy to very many in Wales.)

These contributors embody a marked imbalance of gender as well
as of geography. A disproportionately high number of authors were
women. This partly reflects the high numbers of women missionaries in the field, particularly from the turn of the century. In 1924,
for example, of 56 Welsh missionaries in the field, 37, or 66 percent,
were women, 21 of whom, constituting 38 percent of the total number of missionaries of both sexes, were unmarried women.[49] There
are a number of reasons why this may have been so. One is that male
missionaries in the field had had a troubled history. Dr. Richards, an
early medical assistant to the first of the Welsh missionaries, Thomas
Jones, was expelled in 1845. Then, in October 1847, Jones himself
found his connection with the church abruptly terminated. By all
accounts, he had remarried without church permission, had taken
up farming, and had introduced to the Khasis the distilled form of
alcohol and improved techniques for brewing beer (Jenkins, 230–
41). Twenty years later, William Pryse, who had first extended the
mission south to Sylhet, was excommunicated, though church records are coy about their reasons for doing so.[50] Significantly,
though, both he and Jones remained in their adopted homes until
their deaths. The church was struck by yet another scandal in 1925,
when John Pengwern Jones, who had restarted the Sylheti mission,
was accused by a number of young women in the mission's orphan-
age of undisclosed but inappropriate behaviour. No legal action was
brought, and an internal tribunal eventually exonerated him shortly
before his death in 1927. Nonetheless, men had hardly acquitted
themselves quite as honorably as the church at home had hoped
they might.

But there is another reason, too, why women were deemed to be
more appropriate for the missionary life, especially in Sylhet. There,
missionary energies were chiefly devoted to proselytizing among
Hindus. As one communication from the field had observed,
"women are the real Hindus," and as the "main defenders" (J. H.
Morris, 1907, 312) of the religion, women were regarded not necessarily as the main targets for conversion, but certainly as the essential
agency by means of whose influence Christianity might be normal-

ized or made acceptable in Hindu households. Demand for women missionaries increased as greater priority was given to work in the zenanas, a policy favored by most Christian missionary societies, especially in Bengal, since at least the 1840s,[51] in schools, and in women's hospitals. In addition to the reservoir of enthusiasts generated by the 1904–5 revival, the Welsh church recruited this cohort principally in two places. The first was among those, often from poor rural backgrounds, who had been persuaded of their vocation at evangelical meetings or missionary lectures. These included women such as Elizabeth Williams, born the daughter of a small tenant farmer and Methodist deacon in rural Merionethshire in 1866. Largely self-educated, in 1887 she successfully persuaded the church to approve her as one of their first unmarried woman missionaries in the field. She arrived in Sylhet in December 1889, where, in 1903, she opened the first school for girls. Within a year, the school had sixty pupils. Shortly before the First World War, and following some shrewd lobbying among benefactors in India and in Britain, including M.P.s such as David Lloyd George, Keir Hardie, and Ramsay MacDonald, she also established the first of the mission's women's hospitals in Sylhet. Her diary describes in vivid detail the consequences of the 1897 earthquake in Sylhet, in which her observations on the profligacy of the colonial Residency and the European Club drip with sarcasm. She died of cancer in 1917.

The other source of recruits, which became increasingly important during and after the First World War, were the University Colleges, especially Aberystwyth and Bangor, which from around the turn of the century began to produce a new generation of university-educated women who clearly regarded missionary work not only as a spiritual activity but also as a valid career choice. The vast majority went as teachers. Perhaps the most remarkable of these was Jane Helen Rowlands. Born in Anglesey in 1891, she graduated in French from Bangor in 1911 and studied languages for a year at Newnham College, Cambridge, before withdrawing following a breakdown. She then taught French in Newtown, Montgomeryshire, before applying for a post in the mission. Following a period of training at St. Colm in Edinburgh, she left for India in 1916. In 1918, she was appointed headmistress of Elizabeth Williams's school for girls in Sylhet, then, in 1925, became the first Principal of the Darjeeling Language School for Missionaries before returning to teach at another school for girls in Karimganj in 1931. In the meantime she also did an M.A. in Bengali at Calcutta University, and was awarded a D.Litt. from the Sorbonne for a thesis on women in medieval Bengali literature, completed while on furlough in Paris in 1930.[52] She was subsequently offered chairs in Eastern Languages in universities in the United States, Britain, and India, but refused them all. She died in Karimganj in February 1955.[53] Others included Kitty Lewis, daughter of Sir Herbert Lewis, and Dilys Edmunds, both recruited at Aberystwyth immediately after the First World War.

Women such as these were responsible not only for carrying out missionary work in the theater of the public sermon, the zenanas, the schools, and the hospitals, but also for writing most of the articles printed in *Y Cronicl Cenhadol* and its successor, *Y Cenhadwr.* Though their role in governing the mission field through the District Committees was limited, it can be said that, from the 1890s, they became the mission's most consistent and effective correspondents. It was their constructions of India, and what they made of the missionary presence there, which formed the largest proportion of the missionary journalism consumed by readers at home. Taken together as a package, and particularly when placed alongside the other forms of transmission mentioned earlier, this body of writing appears less zealous and doctrinaire, and more open and exploratory, than other forms of Welsh religious literature at the time.

However, these articles were also functional, both in the sense of communicating the otherness of India, and, thereby, of legitimizing missionary activity there. Mary Louise Pratt describes "the portrait of manners and customs" in travel writing as "a normalizing discourse, whose work is to codify difference, to fix the other in a timeless present where all 'his' actions and reactions are repetitions of 'his' normal habits."[54] Accounts in *Y Cenhadwr* of Indian religious practices caricature Hindu beliefs by essentializing them in the way Pratt suggests. In an article on Kali, one of a series on Hindu deities printed in 1924, Mrs. B. Wynne Jones describes the nakedness of the goddess, her drunken eyes, her delight in violence, her blood lust, and her orgiastic dance on the corpse of her husband, as a means of challenging the moral framework of Hinduism and of the Hindu family and social order (B. Wynne Jones, "Y Dduwies Kali," *Cenhadwr*, Chwefror 1922, 19). Other ethnographic accounts work in similar ways, particularly those that describe dress, social codes of behavior, diet, and occupation, though rarely with the same critical virulence. In "The Indian Barber," which forms part of an ambitious series on work and street life, Dilys Edmunds describes the social and religious significance of the *napit*, but it too "fixes" the intellectual barber in an essentialist way, and attributes his social power to the Hindu "superstitions" which, she seeks to persuade her readers, her school for Hindu girls in Karimganj was gradually eradicating. Religion and caste, as Bernard Cohn has argued, "were the sociological keys to understanding the Indian people," and it would be instructive to set these two series of articles against others in the English missionary press, and in the context of state-sponsored censuses and other exercises in sociological categorization (Thomas, *Colonialism's Culture*, 38). They appear to fit a pattern of colonizing writing.

Other ethnographic accounts may have perplexed rather than reassured their readers. Descriptions of Indian folklore could be particularly problematic, given the efforts the church had made to eradicate so much of Wales's own folk practices. Dancing, for example, had been outlawed by the church's Rules of 1823, yet in 1924 we find Mrs. Robert Jones, from Cherra in the Khasi Hills, excitedly describing Khasi dance as "proverbs in movement" which conveyed secret and profane messages to the initiated. In the past, missionaries had been forbidden to attend these dances, a rule now evidently broken (*Cenhadwr*, Ionawr 1924, 5). Furthermore, while Indian religious beliefs were being derided in the periodical press, examples of Indian religious writing were being made available to readers in Welsh translation. There can be little doubt that texts were chosen that sought to emphasize the holiness, and the proximity to Christianity, of certain aspects of other religions, as Helen Rowlands explained in her introduction to her translations of Rabindranath Tagore (*Cenhadwr*, Mawrth 1923, 37). But Elizabeth Williams had also earlier translated the work of the Hindu priestess Chundra Lela into Welsh in 1908,[55] while in 1924 Helen Rowlands, with Hridesh Ranjan Ghose, published the sermons of the Sadhu Sundar Sing.[56] Readers in Wales were thereby invited to read Hindu religious texts, in their own language and with the approval and authority of the church. Although this may have had interesting cultural and religious consequences, it was not intended to encourage a syncretic dialogue. On the contrary, the reading of such texts was framed by the assumption that they bore powerful testimony to the success of missionary efforts in drawing notable Hindu scholars and priests closer to the Christian God.[57]

Much of *Y Cenhadwr* contains what can only be described as news journalism, especially during the 1930s and 1940s, including articles on the progress of the Congress Party, the activities of Gandhi, the proliferation of symbols of nationhood, and, in 1947, a series of extraordinary accounts of the human cost of Partition, the most notable being Helen Rowlands's reports from Karimganj, positioned on the new border between India and East Pakistan. In other accounts of journeys through the mission field, which included descriptions of landscapes, vegetation, animals, forms of transport, fields, street scenes, markets, and of the men, women, and children they encountered, missionaries employed rhetorical strategies which both emphasized the otherness of India and which encouraged a sympathetic identification with it on the part of their readers. "How different Sylhet is from Wales!" exclaimed Miss E. A. Roberts in 1902 (*Y Drysorfa*, Rhagfyr 1902, 570), yet the very contrast was intended to produce a closer affinity. The missionaries clearly wanted readers at home to care about their work, and about the people they were in contact with. Welsh and Bengali place names are intertwined in these narratives, and comparisons are made between features of the landscape in the two regions. Such self-consciousness becomes most apparent when missionaries describe feelings of loneliness and of homesickness, of *hiraeth*, when they purport to see images of their home country projected on the landscape and the people around them. The employment of such tropes affirmed their sense of belonging to the physical as well as the mental world of their readers.

Other kinds of encounters demanded a different, more subtly nuanced use of language. An essay by Helen Rowlands entitled "the rain," which describes a journey taken downriver with a group of her school pupils during the flood season in Sylhet in 1925, resonated with the vibrancy of color, the scent of flowers, the softness of skin, and the sensual textures of hair and cloth.

> *Yn y bore, fel y mae'r wawr yn torri . . . (m)ae'r dyfroedd i gyd fel pe'n disgwyl yn swil ond yn ffyddiog dawel am gusan gyntaf yr haul. A phwy ar fachlud haul all ddisgrifio'r cysgodau yn y dwr yn ei droi'n rhuddgoch a phorffor? . . . (n)oson leuad ar yr afonydd a'r wlad yn orchuddiedig gan ddwr—mae yn llawn cyfaredd a hud.*[58]

(In the morning, as dawn breaks, . . . the waters wait shyly but with quiet expectation for the first kiss of the sun. And who at sunset could describe the shadows that turn the water ruddy and purple? . . . A moonlit night on the rivers and the land covered by water—it is full of enchantment and magic.)

In the lexicon of Calvinistic Methodism, even in the mid-1920s, "enchantment and magic" were perilous terms that described the vices of a past society the Methodists had done their best to eradicate in their own country. Their use in this context was as distant from contemporary Welsh Calvinistic writing as Thomas Jones's experiments in the distilling of spirits were from its social codes. In describing their encounters with India, missionaries were loosening the bonds

that for more than a century had tied literary style to religious ortho-
doxies.

Missionaries innovated with established cultural forms in other
ways too. John Pengwern Jones in 1901 organized the first Eisteddd-
fod in Sylhet, while Helen Rowlands had later started in Karimganj
an annual eisteddfod in Bengali.[59] Hymns were written in, or translated into, indigenous languages, and these were used in much the
same devotional way within the order of the service in the field as
they were in the home church. J. Arthur Jones, sent to Shillong in
1910 by the *Manchester Guardian,* was struck by the combination of
Indian landscape and Welsh religiosity:

> While I sat at my dinner in the dak bungalow, a familiar strain came to
> my ears. Mingling with the fire-flies . . . floated the minor cadences of
> an old Welsh tune. They were singing in the chapel which stood on the
> hill opposite. The timbre of the voices were a little strange, but apart
> from this I could have imagined myself in some Welsh village where the
> "seiat" was being held in Bethel or Saron. Yet the singers now were
> Khasis, a Mongolian hill folk of Assam, once worshippers of demons . . .
> The Khasis have adopted Welsh Methodism with scarcely a variant.[60]

And in the first issue of *Y Cenhadwr* in 1922, Thomas Charles Edwards could confidently announce that the Welsh Calvinistic Methodists had "to date created in India a Methodist Church in our own
image" (*Cenhadwr,* Ionawr 1922, 2). The recreation of a little Wales
in India went beyond the strictly devotional. In an account of Christmas at her home for orphaned girls in Silchar in 1922, Miss E. M.
Lloyd described how they had "spent an evening in Wales!" Pictures
and maps of the country had been pinned to the walls, the children
were dressed in old Welsh costume, and the choir sang *Hen Wlad fy
Nhadau* and a number of Welsh folk songs, "in Welsh."(*Cenhadwr,*
Rhagfyr 1923, 189–90).[61] While such references to the use of the language and other symbols of Welsh identity are infrequent, this account does suggest another line was being crossed, which, in a very
direct way, raises the question of the colonial context of the mission.

Helen Rowlands herself used the term "a colony of Welsh people"[62] to describe the mission field. While she may have used this
term loosely to denote a specific community of British expatriates, it
could also conceivably be regarded as a reference to the phenomenon of Welsh colonialism. Usually associated with settlement
schemes in the Americas that often sought the cultural preservation
of threatened identities, such scattered Welsh communities formed
an international support and information network that included the

Indian mission.[63] A small non-missionary Welsh presence was also established in northeast India, mainly associated with colonial administration. A Welsh National Society in India (*Cymdeithas Gwladol y Cymru* [sic] *yn yr India*) was established in Calcutta in July 1898, and a Welsh Society of Bengal in July 1909.[64]

But whether the mission formed part of the broader British imperial presence in India, or whether it was engaged in a separate process of colonization of its own, in which case it did so by taking advantage of the colonial structures of the British Empire, the link between the mission and imperialism remains established and incontrovertible. Historians have echoed J. N. Ogilvie's descriptions in 1924 of Christian missions as "the Empire's conscience" and the "soul of the Empire"[65], even though many of them have emphasized the ways in which missionaries objected to its "treatment of subject peoples."[66] Three observations may be made on the Welsh mission as a form of cultural imperialism. The key question here is why were self-conscious members of a linguistic and cultural minority prepared to undermine the cultural autonomy of others? Nigel Jenkins suggests that they did so because they had, during the previous century, so brutally remade their own culture. They were prepared to transform others because they had transformed themselves. This is a powerful argument, though the question could also be approached differently. The ambivalent, even at times contemptuous, attitudes that some missionaries held towards the leadership of the church in Wales suggest that they regarded themselves as role models for evangelists at home. It was precisely the knowledge that they had not won the war in Wales that drove the missionaries, particularly in the early decades of the twentieth century, to regard themselves as the embodiment of the evangelist spirit of early Calvinism. But if they appeared as remote, even formidably austere, figures among their brethren in Wales, they may have been equally incongruous in the mission field. The highly specific nature of their theology, and its cultural and linguistic packaging, is likely to have projected an oddly fragmented or even confused image of the imperial power. The history of the Welsh mission, certainly in the plains but also possibly in the Hills, is broadly consistent with Andrew Porter's evaluation of missionaries generally as being weak agents of British cultural imperialism.[67]

What is clear from the evidence, however, is that missionaries were significant agents of cultural communication. They addressed two audiences, and faced two directions: towards work in the mission field, and towards their church and their readers at home. They formed the link between the two worlds of Wales and the field, and therefore it was, of course, an asymmetrical relationship. While few Assamese or Bengalis toured Wales (and those who did were Christian), it was the missionaries themselves who introduced, through their journalism and their physical presence on furlough, cultural elements of the field. In the interwar years, there are reports of pupils in Welsh primary schools being taught to sing folk songs in Bengali. Women's-only meetings in chapels were known as zenanas, and poems and hymns were composed that eulogized the special relationship between the peoples of Wales and of northeast India.[68] Films, touring exhibitions and missionary journalism kept images of the field continuously in circulation.

It is possible to read this indirect process of cultural communication in one of two ways. One is as a form of propaganda, not only for evangelization, both at home and abroad, but also for the British Empire itself. By simultaneously extolling the spiritual byproducts of Empire, and by celebrating Wales's own collaborative role in Britain's imperial project, it could be argued that missionary activity was part of the ideological apparatus that sought not only to obtain the consent of Welsh Nonconformity for the Empire, but also to obtain the consent of a key Welsh social institution for Wales's own colonization within it. Here, the "multiple identities" that are embodied in missionary self-representations fold into an overarching British and imperial sense of belonging.[69] Yet, while those identities—religious, national, and linguistic—remained indeterminate and contingent, the tensions generated within the "imperial" mindset of Welsh Nonconformity were unresolved. This might lead to an alternative reading that emphasizes the emergence out of these indirect cultural linkages of a set of discourses that point in different directions. These spring from a fundamental element in the missionary belief system which implies that Christianity empowers both individuals and societies, and that its adoption generates social as well as ethical transformation and improvement.[70] Gustav Warneck, in his study of the relationship between missions and culture, first published in English in 1888, referred to Christianity, significantly, as "the Magna Charta of humanity,"[71] and James Dennis's sociological study of missions of 1897 identified this belief as a key component of Christian missionary activity worldwide. It also infused the writing of the Welsh missionaries. Christianity, they argued, was a developmental, modernizing creed that alone could liberate women, provide useful education for children, and free human beings from poverty, caste, communalism, even ultimately from colonial dependency itself. From that fundamental conviction, in this particular case, three rather important issues arise in the missionary literature that appear to have had some effect on political attitudes and forms of thinking in Wales in this period.

One is the modern evolution in Wales of the concept of nationality. In the 1880s, the Young Wales movement had drawn on convert U. Larsing's declarations of love for his Khasi Hills during his tour of Wales twenty years earlier, as a model of patriotism for the Welsh to follow.[72] In 1922, in the opening issue of *Y Cenhadwr*, Thomas Charles Edwards asked whether nations could be "moral agents," and, influenced no doubt by the political rhetoric of David Lloyd George and others Welsh Liberals during the First World War, his answer was unequivocally in the affirmative. "The world owes more of a debt to small nations than to the great empires," he wrote. And of Wales's role as one of those "small nations" he noted that through its missionary activity "our lines of communications are gradually extending through the entire earth." This, he predicted, would in turn lead to "a new International spirit to kill the distrust and hatred of nations . . . The political importance of the Foreign Missions will become more apparent each day. On them depends the peace of the world" (*Cenhadwr*, Ionawr 1922, 2). Shortly afterward, in lecture notes for a furlough tour of Wales, the missionary Rev. Watcyn M. Price argued that

> The world must be treated as a unit and all the nations are equal. . . . We are as nationalist, as selfish as any group of politicians. . . . What would we be saying in Wales to-day if we were put in the position of India or Africa? . . . India is challenging us to be revolutionary in everything.[73]

The emphasis in these texts on the creation of a world community through Christian missionary work was, in the following decade, reiterated even by elements on the Welsh Left. In 1938, David Thomas, a leading member of the I.L.P. in north Wales, regarded missionaries as having raised key international questions of social injustice and imperial oppression, and whose efforts had paved the way for the League of Nations.[74] In the third reading of the Indian Independence Bill in the House of Commons on 15 July 1947, W. R. Williams welcomed Indian Independence as a vindication, and in some respects as a culmination, of the liberating work of the Welsh mission, affirming that "Wales will be second to none in its spirit of elation and thanksgiving on this great day in the history of India."[75] A particular reading of the missionary experience had thus entered Welsh *political* discourse.

Secondly, and allied to this, one could argue that the mission provided a route into the culture for a discussion about race, difference, and power. The experience of missionaries in India enabled some of them to respond positively to the work, for example, of the English missionaries J. H. Oldham and Basil Matthews, on race and the politics of inequality. These mounted critiques of Lothrop Stoddard's national and racial chauvinism[76] and sympathetically discussed Du-Bois's analysis of racial politics in the United States. For Oldham "racial problems . . . (were) to a large extent social, political and economic problems," and in that light he self-reflectedly scrutinized the "ethics of Empire."[77] Both Oldham's *Christianity and the Race Problem* and Basil Matthews's *The Clash of Colour. A study in the problem of race* were published in 1924, and in 1926 the debate entered the pages of *Y Cenhadwr* with articles on "the colour problem" that endorsed Oldham's general position (*Cenhadwr*, Mawrth 1926, 41–44). Few other genres of Welsh-language writing in the interwar period addressed the international politics of race in this way.

Finally, and this has been discussed by Margaret Strobel, Aparnu Basu, and others, the belief in the liberating potential of Christianity was held to apply particularly to the condition of women.[78] As early as in 1887, Sarah Jane Rees (Cranogwen), as editor of *Y Frythones* (The British Woman) had welcomed the church's decision to appoint single women as missionaries as a development that presaged a better future for Welsh women as a whole.[79] Missionary work not only provided women with greater professional opportunities than were available at home, it also gave them greater status, visibility, and a degree of influence, both the field and at home, than they might otherwise have enjoyed. It may be feasible to argue, then, that alongside the imperial message of the mission, its journalism also introduced into Welsh public life a set of discourses on nationhood, international relations, and the politics of race and gender that, while being embedded in a particular Christian ideology, created space for new public forms of conversation.

Meanwhile, back in Assam and Bengal, the missionaries were facing mounting difficulties. The thirty years from the mid-1930s were the most difficult that the mission had ever faced. Laura Evans in 1934 reported "a year of hard fighting with the enemy," when their work was attacked by Muslims and Hindus by means of "persecution, enticements, articles in the newspapers, public meetings addressed by influential leaders" (*Report of the Foreign Mission*, 1934, 55). In 1939, T. W. Reese, admitted that "preaching to non-Christians has never been so difficult as it is now," and blamed "extravagant cultural and national loyalties," for causing difficulties "in and out of the church" (*Report of the Foreign Mission*, 1939, 12). The Second World War militarized virtually the entire area of the mission during the Allied bid to halt the Japanese advance into India, then in 1945 Helen Rowlands, from her base in Karimganj, saw another huge threat to the mission and its ethos. "One day after a visit to a house where many students gathered together to listen to us," she reported, "a young man who had bought a Bengali book from us with St. Mark's Life of Christ in English on the cover, asked "Is this the Communist leader Marx?" Amusing, truly," she added rather dryly, "but also significant" (*Report of the Foreign Mission*, 1945, 28). In August 1947, the Partition of India divided the field, but work in the Assamese sector continued, though at a much reduced level of intensity, until January 1966, when the assets of the mission were transferred to a group of Norwegian Lutherans.

As Wales's missionary "entanglement"[80] with India recedes into the past, how might a reading of its journalism fit into the historiography of modern Wales? Historical writing has, at least since the 1960s, been preoccupied by the shift from Liberalism to Labor, which was also been read as a shift from Nonconformist hegemony to greater secularism, from the Welsh language to English, from agrarian conservatism to industrial and urban modernity, and from a parochial Welsh-speaking nationalism to a socialist English-speaking internationalism. A reading of missionary journalism suggests a more complicated trajectory, one in which new literary styles were being fashioned, and forms of writing were evolving, which at least sought to address issues of difference, power, and the ethics of international relations within Welsh-language Nonconformity itself. But if this reading does amount to a basis for reassessment, we need to recall that it would be only the last of a number of overlapping reinterpretations. In the 1840s, the mission was seen as a sign of the denomination's maturity and responsibility as an evangelical Church, engaged in a broader war of Christian civilization against barbarism. By the 1880s, it was being drawn on to help develop a nascent language of nationality. In the early twentieth century, it was seen as a powerful continuation of the revivalist spirit of 1905. By the 1920s it was also about "small nations" extending outwards in a new postimperial international order. Within the Presbyterian Church today, the history of the mission is being subjected to yet another process of revision. Writing in 1995, Dewi Myrddin Hughes lamented its connection with the British Empire, and with Western power as a whole. "Distance, otherness, discovery and maps were of its essence," he wrote. ". . . The gospel was taken from the centre to the peripheries," from imperial Europe to its colonies.[81] Now, it appears the reverse may be occurring. The church has recently considered canvassing for ministers in Khasia to re-evangelise secularized

Wales.[82] Whatever forms subsequent reassessments may assume, it is surely right to say, with Homi Bhabha, that this history is inescapably "internal" to our own. "The Western metropole must confront its postcolonial history," he writes, ". . . as an indigenous or native narrative *internal to its national identity*."[83] Only by telling their story in this way can the Welsh, finally, bring their missionaries home.

NOTES

This paper was first delivered in the Imperial History Research Seminar, chaired by Professor Andrew Porter, at the Institute of Historical Research, Senate House, University of London, on 13 December 1999, under the auspices of the Currents in World Christianity Project, co-ordinated by the University of Cambridge and financed by the Pew Charitable Trusts. The opinions expressed in this paper are those of the author and do not necessarily reflect the views of the Pew Charitable Trusts. I am grateful for the generous help and advice of Yasmin Ali, Margaret Beetham, Julie Codell, Andrew Cook, John Davidson, Nigel Jenkins, William D. Jones, Paul O'Leary, Peter Marshall, Andrew Porter, Brian Stanley and Jon Wilson.

1. Nigel Jenkins, *Gwalia in Khasia; a visit to the site, in India, of the biggest overseas venture ever sustained by the Welsh 1795–1995* (Llandysul: Gomer Press, 1995). This is an informative and insightful firsthand account, part history, part travelogue, of the impact of the Welsh mission on the Khasi Hills. See also Charlie Pye Smith, *Rebels and Outcasts. A journey through Christian India* (Harmondsworth: Viking, 1998), 259–76.

2. Eastern Bengal was separated from Assam and reunited with Bengal in 1912, *The Imperial Gazetteer of India*, vol. 26, *Atlas* (Oxford, 1909), plate 30.

3. Most histories are by retired missionaries, the most informative being the following three-volume series: Ednyfed Thomas, *Hanes Cenhadaeth Dramor Eglwys Bresbyteraidd Cymru. Cenhadaeth Casia. Y gyfrol gyntaf, Bryniau'r Glaw* (Caernarfon: Gwasg Pantycelyn ar ran Bwrdd y Genhadaeth, 1988); J. Meirion Lloyd, *Hanes Cenhadaeth Dramor Eglwys Bresbyteraidd Cymru. Cenhadaeth Mizoram. Yr ail gyfrol, Y Bannau Pell,* (Caernarfon: Gwasg Pantycelyn ar ran Bwrdd y Genhadaeth, 1989); D. G. Merfyn Jones, *Hanes Cenhadaeth Dramor Eglwys Bresbyteraidd Cymru, Cenhadaeth Sylhet-Cachar. Y drydedd gyfrol, Y Popty Poeth a'i Gyffiniau* (Caernarfon: Gwasg Pantycelyn ar ran Bwrdd y Genhadaeth, 1990). See also two novels by D. G. Merfyn Jones, *Ar Fryniau'r Glaw* (Abertawe, 1980), and *Eryr Sylhet* (Dinbych, 1987), and the memoirs of Gwen Rees Roberts, *Memories of Mizoram. Recollections and Reflections* (n.p.: Presbyterian Church of Wales, 2000). Other useful studies include J. Meirion Lloyd, *Nine Missionary Pioneers. The story of nine pioneering missionaries in North-East India* (Caernarfon, 1989), and Ioan W. Gruffudd (Gol.), *Cludoedd Moroedd. Cofio Dwy Ganrif o Genhadaeth* (Abertawe, 1995). See also Aled Jones, " 'Meddylier am India': tair taith y genhadaeth Gymreig yn Sylhet, 1887–1947," *Transactions of the Honourable Society of Cymmrodorion (THSC),* 1997, n.s. vol. 4, 1998, 84–110, and Jane Aaron, "Slaughter and Salvation: British Imperialism in Nineteenth-century Welsh Women's Writing," *New Welsh Review* 38 (October 1997): 38–46. In an otherwise admirable account of religious movements in modern Wales, D. Densil Morgan, *The Span of the Cross. Christian Religion and Society in Wales 1914–200* (Cardiff: University of Wales Press, 1999), makes only one reference to the Indian mission, 17.

4. Patrick O'Sullivan observes that "aspects of the missionary enterprise are rarely discussed within Irish writing, nor is the concomitant effect on non-European ethnic groups. It might be thought that a nation, part of whose nation-building myth involves criticism of an invader who vilified Irish religion and culture, would at least think twice about so happily doing precisely that to other peoples. . . . This is clearly an area where the sensitivity of the subject matter creates "gaps in the literature," Patrick O'Sullivan, ed., *The Irish World Wide. History, Heritage, Identity. Vol. 5, Religion and Identity* (London: Leicester University Press, 1996), 13.

5. A notable exception, Robert Pope, *Building Jerusalem. Nonconformity, Labour and the Social Question in Wales, 1906–1939* (Cardiff: University of Wales Press, 1998), reinserts the religious impulse into the history of early twentieth-century Welsh labor politics.

6. Important studies of the Welsh outside Wales include William D. Jones, *Wales in America. Scranton and the Welsh* (Cardiff: University of Wales Press; Scranton Pa.: University of Scranton Press, 1993), and Anne Kelly Knowles, *Calvinists Incorporated: Welsh immigrants on Ohio's industrial frontier* (Chicago: University of Chicago Press, 1997).

7. Edward W. Said, *Orientalism* (New York: Vintage Press, 1978). See also Rana Kabbani, *Europe's Myths of the Orient* (Bloomington: Indiana University Press, 1986), Reina Lewis, *Gendering Orientalism: Race, Femininity and Representation* (London: Routledge, 1996), Julie F. Codell and Dianne Sachko Macleod, eds., *Orientalism Transposed: The Impact of the Colonies on British Culture* (Aldershot: Ashgate Press, 1998).

8. See for example Lal Dena, *Missions and colonialism: a study of missionary movement in North East India with particular reference to Manipur and Lushai Hills 1894–1947* (Shillong: Vendrame Institute, 1988).

9. "Before the 1890s . . . opinion-formers . . . were generated by the Nonconformist hegemony itself. It was in this manner that a Nonconformist people emerged as a Welsh 'nation'," Gwyn A. Williams, *When Was Wales? The history, people and culture of an ancient country* (London: Black Raven Press, 1985), 208.

10. *Y Cenhadwr,* Hydref 1922, 148.

11. B. C. Allen, C.S., *Assam District Gazetteers,* vol. 10, *The Khasi and Jaintia Hills, The Garo Hills and The Lushai Hills* (Calcutta: The Baptist Mission Press, 1906), Part 1, 42–53.

12. Allen, 67.

13. B. C. Allen, C.S., *Assam District Gazetteers, vol. ii, Sylhet* (Calcutta: The Baptist Mission Press, 1905), 90.

14. Ibid., *vol i, Cachar* (Calcutta: The Baptist Mission Press, 1905), 59. In 1894 Lorrain and Savidge had found in Lunglei a community of 125 Christians, "the fruit of annual visits by the Welsh missionaries to the north," Brian Stanley, *The History of the Baptist Missionary Society 1792–1992* (Edinburgh: T. and T. Clark, 1992), 270–71.

15. *Report of the Foreign Mission of the Welsh Calvinistic Methodists,* 1910, xv. For other statistics, see *Blwyddiadur, neu Lyfr Swyddogol y Methodistiaid Calfinaidd,* published annually from 1898.

16. John Hughes Morris, *Hanes Cenhadaeth Dramor y Methodistiaid Calfinaidd Cymreig, hyd ddiwedd y flwyddyn 1904* (Liverpool: Llyfrfa y Cymundeb, 1907), 304. For resistance to missionary work in the zenanas, see also Rokeya Sakhawat Hossain, *Sultana's Dream* (Calcutta: 1916; reprint, New York: Feminist Press, 1988).

17. J. Fortis Jyrwa, "Christianity in Khasi Culture: a study of the relationship between Christianity and Traditional Khasi culture with special reference to the

Seng," (D. Miss. diss., Fuller Theological Seminary, School of World Mission, 1984).

18. The Welsh Calvinistic Methodists Foreign Mission Society, *Regulations for the Guidance of the Directors and Missionaries of the Society.* (Salford, 1870), 36–38. See also Nicholas Thomas, *Colonialism's Culture, Anthropology, Travel and Government* (Cambridge: Polity Press, 1994), 39.

19. *Adroddiad Cenhadaeth Dramor y Methodistiaid Calfinaidd Cymreig, 1926,* NLW CMA GZZ/2–14. The success of the Welsh mission among the tribal peoples of the hills may, by 1914, have persuaded other Christian missionaries in the region to rethink their emphasis on the conversion of upper-caste Hindus, see Stanley (1992), 269.

20. Anthony Copley, *Religions in Conflict: Ideology, Cultural Contact and Conversion in Late-Colonial India* (Delhi: Oxford University Press, 1997), 88.

21. *Cenhadaethau Eglwysig: neu Hanes Byr am Weithrediadau y Gymdeithas er Lledaenu yr Efengyl mewn Gwledydd Tramor* (Treffynnon, 1852), 23.

22. Welsh donations to the C.M.S. doubled from £1,450 in 1880 to £2,734 in 1898, Eugene Stock, *The History of the Church Missionary Society. Its Environment, its Men and its Work,* vol. 3 (London: Church Missionary Society, 1899), 713.

23. In 1894, 175 offers of missionary service were received from Wales, 45 from men, 48 from women, *Adroddiad o Gasgliadau yr Eglwys yng Nghymru at y Gymdeithas Genhadol Eglwysig, 1894* (Tremadoc, 1894), iii–iv.

24. E. Thomas Lawson and Robert N. McCauley, *Rethinking Religion. Connecting cognition and culture* (Cambridge: Cambridge University Press, 1990), 1. This study, born of a "frustration with the timidity that characterises so many scholars' discussions of religion," advocates the adoption of more theoretically informed approaches to questions of theology.

25. See Rule XII on Election through Grace, "People beyond number from every tribe, language, people and nation, have been Elected for Holiness and Eternal Life by God" (trans.), *Hanes, Cyfansoddiad, Rheolau Dysgyblaethol ynghyd a Chyffes Ffydd, y corph o Fethodistiaid Calfinaidd yn Nghymru* (Bala, 1825), 68.

26. For the hostility surrounding attempts to launch English language services from 1858, in response to the growth of railway transport, see Frank Price Jones "Yr Achosion Saesneg," *Cylchgrawn Cymdeithas Hanes, Eglwys Methodistaidd Calfinaidd Cymru,* Rhif lvii (October 1972), esp. 66–69.

27. *Rheolau Dysgyblaethol,* rule 40, 98. See also R. Tudur Jones, "Y Genedl Galfinaidd a'i Llen," in D. Densil Morgan (Gol.), *Grym y Gair a Fflam y Ffydd. Ysgrifau ar Hanes Crefydd yng Nghymru,* (Bangor: Gwasg John Penri 1998), 270.

28. D. W. Bebbington, *Evangelicalism in Modern Britain: A history from the 1730s to the 1980s* (Boston: Unwin Hyman, 1989), 30.

29. The number of communicants peaked in 1926 with 189,727, narrowly exceeding the figure for the revival year of 1905, John Williams, ed., *Digest of Welsh Historical Statistics* (Cardiff: Welsh Office, 1985), 2:294–95. For the political and social power of Calvinistic Methodism in nineteenth- and early twentieth-century Wales, see K. O. Morgan, *Wales in British Politics* (Cardiff: University of Wales Press, 1963) and *Wales. Rebirth of a Nation* (New York: Oxford University Press, 1981).

30. Cf. advertisement for "The Calvinistic Methodist Health Insurance Society, Wrexham" in Rev. Watcyn M. Price, *A Guide to the Organization of Missionary Exhibitions* (1932), 42.

31. *Calvinistic Methodism in Wales: Its Present Position and Future Prospects. A Critical Review* (London: Hodder and Stoughton, 1870), 3–4. See also E. T. Davies, *Religion and Society in the Nineteenth Century. A New History of Wales Series.* (Llandybïe: C.

Davies, 1981), 65, on the "debased form" of late nineteenth-century Welsh Non-conformity.

32. Mrs. John Roberts, (Sidney Margaret Roberts), *The Revival in the Khasia Hills* (Newport: Cambrian Printing Works, 1907), 9, 31, 70, 104 and 111.

33. B. T. Vaughan Davies, "Cenhadesau yn Ffwyth y Diwygiad," *Y Gymraes*, Mawrth 1909, 33–34.

34. The Welsh Calvinistic Methodists' Foreign Mission Society, *General Regulations for the Guidance of the Directors and Missionaries of the Society. Adopted by the General Assembly, held at Brecon, July 12–14 1870* (Salford, 1870). See also the clause which stipulates that "marriage without sanction" was "sufficient reason" to terminate a missionary's connection with the Church, The Foreign Mission of the Presbyterian Church of Wales, *General Regulations for the guidance of the committee and the missionaries in India* (Aberdare, 1928), 57.

35. "No Missionary shall continue to labour in a foreign country for a longer period than fifteen years, without revisiting his native land, and holding personal intercourse with the Directors of the Society," 30.

36. *Y Drysorfa*, Awst 1908, 383–84.

37. Miss E. A. Roberts, "Y Cronicl Cenhadol," *Y Drysorfa* (Rhagfyr, 1902), 570.

38. *Comisiwn Ymchwil y Genhadaeth Dramor. Adroddiad y Ddirprwyaeth a Ymwelodd a'r India* (Bala: Eglwys Bresbyteraidd Cymru 1936), 5, NLW CMA GZ/35. See also Jenkins, *Gwalia in Khasia*, 52.

39. Missionary work was to include the " Christian training of young people, male and female, who are not Christian . . . (and) . . . the advancement of Christian civilisation," *General Regulations* (1870), 37.

40. Many of these schools are still open, though they operate under new names. The Welsh Mission High School in Shillong, for example, was still operational in 1967. Gillian Wilson, ed., *Theodore. Letters from the Oxford Mission in India 1940–1993* (Romsey: Oxford Mission, 1997), 215, see the reference to its then headmaster, "the Patriarch of these hills . . . Wilson Reade." The location of the Shillong Welsh Mission Hospital is marked on map British Library IOR Y/1/125/NE/1873/1901.

41. *Llawlyfr yr Arddangosfa Genhadol Y Bala*, Mai 26–28, 1926, 54.

42. *Adroddiad Cenhadaeth Dramor*, 1928, 36.

43. Dr. H. Gordon Roberts, "Christ and the Healing of India," notes for a lantern lecture, (n.d.), NLW CMA GZ/53.

44. R. J. Williams, "Un o'r Arloeswyr. Elizabeth Williams, Sylhet," *Y Goleuad*, Medi 7, 1917, 5. See occasional series on "Yr Oriel Genhadol" in *Y Cenhadwr* for biographies and photographic portraits.

45. Numbers of Welsh speakers in Wales over the age of three totalled 766,103 in 1921, peaking at 811,329 in 1931. For further details, consult Williams, *Digest* 1 (1985): 86–88. The C.M.S., founded in 1799, published its Annual Proceedings from 1800 to 1922. See also *The Missionary Register* 1813–55 and *The Church Missionary Paper* and *Record* from 1830. Both *The Church Missionary Gleaner*, established 1841, and *Mercury and Truth*, established 1897, ended in the early 1920s, Joseph L. Altholz, The *Religious Press in Britain* (New York: Greenwood Press, 1989), 20.

46. The circulation of Irish missionary journals bore "testimony to the missionary movement's popular base" in Ireland due to lay support in distribution and fund-raising; also Edmund Hogan, *The Irish Missionary Movement: a Historical Survey 1830–80* (Dublin: Gill and Macmillan, 1990), 127.

47. There is some evidence of editing, though the example cited was never published, see Dienw, "Erthygl ar India . . . gan un o'n hen genhadon" (n.d.), NLW CMA GZ/98, in particular 4, of twelve manuscript pages of an article submitted ostensibly for publication in *Y Cenhadwr*.

48. *Adroddiad Cymdeithas Genhadol Dramor y Methodistiaid Calfinaidd Cymreig, 1895,* NLW CMA G2/1

49. NLW CMA/GZ/2–14.

50. For further information on the expulsion of William Pryce, see Morris, 1907, 300. Pryce died in India on 2 August 1869.

51. Aparnu Basu, "Mary Ann Coote to Mother Teresa: Christian Women and the Indian Response," in *Women and Missions Past and Present. Anthropological and Historical Perceptions,* ed. Fiona Bowie, Deborah Kirkwood, and Shirley Ardener (Providence, R.I.: Berg, 1993), 199.

52. J. H. Rowlands, *La Femme Bengalie dans la Littérature du Moyen-Age* (Paris: A. Maisonneuve, 1930), *v.* of the Introduction is particularly revealing of her intentions.

53. Griffith Wynne Griffith, *Cofiant Cenhades. Miss J. Helen Rowlands, M.A., D. Lit., (Helen o Fon)* (Caernarfon: Llyfrfa'r Methodistiaid Calfinaidd, 1961), passim. See also W. R. Owain-Jones, "The Contribution of Welshmen to the Administration of India," *TH SC* (1970), Part 1, 260–61; *Dictionary of Welsh Biography 1941–1970* (Cardiff: University of Wales Press, 2001), 237–38.

54. Mary Louise Pratt, "Scratches on the Face of the Country; or, what Mr. Barrow saw in the land of the Bushmen," *"Race," Writing and Difference,* ed. Henry Louis Gates Jr. (Chicago: University of Chicago Press, 1986), 139.

55. Ada Lee and Elizabeth Williams, *Y Offeiriades Hindwaidd. Hanes Bywyd Chundra Lela* (Caernarfon: Llyfrau'r Cyfundeb, 1908). This text had previously been translated into English by Ada Lee in 1903.

56. Helen J. Rowlands and Hridesh Ranjan Ghose, *Sermons and Sayings of Sadhu Sundar Singh during his visit to the Khasi Hills, Assam, March 1924* (Sylhet: Published by the Authors, 1924).

57. Tagore was skeptical of missionary attempts to translate and evaluate his writing. Responding to Edward Thompson's biography of him, *Rabindranath Tagore: Poet and Dramatist* (London: Oxford University Press, 1926), he wrote that "being a Christian Missionary, his [Thompson's] training makes him incapable of understanding some of the ideas that run through all my writings . . . ," quoted in Krishna Dutta and Andrew Robinson, *Rabindranath Tagore. The Myriad Minded Man* (London: Bloomsbury, 1995), 277. See also E. P. Thompson, *Alien Homage. Edward Thompson and Rabindranath Tagore* (Delhi: Oxford University Press, 1993). The first biography of Tagore published in English was by Carmarthen-raised Ernest Rhys in 1915.

58. *Y Cenhadwr,* Ionawr 1925, 8–9.

59. John Pengwern Jones introduced the Eisteddfod to Sylhet in 1904, and Helen Rowlands later held eisteddfodau in Bengali at Karimganj (Lloyd, 1989, 7).

60. *Report of the Foreign Mission,* 1910, 13.

61. See also Susan Fleming McAllister, "Cross-cultural dress in Victorian British Missionary Narratives: Dressing for Eternity," *Historicizing Christian Encounters with the Other,* ed. John C. Hawley (Basingstoke: Macmillan, 1998), esp. 123–24.

62. *The Link,* March–April 1935, 18.

63. See for example coverage of the Indian Mission in such Welsh-American periodicals as *Y Cyfaill* (The Friend), Rhagfyr 1923. See also Aled Jones and Bill Jones, *Welsh Reflections. Y Drych and America 1851–2001* (Llandysul: Gomer Press, 2001), 50, 89.

64. D. E. Lloyd Jones, "David Edward Evans. A Welshman in India," *THSC* (1967), Part 1, 136–40.

65. J. N. Ogilvie, *Our Empire's Debt to Missions. The Duff Missionary Lecture 1923*

(London: Hodder and Stoughton, 1924), 10, 253. See, for example, Donald Harman Akenson, *The Irish Diaspora. A Primer* (Toronto: P. D. Meany, 1993), 146.

66. Brian Stanley, *The Bible and the Flag. Protestant missions and British imperialism in the nineteenth and twentieth centuries*, (Leicester: Apollos, 1990), 179.

67. A. N. Porter, "Cultural Imperialism and Protestant Missionary Enterprise 1780–1914," *Journal of Imperial and Commonwealth History*, 25 (1997): 367–91.

68. Maldwyn C. John, *Hanes Bywyd a Gwaith Mrs. Esther Lewis—Cenhades 1887–1958* (Swansea: Gwasag John Penri, 1996), 15–16.

69. See Laurence Brockliss and David Eastwood, eds., *A Union of multiple identities. The British Isles, c.1750–1850* (Manchester: Manchester University Press, 1997), esp. 208 on the "more positive" British identity that emerged in the late nineteenth century with the "experience and management of Empire." In Scotland, "(m)issionaries unquestionably stimulated a belief in a profoundly Scottish contribution to empire-building," John M. Mackenzie, "Essay and Reflection: On Scotland and the Empire," *International History Review* 15 (1993): 728.

70. James S. Dennis, *Christian Missions and Social Progress. A sociological study of foreign missions.* 3 vols. (New York: Fleming H. Revell, 1897–1906), 1: 408.

71. Gustav Warneck, *Modern Missions and Culture: their mutual relations.* trans. Thomas Smith (Edinburgh: J. Gemmell, 1883), *xxii.*

72. S. T. Jones, "Cymry Cymreig," *Cymru Fydd*, Ebrill 1889, 381. U. Larsing was, in 1846, among the first to be converted by Welsh missionaries in Khasia. He travelled to Wales in 1860, where he died in 1863. He is buried in Chester, see *Y Cenhadwr* (Tachwedd 1922), 164.

73. Rev. Watcyn M. Price, "The Call of India, notes for a lecture" (n.d.), NLW CMA GZ/53

74. David Thomas, *Y Ddinasyddiaeth Fawr* (Wrecsam: Hughes a'i Fab, 1938), 79–82.

75. *Parliamentary Debates (Hansard)*, 5th ser., vol. 440, 271. Williams was MP for Heston and Isleworth.

76. Stoddard (1883–1950) had proposed that "civilization is the body, the race is the soul"; see Lothrop Stoddard, *The Rising Tide of Colour Against White World-Supremacy* (London: Chapman and Hall, 1920). See also his *Revolt against Civilization: the menace of the under man* (London: Chapman and Hall, 1922).

77. J. H. Oldham, *Christianity and the Race Problem* (London: Student Christian Movement, 1924), 248 and 94. Oldham was Secretary to the International Missionary Council and editor of the *International Review of Missions*. See also Basil Matthews, *The Clash of Colour. A study in the problem of race* (London: Edinburgh House Press, 1924), published by the United Council for Missionary Education. For his treatment of DuBois and Marcus Garvey, see 75–76. C.M.S., "Schemes of Study" are also revealing in this respect, see in particular *Indian Problems and the Christian Message. A Scheme of Study* (London: Church Missionary Society, 1926) on "the national ideal," and *India-Whither Bound? A Scheme of Study* (London: Church Missionary Society, 1930), especially "India's women: discuss 'the women's movement in India holds the key to progress,'" 8.

78. Margaret Strobel, *European Women and the Second British Empire* (Bloomington: Indiana University Press, 1991). Also Nupur Chaudhuri and Margaret Strobel, eds., *Western Women and Imperialism: Complicity and Resistance* (Bloomington: Indiana University Press, 1992).

79. Cranogwen, "Dyfodol Merched Cymru," *Y Frythones*, Gorphenaf, 1887, 202.

80. For the concept of colonial "entanglement," see Nicholas Thomas, *Entangled Objects. Exchange, Material Culture, and Colonialism in the Pacific* (Cambridge: Harvard University Press, 1991).

81. Dewi Myrddin Hughes, "Dealltwriaeth Genhadol C.W.M.," *Cludoedd Moroedd. Cofion Dwy Ganrif o Genhadaeth 1795–1995.* Ioan W. Gruffydd (Gol.) (Abertawe: Bwrdd y Genhadaeth, Undeb yr Annibynwyr Cymraeg, 1995), 91.

82. For a recent report on the continuing connections between Wales and Khasia, see Garmon Rhys, "Draw, draw yn Khasia," *Golwg,* cyf. 12, rhif. 19, 20 (Ionawr 2000): 10–11.

83. Homi K. Bhabha, *The Location of Culture* (London: Routledge, 1994), 6.

"There is Nothing More Poetical than War": Romanticism, Orientalism, and Militarism in J. W. Kaye's Narratives of the Conquest of India

DOUGLAS M. PEERS

J. W. KAYE WAS THE PRE-EMINENT HISTORIAN AND BIOGRAPHER OF BRITISH India in the early- to mid-Victorian era, an author who not only profoundly shaped contemporary impressions of India but who would also lay the foundations for future historians as well. The writings of J. W. Kaye provide unique opportunities to test the ideological and material processes at work in the production of colonial discourse, for his writings not only straddled a range of genres, but Kaye himself was variously located in a number of different communities. Much of his writing was done in England and for British periodicals, yet he spent considerable time in India where he wrote for Anglo-Indian journals. During the course of his life, Kaye produced five novels, a selection of poems, a collection of essays, four histories of different periods of British India (two of which were multivolume productions), five biographies, one biographical collection, and a staggering 143 articles and reviews for some of the leading periodicals of the day, including *Blackwood's, North British Review, Cornhill Magazine,* and *Bentley's Miscellany*. In many cases, his books were either first serialized in journals, or crucial elements in them had been given an initial airing in the periodical press. His novel *Peregrine Pulteney,* for example, made its first appearance in the pages of the *Calcutta Literary Gazette*. He also provided the text to accompany two lavishly illustrated works on the landscapes and peoples of India, was founding editor of the *Calcutta Review,* and served as editor of one Calcutta and two British newspapers. No wonder then that one newspaper opined on his death that he was "one of the greatest authorities on Indian questions."[1] Another spoke of "the extraordinary powers displayed by one who could write graceful essays and verses at nineteen and twenty, and striking romances before the morning of life had fled; and who in later years became the stern Calcutta reviewer of facts and fallacies, the historian of wars, and the biographer of eminent men whose like, take them for all in all, we shall not look upon again."[2] More recently, Ranajit Guha, the founder of the Subaltern Studies project, has described Kaye's *History of the Sepoy War* as "that truly brilliant work of imperial historiography," singling out in particular how powerfully Kaye's accounts drew upon the epic narratives of war and revolution.[3]

A close reading of Kaye's writings confirms Guha's assessment: a conquest narrative is the thread that runs through and unites Kaye's works, whether they were novels, biographies, or articles and reviews for the Victorian press. It is the latter two that will most concern us, for the popularity of his books was grounded in his success as a journalist and editor. For as Ann Parry has noted about Kipling, "The periodical press was a crucial site in the ideological processes of the nineteenth-century, clearly instrumental in positioning the reader in relation to dominant ideas and values."[4] Kaye's articles and reviews established his credentials as the key communicator for the Anglo-Indian community. Journalism allowed him to test his ideas, expand his contacts in the military, official, political, and publishing worlds, and place certain events and ideas before the public. Periodicals also provided Kaye with a safe and solid platform from which he could publicize his interpretations of the British in India, for many of his writings appeared anonymously. Anonymity served Kaye well, especially in his early career as a writer, for it enabled him to capitalize on his privileged access to information without jeopardizing either his career or his contacts. And in one instance, anonymity allowed him to review one of his own works.[5]

If reasons and rationalizations for the British conquest of India were the predominant themes in Kaye's writings, how he dealt with such themes can best be understood by locating Kaye within the information networks that bound India and Britain together, and then by appreciating the extent to which that position fostered certain tensions in his writing. Anglo-Indian society was not simply an offshoot of British society. The two worlds had much in common, yet Anglo-Indian society had acquired certain distinctive traits, such as a very militarized view of the world and a propensity to identify itself in terms of its Indian surroundings. The latter contributed to the rise of orientalist scholarship, and in particular the practice of defining Britishness in terms of an Indian otherness. At the same time, this blend of orientalism and militarism was most often captured through romanticism. J. W. Kaye, having spent considerable time in India and having maintained close ties with Anglo-Indian society, was very much influenced by such positions. But he also had one foot firmly planted in Britain, and worked hard to explain India and the Anglo-Indian worldview to a domestic audience. Moreover, the values he espoused were often those we now associate with the Victorian middleclasses. The end result was that Kaye often trimmed and tacked between British and Anglo-Indian cultures, and between Victorian and Romantic literary and philosophical traditions. He produced narratives of conquest and heroic biographies that were informed by, and in turn informed, each of these worlds. He was himself an Anglo-Indian, yet directed much of his writings to a British audience. His definition of progress, character, and providence were undeniably Victorian, yet he sought to explain them by resorting to romanticism. As he poignantly declared in one review, "Our modern warriors have really achieved what the ancients only dreamt of."[6] And his heroes, thoroughly domesticated according to Victorian conventions, operated in a womanless world.

J. W. Kaye wrote at a time, as Robin Gilmour has so evocatively put it, of "pervasive time-hauntedness."[7] The Victorians were fascinated with time and their place in it, and none more so than J. W. Kaye who turned to history, after experimenting first with poetry and novels, as a means of both making sense of Britain's place in the world and seeking the basis for stability within the British Empire. The acquisition of an empire confronted Britain with societies and civilizations that appeared so different, so dated, as to confirm Britain's place on the cutting edge of modernity. And if the fixation on time was one defining feature of the Victorian era, the second was the growing political, cultural, and economic clout claimed by groups who had hitherto been excluded from positions of power within British society. The emerging middle and professional classes as well as the Evangelicals were gaining ground politically, economically, and socially, and, not surprisingly, the empire became the place where their status and future aspirations could be vouchsafed. The empire gave them not only opportunities to create wealth, but it also enabled them to acquire the trappings of status which had until then been the monopoly of the aristocracy. Kaye unabashedly identified with these groups, yet his writings betrayed the presence of alternative voices, particularly those which stemmed from romanticism, and a fascination with the medieval, two influences that were especially pervasive in Anglo-Indian society.

Furthermore, Kaye's writings straddled a number of key intersections in nineteenth-century British Imperial culture. Chronologically his work bridged the period between the eras of conquest and consolidation in India, and between Company and Crown rule. Aesthetically, he occupied the interstices between the Romantic and the Victorian. Kaye's position on the cusp between the two is well illustrated when, after proclaiming "there is nothing more poetical than war," he laments, "Science has deprived war of much of its old poetical aspect."[8] The industrialization of warfare had stripped it of its chivalry. Yet there is some hope that these poetic qualities can be kept alive in India, for "there is a halo of barbaric romance ever surrounding our oriental wars, which sends back the imagination to those remote ages when the Macedonian conqueror appeared on the scene of our recent triumph . . . the environments of an Afghan or Punjabi war are necessarily romantic and picturesque" (Kaye, "Poetry of Indian Warfare," 222).

Yet as a historian, Kaye not only subscribed to a very modern view of history, namely that history was all about the march of progress, but he also adopted what could best be described as modern methods of doing history. His work relied on an extensive range of original documents from which he frequently quoted and to which he often had unique access. Moreover, he could call upon his own personal experience in India to help authenticate his works. As first an artillery officer in India, and then an editor, he developed close links with the Anglo-Indian community and he would foster these links long after he had left India in 1845. To these personal sources of information he added access to official reports and memoranda, for in the mid-1850s he joined the home office of the East India Company, and when it was wrapped up in the aftermath of the Indian Rebellion of 1857–58, he moved across town to the India Office where he occupied one its most senior positions.

J. W. Kaye was thus uniquely placed to broker information between India and Britain, and he did so with a very clear purpose: he wanted to instruct British and Anglo-Indian society about their obligations as much as he wished to entertain them. In a review article that reflected back upon the first six years of the *Calcutta Review,* he claimed, "It is, certainly, our first object to instruct the reader; but we rejoice greatly in an opportunity of amusing him."[9] Review articles were especially well suited to these tasks, for they enabled Kaye to bring to the attention of his readers in India and Britain recent books that he felt merited attention, while also allowing him to critique those that he felt undermined Britain's position and role in India[10] (Kaye, "Illustrations of Anglo-Indian Society"). But as he told his readers in India, Anglo-Indian periodicals like the *Calcutta Review* had to contend with a dearth of what he termed "light literature," and so entertaining readers was more difficult than it was in Britain where reviewers were overwhelmed with lighter fare.[11] Not surprisingly then, Kaye turned to accounts of military operations in India as a means of combining instruction with entertainment. As Kaye informed his readers, "the war-maker is sure of popular applause" because his actions are "ever intelligible to the multitude."[12] War made for gripping reading, especially when it was set in an exotic location, for it provided dramatic stories of bravery, villainy, comedy, and tragedy. Even parody was included, for the army included all types of characters in all types of situation. In another piece in the *Calcutta Review*, he wrote of the Afghan and Sikh wars that "there is scarcely a work, great or small, illustrative of the operations, or the country traversed in the course of them, which we have not amply reviewed" (Kaye, "Poetry of Recent Indian Warfare," 220). So great was the demand for information on these wars that Kaye was prompted to write several histories himself.

Kaye attributed the rise of British power to character traits unique to the British gentleman, and hence much of his writing was dedicated to identifying and celebrating them. When reviewing some recent writings on history of the conquest of India, Kaye remarked that British officers in India "afforded some of the noblest examples of Christian heroism in the annals of chivalry, as they are written in the great book of the world" (Kaye, "The Romance of Indian Warfare," 224). Similarly, in the preface to *Lives of Indian Officers,* a book that was first serialized in *Good Words,* he declared his duty to be to show "how youths from middle class families carved their way to fame and fortune."[13] He went on to claim that his ultimate goal was to produce a "Biographical History of India," one that would reveal "the lives of the Great Men who make history" (Kaye, *Lives of Indian Officers* 1: xi–xii). His articles, reviews, histories, and historical biographies were intended to publicize imperial heroes who would in turn serve as role models for future generations. His didactic aim was made even more explicit when he reflected, "If I have induced even a few [youths], contemplating these heroic examples, to endeavour to do likewise, I shall not have written in vain" (Kaye, *Lives of Indian Officers* 1: xiv). His heroes were described in terms redolent of an earlier age, yet their virtues were unmistakably Victorian. No matter whether they were dispensing justice to peasants along the Ganges, or fending off tribal attacks along the northwest frontier, Kaye's heroes (who included, among others, Henry Lawrence, Charles Metcalfe, Mountstuart Elphinstone, John Malcolm, and James Outram) are recognizable by their industriousness, manliness, piety, and self-sacrifice. In other words, they became the quintessential Victorian imperial heroes.

Kaye's career as a writer began at a time of profound social, political, and cultural change, an era when the clash between the Ancien Regime and the modernizing world of industrialization and empire was reaching its crescendo. Urbanization was reshaping the British landscape; industrialization and commercialization were transforming the British economy, while society had to contend with the emergence of new social groups. The struggles for parliamentary reform and Catholic emancipation, and the rise of Chartism in Britain threatened to alter irrevocably the political landscape. And all this was set against the backdrop of the revolutions of 1830 and 1848 in Europe.

Historians have come to view these as years of reform, and certainly efforts at and interest in reform were there. But for many of the years commonly associated with reform, and particularly the 1820s and 1830s, anxiety and uncertainty prevailed as British society struggled to make sense of the social, political, cultural, and economic upheavals stemming from the French and Industrial Revolutions.[14] These anxieties were aggravated still further by the paradox that Britain had become a world power without possessing a coherent worldview on account of the crisis that had befallen Christianity in Britain. By the late nineteenth century, science would fill part of that gap, but Gilmour suggests that before then, there was nothing from which society as a whole could seek reassurance (Gilmour, 19).

This image of a society adrift requires some modification. Religion might have lost much of its binding potential, but the idea of empire and the unity it provided was gaining ground. Contrary to what earlier generations of historians have suggested, the mid-nineteenth century did experience a renewed bout of imperial expansion, and with it, a growing identification with Britain's imperial mission. Historians commonly speak of a first British empire and a second British empire, with the first being anchored in the Atlantic and covering the period up to the end of the American Revolution, and the second being a tropical empire that is often dated from the scramble for Africa in the 1880s. The period in between has often been characterized as a period of imperial apathy, or even antipathy with the growth of the Little Englanders. Such a chronology overlooks the fact that not only was British rule becoming more deeply embedded in India, but its frontier was rolling inexorably forward.[15] And more to the point, there was little sign of any diminished enthusiasm for Britain's empire in India. The public reaction to the Indian Rebellion of 1857–58 is proof of just how central India had become to Greater Britain.[16]

Imperial narratives of empire framed in terms of progress were an important means by which Britons could locate themselves historically. As Kaye remarked, "We must look to the East now as the nour-isher of great military renown."[17] The past was ransacked, not only to provide the necessary proof that history was unfolding as it should, but also to provide universal models of heroic conduct that enabled the actions of contemporary figures to be made intelligible. And the impact was not confined to the imperial periphery, for the ideological rationalizations and explanations for colonial rule en-couraged the growth within Britain of certain beliefs and institu-tions that drew upon the racial, gender, and class hierarchies that flourished in the empire in general and in India in particular. These in turn had important consequences for the evolution of British so-ciety and its identities.

The anxieties, which were such an important feature of early- and mid-Victorian Britain, can also be traced to India where they were given added poignancy by the demands of ruling over a large, var-ied, and all too often unknown population. The clash between those defending continuity and those pushing for change manifested it-self in India in what historians have customarily labeled the Orien-talist-Anglicist debate. In its simplest guise, orientalists favored working through Indian institutions and respecting Indian customs and traditions (real or invented)—for pragmatic as well as doctri-naire reasons—whereas the Anglicists believed that Indian customs and traditions were nothing more than barriers to progress, and hence they should be jettisoned and replaced with western institu-tions and ideologies.[18]

Historians are now faced with a richer, yet more complex picture of British policy in terms of its intellectual and cultural contexts, owing in part to the realization that there was a considerable gap between the rhetoric of colonial rule and its reality. Recently it has come to be understood that the culture of colonial rule contained within it a fundamental paradox: official rhetoric and traditional his-toriography have played up the interventionist character of colonial rule, emphasizing (for good or bad) its capacity to reform and mod-ernize Indian society. Yet the historical record suggests something quite different: colonial rule all too often had the opposite effect, that in fact British rule froze social and political institutions and frus-trated indigenous development (Washbrook). Kaye's writings exem-plify this paradox, for many of his heroic figures would, under previous nomenclature, be labeled as orientalists as they strove to understand and administer India in Indian terms, yet the policies which Kaye himself advocated were those that would normally be termed Anglicist, such as western education and increased scope for missionaries.

This contradiction between rhetoric and reality was to a large extent the consequence of one of the most salient characteristics of the British Raj: it was a conquest state, one that was not only structurally geared towards conquest but was moreover culturally and ideologically grounded in conquest (Peers, *Between Mars and Mammon*). As one historian has recently noted, "the dominant ideologies of the imperial projects of the period (1760–1830) were informed by its military and aristocratic character."[19] The military was able to exert a profound influence on imperial policy-making, not by conflict with the civil authorities, but rather through alliance with them, because the Anglo-Indian community was acutely conscious of its beleaguered state. As Kaye reminded his readers, "In India every war is more or less popular. The constitution of Anglo-Indian society renders it almost impossible that it would be otherwise."[20] Canonical figures like Thomas Munro, Mountstuart Elphinstone, and John Malcolm (all of whom were not only admired by Kaye but about whom he would pen biographical sketches) constantly reminded their listeners that European notions of the separation of the sword from the state, like European notions of a balance of power, were inapplicable to India.[21] The most commonly chanted mantra was that of John Malcolm: "Our Indian Empire has been acquired and must be maintained by the sword."[22]

This "truth" about British rule, that is to say its dependence upon the military to secure its future, helped foster certain images of India in the public mind, particularly that India was a land of endemic warfare. Consequently, the wider public came to appreciate India at least in part through the optics of the army. It manifested itself in highly romanticized accounts of warfare and society in India such as those written by Kaye.[23] Part of his urge to write in this manner was utilitarian in inspiration: as an editor and author in India, Kaye was all too familiar with the military's dominance in the literary marketplace. As he noted in one of his reviews, "The Indian journalist who systematically maligns [the army], presents no other spectacle than that of a martyr deliberately walking up to the stake, and with his own hand igniting the faggots which he himself has piled around it."[24]

But it would be wrong to reduce the popularity of certain genres to purely material considerations. Romanticism, by accentuating the difference between tradition and modernity, was ideally suited to differentiating between the British and the growing numbers of people falling under their control, for it was during the years covered by this study that the empire in India grew most rapidly. The British conquest of India, with its epic quality, readily lent itself to romanticization.[25] Authors like Walter Scott were often more popular in India than they were in Britain, and their works set literary standards which writers in India sought to emulate. Historical romances were especially popular. For example, Charles Masson, known in India as a writer of popular histories and travelogues, produced what he anticipated would become an epic poem about Afghanistan (Kaye, "Poetry of Recent Indian Warfare," 220–56). Henry Lawrence also tried his hand at writing a historical romance that was inspired by Walter Scott.[26] While most of Kaye's novels were influenced by the conventions of historical romance, his last novel, *Long Engagements* (1846) marked his most systematic attempt at writing in this genre.

One crucial reason for the popularity of historical romance in India, and particularly when written in the style of Walter Scott, was that it was widely believed that it best encapsulated the values and self-identity of the army who were so instrumental in determining Anglo-Indian culture. As one writer put it, "No writer of fiction, not even Shakespeare himself, has done so much to illustrate the military character as Walter Scott."[27] That this sentiment was widely shared was confirmed by the army's choice of books for its regimental libraries. A surviving letter from the Adjutant General in Bengal lists the books that he recommended be purchased for soldier's libraries. Not surprisingly, religious works such as bishops' lives and homilies figured in his wish list, along with biographies of military worthies, campaign narratives, and patriotic histories. The only fictional works that he requested were ones by Walter Scott.[28] Several years before, a similar request had been made from Bombay for books for soldiers' libraries, and once again after reeling off a number of religious, biographical, and historical works, it requested "Waverly and all the works by the same author."[29] No other fictional works were indicated.

Scott's writings were accepted as compatible with the culture and ideology of the British in India largely because his view of history so neatly met the needs of the Anglo-Indian community in India, particularly his racializing of history.[30] Scott's writings accepted and even venerated the types of social hierarchy that prevailed in the army as well as in the empire. His love of feudal and medieval imagery was easily transferred to India where such images were often used in efforts both to capture the essence of Indian society and locate British officials within it. As Thomas Metcalf has noted, "In an age of industrialism and individualism, of social upheaval and laissez faire, marked by what were perceived as the horrors of continental revolution and the rationalist excesses of Benthamism, the Middle Ages stood forth as a metaphor for paternalist ideals of social order and proper conduct."[31] We can see this most clearly in descriptions of martial communities like the Rajputs where medieval-feudal motifs were employed to reflect contemporary ideas of loyalty by playing up the themes of personal fealty and obligation.[32] In Kaye's writings, Rajputs were singled out as proof of the timelessness of the east: "There is no part of India to which more historical interest attaches, none more instinct with ancient traditions and chivalrous associations, than Rajpootana; but none, also, which, regarded from a political view, is surrounded with greater difficulties, and is more suggestive of despair."[33] Authors like Kaye found much to admire in the Rajput sense of honor, but tempered their admiration by denying Indians access to such foundational Victorian virtues as charity, thrift, duty, and Christian devotion. Ultimately, Kaye's fascination with medieval themes owed less to an interest in the past for its own sake and more to its value in differentiating between societies living in the present, such as Britain, and those that continued to be mired in the past, like India.

Kaye was ideally positioned to capture and translate the moods of Anglo-Indian society for domestic readers, for not only was he a determined and capable writer, well-connected in Calcutta as well as in London, but he also exemplified, at least outwardly, many of the attributes that that society valued. He had a military background and was solidly middleclass, yet believed firmly in the very rigid social, gender, and racial hierarchies of Anglo-Indian society. He was also emphatically Evangelical, yet wary of the damage that overly enthusiastic missionaries could cause in India. He extolled the virtues of the self-made men who had made British India, at least according to his readings of history, yet was convinced that Indians lacked that very capacity and therefore needed to be ruled with strict discipline. Like many other Anglo-Indians, his political position shifted dramatically as he moved from Britain to India and then back to Britain. His political views on domestic issues clearly aligned him with the Whigs (and later the Liberals) yet in India he advocated positions that were ideologically closer to the Tories.[34] Kaye was born and raised in London in a family with impeccable middle-class credentials: his father and grandfather both had worked as solicitors for the Bank of England. His early education was given over to Rugby and Repton, before being sent on to Eton in 1823. But his time at Eton was cut short when his father was nearly bankrupted by the commercial crisis of 1826. A brief period in a smaller and more affordable school in Salisbury followed. Plans for him to go on to Oxford were also dashed, and he instead secured through family connections a cadetship with the East India Company army. The East India Company was a popular route for middle-class families seeking lucrative and respectable careers for their sons. The Company offered material rewards as well as the less tangible yet equally important rewards in the form of status, for in India a Company official could live like the aristocracy.

J. W. Kaye entered the Company's military college of Addiscombe in 1831, passing into the artillery in 1832 and from there being posted to the Bengal army. However, he fell sick shortly after arriving in 1833 at the headquarters of the Bengal artillery at Dum Dum, and returned to England in 1834 on sick leave. It was only after three years that he was able to return to India where, besides a very brief stint along the Arakan border with Burma and another brief sick leave, he spent most of his Indian career in cantonments close to Calcutta. It was during this time that Kaye began to write, at first anonymously, placing articles in the *Calcutta Literary Gazette* in 1834 and arranging for the private publication of a collection of his poems shortly after returning to England in 1835. Then followed a number of novels that enjoyed limited success. As he ruefully noted in one of the novels in which the hero was a thinly disguised variant of himself, his literary ventures to date "were only moderately successful" for "there was too much ballast in them;—overloaded with speculative disquisition, though for the most part these disquisitions were clothed in eloquent language, and interwoven with the interest of the story; my writings were too heavy and didactic for the excitement-loving taste of the times."[35] However unsuccessful these novels were from a commercial or even literary standpoint, they are very valuable for the light they shed on Kaye's sense of his own surroundings as well as his aesthetic values, such as his admiration for Wordsworth.

It was after his return to India following his first sick leave that he began to turn his energies to journalism. For a time he served as editor of the *Bengal Hurkaru,* one of the most popular newspapers in Bengal. It was through the *Hurkaru* that he developed the contacts that helped him with his next venture, publishing and editing the *Calcutta Review.* Appearing for the first time in 1843, the *Calcutta Review* was intended to give Anglo-Indians a literary journal that would be the Indian equivalent of periodicals like the *Edinburgh Review* and the *Quarterly Review.* Two missionaries, Alexander Duff and J. C. Marshman, and the soldier-administrator Henry Lawrence, whose heroic death at the siege of Lucknow led to his becoming one of the heroes of the nineteenth century, assisted him in this venture. Marshman was especially important to the success of the *Calcutta Review* for he actively recruited writers such as Henry Lawrence. To the latter he wrote, "Kaye, the spirited editor of the *Hurkaru* has this week written to me to say that he has projected such a publication, and will have the first number through the press. . . . He is a very fine writer himself and improves rapidly with age."[36]

Kaye would later recollect that the *Calcutta Review* "was a bold and seemingly a hopeless experiment, and I expected that it would last out a few numbers and then die, leaving me perhaps a poorer man than before. Its success astonished no one more than myself."[37] Part of its success stemmed from the lack of competition; while there was no shortage of newspapers in India, though they were often short-lived, there was no other journal in Calcutta that provided timely reviews of recently-published books. The *Calcutta Review* was therefore well-positioned to play a leading role in the political, cultural, and religious debates of the time. It success was also due to its timing: the blend of liberalism and Evangelicalism which marked the *Calcutta Review* in its early years was well-suited to the growing demands that Indian government be reformed and conducted according to Christian principles.[38] The *Calcutta Review* soon proved to be a financial as well as a critical success. Kaye even toyed briefly with the idea of trying to edit and publish the *Calcutta Review* from London once he had returned to England in 1845, but he was persuaded otherwise. He nevertheless continued as proprietor and would continue to send articles to it for another ten years.

It was upon his return to England in 1845 that Kaye shifted to the genres that would prove to be his most influential and lucrative: history and historical biography. Shortly after landing in Britain, he began his *History of the War in Afghanistan* (1851), a book that took him six years to write. Once completed, it clearly established his reputation in Britain as one of the leading public authorities on India. But its success was in turn largely due to his ability to continue to educate his readers through his many articles and reviews. Between his return to England and the publication of his *History of the War in Afghanistan*, Kaye published no less than eight articles on recent events in India in the *North British Review* as well as a further twenty-nine articles in the *Calcutta Review*. His view of the justice and need for the war in his *History* was similar to what he wrote in the Anglo-Indian press, namely that the British had seriously blundered into this war. Yet these mistakes and blunders paled into insignificance when compared to the many acts of heroism he recounted. Arguably, the blunders only made heroes appear in sharper relief for they alone could restore British reputations. In his idealization of James Outram, he described his actions in Afghanistan as "one of the most romantic passages of a war full of romantic passages."[39]

There was also a steady stream of articles in the Anglo-Indian and

British press on the more recent Sikh wars. His writings on these campaigns turned again on their intoxicating blend of the exotic, the tragic, and the romantic. In the opening paragraph to a review of recent works on the Sikh Wars, he announced, "The Recent history of the Punjaub, with all its interwoven tragical plots, vividly reminds us of the last act of one of those extravagantly bloody tragedies of the Hieronomo or Titus Andronicus school."[40] In another review article he returned to this theme, insisting "There is nothing in ancient history to compete in military grandeur or in romantic interest with the Afghan and Sikh campaigns" (Kaye, "The Romance of Indian Warfare," 194).

Campaign histories provided the perfect setting for epic narratives. As he explained in the preface to the second edition of his *History of the War in Afghanistan,* which came out in 1857, he had made some revisions so as to provide the "epic completeness of a beginning, a middle and an end."[41] Elsewhere he noted that, "War is the grand style of poetry in is highest form of development . . ." for "at the head of all poetry stands the heroic" (Kaye, "Poetry of Recent Indian Warfare," 220). For Kaye this was particularly true in India where heroes were in abundance, exotic backgrounds were easily produced, and villains were everywhere to be found. As Kaye noted, "the nature of the country, the character of the people, their mode of warfare, their dress—are all surrounded with poetical association" (Kaye, "Poetry," 222). In the same article, Kaye invokes Shakespeare to describe the Sikh Wars that were then occurring on "the vast theatre of the East"(Kaye, "Poetry," 247). Kaye would repeatedly return to these themes, in one case titling an article "The Romance of Indian Warfare" even though one of the books under review consisted of nothing more than published official dispatches (Kaye, "The Romance of Indian Warfare," 1849).

The History of the War in Afghanistan was soon followed by his *History of the Administration of the East India Company,* a nakedly partisan defense of the Company, and one which led to his succeeding John Stuart Mill as political secretary in the examiner's office of the East India Company, one of the most senior positions in the Company's permanent bureaucracy. When the East India Company was abolished in 1858, Kaye moved over to its successor—the India Office—where he continued in much the same role. These appointments not only furnished him with an income, but they also gave him unmatched access to the flow of information between India and Britain. It was during his employment at the India Office that Kaye began his largest and perhaps most famous work, *A History of the Sepoy War in India,* first published in 1864 and later reprinted on several occasions. It is still a standard reference work today. But like his earlier books, he prepared his audiences for his *History of the Sepoy War* through his writings for British periodicals. The Indian Rebellion of 1857/58 quickly captured the British imagination, and it soon began to figure prominently in the daily, weekly, monthly, and quarterly press. Kaye was by then one of the leading experts on India, and with this increased interest in India came new opportunities and new venues for his views. He penned at least eighteen substantial articles on the Rebellion before his history appeared. His position as an authority on India also led to him writing for journals in which he had not appeared before, including *Blackwood's* and *Edinburgh Review.* The Indian Rebellion brought out most clearly his orientalist perspectives on India. In one article he declared that "Our sepoy army revolted, not because it was an army of blacks under a white master, but simply because it was an Oriental army, and all Oriental armies revolt."[42] By way of contrast, the Anglo-Saxons appeared in much better light. In the same article he wrote, "I really believe that the Mutiny was trampled out by the indomitable courage of the Anglo-Saxon race." (Kaye, "The Future of India and her Army," 633)

Soon after, he published a series of brief biographies of eminent Anglo-Indians in 1865 in *Good Words* (a magazine with a decidedly middle-class readership). These laid the foundations for another of his better-known works, *The Lives of Indian Officers* (1867). Kaye's ability to tap into the flow of information between India and Britain was consolidated still further by his editorship of the *Overland Mail* (1855–68), a magazine published in London and pitched at Anglo-Indians eager to be kept abreast of developments in India. He would in turn use his position at the *Overland Mail* to enhance his credibility when writing for other periodicals. In one article for *Blackwood's* on the future of the Indian army, a very controversial topic in the aftermath of the revolt, Kaye wrote under the byline of "A friendly letter by the *Overland Mail*" (Kaye, "The Future of India and her Army," 633). Ill health forced him to resign from the India Office in 1874, and he died shortly after in 1876.

It is important to note that while Kaye was deeply integrated into the institutions and information networks of Anglo-Indian society, his own first-hand experience of India was actually quite limited. This was wryly noted in one of his obituaries, where it was said, "There is no Knight of the Star of India so well known to Orientals by repute, of whom they have seen so little."[43] While Kaye spent about a decade in India, most of that time was in Calcutta, and hence his familiarity was with Anglo-Indian society, not Indian society, and this shows in his writings. Unlike writers like Meadows Taylor, Kaye did not go to great lengths to locate his stories within an Indian context. He did not even make much of an effort to employ India as an exotic backdrop for his stories (which might explain their relative lack of success). In part this was the consequence of his having taken on the role of spokesman for the Anglo-Indian community, a group that he felt was either ignored or caricatured at home. He complained in one review article that "a work containing a true account of Anglo-Indian society . . . is even in the year 1847 a desideratum which has yet to be supplied."[44] It was only with his work on the Afghan War, and particularly frontier warfare, that Kaye appears to have fully grasped the dramatic potential of India itself, but even then it was little more than a foil against which he could develop his heroes. *Long Engagements; a Tale of the Affghan Rebellion* (1846) was the closest thing he wrote to a historical romance grounded in India.

If success with fiction and poetry eluded Kaye, he did enjoy great success with contemporary history and biography. Like many of his countrymen, he believed that history was linear and about progress. And he understood progress in terms with which most of his readers would be familiar: good government, Christian faith, individualism, and commercial prosperity. The history of British rule in India was one of slow but inexorable progress, punctuated by the occasional blunder, but most of all one in which the corruption, oppression, and venality of the past had presumably been replaced by a far nobler mission. The march of civilization was most clearly glimpsed in such 'triumphs' as the abolition of *sati* and the eradication of *thagi*— the two touchstones to which the British defense of imperialism turned.[45] *Sati*, or the practice of widows taking their own lives on the death of their husband, and *thagi*, the custom whereby robbers of an alleged religious cult murdered their victims, were invoked by Kaye and others as the ultimate proof of just how degraded Indian society had become, and hence their eradication was heralded as proof positive of the benefits of colonial rule. Nearly fifty years after its first publication, extracts from his history of the East India Company's Administration regarding the Company's role in ending *sati* were still being reprinted. In it, Kaye had praised the Company for bringing about the "humanising tendency of British rule."[46]

Perhaps the most strikingly modern aspect of Kaye's writings was the degree to which they conformed, at least on first appearance, to present-day historical conventions and practices with regards to sources. In his preface to *Lives of Indian Officers*, Kaye reports that he had worked from "many large manuscript volumes, the growth of past years of historical research, full of personal correspondence and biographical notes, [and also] extensive collections of original papers, equally serviceable, which had not been transcribed" (Kaye, *Lives of Indian Officers*, viii). When writing his biography of John Malcolm, Kaye frequently consulted Mountstuart Elphinstone who had worked closely with Malcolm and knew him well (N. N. Singh, 154). Kaye not only used original sources, but also peppered his works with lengthy quotes, thereby enhancing his claims to authenticity. He shared with Thomas Babington Macaulay a deep-seated belief in the capacity of the historian to capture the spirit of the age through careful and faithful archival work (N. N. Singh, 27).

But a word of caution is in order for it is not always possible to verify Kaye's sources. In many instances the originals appear to have not survived. Sometimes, Kaye never returned letters to the people who had lent them to him and these letters have to all intents and purposes disappeared.[47] In other instances, Kaye may have destroyed the originals at the request of the sender. We must remember that Kaye gleaned a lot of information from army officers and high-ranking officials, and much of that was sent to him only after he had assured his contacts that he would respect their wish for anonymity. This was certainly the case with Henry Lawrence who had informed Kaye on at least one occasion that he wanted some of his letters destroyed.[48] Without confirmation from the originals, the accuracy of his quotations can never be taken as proven, and while there is no evidence to suggest that he deliberately massaged his data, at least one of his contemporary Anglo-Indian biographers, G. R. Gleig, was not above tampering with the original text.[49]

There are also important items that Kaye neglected to include in his histories and biographies. On a number of occasions it is clear that he deliberately chose not to address controversial or questionable actions on the part of his subjects. We see an example of this in his biography of Henry St. George Tucker, a powerful and influential director of the Company, and a self-made man of the kind that Kaye admired. But Tucker had also been convicted early in his career with assault and attempted rape, a crime for which he served four months and paid a fine.[50] Kaye never mentioned it. Nor did Kaye in his biography of Metcalfe acknowledge that he had two sons by a Sikh woman. Singh attributes this omission to Kaye's Christianity and the fact that Metcalfe's marriage had not been solemnized. Much more likely though is the fact that interracial relationships, commonplace in the eighteenth century, had passed beyond the pale.[51] As one who had spent the better part of a decade in Calcutta, Kaye would have been only too well aware of these prejudices and the damage they could do to the reputation of someone as eminent as Charles Metcalfe.

History, for Kaye, was ultimately inseparable from biography, for history was about individuals fulfilling God's design.[52] His 1846 article on the Sikh war was in reality grounded in an assessment of Henry Lawrence (Kaye, "The War on the Sutlej"). Similarly, an article in 1852 used Sir Charles Napier to address wider issues of imperial governance.[53] He claimed in the preface to his *History of the Sepoy War*, "If it be true that the best history is that which most nearly resembles a bundle of biographies, it is especially true when said with reference to Indian history."[54] His focus was on identifying individuals who best demonstrated the characteristics necessary to protect and preserve the empire, so Indians were given short shrift. Several years after his death, and following the publication of a biography of James Outram by another author, one reviewer was moved to declare, "Since Kaye's death, Anglo-Indian biography seems to have fallen upon evil days" (N. N. Singh, 115).

His first foray into historical biography was to write the life of an important but strikingly unheroic figure, Henry St. George Tucker, who rose from being an auditor in India to chairman of the East India Company's Court of Directors. From there, Kaye moved on to much more stirring figures, such as Charles Metcalfe and John Malcolm, before turning his pen to writing a series of shorter sketches of key individuals for *Good Words*. The explanation he offered for publishing these biographies initially in a magazine aimed at a more popular market is worth quoting:

> The temptations, indeed, were very great . . . awakening, through a popular periodical counting its readers by hundreds of thousands, the interests of an immense multitude of intelligent people, whom every writer on Indian subjects is painfully conscious of being unable to reach through the medium of bulky and high-priced books (Kaye, *Lives of Indian Officers* 1: *viii*).

These potted biographies would later be gathered, revised, and published in *Lives of Indian Officers* (1867). This work would in turn provide the inspiration for later efforts at trying to capture the essence of imperial rule through biography, including the Rulers of India series—some twenty-five biographies published at the turn of the century by Clarendon Press—as well as Philip Mason's paean to British rulers, *The Men Who Ruled India*.[55]

Kaye's biographies were designed to provide examples of what it took to conquer and maintain an empire, and to do so they relied

upon a clear narrative of progress. Kaye's heroes were depicted as
dedicated, self-sacrificing Christians. This image is set against their
eighteenth century forebears; the nobs, nabobs, and dandies who in
their avarice conquered an empire but nearly lost it. It was within
that context that Kaye harshly criticized Hicky's *Gazette*, the first
newspaper in India (1780), for its lack of decorum and its focus on
scandal and gossip.[56] His choice of heroes also reflects the march of
progress in India—noticeably absent from his collective biography
are Clive and Hastings. They may well have been instrumental in
founding the empire, but their conduct did not measure up to
Kaye's moral yardstick. In his review of W. D. Arnold's *Oakfield; or
Fellowship in the East*, Kaye commented favorably on its solemnity and
obvious Christian groundings as compared to other recent memoirs
of service in India in which accounts of drinking and gambling
stood out.[57] In another review, he fulminated against the stereotype
of "the ignorant blundering old nabob."[58] Kaye wished to quash
such stereotypes of Anglo-Indian society by stressing just how cul-
tured Anglo-Indian society had become. He insisted that "people
have time to read and they do read" (Kaye, "English Literature in
India," 203). He was not alone in his frustration against such stereotypes. One of his contemporaries at the *Calcutta Review* complained
that until well into the nineteenth century, India "only existed in
the popular imagination as a kind of Eldorado of irresponsibility."[59]

It was this emphasis on duty and disinterestedness that led Kaye
to defend so vigorously the East India Company, for it had over time
addressed its own failings, and had become an efficient and just organization. In his review of Edmond Thornton's popular history of
British India, Kaye highlighted the virtues of Company rule (Kaye,
"Mr. Thornton's Last Volume"). Many of these virtues were attribut-
able to the fact that the Company made available opportunities for
the middleclasses whom had hitherto been practically barred from
the corridors of the British government. In Kaye's eyes, the East
India Company was the closest thing extant to a meritocracy, or in
his works a "great 'Monarchy of the Middle Classes'" (Kaye, *Lives of
Indian Officers* 1: xiii). He idealized the East India Company: when
talking about its demise and the tearing down of its offices, Kaye
lamented that "Mr. Company was above foppery. . . . He had an eye
to business, not to show; and his house was good for business purposes."[60] Kaye continued to defend the Company even after it had
gone, comparing it favorably to what came in its place—the British
government (his new employer) as represented by the Secretary of
State for India. Not surprisingly he chose not to identify himself pub-

licly as the author of such pieces, preferring instead to leave them as anonymous contributions.[61]

Kaye's heroes clearly conformed to what has become known as muscular Christianity, not surprisingly given his Evangelical beliefs. Yet at times it appears that Kaye rated physique over faith. He might have purposefully avoided any reference to Metcalfe's liaison with a Sikh woman and their having had children, but he did register surprise at Metcalfe's lack of athleticism (N. N. Singh, 152). The stress that he placed on outdoor pursuits is also evident in his review of a clergyman's memoir (Reverend T. Acland, *Manners and Customs of the Hindus,* London: Murray, 1847). What Kaye liked best about it was the attention that this minister gives to sporting life, especially hunting. "With a gun in his hand and a solah hat on his head, he appears to have been perfectly contented" (Kaye, "Illustrations of Anglo-Indian Society," 549). Kaye did not even complain when the author continued to hunt monkeys after learning that they were sacred to the local inhabitants. Sports were also at the heart of what Kaye identified as the ideal training for imperial servants.[62] "The true eye, that steady hand, that firm seat in the saddle, with all the cool courage of the hunting-field—these are the aids which will find him out in the hour of trial, and help him to the front in the grand Indian career."[63] Kaye used Outram to illustrate how crucial sportsmanship was to imperial service. When Outram was sent out to subdue the Bhils, a forest dwelling community in western India, he discovered that:

> You might address them in all the languages of the earth, and demonstrate the immorality of their habits with a force of logic worthy of Mill; you might go among them with all the learning of all the schools, explain the solar system, and produce no greater impression upon them than you would upon the rock-temples of Ellora or Bameean. But show them how to shoot a tiger, and lo! They worship you at once (Kaye, "Career of an Indian Officer," 76).

If race and class, in this case an idealized middleclass, provided two important sets of parameters for Kaye's heroes, gender was also very much at work. For Kaye, the British Empire was a masculine empire, one that offered little scope for women. Of Malcolm, Kaye said, "he was a Man and on a large scale" (N. N. Singh, 154). Interestingly, however, Kaye did advocate expanded employment opportunities for women in Britain.[64] But there were limits to such opportunities: "It need not be said that the practical equality of the sexes is contended for by very few, or that those few know not what they are asking."[65]

Masculinity of a particular type was the essential ingredient in making imperial rulers, a masculinity that was defined in unmistakably middle-class and evangelical terms. It relied upon the kind of rigorous self-discipline that had become a defining characteristic of the white, male and middle-class Briton—the same individuals who filled the officer ranks and also imperial offices.[66] Women are noticeably absent from much of Kaye's writings, especially those that addressed the northwest frontier. It was along that frontier that Kaye was able to depict his heroes most clearly in an exotic location amid ever-present fighting, and in an arena uncomplicated by the presence of women. It was on the frontier that men were "removed from all accidental environments, and [must] trust only to his naked manhood" (Kaye, "The Romance of Indian Warfare," 197). As Kaye reminded his readers in another article that was framed by questions of gender difference, "The want of courage, which disgraces a man, is no slur upon the reputation of a woman" (Kaye, "The Non-Existence of Women," 541).[67]

If European women rated barely a mention in his writings, Indian women were rarely glimpsed save to prove how degraded Indian society had become, as in Kaye's use of *sati*. Indian women were largely silenced in his accounts because, "whilst the country seems to swarm with women, there is a total absence of ladies" (Kaye and Simpson, 1: 21). For Kaye gender was entangled with race and class.

Yet the romantic in Kaye led him to idealize a most unlikely symbol of Indian womanhood—those women who had committed themselves (voluntarily in some but not all cases) to the funeral pyres of their husbands. *Sati* was simultaneously the site of one of Britain's greatest triumphs and a place where the virtues of wifely devotion were expressed in their starkest form. As he informed his readers, "No martyr, in the grand old times of Apostolic Christianity, died with a nobler fortitude, than often did these unhappy women, under the curse of a degrading superstition" (Kaye, *The Suppression of Human Sacrifice*, 24). It is worth noting that in giving his readers an example of *sati*, from which there were many to choose, Kaye settled on one from 1742–43. The choice is interesting for it is one from the distant past and it is one in which the widow of a high caste Maratha official did so of her own choice. The English factor's wife Lady Russell implored her to change her mind but to no avail. Kaye used this distant example to show not only how deeply rooted *sati* was in Indian society, but also to signal how much British attitudes had changed.

However, for the most part, Kaye's understanding of appropriate roles and conduct for women were couched in terms of British middle-class conventions, conventions which effectively excluded Indian women. As Leonore Davidoff and Catherine Hall have argued, "The belief in the national difference and complementary roles of men and women which had originally been linked to Evangelicalism had become the common sense of the middle class."[68] The problem for Kaye was that India offered few complementary roles for European women. When European women did appear in his histories and biographies, they were depicted as a destabilizing and even destructive force. In *The Story of Basil Bouverie* (1842), women are the instigators of much of the trouble. Too much femininity threatened to erode the imperial edifice. This was one of the themes of *Peregrine Pulteney* as well as his article entitled *Romance of Indian Warfare*. In both cases femininity (or the absence of appropriate masculinity) was what placed Indian males below Europeans.[69] In *Peregrine Pulteney*, one character's masculinity was stunted by too long and too close a proximity to female company (Kaye, *Peregrine Pulteney*, 2: 26). In a review article that looked, among other things, at the state of Indian princes, the slow incapacitation of the Nawabs of Awadh was accounted for by the overpowering presence of the "Queen Mother, a woman of masculine energy" (Kaye, "The Annexation of Oude," 542). The latter article reveals a common feature of much oriental scholarship, namely the denial of appropriate masculine qualities to Indian males. In this case, the most masculine person was the Queen Mother, a clear perversion of proper gender roles.

There are clear echoes in Kaye's writings of what Margaret Strobel has aptly termed the "myth of the destructive female," or the commonplace belief that it was the arrival of European women that strained relations between rulers and the ruled.[70] Too many women in the barracks, for example, were seen to be harmful to military efficiency, for they threatened to sap men of their courage (Kaye, "Military Society in India"). European women also undermined the bonds of loyalty and understanding that had existed between colonial rulers and their Indian subjects. Yet Kaye was sufficiently Victorian to believe that middle-class domesticity had much to offer, and consequently there is a marked tone of ambivalence in his writings. While he tended to idealize the homosociability of Anglo-Indian military culture, he was nevertheless also convinced of the virtues of middle-class domesticity, and in particular its role in elevating the tone of European society in India. As a result he found himself in a quandary as is revealed in the following quote: "European female society, to which under Providence we owe the salvation of our morality, has severed the officer from his men, and weakened the discipline of the native army. There is little unmixed good in this world.

The man rises upon the ruins of the officer; but how can we deplore this elevation. We cannot expect, we cannot wish to see the old type of Hinduized Englishman revived" (Kaye, "Civis on Indian Affairs," 426). He would return to this theme in a later article, again commenting on how better domestic conditions for European officers had constrained their relationships with the sepoys under their command, "The tendency of that improved domestic life, which is to be regarded on all accounts with so much satisfaction, is certainly not to strengthen the bonds between the Europeans and the native" (Kaye, "Military Society in India," 432). But again he could not recommend a return to the old ways.

J. W. Kaye's articles, reviews, and books collectively reveal the often hybrid quality of imperial discourse. It could never be hegemonic when it had to contend with so many voices, ideologies and positions. In Kaye's case, his ambivalence can be partly explained by his liminal position, caught between Britain and India, and between the Romantic and Victorian eras. He subscribed to the Victorian faith in progress, providence, and domesticity yet succumbed to highly romanticized readings of British activity in India. The end result was best captured in the ways in which he chose to present his heroic characters. He especially liked to dwell on the "romantic achievements of the Christian warriors of the 19th century" (Kaye, "The Romance of Indian Warfare," 194). Ultimately, his archetypal imperial heroes conformed to what John MacKenzie has identified as one of the foundational ideologies of Victorian imperialism, namely that "national character as formulated in the nineteenth century was a myth that was essentially English and masculine, represented as phlegmatic, unemotional, unintellectual, individualist, eccentric, sporting (both literally and metaphorically), fair-minded and essentially youthful."[71] It is therefore not surprising that Kaye believed that the best representatives of British service in India were either military officers seconded to civil or political duties or civilians who demonstrated martial qualities (Kaye, "Military Society in India"). The popularity of such images and their ability to resonate through time can be understood best in terms of their ability to draw on dominant discourses of gender, race, and class while playing upon some of the prevailing literary fashions of the time, particularly romanticism and a fascination with history. Kaye's accounts helped legitimate middle-class claims to respectability by demonstrating that it was middle-class virtues that would ensure the survival of the British Empire. Yet for all its Victorian overtones, Kaye could never break completely from the romanticized views of society that prevailed in India. His ambivalence on that score appears most clearly when he has to contend with the domestication of colonial society. Like many of his contemporaries, Kaye idealized the middle-class family and saw the future of Britain in its domesticity. But in an Indian context, such domesticity threatened to erode the homoso-ciability of frontier society, the same society that was responsible for creating the necessary heroes. Manly vigor had to be continually re-asserted; otherwise, he fretted, "the gradual deterioration of the dominant race by which our Indian empire will be slowly destroyed" (Kaye, "The Future of India and her Army," 642). And he was not alone in these fears. His long-time friend and colleague, Sir Bartle Frere lamented that:

> But nothing can make up for the loss of such a noble school of frontier officers as John Jacob founded and which the Government of India so persistently discouraged and ultimately abolished. You will find it every day more difficult to form men such as your Punjab frontier has fur-nished, and of which you still have some left. But if you intend to keep India, you must manage to train up men in the spirit for your Malcolms, Elphinstones, and Metcalfes of times past, and of Sir George Clerk in later days, men who by their character, and the confidence the Natives have in them, can hold their own without the immediate presence of battalions and big guns.[72]

NOTES

John William Kaye. "Poetry of Recent Indian Warfare," *Calcutta Review* 11 (1848): 220. Over the course of my explorations into the relationships between imperial ideology, the military and print culture, I have amassed a number of debts. I would like to thank in particular the following for their stimulating and critical commen-tary: Antoinette Burton, David Finkelstein, Mark Harrison, Philippa Levine, Javed Majeed and P. J. Marshall. I would also like to thank Julie Codell for undertaking this project and for her helpful comments on this essay.

1. The *Bengalee*, 29 July 1876, quoted in Nihar Nandan Singh. *British Historiogra-phy on British Rule in India; the Life and Writings of Sir John William Kaye, 1814–1876* (Patna: Janaki Prakashan, 1986). Singh's biography is the only scholarly study of Kaye and deserves to be much better known. However, Singh concentrates for the most part on Kaye's books and does not address his journalism, nor does Singh interpret Kaye in terms of wider issues of imperial discourse.

2. W. F. B. Laurie, *Sketches of Some Distinguished Anglo-Indians with an Account of Anglo-Indian Periodical Literature.* (London: John Day, 1875), 196.

3. Ranajit Guha, "Not at Home in Empire." *Critical Inquiry* 23 (1997): 485.

4. Ann Parry, "Reading Formations in the Victorian Press: the Reception of Kipling, 1888–1891." *Literature and History* 11 (1985): 254.

5. Kaye, "Kaye's War in Afghanistan," *Calcutta Review* 15 (1851): 423–55.

6. Kaye, "The Romance of Indian Warfare," *North British Review* 12 (1849): 195.

7. Robin Gilmour, *The Victorian Period: the Intellectual and Cultural Context of English Literature, 1830–1890* (Harlow: Longman, 1993): *xiii.*

8. Kaye, "Poetry of Recent Indian Warfare," *Calcutta Review* 11 (1848): 221.

9. Kaye, "Recent Military Memoirs," *Calcutta Review* 14 (1850): 265.

10. Kaye, "Illustrations of Anglo-Indian Society," *Calcutta Review* 8 (1847): 548–68.

11. Kaye, "Recent Military Memoirs," *Calcutta Review* 14 (1850): 265–95.

12. Kaye, "The War on the Sutlej," *North British Review* 5 (1846): 258.

13. Kaye, *Lives of Indian Officers, Illustrative of the History of the Civil and Military Services of India.* 2 vols. (London: A. Strahan, 1867), 1: xi.

14. For a recent evaluation of this period, see David Eastwood, "The Age of Uncertainty: Britain in the Early-Nineteenth Century," *Transactions of the Royal Historical Society* 8 (1998): 91–116.

15. See C. A. Bayly, *Indian Society and the Making of the British Empire: the New Cambridge History of India,* vol. 2, bk. 1 (Cambridge: Cambridge University Press, 1988) and David Washbrook, "India, 1818–1860: The Two Faces of Colonialism," *The Oxford History of the British Empire: The Nineteenth Century,* edited by A. Porter (Oxford: Oxford University Press, 1999).

16. For a discussion of responses to the Indian Rebellion, or Mutiny, see Manu Goswami, "'Englishness' on the Imperial Circuit: Mutiny Tours in Colonial South Asia," *Journal of Historical Sociology* 9 (1996): 54–84; Thomas R. Metcalf, *Ideologies of the Raj: the New Cambridge History of India,* vol. 3, bk. 4. (Cambridge: Cambridge University Press, 1994); Rudrangshu Mukherjee, *Spectre of Violence: the 1857 Kanpur Massacres* (New Delhi: Viking, 1998); William Oddie, "Dickens and the Indian Mutiny," *Dickensian* 68 (1972): 3–15; E. M. Palmegiano, "The Indian Mutiny in the Mid-Victorian Press," *Journal of Newspaper and Periodical History* 7 (1991): 3–11; Nancy L. Paxton, *Writing under the Raj: Gender, Race, and Rape in the British Colonial Imagination, 1830–1947* (New Brunswick, N.J.: Rutgers University Press, 1998); and Jenny Sharpe, *Allegories of Empire: the Figure of Woman in the Colonial Text* (Minneapolis: University of Minnesota Press, 1993).

17. Kaye, "Sir Walter Gilbert and the Indian Army." *Bentley's Miscellany* 33 (1853): 627.

18. There is considerable literature on the so-called Age of Reform in India. See for example G. D. Bearce, *British Attitudes towards India, 1784–1858* (Oxford: Oxford University Press, 1961); Eric Stokes, *The English Utilitarians and India* (Oxford: Oxford University Press, 1959); and David Kopf, *British Orientalism and the Bengal Renaissance; the Dynamics of Indian Modernization, 1773–1835* (Berkeley and Los Angeles: University of California Press, 1969). For the beginnings of a critical reappraisal, see the essays in C. H. Philips and M. D. Wainwright, eds., *Indian Society and the Beginnings of Modernization* (London: Curzon Press, 1976).

19. C. A. Bayly, "The First Age of Global Imperialism, c. 1760–1830," *Journal of Imperial and Commonwealth History* 26 (1998): 39. Militarism is a term which can all too easily lead to apoplectic fits among British historians, for they have assumed that of all the characteristics that have come to define the British state, a deeply-rooted suspicion of the army is one of the most persistent, and consequently the army in Britain, at least since 1688, has never been as politicized as armies have become in Europe, Latin America, or elsewhere. While it is true that the British army did prefer the barracks to the barricades, this is not the same thing as arguing that it was apolitical. See also Douglas M. Peers, *Between Mars and Mammon* (London: I.B. Tauris, 1995), and Hew Strachan, *Politics of the British Army* (Oxford: Clarendon, 1997). For an example of just how resilient the myth is of the apolitical

nature of the British army, see John Keegan's acerbic review of Strachan's *Politics of the British Army* in the *Times Literary Supplement*, 24 July 1998, 26.

20. Kaye, *History of the War in Afghanistan* (London: Richard Bentley, 1851), 1: 361.

21. Peers, *Mars and Mammon*, especially chapters 1–3. The marquis of Hastings, governor general from 1813 to 1823 and likely the most aggressive advocate of this colonial variant of militarism, proclaimed: "The subjection of the military to the civil power is a most just principle, but in its application advertence should be made to local peculiarities." See also Oriental and India Office Collections [hereafter OIOC], Hastings to William Fullerton Elphinstone, 20 March 1821, MSS Eur F89/2A/1/4 (Elphinstone Papers).

22. There are at least three different writers who call upon Malcolm's axiom. "The Military Constitution of Our Indian Empire," *United Service Journal* 3, no. 1 (1845, 1846): 237–44; 409–16; 60–67; "The History of the Bengal Army," *Colburn's United Service Magazine* 3 (1850): 446–54; 589–94; and A. Andrews, "The Indian Army," *Fraser's Magazine* 56 (1857): 164–72. Not even the much-vaunted (or condemned) reformers like Bentinck or Macauley could make much headway against such beliefs, for they too yielded to the strategic imperative that British India was always under threat, if not from without, then most certainly from within.

23. Recent work has highlighted the extent to which romanticism was the imperial genre par excellence, and nowhere was this more apparent than in India where romanticism and medievalism were particularly popular cultural forms. See for example Nigel Leask, *British Romantic Writers and the East, Anxieties of Empire* (Cambridge: Cambridge University Press, 1992); Saree Makdisi, *Romantic Imperialism: Universal Empire and the Culture of Modernity* (Cambridge: Cambridge University Press, 1998): and Katie Trumpener, *Bardic Nationalism: the Romantic Novel and the British Empire* (Princeton: Princeton University Press, 1997). According to Priya Joshi, "Gothic, melodrama, romance and sensational fiction: each were forms that challenged, then lost out to, high realism in nineteenth-century Britain, yet they found an enthusiastic and continuing market among colonial readers." See Joshi, "Culture and Consumption: Fiction, the Reading Public, and the British Novel in Colonial India." *Book History* 1 (1998): 212.

24. John William Kaye, "Mr. Thornton's Last Volume: The Indian Press, Afghanistan, Sindh and Gwalior," *Calcutta Review* 5 (1846): 157.

25. This can be gauged in this excerpt from an 1827 article on the Indian army, in which the history of that army is declared to be:

As lively and as improbable a romance, as ever came from the pen of a Radcliffe, a Cervantes, or a Scott. What can be more astonishing, than that a handful of Europeans, impelled, not by the love of conquest, but by circumstances over which they had no control, should have risen, within a short space of half a century, from the situation of mere adventurers . . . to the lordship of the greatest, the most populous, and the most extensive empire, upon the face of the whole earth?

And then with a rhetorical flourish, the author concluded "There is nothing in the career of Rome herself at all to be compared with the English nation in India." G. R. Gleig, "The Indian Army," *Blackwood's Edinburgh Magazine* 21 (1827): 563.

26. Henry Lawrence, *Adventures of an Officer in the Service of Runjeet Singh* (1845; reprint, Karachi: Oxford University Press, 1845). Historical romance, Lawrence wrote, "offers pictures of men and manners, and seeks to sketch the interior scenes of life, and details that escape the casual observer, rather than to chronicle occurrences already recorded in official documents," p. 261.

27. Portfire, "The Military Character, as Exhibited by Works of Fiction," *Colburn's United Service Magazine* 2 (1857): 389–400.

28. OIOC, Military Letter from Bengal, 29 Aug 1834, F/4/1486 (Board's Collections).

29. OIOC, Military Letter from Bombay, 29 Jan 1823, L/Mil/5/384/85(a).

30. Tim Fulford and Peter J. Kitson, eds., *Romanticism and Colonialism: Writing and Empire, 1780–1830* (Cambridge: Cambridge University Press, 1998).

31. Thomas R. Metcalf, *Ideologies of the Raj* (Cambridge: Cambridge University Press, 1994), 75.

32. For the Rajputs, see Norbert Peabody, "Tod's Rajasthan and the Boundaries of Imperial Rule in Nineteenth-Century India," *Modern Asian Studies* 30 (1996): 185–220.

33. Kaye and William Simpson, *India, Ancient and Modern: A Series of Illustrations of the Country and People of India and Adjacent Territories, Executed in Chromo-Lithography from Drawings by William Simpson with Descriptive Literature by John William Kaye*, 2 vols., (London: Day and Son, 1867), 1: 2.

34. Of particular value are his early novels for he frequently wrote himself into the story. This is especially the case with *Peregrine Pulteney* in which its hero experiences a childhood that mirrors that of Kaye (Kaye 1842).

35. John William Kaye, *Jerningham; or, the Inconsistent Man*. 3 vols., (London: Smith, Elder and Co., 1836), iii, 144.

36. OIOC, Marshman to Lawrence, 26 April 1844, MSS Eur F85/27 (Lawrence Papers).

37. Herbert Edwardes and Herman Merivale, *Life of Sir Henry Lawrence*, 2 vols., (London: Smith, Elder and Co, 1872), 2: 17.

38. Kaye, "The Administration of Lord Ellenborough," *Calcutta Review* 1 (1844): 508–62.

39. Kaye, "Career of an Indian Officer," *Cornhill Magazine* 3 (1861): 77.

40. Kaye, "The War on the Sutlej," *North British Review* 5 (1846): 246.

41. Kaye, *History of the War in Afghanistan*. 2nd ed., (London: Richard Bentley, 1851), *ix*.

42. Kaye, "The Future of India and Her Army," *Blackwood's* 86 (1859): 636.

43. *Athenaeum*, 29 July 1876.

44. Kaye, "Illustrations of Anglo-Indian Society," *Calcutta Review* 8 (1847): 566.

45. The discrepancy between the discursive treatments of *thagi* and *sati* and their historical reality has been the subject of recent attention. See Lata Mani, *Contentious Traditions: The Debate on Sati in Colonial India* (Berkeley and Los Angeles: University of California Press, 1998) and Radhika Singha, "Providential Circumstances: the Thuggee Campaign of the 1830s and Legal Innovation," *Modern Asia Studies* 27 (1993): 83–146.

46. Kaye, *The Suppresson of Human Sacrifice, Suttee and Female Infanticide*. 2nd ed. (London: Christian Literature Society for India, 1898).

47. OIOC, Outram to E.A. Reade, 23 July 1880, MSS Eur E123 (Reade Papers).

48. OIOC, Lawrence to Kaye, 29 June 1844, MSS Eur F85/5A (Lawrence Papers).

49. Gleig rewrote some passages in a letter from Arthur Wellesley to Thomas Munro. See Douglas M. Peers, "'Those Noble Exemplars of the True Military Tradition'; Constructions of the Indian Army in the Mid-Victorian Press," *Modern Asian Studies* 31 (1997): 109–42.

50. Singh, 133.

51. As Emma Roberts explained in 1835, "To be seen in public with, or to be

known to be intimate in the houses of Indo-Britons, was fatal to a new arrival in Calcutta; there was no possibility of emerging from the shade, or of making friends or connection in a higher sphere." Emma Roberts, *Scenes and Characteristics of Hindos.* 3 vols. (London: W.H. Allen, 1835), 3: 95. Roberts also warned her readers that, "The prejudices against 'dark beauties' (the phrase usually employed to designate those who are the inheritors of the native complexion) are daily gaining ground, and in the present state of female intellectuality their uncultivated minds form a decided objection." See Roberts, 1: 43.

52. As he explained to his readers, "The fiat of a superior power has determined the time and the extent of our progression, and we have nothing to do but recognize God in History and bow to his behests." J. W. Kaye, "Civis on Indian Affairs," *Calcutta Review* 13 (1850): 407.

53. Kaye, "Sir Charles Napier and the Unhappy Valley," *Bentley's Miscellany* 31 (1852): 82–88.

54. Kaye, *A History of the Sepoy War in India, 1857–58.* 1st ed. 3 vols. (London: W. H. Allen, 1864),1: xii.

55. Philip Mason, *The Men Who Ruled India,* abridged ed. (London: Jonathan Cape, 1985). This was originally published in two volumes: *The Founders* (1953) and *The Guardians* (1954).

56. Brahma Chaudhuri, "India," *Periodicals of Queen Victoria's Empire: an Exploration,* ed. J. Don Vann and R. VanArsdel (Toronto: University of Toronto Press, 1996), 176–77.

57. Kaye, "Military Society in India—and Chapters of Indian Experience," *Calcutta Review* 22 (1854): 442.

58. Kaye, "English Literature in India," *Calcutta Review* 5 (1846): 203.

59. H. G. Keene, "India in English Literature," *Calcutta Review* 33 (1859): 37.

60. Kaye, "The House That John Built," *Cornhill Magazine* 2 (1860): 113.

61. Kaye, "The Demise of the Indian Army," *Blackwood's* 90 (1861): 100–114.

62. J. A. Mangan has written extensively on the subject of imperialism and sportsmanship. See for example J. A. Mangan, *The Games Ethic and Imperialism: Aspects of the Diffusion of an Ideal* (London: Viking, 1986) and J. A. Mangan, " 'Muscular, Militaristic and Manly': the British Middle-Class Hero as Moral Messenger," *International Journal of the History of Sport* 13 (1996): 28–47.

63. Kaye, "Career of an Indian Officer," *Cornhill Magazine* 3 (1861): 74.

64. Kaye, "The Employment of Women," *North British Review* 26 (1857): 293.

65. Kaye, "The Non-Existence of Women," *North British Review* 23 (1855): 539.

66. James Eli Adams, *Dandies and Desert Saints; Styles of Victorian Masculinity* (Ithaca: Cornell University Press, 1995), 2. See also the essays in Catherine Hall, *White, Male and Middle Class: Explorations in Feminism and History* (Cambridge: Polity Press, 1992).

67. He said much the same thing in *Peregrine Pulteney,* "they were women; and courage with women is not the thing needful, as with men." Kaye, *Peregrine Pulteney: or, Life in India.* 3 vols. (London: John Mortimer, 1844), 2: 247.

68. Leonore Davidoff and Catherine Hall, *Family Fortunes, Men and Women of the English Middle Class* (London: Routledge, 1987), 149.

69. The extent to which masculinity defined imperial discourse is the subject of Mrinalini Sinha, *Colonial Masculinity; the 'Englishman' and the 'Effeminate Bengali' in the Late Nineteenth-Century* (Manchester: Manchester University Press, 1995). See also Metcalf, *Ideologies of the Raj.*

70. Margaret Strobel, *European Women and the Second British Empire* (Bloomington: Indiana University Press, 1991).

71. John M. MacKenzie, "Empire and National Identities: the Case of Scotland," *Transactions of the Royal Historical Society* 8 (1998): 215–32.

72. Sir Bartle Frere, *Letter to Sir John Kaye* (London: n.p., 1874), 5.

Notes on Contributors

HELEN CALLAWAY, anthropologist and former Director of the Centre for Cross-Cultural Research on Women at the University of Oxford, is the author of *Gender, Culture and Empire: European Women in Colonial Nigeria* (1987) and co-editor of *Anthropology and Autobiography* (1990) and *Caught Up in Conflict: Women's Responses to Political Strife* (1986). With Dorothy Helly she co-authored "Crusader for Empire: Flora Shaw, Lady Lugard," *Western Women and Imperialism*, eds. N. Chaudhuri and M. Strobel (1992) and "Journalism as active politics: Flora Shaw, *The Times* and South Africa," *The South African War Reappraised*, ed. D. Lowry (2000), and is currently writing a biography of Flora Shaw, Lady Lugard (1852–1929).

JULIE F. CODELL is Professor of Art History and English at Arizona State University. Her numerous articles and reviews on Victorian art and culture have appeared in many scholarly journals, anthologies, and encyclopedias. She wrote *The Victorian Artist: Artists' Public Images in British Biographical Literature, c. 1870–1910* (2003), and co-edited *Orientalism Transposed: The Impact of the Colonies on British Culture* (1998). She is currently preparing a book on visuality and imperial cultures in the Delhi Coronation Durbars and their exhibitions of Indian art, 1877–1911, and is guest editor for a special issue of *Victorian Periodicals Review* on the press in late nineteenth-century India (2004).

DEEPALI DEWAN is Associate Curator of South Asian Civilizations at the Royal Ontario Museum and teaches at the University of Toronto. She received her Ph.D. from the University of Minnesota in South Asian Art History with a dissertation on colonial art education and the production of disciplinary knowledge. She has received research fellowships from the Social Science Research Council, American Institute for Indian Studies, College Art Association, and the Macarthur Interdisciplinary Program for the Study of Global Change.

DAVID FINKELSTEIN is Head of the Media and Communication Department at Queen Margaret University College, Edinburgh. He is co-editor of *Nineteenth-Century Media and the Construction of Identities* (2000), *Negotiating India in the Nineteenth-Century Media* (2000), and *The Book History Reader* (2001), and author of *The House of Blackwood: Author-Publisher Relations in the Victorian Era* (2002).

MICHAEL HANCHER, a professor of English at the University of Minnesota, has published many essays on Victorian writers and artists, as well as articles on speech-act theory, pragmatics, and the law. His work on pictorial illustration ranges from *A Christmas Carol* and the *Alice* books to illustrated dictionaries—including an account of Blackie's *Imperial Dictionary*, which preceded *The Imperial Gazetteer.*

DOROTHY O. HELLY, Professor Emerita of History and Women's Studies, Hunter College and The Graduate School, The City University of New York, is the author of *Livingstone's Legacy: Horace Waller and Victorian Mythmaking* (1987), co-editor of *Gendered Domains: Rethinking Public and Private in Women's History* (1982), and co-author of *Women's Realities, Women's Choices: An Introduction to Women's Studies* (2d ed., 1995). With Helen Callaway she co-authored "Crusader for Empire: Flora Shaw, Lady Lugard," *Western Women and Imperialism,* N. Chaudhuri and M. Strobel, eds. (1992) and "Journalism as active politics: Flora Shaw, *The Times* and South Africa," *The South African War Reappraised,* ed. D. Lowry (2000), and is currently writing a biography of Flora Shaw, Lady Lugard (1852–1929).

TONY HUGHES-d'AETH is a lecturer in English, Communications and Cultural Studies at the University of Western Australia. He is the author of *Paper Nation: The Story of The Picturesque Atlas of Australasia, 1886–1888* (Melbourne University Press, 2001).

ALED JONES is Sir John Williams Professor of Welsh History at the University of Wales, Aberystwyth and Head of its Department of History and Welsh History. He writes on British newspaper history and the Welsh engagement with Empire. He is the author of *Press, Politics and Society. A history of journalism in Wales* (Cardiff, 1993), *Powers of the Press. Newspapers power and the public in nineteenth-century England* (Aldershot, 1996), and, with Bill Jones, *Welsh Reflections. Y Drych and America 1851–2001* (Llandysul, 2001).

ALEX NALBACH is an Assistant Professor of Modern European and Asian History at Sagninaw Valley State University in Michigan. His research interests include the development of information regimes and the effects of publicity on statecraft in the nineteenth century.

CATHERINE PAGANI is Associate Professor of Asian art history in the Department of Art at The University of Alabama. She is interested in Sino-Western contacts in the seventeenth and eighteenth centuries; her monograph, *"Eastern Magnificence and European Ingenuity": Clocks of Late Imperial China*, examines the resulting cross-cultural influences in technology and the arts.

DOUGLAS PEERS is Associate Professor of History at the University of Calgary and author of *Between Mars and Mammon: Colonial Armies and the Garrison State in Early-Nineteenth Century India* (1995), co-editor (with David Finkelstein) of *Negotiating India in the Nineteenth Century Media* (2000) as well as the author of articles on the cultural, medical, and political impact of the military in colonial India. He is currently working on a study of the historiography of colonial rule in India.

DENISE P. QUIRK, a Ph.D. candidate at Rutgers University, is completing a dissertation on gender, feminism, and the women's press as key factors in Victorian imaginings of nation and empire, and teaching European history and women's studies. She is the author of "Eliza Cook," in *Nineteenth-Century British Women Writers: A Bio-Bibliographical Critical Sourcebook*, edited by Abigail Burnham (2000), and the co-editor, with Lisa Merrill, of *Nothing but a Memory: Selected Letters of American Actress Charlotte Cushman* (forthcoming).

J. LEE THOMPSON is Associate Professor of History at Lamar University, where he teaches British and European political and imperial history. He is currently at work on two books on the career of the imperial proconsul Alfred, Lord Milner: *Milner: Civilian Soldier of Empire* and *Failed Imperialism: Lord Milner in South Africa, 1897–1905*.

BIBLIOGRAPHY

Archival Sources and Periodicals

Archives nationales, Paris.
Bengal Hurkaru.
The Bengalee.
Blackwood Papers. National Library of Scotland.
Blackwood's Edinburgh Magazine.
Sir Harry Brittain Papers, British Library of Economic and Political Science, Northcliffe Add. Mss., British Library.
Bulletin, Sydney.
Calcutta Review.
Cape Argus (Weekly Edition), 1892.
Y Cenhadwr.
Colburn's United Service Magazine.
Collier's.
Contemporary Review (London).
Cornhill Magazine.
Y Cronicl Cenhadol.
Cymry Fydd.
Daily Graphic, 1890–1892.
Daily Mail (London).
Davies Collection (Emily Davies), Girton College.
Y Drysorfa.
Elphinstone Papers, OIOC, British Library.
English Woman's Journal.
Englishwoman's Domestic Magazine.
Englishwoman's Review.
Fortnightly Review.
Fraser's Magazine.
Y Frythones.
Y Goleuad.
Good Words.
The Graphic (illustrated weekly), 1889.
Y Gymraes.
Homeward Mail (Allahabad).

303

Illustrated London News.

Indian Association Collection, Bristol and London, OIOC, British Library.

Journal of Indian Art and Industry. 10 vols, 10 nos., 1884–1917.

Lawrence Papers, OIOC, British Library.

The Link.

Macleod, William. Sketchbooks, Mitchell Library, State Library of New South Wales.

Macmillan's.

Melbourne Age.

National Review.

New Review.

The Nineteenth Century.

The Nineteenth Century and After.

North British Review.

The Ottawa Citizen.

Overland Mail.

Pall Mall Gazette, 1890.

Queen, The Lady's Newspaper.

Reade Papers, OIOC, British Library.

Reuters Archive, London.

Review of Reviews (London).

Saturday Review.

Shaw [Flora Louise, Lady Lugard] Papers, Rhodes House, Oxford.

Sydney Daily Telegraph.

Sydney Morning Herald.

The Times (London), 1892.

United Service Journal.

Victoria Magazine.

Westminster Review.

PUBLISHED SOURCES

Aaron, Jane. "Slaughter and Salvation: British Imperialism in Nineteenth-Century Welsh Women's Writing." *New Welsh Review* 38 (October 1997): 38–46..

Adams, James Eli. *Dandies and Desert Saints: Styles of Victorian Masculinity.* Ithaca: Cornell University Press, 1995.

Adas, Michael. *Machines as the Measure of Men: Science, Technology, and Ideologies of Western Dominance.* Ithaca: Cornell University Press, 1989.

Afghani, Jamal al-Din al-. "The Reign of Terror in Persia." *Contemporary Review* 61 (February 1892): 238–48.

Ahmad, Maulvi Rafiūddin. "The Battle of Omdurman and the Mussulman World." *The Nineteenth Century* 44 (October 1898): 688–696.

———. "In defence of Islam." *Fortnightly Review* 65 o.s., 59 n.s. (January 1896): 165–76.

———. "England in relation to Mohamedan States." *National Review* 21 (April 1893): 187–95.

———. "The future of the Anglo-Afghan alliance." *The Nineteenth Century* 43 (February 1898): 24–49.

———. "India II: Is the British 'Raj' in danger?" *The Nineteenth Century* 42 (September 1897): 493–500.

———. "A Moslem view of Abdul Hamid and the Powers." *The Nineteenth Century* 38 (July 1895): 156–64.

———. "A Moslem's view of the Pan-Islamic revival," *The Nineteenth Century* 42 (October 1897): 517–26.

Ahmed Riza. "The Caliph and his duties." *Contemporary Review,* 17 (September 1896): 206–09.

Ahvenainen, Jorma. *The Far Eastern Telegraphs: The History of Telegraphic Communication between the Far East, Europe and America before the First World War.* Helsinki: Suomalainen Tiedeakatemia, 1981.

Alcoff, Linda. "The Problem of Speaking for Others." *Cultural Critique* 12 (Winter 1991): 5–32.

Allen, B. C. *Assam District Gazetteers.* Volumes 1, 2, 10. Calcutta: The Baptist Missionary Press, 1905–06.

Altholz, Joseph L. The *Religious Press in Britain.* New York: Greenwood Press, 1989.

Altick, Richard D. *The English Common Reader: A Social History of the Mass Reading Public, 1800–1900.* Chicago: University of Chicago Press, 1957.

———. *The Shows of London.* Cambridge: Harvard University Press, 1978.

Ameer Ali, Syed, "A cry from the Indian Mohammedans." *The Nineteenth Century* 12 (August 1882): 193–215.

———. "The influence of women in Islam." *The Nineteenth Century* 45 (May 1899): 755–74.

———. "Islam and Canon MacColl." *The Nineteenth Century* 38 (November 1895): 778–85.

———. "Islam and its critics." *The Nineteenth Century* 38 (September 1895): 361–80.

———. "The life problem of Bengal." *The Nineteenth Century* 14 (September 1883): 421–40.

———. "The real status of women in Islam." *The Nineteenth Century* 20 (September 1891): 387–99.

———. "The rupee and the ruin of India." *The Nineteenth Century* 33 (March 1893): 515–24.

———. "Some Indian suggestions for India." *The Nineteenth Century* 7 (June 1880): 963–78.

Amos, Valerie, and Pratibha Parmar. "Challenging Imperial Feminism." *Feminist Review* 17 (Autumn 1984): 3–17.

Anagol-McGinn, Padma, "The Age of Consent Act (1891) Reconsidered: Women's Perspectives and Participation in the Child Marriage Controversy in India." *South Asia Research* 12 (November 1992): 100–18.

Anderson, Benedict. *Imagined Communities: Reflections on the Origin and Spread of Nationalism.* London: Verso, 1983.

Anderson, Margaret and Andrew Reeves. "Contested Identities: Museums and the Nation in Australia." In *Museums and the Making of "Ourselves": The Role of Objects in National Identity*, ed. Flora E.S. Kaplan. London and New York: Leicester University Press, 1994, 79–124.

Art and Industry through the Ages: Monograph Series on Bengal. New Delhi: Navrang, 1976.

Art and Industry through the Ages: Monograph Series on Bombay Presidency. New Delhi: Navrang, 1976.

Art and Industry through the Ages III: Monograph Series on Madras Presidency/Southern India. New Delhi: Navrang, 1982.

Asad, Talal and John Dixon, "Translating Europe's Others." In *Europe and its Others*, ed. F. Barker, P. Hulme, M. Iversen, and D. Loxley. Colchester: University of Essex, 1985, 170–77.

Asher, Catherine and Thomas Metcalf, ed. *Perceptions of South Asia's Visual Past.* New Delhi: American Institute of Indian Studies, 1994.

Askew, M. and B. Hubber. "The Colonial Reader Observed: Reading in its Colonial Context." In *The Book in Australia: Essays Towards a Cultural and Social History*, ed. D. H. Borchardt and W. Kirsop. Melbourne: Australian Reference Publications, 1988, 110–38.

Atkinson, George. *Curry and Rice.* London: Day and Son, 1859.

Ausland-Deutschen, *Die Presse und die deutsche Weltpolitik.* Zurich: Zürcher und Furrer, 1906.

Australian Men of Mark, 2 vols. Sydney and Melbourne: Charles F. Maxwell, 1888.

Ballaster, Ros, Margaret Beetham, Elizabeth Frazer, and Sandra Hebron. *Women's Worlds: Ideology, Femininity and the Woman's Magazine.* London: Macmillan, 1991.

Barakatüllah, Mohammad, "Islam and Soofeeism." *Westminster Review* 144 (December 1895): 674–78.

Balzac, Honore-de, *Oeuvres.* Paris: Michel Lévy Frères, 1869–76.

Barringer, Tim and Tom Flynn, ed. *Colonialism and the Object: Empire, Material Culture and the Museum.* London and New York: Routledge, 1998.

Barthes, Roland. *Camera Lucida.* Trans. Richard Howard. London: Fontana, 1984 [1980].

Basse, Dieter. *Wolff's Telegraphisches Bureau. Agenturpublizistik zwischen Politik und Wirtschaft.* Munich, London, New York, Paris: K. G. Saur, 1991.

Basu, Aparna. "Mary Ann Cooke to Mother Teresa: Christian Women and the Indian Response." In *Women and Missions Past and Present. Anthropological and Historical Perceptions*, ed. Fiona Bowie, Deborah Kirkwood and Shirley Ardener. Providence, R. I.: Berg, 1993, 187–208.

Baucom, Ian. *Out of Place: Englishness, Empire, and the Locations of Identity.* Princeton: Princeton University Press, 1999.

Bayly, C.A. *Empire and Information: Intelligence Gathering and Social Communication in India, 1780–1870.* Cambridge: Cambridge University Press, 1996.

———. *Imperial Meridian; the British Empire and the World, 1730–1830.* London: Longman, 1989.

———. *Indian Society and the Making of the British Empire: The New Cambridge History of India*, II.1. Cambridge: Cambridge University Press, 1988.

———. *The Raj.* London: National Portrait Gallery, 1990.

———. "The First Age of Global Imperialism, c. 1760–1830," *Journal of Imperial and Commonwealth History* 26 (1998): 28–47.

Bebbington, D. W. *Evangelicalism in Modern Britain: A history from the 1730s to the 1980s.* Boston: Unwin Hyman, 1989.

Beetham, Margaret. *A Magazine of Her Own?: Domesticity and Desire in the Woman's Magazine, 1800–1914.* London: Routledge, 1996.

Beveridge, Henry. *A Comprehensive History of India, Civil, Military, and Social.* London, Blackie and Son, 1862.

Beveridge, William Henry. *India Called Them.* London: Allen and Unwin, 1947.

Bhabha, Homi K. *The Location of Culture.* London: Routledge, 1994.

Bhownaggree, Sir Mancherjee Merwanjee, "The present agitation in India and the vernacular press." *Fortnightly Review* 68 o.s., 62 n.s. (August 1897): 304–13.

Blackburn, William, ed. *Joseph Conrad: Letters to William Blackwood and David S. Meldrum.* Durham, N. C.: Duke University Press, 1958.

Blake, Robert. *The Conservative Party from Peel to Churchill.* London: Eyre and Spottiswood, 1970.

Blackie, Agnes A. C. *Blackie and Son, 1809–1959.* London: Blackie and Son, 1959.

Blackie, W. G., ed. *The Imperial Gazetteer: A General Dictionary of Geography, Physical, Political, Statistical and Descriptive.* 2 vols. Glasgow: Blackie and Son, 1855.

———, ed. *The Imperial Gazetteer: A General Dictionary of Geography, Physical, Political, Statistical, and Descriptive; With a Supplement, Bringing the Geographical Information Down to the Latest Dates.* 2 vols. London: Blackie and Son, 1876.

———. *Remarks on the East India Company's Civil Service Examination Papers, As Illustrative of Some Defects in the Course of Academical Education in Scotland.* Glasgow: printed for private circulation, 1858.

———. *Sketch of the Origin and Progress of the Firm of Blackie and Son.* Glasgow: printed for private circulation, 1897.

Blackie's Literary and Commercial Almanack, 1854. Glasgow: Blackie and Son, 1853.

Blackie, Walter W. *Walter Graham Blackie, Ph.D., LL.D. (1816–1906).* London and Glasgow: printed for private circulation by Blackie and Son, 1936.

Blainey, Geoffrey. *A Land Half Won.* Melbourne: Macmillan, 1980.

Blondheim, Menahem. *News Over the Wires: The Telegraph and the Flow of Public Information in America, 1844–1897.* Cambridge: Harvard University Press, 1994.

Borthwick, Meredith. *The Changing Role of Women in Bengal, 1849–1905.* Princeton: Princeton University Press, 1984.

Boutbouqalt, Tayeb. *Les agences mondiales d'information: Havas Maroc (1889–1940)* Casablanca: Editions maghrébines, 1996.

Bowler, Peter J. *The Invention of Progress: the Victorian and the Past.* Oxford: Basil Blackwell, 1989.

Brake, Laurel. *Subjugated Knowledges: Journalism, Gender and Literature in the Nineteenth Century.* London: Macmillan, 1994.

———. "Theories of Formation: *The Nineteenth Century:* Vol. I, No. I, March 1877, Monthly. 2/6." *Victorian Periodicals Review* 25 (Spring 1992): 16–21.

———. Aled Jones, and Lionel Madden, ed. *Investigating Victorian Journalism.* Basingstoke: Macmillan, 1990.

Brett, Maurice. *The Journals and Letters of Reginald, Viscount Esher.* vol. 2. London: Ivor Nicholson and Watson, 1934.

Brilliant, Richard. *Portraiture.* London: Reaktion Books, 1991.

Brittain, Sir Harry. *Pilgrims and Pioneers.* London: Hodder and Stoughton, 1946.

Brockliss, Laurence and David Eastwood, eds. *A Union of Multiple Identities. The British Isles, c.1750–1850.* Manchester: Manchester University Press, 1997.

Brody, Jennifer DeVere. *Impossible Purities: Blackness, Femininity, and Victorian Culture.* Durham: Duke University Press, 1998.

Browning, Robert. *The Poems.* 2 vols. Ed. John Pettigrew and Thomas J. Collins. New Haven: Yale University Press, 1981.

Bryant, W. C., ed. *Picturesque Canada.* 2 vols. New York: D. Appleton, 1872–74.

Burton, Antoinette. *At the Heart of the Empire: Indians and the Colonial Encounter in Late-Victorian Britain.* Berkeley: University of California Press, 1998.

———. *Burdens of History: British Feminists, Indian Women, and Imperial Culture, 1865–1915.* Chapel Hill: University of North Carolina Press, 1994.

———. "Tongues Untied: Lord Salisbury's 'Black Man' and the Boundaries of Imperial Democracy." *Comparative Study of Society and History* (2000): 632–61.

Busch, Briton Cooper. *Hardinge of Penshurst: A Study in the Old Diplomacy.* Hamden, Conn.: Shoe String-Archon, 1980.

Butler, Judith. *Gender Trouble.* New York: Routledge, 1990.

———. *Bodies That Matter.* New York: Routledge, 1994.

Caine, Barbara. *English Feminism, 1780–1980.* New York: Oxford University Press, 1998.

Callaway, Helen. *Gender, Culture and Empire: European Women in Colonial Nigeria.* Urbana: University of Illinois Press, 1987.

Calvinistic Methodism in Wales: Its Present Position and Future Prospects. A Critical Review, London: Hodder and Stoughton, 1870.

"Canada and the Empire," *Citizen* (Ottawa), 19 November 1906.

Carlyle, Thomas. "On Heroes, Hero-Worship, and the Heroic in History," *Thomas Carlyle's Works.* Standard Edition, vol. 4. London: Chapman and Hall, 1913.

Carpenter, Francis Ross. *The Old China Trade: Americans in Canton, 1784–1843.* New York: Coward, McCann and Geoghegan, 1976.

Carpenter, J. Estlin. *The Life and Work of Mary Carpenter.* 2nd ed. London: Macmillan, 1881.

Carpenter, Mary. *Six Months in India.* London: Longmans, Green, 1868.

Carter, Paul. "Strange Seas of Thought." *The Australian's Review of Books* (June 1998), 20.

———. *The Road to Botany Bay: An Essay in Spatial History.* London: Faber and Faber, 1987.

Catalogue d'une précieuse collection d'objets d'art et de curiosité de la Chine provenant du Palais d'été de Yuen-ming-yuen. Paris: Imprimerie de Pillet fils anié, 1861.

Catterall, Peter, Colin Seymour-Ure, and Adrian Smith, eds. *Northcliffe's Legacy.* London: Macmillan, 2000.

Certeau, Michel de. *The Practice of Everyday Life.* Trans. Stephen Rendall. Berkeley: University of California Press, 1984.

———. *The Writing of History.* Trans. Tom Conley. New York: Columbia University Press, 1988.

Chamberlayne, P. C. *Compendium Geographicum; or, a More Exact, Plain, and Easie Introduction into All Geography, Than Yet Extant, After the Latest Discoveries, or Alterations; Very Useful, Especially for Young Noblemen and Gentlemen.* 2nd ed. London: William Crook, 1685.

Chatterjee, Partha. "Colonialism, Nationalism and Colonialized Women: The Contest in India." *American Ethnologist* 16 (November 1989): 622–33.

Chaudhuri, Brahma. "India." In *Periodicals of Queen Victoria's Empire: an Exploration*, ed. J. Don Vann and R. VanArsdel. Toronto: University of Toronto Press, 1996, 176–77.

Chaudhuri, Nupur. "Memsahibs and Their Servants in Nineteenth-Century India." *Women's History Review* 3 (1994): 549–62.

———— and Margaret Strobel, eds. *Western Women and Imperialism: Complicity and Resistance*. Bloomington: Indiana University Press, 1992.

————. "Shawls, Jewelry, Curry, and Rice in Victorian Britain." In *Western Women and Imperialism*, ed. N. Chaudhuri and M. Strobel. Bloomington: Indiana University Press, 1992, 231–46.

"The Chinese War." In *The Comic Album: A Book for Every Table*. London: Orr and Co., 1842.

Clark, Alan M. *Catalogue: Exhibition, 150 Years of Publishing—Blackie and Son, 1809–1959*. Glasgow: W. and J. Mackay, 1959.

Codell, Julie F. "Resistance and Performance: Native Informant Discourse in the Biographies of Maharaja Sayaji Rao III of Baroda." In *Orientalism Transposed: The Impact of the Colonies on British Culture*, ed. Julie F. Codell and Dianne Sachko Macleod. Aldershot: Ashgate, 1998, 13–45.

Cohn, Bernard S. "Representing Authority in Victorian India." In *The Invention of Tradition*, ed. Eric Hobsbawm and Terence Ranger. Cambridge: Cambridge University Press, 1983, 165–209.

———— *Colonialism and Its Forms of Knowledge: The British in India*. Princeton: Princeton University Press, 1996.

Collins, H. M. *From Pigeon Post to Wireless*. London: Hodder and Stoughton, Ltd., 1925.

Comaroff, John and Jean Comaroff. *Ethnography and the Historical Imagination*. Boulder, Colo.: Westview Press, 1992.

Cook, E. T. *Edmund Garrett, a Memoir*. London: Edwin Arnold, 1909.

Coombes, Annie E. *Reinventing Africa: Museums, Material Culture and Popular Imagination*. New Haven and London: Yale University Press, 1994.

Cooper, Frederick, and Ann Laura Stoler, eds. *Tensions of Empire: Colonial Cultures in a Bourgeois World*. Berkeley: University of California Press, 1997.

Copley, Anthony. *Religions in Conflict: Ideology, Cultural Contact and Conversion in Late-Colonial India*. Delhi: Oxford University Press, 1997.

Cowell, Herbert. "The Opening of Parliament." *Blackwood's Magazine* 127 (March 1880): 398–410.

Cowtan, Robert. *Memories of the British Museum*. London: Richard Bentley and Son, 1872.

Culler, A. Dwight. *The Victorian Mirror of History*. New Haven: Yale University Press, 1985.

Curtis, Gerard. "Dickens in the Visual Market." In *Literature in the Marketplace: Nineteenth-Century Publishing and Reading Practices*, ed. John O. Jordan and Robert L. Patten. Cambridge: Cambridge University Press, 1995.

Das, Devendra N. [or Devendranath Das, or Devendra, N. Das]. "The Hindu widow." *The Nineteenth Century* 20 (September 1886): 364–73.

David, Dierdre. *Rule Britannia: Women, Empire, and Victorian Writing.* Ithaca: Cornell University Press, 1995.

Davidoff, Leonore, and Catherine Hall. *Family Fortunes: Men and Women of the English Middle Class, 1780–1850.* Chicago: University of Chicago Press, 1987.

Davison, Graeme. "Historic Time and Everyday Time." *Australia, 1888* 7 (April 1981): 5–10.

———. *The Rise and Fall of Marvellous Melbourne.* Melbourne: Melbourne University Press, 1978.

———. "The Use and Abuse of Australian History." *Australian Historical Studies* 23 (October 1988): 56–58.

———, et al., eds. *Australians, 1888.* Melbourne: Fairfax, Syme and Weldon, 1987.

Dehejia, Vidya, ed. *India Through the Lens: Photography 1840–1911*, Washington D. C.: Freer Gallery of Art and Arthur M. Sackler Gallery with Mapin and Prestel, 2000.

Dena, Lal. *Missions and Colonialism: A Study of Missionary Movement in North East India with Particular Reference to Manipur and Lushai Hills 1894–1947.* Shillong: Vendrame Institute, 1988.

Dening, Greg. *Performances.* Melbourne: Melbourne University Press, 1996.

Dennis, James S. *Christian Missions and Social Progress. A sociological study of foreign missions.* 3 vols. New York: Fleming H. Revell, 1897–1906.

Desmond, Ray. *The India Museum 1801–1879.* London: Her Majesty's Stationary Office and India Office Library and Records, 1982.

Dewan, Deepali. "The Body at Work: Colonial Art Education and the Figure of the 'Native Craftsman.'" *Confronting the Body: The Politics of Physicality in Colonial and Post-Colonial India*, ed. Satadru Sen and James Mills. London: Anthem Press (forthcoming).

———. "Crafting Knowledge and Knowledge of Crafts: Art Education, Colonialism and the Madras School of Arts in Nineteenth-Century South Asia." Ph.D. dissertation, University of Minnesota, 2001.

Dharwadker, Vinay. "Print Culture and Literary Markets in Colonial India." In *Language Machines*, ed. J. Masten, P. Stallybrass, and N. Vickers. London: Routledge, 1997, 108–33.

Dictionary of National Biography, Second Supplement, vol. 1, January 1901–December 1911, ed. Sir Sidney Lee. London: Oxford University Press, rpt. 1920.

Dictionary of National Biography: The Concise Dictionary, Part 2, 1901–70. Oxford: Oxford University Press, 1982.

Dirks, Nicholas, ed. *Colonialism and Culture.* Ann Arbor: University of Michigan Press, 1992.

———. "The Policing of Tradition: Colonialism and Anthropology in Southern India." *Comparative Studies in Society and History* 39 (1997): 182–212.

Dixon, Robert. *Writing the Colonial Adventure: Race, Gender and Nation in Anglo-Australian Popular Fiction, 1825–1914.* Cambridge: Cambridge University Press, 1995.

Docker, John. *The Nervous Nineties: Australian Cultural Life in the 1890s.* Oxford: Oxford University Press, 1991.

Driver, Felix. *Geography Militant: Cultures of Exploration and Empire.* Oxford: Blackwell, 2001.

Dunn, Nathan. *"Ten Thousand Chinese Things." A Descriptive Catalogue of the Chinese*

Collection in Philadelphia with Miscellaneous Remarks Upon the Manners, Customs, Trade, and Government of the Celestial Empire. Philadelphia: Printed for the Proprietor, 1839.

Dutt, Romesh Chunder. "Famines in India and their remedy." *Fortnightly Review* 68 o.s., 62 n.s. (August 1897): 198–214 (signed "A Hindu," ascribed by *Wellesley Index*).

———. "The grievances of India," *Dark Blue* 3 (May 1872): 325–41 (signed "A Hindu," ascribed by *Wellesley Index*).

Dutt [or Datt], Shoshee Chunder, Raî Báhádur, [or Sasi Chandra]. "Taxation in India," *Fraser's* 94 o.s., 14 n.s. (Sept. 1876): 302–24.

Dutta, Krishna and Andrew Robinson, *Rabindranath Tagore: The Myriad Minded Man.* London: Bloomsbury, 1995.

Edwardes, Herbert, and Herman Merivale. *Life of Sir Henry Lawrence.* 2 vols. London: Smith, Elder and Co, 1872.

Efland, Arthur. *A History of Art Education: Intellectual and Social Currents in Teaching the Visual Arts.* New York: Teachers College, Columbia University, 1990.

Elgin, James Lord. *Letters and Journals of James, Eighth Earl of Elgin.* Ed. Theodore Warland. London: John Murray, 1872.

Embree, Ainslie T. "Comment: Widows as Cultural Symbols." In *Sati, the Blessing and the Curse,* ed. John Stratton Hawley. Oxford: Oxford University Press, 1994, 149–59.

Engels, Dagmar, "The Age of Consent Act of 1891: Colonial Ideology in Bengal," *South Asia Research* 3 (1983): 107–34.

———. "The Limits of Gender Ideology: Bengali Women, the Colonial State, and the Private Sphere, 1890–1930." *Women's Studies International Forum* 12 (1989): 425–37.

Fabian, Johannes. *Time and the Other.* New York: Columbia University Press, 1983.

Fanon, Frantz. *The Wretched of the Earth.* Trans. Constance Farrington. New York: Grove Press, 1963.

Fenby, Jonathan. *The International News Services.* New York: Shocken Books, 1986.

Fetter, Frank W. "The Economic Articles in Blackwood's Edinburgh Magazine and their Authors 1817–1853." *Scottish Journal of Political Economy* 7 (1960): 85–107; 213–31.

Finkelstein, David. *The House of Blackwood: Author-Publisher Relations in the Victorian Era.* University Park: Penn State University Press, 2002.

———. *An Index to Blackwood's Magazine, 1901–1980.* Aldershot: Scolar Press, 1995.

——— and Douglas Mark Peers, eds. *Negotiating India in the Nineteenth-Century Media.* Basingstoke: Macmillan Press, 2000.

Fitzpatrick, J. Percy. *Through Mashonaland with Pick and Pen.* Ed. A. P. Cartwright. Johannesburg: Argus Printing and Publishing Company, 1892; Ad. Donker Publishing, rev. ed., 1973.

Forbes, Geraldine. "Women and Modernity: The Issue of Child Marriage in India." *Women's Studies International Quarterly* 1 (1979): 407–19.

Ford, Jane. "An African Encounter, A British Traitor, and *Heart of Darkness.*" *Conradiana* 27 (1995): 123–34.

Fortune, Robert. *Three Years' Wanderings in the Northern Provinces of China, Including a Visit to the Tea, Silk, and Cotton Countries: with an Account of the Agriculture and*

Horticulture of the Chinese, New Plants, Etc. London: John Murray, 1847; reprinted New York: Garland Publishing, 1979.

Foster, R. F. *Lord Randolph Churchill.* Oxford: Clarendon Press, 1981.

Foucault, Michel. *The Order of Things: an Archaeology of the Human Sciences.* New York: Vintage Books, 1994 [1970]).

———. "History of Systems of Thought." In *Language, Counter-memory, Practice,* ed. D. F. Bouchard. Ithaca: Cornell University Press, 1977.

Fraser, Angus. "John Murray's Colonial and Home Library." *Papers of the Bibliographical Society of America* 91 (1997): 339–408.

Frédérix, Pierre. *Un Siècle de Chasse aux Nouvelles de l'Agence d'Information Havas a l'Agence France-Presse. (1837–1957).* Paris: Flammarion, 1959.

Fuchs, Friedrich. *Agence Havas und das Reutersbureau.* Dissertation at Erlangen, 1918.

———. *Telegraphische Nachrichtenbüros. eine Untersuchung über die Probleme des internationalen Nachrichtenwesens.* Berlin: D. Reimer-E. Vohsen, 1919.

Fulford, Tim and Peter J. Kitson, ed. *Romanticism and Colonialism: Writing and Empire, 1780–1830.* Cambridge: Cambridge University Press, 1998.

Gaekwad, Sayaji Rao. "My Ways and Days in Europe and in India." *The Nineteenth Century and After* 49 (February 1901): 215–25.

Garrett, F. Edmund. *In Afrikanderland and the Land of Ophir, being Notes and Sketches in Political, Social, and Financial South Africa.* London: *Pall Mall Gazette* Extra No. 58, 2d ed., 1891.

Ghosh, A. Sarathkumar. "The financial relation between England and India." *Westminster Review* 148 (October 1897): 401–12.

———. "Great Britain's Duty: India." *National Review* 30 (November 1897): 405–11.

———. "A remedy for Indian famines." *Contemporary Review* 72 (August 1897): 268–71.

Ghosh, Nanda. "Social reforms in India." *National Review* 8 (November 1886): 361–68.

Ghulam-us-Saqlain. "The Musselmans of India and the Armenian question." *The Nineteenth Century* 37 (June 1895): 926–39.

Gikandi, Simon. *Maps of Englishness: Writing Identity in the Culture of Colonialism.* New York: Columbia University Press, 1996.

Gilmour, Robin. *The Victorian Period: The Intellectual and Cultural Context of English Literature, 1830–1890.* Harlow: Longman, 1993.

Gleig, G. R. "The Indian Army." *Blackwood's Edinburgh Magazine* 21 (1827): 563–74.

Goffman, Erving. *The Presentation of Self in Everyday Life.* New York: Anchor, 1959.

Gour, Hury Singh. "Hindu theory of marriage." *National Review* 18 (December 1891): 502–06.

Greenberger, Allen K. *The British Image of India: A Study in the Literature of Imperialism, 1880–1960.* Oxford: Oxford University Press, 1969.

Greene, D. Sarsfield. *Views in India, from Drawings Taken during the Seapoy Mutiny.* London: Thomas McLean, 1859.

Greenhalgh, Paul. *Ephemeral Vistas: The Expositions Universelles, Great Exhibitions and World's Fairs, 1851–1939.* Manchester: Manchester University Press, 1988.

Grewal, Inderpal. *Home and Harem: Nation, Gender, Empire, and the Cultures of Travel.* London: University of Leicester Press, 1996.

Griffith, Wynne Griffith. *Cofiant Cenhades. Miss J. Helen Rowlands, M.A., D.Lit., (Helen o Fon)*. Caernarfon, Wales: Llyfrfa'r Methodistiaid Calfinaidd, 1961.

Griffiths, Tom. *Hunters and Collectors: The Antiquarian Imagination in Australia*. Melbourne: Cambridge University Press, 1996.

———. "Part Silences: Aborigines and Convicts in Our History Making." In *Pastiche I: Reflections on Nineteenth-Century Australia*, ed. Penny Russell and Richard White. Sydney: Lalen and Unwin, 1989.

Griggs, W. *Illustrated Pamphlet of Photo-Chromo-Lithography*. London: Griggs, 1882.

Groth, Otto. *Die Zeitung*. Mannheim: J. Bensheimer, 1928.

Guha, Ranajit. "Not at Home in Empire," *Critical Inquiry* 23 (1997): 482–93.

Guha-Thakurta, Tapathi. "Tales of the Bharhut Stupa: Archaeology in the Colonial and Nationalist Imaginations." In *Paradigms of Indian Architecture: Space and Time in Representation and Design*, ed. G. H. R. Tillotson. London: SOAS, 1998, 26–58.

Gwynn, Stephen. *The Irish Statesman* (November 10, 1923): 279.

Habermas, Jürgen. *The Structural Transformation of the Public Sphere*. Trans. Burger and Lawrence. Cambridge: Harvard University Press, 1989.

Halim Pasha, Muhammad 'Abd al. "A reply to my critics." *The Nineteenth Century* 18 (September 1885): 485–92.

Hancher, Michael. "Gazing at *The Imperial Dictionary*." *Book History* 1 (1998): 156–81.

Hardie, Martin. *English Coloured Books*. London: Methuen and Co., 1906. Totowa, N.J.: Rowman and Littlefield, 1973.

Hardinge, Charles Stewart. *Recollections of India, Drawn on Stone by J. D. Harding from the Original Drawings by the Honourable Charles Stewart Hardinge*. London: Thomas M'Lean, 1847.

Hardinge, Charles Viscount. *Viscount Hardinge*. Rulers of India 19. Oxford: Clarendon Press, 1892.

Hardman, Thomas. *A Parliament of the Press: The First Imperial Press Conference*. London: Constable, 1909.

Harris, José. *William Beveridge: A Biography*. 2nd ed. Oxford: Clarendon Press, 1997.

Harris, Walter B. "Sea Fishing at the Cape." *Blackwood's Magazine* 148 (November 1890): 626–36.

Harrow, Alvin F. *Old Wires and New Waves: The History of the Telegraph, Telephone and Wireless*. New York and London: D. Appleton-Century Company, Inc., 1936.

Hawkins, Hunt. "Joseph Conrad, Roger Casement and the Congo Reform Movement." *Journal of Modern Literature* 9 (1981–82): 65–80.

Healy, J. J. "The Lemurian Nineties." *Australian Literary Studies* 8 (1978): 307–316.

Hevia, James L. "Loot's Fate: The Economy of Plunder and The Moral Life of Objects 'From The Summer Palace of The Emperor of China.'" *History and Anthropology* 6 (1994): 319–45.

The History of The Times, vol. 2, *The Tradition Established, 1841–1884*, and vol. 3, *The Twentieth Century Test, 1884–1912*. London: The Times, 1939 and 1947.

Hobsbawm, Eric, and Terence Ranger, eds. *The Invention of Tradition*. Cambridge: Cambridge University Press, 1983.

Hogan, Edmund. *The Irish Missionary Movement: a Historical Survey 1830–80*. Dublin: Gill and Macmillan, 1990.

Homans, Margaret. *Royal Representations: Queen Victoria and British Culture, 1837–1876*. Chicago: University of Chicago Press, 1998.

Hughes, Dewi Myrddin. "Dealltwriaeth Genhadol C.W.M.," *Cludoedd Moroedd. Cofion Dwy Ganrif o Genhadaeth 1795–1995*. Ioan W. Gruffydd (Gol.) Abertawe, Wales: Bwrdd Y Genhadaeth, Undeb Yr Annibynwyr Cymraeg, 1995.

Hughes, Robert. *The Fatal Shore: a History of the Transportation of Convicts to Australia.* London: Collins, Harvill, 1987.

International Exhibition of 1862. Illustrated Catalogue. 4 vols. London, n. p., 1862.

Jameson, Anna. *Diary of an Ennuyée.* London: Henry Colburn, 1826.

Jayawardena, Kumari. *The White Woman's Other Burden.* New York: Routledge, 1996.

Jenkins, Nigel. *Gwalia in Khasia; a visit to the site, in India, of the biggest overseas venture ever sustained by the Welsh 1795–1995.* Llandysul: Gomer Press, 1995.

John, Maldwyn C. *Hanes Bywyd a Gwaith Mrs. Esther Lewis—Cenhades 1887–1958.* Swansea: Gwasg John Penri, 1996.

Johnson, Samuel. *A Dictionary of the English Language.* 2 vols. 1755. Reprint, New York: AMS Press, 1967.

Jones, Aled. *Press, Politics and Society. A History of Journalism in Wales.* Cardiff: University of Wales Press, 1993.

———. *Powers of the Press.* Aldershot: Scolar, 1996.

Jones, D. E. Lloyd. "David Edward Evans. A Welshman in India." *THSC* (1967): Part 1, 136–40.

Jones, D. G. Merfyn *Hanes Cenhadaeth Dramor Eglwys Bresbyteraidd Cymru, Cenhadaeth Sylhet-Cachar. Y drydedd gyfrol, Y Popty Poeth a'i Gyffiniau.* Caernarfon, Wales: Gwasg Pantycelyn ar ran Bwrdd y Genhadaeth, 1990.

Jones, S. T. "Cymry Cymreig," *Cymry Fydd* (Ebrill 1889): 381.

Joshi, Priya. "Culture and Consumption: Fiction, the Reading Public, and the British Novel in Colonial India." *Book History* 1 (1998): 206–07.

Jyrwa, J. Fortis. "Christianity in Khasi Culture: A Study of the Relationship between Christianity and Traditional Khasi Culture with Special Reference to the Seng," D. Miss. diss., Fuller Theological Seminary, School of World Mission, 1984.

Kabbani, Rana. *Europe's Myths of the Orient.* Bloomington: Indiana University Press, 1986.

Karl, Frederick and Laurence Davies, eds. *The Collected Letters of Joseph Conrad,* vol. 4: 1908–1911. Cambridge: Cambridge University Press, 1990.

Kaye, John William. "The Administration of Lord Ellenborough." *Calcutta Review* 1 (1844): 508–62.

———. *The Administration of the East India Company; a History of Indian Progress.* London: Richard Bentley, 1853.

———. "The Annexation of Oude." *North British Review* 25 (1856): 515–53.

———. "Career of an Indian Officer." *Cornhill Magazine* 3 (1861): 72–89.

———. *Christianity in India: An Historical Narrative.* London: Smith, Elder, 1859.

———. "Christianity in India." *North British Review* 13 (1850): 583–620.

———. "Civis on Indian Affairs." *Calcutta Review* 13 (1850): 406–41.

———. "The Conquest of Oude." *Edinburgh Review* 107 (1858): 513–40.

———. "The Demise of the Indian Army." *Blackwood's* 90 (1861): 100–14.

――――. *Doveton: Or the Man of Many Impulses. By the Author of "Jerningham."* 3 vols. London: Smith, Elder and Co, 1837.

――――. "Employment of Military Men in Civil Life." *North British Review* 12 (1850): 499–531.

――――. "The Employment of Women." *North British Review* 26 (1857): 291–338.

――――. "English Literature in India." *Calcutta Review* 5 (1846): 202–20.

――――. *Essays of an Optimist.* London: Smith, Elder and Co, 1870.

――――. "A Familiar Epistle from Mr John Company to Mr John Bull." *Blackwood's* 83 (1858): 245–58.

――――. "A Few More Words from Mr John Company to Mr John Bull." *Blackwood's* 83 (1858): 370–84.

――――. "The Future of India and Her Army," *Blackwood's* 86 (1859): 633–46.

――――. *A History of the Sepoy War in India, 1857- 58.* 1st ed. 3 vols. London: W. H. Allen, 1864.

――――. *History of the War in Afghanistan.* London: Richard Bentley, 1851.

――――. "The House That John Built." *Cornhill Magazine* 2 (1860): 113–21.

――――. "Illustrations of Anglo-Indian Society." *Calcutta Review* 8 (1847): 548–68.

――――. *Jerningham; or, the Inconsistent Man.* 3 vols. London: Smith, Elder and Co., 1836.

――――. "John Company's Farewell to John Bull." *Blackwood's* 84 (1858): 338–51.

――――. "Kaye's War in Afghanistan." *Calcutta Review* 15 (1851): 423–55.

――――. *The Life and Correspondence of Charles, Lord Metcalfe . . . From Unpublished Letters and Journals.* 2 vols. London: R. Bentley, 1854.

――――. *The Life and Correspondence of Henry St. George Tucker, Late Accountant General of Bengal and Chairman of the East India Company.* London: R. Bentley, 1854.

――――. *Lives of Indian Officers, Illustrative of the History of the Civil and Military Services of India.* 2 vols. Vol. 1. London: A. Strahan, 1867.

――――. *Long Engagements; a Tale of the Affghan Rebellion.* London: Chapman and Hall, 1846.

――――. "Marriage and Divorce Bill." *North British Review* (1857): 162–93.

――――. "Military Society in India—and Chapters of Indian Experience." *Calcutta Review* 22 (1854): 429–58.

――――. "Mountstuart Elphinstone: In Memoriam." *Once a Week* 1 (1859): 502–4.

――――. "Mr. Thornton's Last Volume: The Indian Press, Afghanistan, Sindh and Gwalior." *Calcutta Review* 5 (1846): 145–80.

――――. "The Non-Existence of Women." *North British Review* 23 (1855): 536–62.

――――. "Our Indian Heroes." *Good Words* 6 (1865): 69–80; 165–76; 246–56; 327–36; 98–408; 67–78; 543–52; 621–32; 99–708; 71–80; 841–52;.

――――. *Peregrine Pultuney: Or, Life in India.* 3 vols. London: John Mortimer, 1844.

――――. *Poems and Fragments.* Jersey: privately printed, 1835.

――――. "Poetry of Recent Indian Warfare." *Calcutta Review* 11 (1848): 220–56.

――――. "Recent Military Memoirs." *Calcutta Review* 14 (1850): 265–95.

――――. "The Romance of Indian Warfare." *North British Review* 12 (1849): 193–224.

――――, ed. *Selections from the Papers of Lord Metcalfe . . .* London: Smith, Elder and Co., 1855.

———. "Sir Charles Napier and the Unhappy Valley." *Bentley's Miscellany* 31 (1852): 82–88.

———. "Sir Walter Gilbert and the Indian Army." *Bentley's Miscellany* 33 (1853): 627–32.

———. "Society in India." *Bentley's Miscellany* 31 (1852): 242–49.

———. *The Story of Basil Bouverie. By the Author of "Peregrine Pultuney."* 3 vols. Calcutta: privately printed, 1842.

———. *The Suppresson of Human Sacrifice, Suttee and Female Infanticide.* 2nd ed. London and Madras: Christian Literature Society for India, 1898.

———. "The War on the Sutlej." *North British Review* 5 (1846): 246–80.

Kaye, John William, and William Simpson. *India, Ancient and Modern: A Series of Illustrations of the Country and People of India and Adjacent Territories, Executed in Chromo-Lithography from Drawings by William Simpson with Descriptive Literature by John William Kaye.* 2 vols. London: Day and Son, 1867.

Keene, H. G. "India in English Literature," *Calcutta Review* 33 (1859): 29–48.

Kendle, John. *The Colonial and Imperial Conferences 1887–1911.* London: Macmillan, 1967.

Koss, Stephen. *The Rise and Fall of the Political Press in Britain.* London: Fontana Press, 1990.

Krebs, Paula. *Gender, Race, and the Writing of Empire.* Cambridge: Cambridge University Press, 1999.

Lalvani, Suren. "Photography, Epistemology, and the Body." *Cultural Studies* 7 (1993): 442–65.

Langdon, William B. *"Ten Thousand Chinese Things": A Descriptive Catalogue of the Chinese Collection, Now Exhibiting at St. George's Place, Hyde Park Corner, London, with Condensed Account of the Genius, Government, History, Literature, Agriculture, Arts, Trade, Manners, Customs and Social Life of the People of the Celestial Empire.* London: Printed for the Proprietor, 1843.

Laurie, W. F. B. *Sketches of Some Distinguished Anglo-Indians with an Account of Anglo-Indian Periodical Literature.* London: John Day, 1875.

Lawrence, Henry. *Adventures of an Officer in the Service of Runjeet Singh.* 1845. Reprint, Karachi: Oxford University Press, 1975.

Lawson, E. Thomas and Robert N. McCauley. *Rethinking Religion. Connecting cognition and culture.* Cambridge: Cambridge University Press, 1990.

Lee, Ada and Elizabeth Williams. *Y Offeiriades Hindwaidd. Hanes Bywyd Chundra Lela.* Caernarfon, Wales: Llyfrau'r Cyfundeb, 1908.

Lee, Jean Gordon. *Philadelphians and the China Trade.* Philadelphia: Philadelphia Museum of Art, 1984.

Lee, Jenny and Charles Fahey. "A Boom for Whom? Some Developments in the Australian Labour Market, 1870–1891," In *Pastiche I: Reflections on Nineteenth-Century Australia,* ed. Penny Russell and Richard White. Sydney: Allen and Unwin, 1994, 162–184.

Lefebure, Antoine. *Havas: les arcanes de pouvoir.* Paris: B. Grasset, 1992.

Lefebvre, Henri. *The Production of Space.* London and Cambridge, Mass: Blackwell, 1991.

Levine, Philippa. "'The Humanising Influences of Five O'Clock Tea': Victorian Feminist Periodicals." *Victorian Studies* 33 (1990): 293–306.

Linton, Eliza Lynn. *The Girl of the Period and Other Social Essays.* London: R. Bentley, 1883.

Loch [Sir Henry, afterwards, Lord] Muniments. Scottish Record Office, Edinburgh.

Locke, John. "Some Thoughts Concerning Reading and Study for a Gentleman." In *Works of John Locke.* 10th ed. Vol. 3. London, 1801.

Lorimer, Douglas. *Colour, Class and the Victorians.* London: Leicester University Press, 1978.

Lowe, Lisa. *Critical Terrains: French and British Orientalisms.* Ithaca and London: Cornell University Press, 1991.

Luard, John. *Views in India, Saint Helena and Car Nicobar, Drawn from Nature and on Stone.* London: J. Graf, 1838.

Lugard, Frederick Dealtry. "A Glimpse of Lake Nyassa." *Blackwood's Magazine* 147 (January 1890): 18–29.

Lunt, James. *Scarlet Lancer.* London: Rupert Hart-Davis, 1964.

Macdonald, Stuart. *The History and Philosophy of Art Education.* London: University of London Press, 1970.

Macintyre, Stuart. *A Colonial Liberalism: The Lost World of Three Victorian Visionaries.* Oxford: Oxford University Press, 1991.

MacKenzie, John. *Imperialism and Popular Culture.* Manchester: Manchester University Press, 1986.

———. *Propaganda and Empire.* Manchester: Manchester University Press, 1984.

———. "Essay and Reflection: On Scotland and the Empire." *International History Review* 15 (1993).

———. "Empire and National Identities: the Case of Scotland." *Transactions of the Royal Historical Society* 8 (1998): 215–32.

Macleod, Conor. *Macleod of "The Bulletin": The Life and Work of William Macleod by his Wife.* Sydney: Snelling, 1931.

Macleod, William. Sketch Notebook, c. May 1886, ML A2147, Item 1. Mitchell Library, State Library of New South Wales.

Macmillan, Margaret. *Women of the Raj.* London: Thames and Hudson, 1988.

Malabari, B. M. *An Appeal from the Daughters of India.* London: Farmer and Sons, 1890.

Mangan, J. A. *The Games Ethic and Imperialism: Aspects of the Diffusion of an Ideal.* London: Viking, 1986.

———. "'Muscular, Militaristic and Manly': the British Middle-Class Hero as Moral Messenger," *International Journal of the History of Sport* 13 (1996): 28–47.

Mani, Lata. *Contentious Traditions: The Debate on Sati in Colonial India.* Berkeley: University of California Press, 1998.

———. "Contentious Traditions: The Debate on Sati in Colonial India." In *Recasting Women: Essays in Colonial History,* ed. Kumkum Sangari and Sudesh Vaid. New Delhi: Kali for Women, 1989, 88–126.

———. "The Production of an Official Discourse on *Sati* in Early Nineteenth-Century Bengal." In *Europe and its Others,* ed. Francis Barker. Vol. 1 Colchester: University of Essex, 1979, 107–27.

Marder, Arthur J. *Fear God and Dread Nought: The Correspondence of Lord Fisher of Kilverstone.* Vol. 2. London: Jonathan Cape, 1956.

Marryat, Florence (Mrs. Ross Church). *Gup: Sketches of Anglo-Indian Life and Character.* London, 1868.

Mason, Philip. *The Men Who Ruled India,* abridged ed. London: Jonathan Cape, 1985.

Mathews, Joseph J. *Reporting the Wars.* Minneapolis: University of Minnesota Press, 1957.

McCelland, Keith, Catherine Hall, and Jane Rendall, eds. *Defining the Victorian Nation: Gender, Class, and Race and the Reform Act of 1867.* Cambridge: Cambridge University Press, 1999.

Metcalf, Thomas R. *Ideologies of the Raj.* Cambridge: Cambridge University Press, 1994.

Meyers, Jeffrey. "Conrad and Roger Casement," *Conradiana* 5 (1973): 64–69.

Midgley, Clare, ed. *Gender and Imperialism.* London: Routledge, 1997.

Misra, Uma Sankar. "Lord Dufferin and the Indian National Congress." *Westminster Review* 132 (July 1889): 92–96.

Mitter, Partha. *Art and Nationalism in Colonial India, 1850–1922: Occidental Orientations.* Cambridge: Cambridge University Press, 1994.

———. *Much Maligned Monsters* (Oxford: Oxford University Press, 1977).

Moberly Bell, E. H. C. *The Life and Letters of C.F. Moberly Bell.* London: Richards Press, 1927.

Mohanty, Chandra. "Under Western Eyes." *Feminist Review* (Autumn 1988): 61–88.

Mohsin-ul-Mulk, Nawab [Syed Maulvi Mehdi Ali]. "Attack on the Native States of India." *The Nineteenth Century* 26 (October 1889): 545–60.

Morris, E. E., ed. *Cassell's Picturesque Australasia.* 4 vols. London: Cassell, 1887–1889.

Morris, John Hughes. *Hanes Cenhadaeth Dramor y Methodistiaid Calfinaidd Cymreig, hyd ddiwedd y flwyddyn 1904.* Liverpool: Llyfrfa y Cymundeb, 1907

Mozoomdar, Protap Chunder. "Present-day progress in India." *The Nineteenth Century* 48 (December 1900): 993–1000.

Le Musée Chinois de l'Imperatrice Eugénie. Paris: Réunion des Musées Nationaux, 1994.

Nair, Janaki. "Uncovering the Zenana: Visions of Indian Womanhood in English-women's Writings, 1813–1940." *Journal of Women's History,* 2 (Spring 1990): 8–34.

Nawangar, Maharaja Shri Ranjitsinhji Vibhaji. "Cricket and the Victorian Era." *Blackwood's Magazine* 162 (July 1897): 1–16.

Northcote, Henry Stafford. "Paulo Paulo post futurum policy." *Blackwood's Magazine* 128 (December 1880): 767–774.

Nowell-Smith, Simon. *The House of Cassell.* London: Cassell, 1958.

———. *International Copyright Law and the Publisher in the reign of Queen Victoria.* Oxford: Oxford University Press, 1968.

Ogilvie, J. N. *Our Empire's Debt to Missions. The Duff Missionary Lecture 1923.* London: Hodder and Stoughton, 1924.

Ogilvie, John, ed. *The Imperial Dictionary, English, Technological and Scientific.* 2 vols. Glasgow: Blackie and Son, 1850.

O'Hanlon, Rosalind. "Recovering the Subject: Subaltern Studies and Histories of Resistance in Colonial South Asia." *Modern Asian Studies* 22 (1988): 189–224.

Oldham, J. H. *Christianity and the Race Problem.* London: Student Christian Movement, 1924.

Orwell, George. *A Collection of Essays*. New York: Bantam Press, 1954.

O'Sullivan, Patrick, ed. *The Irish World Wide: History, Heritage, Identity*. Vol. 5, *Religion and Identity*. London and New York: Leicester University Press, 1996.

Oxford English Dictionary. 13 vols. Oxford: Clarendon Press, 1933.

Papers Relating to Maintenance of Schools of Art in India as State Institutions, 1893–96. Selections from the Records, 341. Calcutta: Home Department, 1898.

Parry, Ann. "Theories of Formation: *Macmillan's Magazine*. Vol. 1, November 1859. Monthly. 1/0." *Victorian Periodicals Review* 26 (1993): 100–04.

Parry, Benita. *Delusions and Discoveries: Studies on India in the British Imagination, 1880–1930*. Berkeley: University of California Press, 1972.

Patterson, R. H. "The Crisis Abroad." *Blackwood's Magazine* 127 (April 1880): 518–29.

Peers, Douglas M. *Between Mars and Mammon: Colonial Armies and the Garrison State in Early Nineteenth Century India*. London: Tauris, 1995.

———. "'The Habitual Nobility of Being': British Officers and the Social Construction of the Bengal Army in the Early Nineteenth Century." *Modern Asian Studies* 25 (1991): 545–70.

———. "'Those Noble Exemplars of the True Military Tradition'; Constructions of the Indian Army in the Mid-Victorian Press." *Modern Asian Studies* 31 (1997): 109–42.

Pollock, Della, ed. *Exceptional Spaces: Essays in Performance and History*. Chapel Hill: University of North Carolina Press, 1998.

Pope, Robert. *Building Jerusalem: Nonconformity, Labour and the Social Question in Wales, 1906–1939*. Cardiff: University of Wales Press, 1998.

Porter, A. N. "Cultural Imperialism and Protestant Missionary Enterprise 1780–1914." *Journal of Imperial and Commonwealth History* 25 (1997): 367–91.

Portfire [pseud.]. "The Military Character, as Exhibited by Works of Fiction." *Colburn's United Service Magazine* 2 (1857): 389–400.

Pound, Reginald and Geoffrey Harmsworth. *Northcliffe*. London: Cassell, 1959.

Pratt, Ambrose. *David Syme: The Father of Protection in Australia*. London: Ward Lock, 1908.

Pratt, Mary Louise. "Scratches on the Face of the Country; or, What Mr. Barrow Saw in the Land of the Bushmen," *"Race," Writing and Difference*. Ed. Henry Louis Gates Jr. Chicago: University of Chicago Press, 1986.

Pye Smith, Charlie. *Rebels and Outcasts. A Journey through Christian India*. Harmondsworth: Viking, 1998.

Pykett, Lyn. "Reading the Periodical Press: Text and Context." In *Investigating Victorian Journalism*. Ed. Laurel Brake, Aled Jones, and Lionel Madden. London: Macmillan, 1990, 3–18.

Raheja, Gloria Goodwin. "The Ajaib-Gher and the Gun Zam-Zammah: Colonial Ethnography and the Elusive Politics of 'Tradition' in the Literature of the Survey of India," *South Asia Research* 19 (1999): 29–51.

Ramusack, Barbara. "Cultural Missionaries, Maternal Imperialists, Feminist Allies: British Women Activists in India, 1865–1945." In *Western Women and Imperialism Complicity and Resistance*, ed. Nupur Chaudhuri and Margaret Strobel. Bloomington: Indiana University Press, 1992, 119–36.

Rantanen, Terhi. "Foreign News in Imperial Russia: The Relationship between International and Russian News Agencies, 1856–1914." Helsinki: *Annales Academiae Scientarum Fennicae. Dissertationes Humanum Litterary* 58 (1990).

Rashid, Salim. "David Robinson and the Tory Macroeconomics of *Blackwood's Edinburgh Magazine.*" *History of Political Economy* 10 (1978): 259–70.

Read, Donald. *The Power of News: The History of Reuters, 1849–1989.* Oxford: Oxford University Press, 2000.

Reichardt, Annie. "Mohammedan Women." *The Nineteenth Century* 20 (June 1891): 941–52.

Rendall, Jane. "'A Moral Engine'? Feminism, Liberalism and the *English Woman's Journal.*" In *Equal or Different: Women's Politics 1800–1914,* ed. Jane Rendall. London: Basil Blackwell, 1987, 112–137.

———. "Friendship and Politics: Barbara Leigh Smith Bodichon (1827–91) and Bessie Rayner Parkes (1829–1925)." In *Sexuality and Subordination: Interdisciplinary Studies of Gender in the Nineteenth Century,* ed. Susan Mendus and Jane Rendall. London: Routledge, 1989, 136–170.

Review of *A Comprehensive History of India* by Henry Beveridge. *Athenaeum* (12 April 1862): 495–96.

Review of *Imperial Gazetteer,* vol. 1., edited by W. G. Blackie. *Athenaeum* 7 (May 1853): 561.

Richards, Thomas. "Archive and Utopia." *Representations* 37 (Winter 1992): 104–37.

Ricouer, Paul. "The Model of the Text: Meaningful Action Considered as a Text." *Social Research* 38 (1971): 529–62.

———. *Time and Narrative.* 2 vols. Trans. Kathleen McLaughlin and David Pellauer. Chicago: The University of Chicago Press, 1984 [1983].

Roberts, Brian. *Churchills in Africa.* London: Hamish Hamilton, 1970.

Roberts, Emma. *Scenes and Characteristics of Hindos.* 3 vols. London: W. H. Allen, 1835.

Roberts, Gwen Rees. *Memories of Mizoram. Recollections and Reflections.* N.p.: The Mission Board of the Presbyterian Church of Wales, 2000.

Roberts, Mrs John [Sidney Margaret Roberts]. *The Revival in the Khasia Hills.* Newport: Cambrian Printing Works, 1907.

Rowlands, Helen J. and Hridesh Ranjan Ghose. *Sermons and Sayings of Sadhu Sundar Singh during his visit to the Khasi Hills, Assam, March 1924.* Sylhet: The Authors, 1924.

Rowlands, J. H. *La Femme Bengalie dans la Littérature du Moyen-Age.* Paris: A. Maisonneuve, 1930.

Rukhmabai. "Indian child marriages: an appeal to the British Government." *New Review* 3 (September 1890): 263–91.

Russell, John C. "Bison Stalking in India." *Blackwood's Magazine* 141 (June 1887): 795–806.

Ryan, Simon. *The Cartographic Eye: How Explorers Saw Australia.* Melbourne: Cambridge University Press, 1996.

Said, Edward W. *Orientalism.* New York: Vintage Press, 1978.

———. "Representing the Colonized: Anthropology's Interlocutors." *Critical Inquiry* 15 (1989): 205–25.

Sangari, Kumkum, and Sudesh Vaid, eds. *Recasting Women: Essays in Indian Colonial History.* New Brunswick: Rutgers University Press, 1990.

Sarkar, Tanika. "Talking about Scandals: Religion, Law and Love in Late Nineteenth-Century Bengal." *Studies in History* 13 (1997): 63–95.

Schultz, Raymond L. *Crusader in Babylon: W.T. Stead and the Pall Mall Gazette.* Lincoln: University of Nebraska Press, 1972.

Schwarzlose, Richard. *The Nation's Newsbrokers.* 2 vols. Evanston: Northwestern University Press, 1989–90.

Scott, Joan. *Gender and the Politics of History.* New York: Columbia University Press, 1988.

Sekyi-Otu, Ato. *Fanon's Dialectic of Experience.* Cambridge: Harvard University Press, 1996.

Sévasly, Mihran [or Sivazlin, Mihran]. "The Armenian question." *New Review* 1 (September 1889): 305–16.

Shand, A. Innes. "Big Game Shooting." *Blackwood's Magazine* 155 (April 1894): 582–590.

Shattuck, J. and M. Wolff, eds. *The Victorian Periodical Press.* Leicester: Leicester University Press, 1982.

Shaw, George. "Bicentennial Writing: Revealing the Ash in the Australian Soul," *1888 and All That: New Views of Australia's Past.* Ed. George Shaw. St. Lucia: University of Queensland Press, 1988.

Shaw, Gerald. *The Garrett Papers.* Cape Town: Van Riebeeck Society, 1984.

Singh, Joytsna G. *Colonial Narratives, Cultural Dialogues: "Discoveries" of India in the Language of Colonialism.* London: Routledge, 1996.

Singh, Nihar Nandan. *British Historiography on British Rule in India; the Life and Writings of Sir John William Kaye, 1814–1876.* Patna: Janaki Prakashan, 1986.

Singh, Odai Partab [Oday Pertap], Rajah of Bhinga. "The cow agitation, or the mutiny-plasm in England." *The Nineteenth Century* 35 (April 1894): 667–72.

———, "The decay of landed aristocracy in India." *The Nineteenth Century* 31 (May 1892): 830–38.

Sinha, Mrinalini. *Colonial Masculinity: The "Manly Englishman" and the "Effeminate Bengali" in the Last The Nineteenth Century.* Manchester: Manchester University Press, 1995.

Sinnema, Peter. *Dynamics of the Pictured Page: Representing the Nation in the* Illustrated London News. Aldershot: Ashgate, 1998.

Sinnett, Frederick. *The Fiction Fields of Australia.* Ed. Cecil Hadgraft. St. Lucia: University of Queensland, 1966 [1856].

Smiles, Samuel. *Self-Help.* London: J. Murray, 1859,

Smith, Jonathan M. "State Formation, Geography, and a Gentleman's Education." *Geographical Review* 86 (1996): 91–100.

Smith, Sidonie. *Moving Lives: Twentieth Century Women's Travel Writing.* Minneapolis and London: University of Minnesota Press, 2001.

Sorabji, Cornelia. "Behind the Purdah." *Macmillan's* 82 (July 1900): 193–200.

———. "The legal status of women in India." *The Nineteenth Century* 44 (November 1898): 854–66.

Sparkes, John. *Schools of Art: Their Origin, History, Work and Influence.* London: William Clowes and Sons, 1884.

Spivak, Gayatri Chakravorty. *The Post-Colonial Critic: Interviews, Strategies, Dialogues.* Ed. Sarah Harasym. New York : Routledge, 1990.

Spurr. David. *The Rhetoric of Empire. Colonial Discourse in Journalism, Travel Writing, and Imperial Administration.* Durham, N.C. and London: Duke University Press, 1993.

Stanley, Brian. *The Bible and the Flag. Protestant missions and British Imperialism in the Nineteenth and Twentieth centuries.* Leicester: Apollos, 1990.

———. *The History of the Baptist Missionary Society, 1792–1992.* Edinburgh: T. and T. Clark, 1992.

Startt, James. *Journalists For Empire: The Imperial Debate in the Edwardian Stately Press.* New York: Greenwood Press, 1991.

Stetz, Margaret Diane. "Sex, Lies, and Printed Cloth: Bookselling at the Bodley Head in the Eighteen-Nineties." *Victorian Studies* 35 (1991): 71–86.

Stock, Eugene. *The History of the Church Missionary Society: Its Environment, its Men and its Work.* Vol. 3. London, 1899.

Stoddard, Lothrop. *The Rising Tide of Colour Against White World-Supremacy.* London: Chapman and Hall, 1920.

Stoler, Ann Laura. "Carnal Knowledge and Imperial Power: Gender, Race, and Morality in Colonial Asia." In *Feminism and History*, ed. Joan Scott. New York: Oxford University Press, 1998, 209–66.

———. *Race and the Education of Desire: Foucault's History of Sexuality and the Colonial Order of Things.* Durham, N.C.: Duke University Press, 1995.

Stone, Melville. "The Associated Press. Fifth Paper: Its Work in War." *Century Magazine* 70 (1905): 505.

Storey, Graham. *Reuters: The Story of a Century of News-Gathering.* New York: Greenwood Press, 1969.

Strobel, Margaret. *European Women and the Second British Empire.* Bloomington: Indiana University Press, 1991.

Sullivan, Alvin, ed. *British Literary Magazines: The Victorian and Edwardian Age, 1837–1913.* Westport, Conn.: Greenwood Press, 1984.

Sutherland, Alexander, ed. *Victoria and its Metropolis: Past and Present.* 2 vols. Melbourne: McCarron, Bird, 1888.

Symon, J. D. *The Press and its Story.* London: Seeley, Service and Co., 1914.

Tagg, John. *The Burden of Representation: Essays on Photographies and Histories.* London: Macmillan, 1988.

Tallis, John. *Tallis's History and Description of the Crystal Palace, and the Exhibition of the World's Industry in 1851.* London and New York: John Tallis and Co., 1851.

Tartakov, Gary Michael. "Changing Views of India's Art History." In *Perceptions of South Asia's Visual Past*, ed. Catherine B. Asher and Thomas R. Metcalf. New Delhi: American Institute of Indian Studies, 1994, 15–36.

Thomas, David. *Y Ddinasyddiaeth Fawr.* Wrecsam, Wales: Hugheas a'i Fab, 1938.

Thomas, Nicholas. *Entangled Objects. Exchange, Material Culture, and Colonialism in the Pacific.* Cambridge: Harvard University Press, 1991.

———. *Colonialism's Culture: Anthropology, Travel and Government.* Cambridge: Polity Press, 1994.

Thompson, Andrew S. *Imperial Britain: The Empire in British Politics c. 1880–1932.* London: Longman, 2000.

Thompson, J. Lee. *Northcliffe: Press Baron in Politics, 1865–1922.* London: John Murray, 2001.

Thompson, Leonard, "Great Britain and the Afrikaner Republics, 1870–1899." In *The Oxford History of South Africa.* Vol. 2: *South Africa, 1870–1966,* ed. Monica Wilson and Leonard Thompson. Oxford: Clarendon Press, 1971.

Trainor, Luke. *British Imperialism and Australian Nationalism.* Melbourne: Cambridge University Press, 1994.

Tucker, Maya. "Centennial Celebrations 1888." *Australia, 1888* 7 (April 1981): 11–25.

Twain, Mark. *Following the Equator: A Journey Around the World.* 2 vols. New York and London: Harper and Brothers, 1925 [1897].

Vann, J. D. and R. VanArsdel. *Periodicals of Queen Victoria's Empire.* Toronto: University of Toronto Press, 1996.

Vijaya-Raghavan, T. "Hindu marriage customs and British law," *National Review.* 17 (March 1891): 80–90.

Viswanathan, Gauri. "Currying Favor: The Politics of British Educational and Cultural Policy in India, 1813–54." In *Dangerous Liaisons: Gender, Nation, and Postcolonial Perspectives,* ed. A. McClintock, A. Mufti, and E. Shohat. Minneapolis: University of Minnesota Press, 1997, 113–29.

Warneck, Gustav. *Modern Missions and Culture: their mutual relations.* Trans. Thomas Smith. Edinburgh: J. Gemmell, 1883.

Washbrook, David. "India, 1818–1860: The Two Faces of Colonialism." In *The Oxford History of the British Empire: The Nineteenth Century,* ed. Andrew Porter. Oxford: Oxford University Press, 1999.

Watts, Thomas. "On the Probable Future Position of the English Language." *Transactions of the Philological Society* 4 (1848–50): 207–14.

Webby, Elizabeth. "Journals in the Nineteenth Century." In *The Book in Australia,* ed. D. H. Borchardt and W. Kirsop. Melbourne: Australian Reference Publications, 1988, 43–65.

Webster, Noah. *An American Dictionary of the English Language.* 2 vols. 1828. Reprint, New York: Johnson Reprint Corporation, 1970.

Weiner, Joel, ed. *Innovators and Preachers: The Role of the Editor in Victorian England.* Westport, Conn.: Greenwood Press, 1985.

Whibley, Charles. "A Retrospect." *Blackwood's Magazine* 201 (April 1917): 433–46.

White, Hayden. *The Content of the Form: Narrative Discourse and Historical Representation.* Baltimore and London: Johns Hopkins University Press, 1987.

White, Llewellyn and Robert D. Leigh. "The Growth of International Communications." In *Mass Communications,* ed. Wilbur Schramm. Urbana: University of Illinois Press, 1960.

Whitlock, Gillian and Gail Reekie. *Uncertain Beginnings: Debates in Australian Studies.* St. Lucia: Queensland University Press, 1993.

Whyte, Frederic. *The Life of W. T. Stead.* 2 vols. New York and London: Garland, 1971.

Wiener, Joel H., ed. *Innovators and Preachers: The Role of the Editor in Victorian England.* Westport, Conn.: Greenwood Press, 1985.

Williams, Francis. *Transmitting World News: A Study of Communications and the Press.* Paris: UNESCO, 1953.

Williams, Gwyn A. *When Was Wales? The History, People and Culture of an Ancient Country*. London: Black Raven Press, 1985.

Williams, John, ed. *Digest of Welsh Historical Statistics*. Cardiff: Welsh Office, 1985.

Williams, Raymond. *The Country and the City*. New York: Oxford University Press, 1973.

Wilson, Gillian, ed. *Theodore. Letters from the Oxford Mission in India 1940–1993*. Romsey: Oxford Mission, 1997.

Wolff, Michael, "Charting the Golden Stream." *Victorian Periodicals Newsletter* 13 (1971): 23–38.

Young, Robert. *Colonial Desire: Hybridity in Theory, Culture and Race*. New York: Routledge, 1995.

Yule, Henry and A. C. Burnell. *Hobson-Jobson*. Ed. William Crooke. London: Routledge and Kegan Paul, 1968.

Index